Galati

Braila

Danube

To Russia 1829-56

DOBRADZHA

□BUCHAREST

Cherna Voda

Constanța

Silistra

rgiu

Rusé

1867

Dobrich

Razgrad

Popovn

Provadiya

ov

Yantra

Shumen

Samovodené

Preslav

Varna

Gorna Oryakhovitsa

Kamchiya

Türnovo

ovo

Elena

Kotel

ryarna

rovo

Neikovo

Zheravna

Gradets

pka

Sliven

Karnobat

zanlŭk

Burgas

Nova Zagora

Yambol

Sozopol

a Zagora

rpan

Uzundzhovo

Tundzha

Kharmanli

skovo

Adrianople

Arda

Black

Sea

Constantinople

San Stefano

Sea of
Marmara

a

D1269723

E.G.M.

A HISTORY OF BULGARIA
1393–1885

The Church at Shipka built as a memorial to the Russian soldiers who
died to liberate Bulgaria from the Turks

A HISTORY OF BULGARIA
1393–1885

MERCIA
MACDERMOTT

Ruskin House
GEORGE ALLEN & UNWIN LTD
MUSEUM STREET   LONDON

*Printed in Great Britain
in 10 on 12 point Plantin type
by Unwin Brothers Limited
Woking and London*

ACKNOWLEDGEMENTS

I would like to express my special gratitude to the late Professor R. R. Betts and to my husband for their help in correcting the manuscript.

Grateful acknowledgements are also due to Miss Honor Levine, owner of the silver buckle in Illustration 1b; to the proprietors of *Punch* for permission to reproduce the drawing in Illustration 12b; to the proprietors of the *Illustrated London News* for permission to reproduce the drawings in Illustrations 12a, 13, and 14; to J. Allan Cash for permission to reproduce Illustrations 3 and 4a; to Douglas Greene for Illustration 1b; and to the Press Department of the Bulgarian Legation in London, the Committee for Friendship and Cultural Relations with Foreign Countries (Sofia) and the Society for Friendship with Bulgaria for supplying the remainder of the illustrations.

CONTENTS

A*

ILLUSTRATIONS

CHAPTER I

BULGARIA BEFORE 1393

The epoch of Turkish rule in Bulgaria had so profound an effect upon the pattern of national life, and lasted so long, that even the Bulgarians themselves began to forget that things had ever been different. Yet, before the Turkish Conquest, mediaeval Bulgaria had been one of the foremost states in Europe in the field of culture and education, while militarily her power had attained heights which made Tsar Simeon's claim to the imperial crown of Byzantium by no means impertinent.

The territory which we now call Bulgaria has been inhabited from the earliest times. Remains dating from the Old Stone Age have been found in the caves of the Stara Planina, or Balkan Range. In the second or third millennium BC the territory was settled by Thracian tribes, and in the sixth century BC the slave-owning Greek states began colonizing the Black Sea coast, where they set up trading centres at Odessos (Varna), Apolonia (Sozopol), and Mesembria (Nesebŭr). The Thracian State was conquered first by Philip of Macedon and later by the Romans. Owing to their fine fighting qualities, many Thracian slaves took part in Roman spectacles as gladiators. Spartacus, the leader of the Slaves' Revolt, was himself born within the borders of present-day Bulgaria. When the Roman Empire was divided into two, the territory of Bulgaria was included in the eastern half with its capital at Constantinople, and subsequently formed part of the Byzantine Empire.

During the sixth and seventh centuries AD pagan Slavonic tribes invaded and settled in the Balkans in spite of Byzantine opposition. The Slavs were a freedom-loving, agricultural people, loosely knit into tribes based on the *zadruga* or large patriarchal family, which owned and cultivated the land in common. A feature of their tribal life was the absence of private property or any single permanent leader. Temporary leaders might be elected in time of war or danger, but normally decisions were taken by popular assemblies. During the seventh and eighth centuries, however, the growth of private property and a tribal aristocracy led to the disintegration of the old democratic communal society and to the development of elements of feudalism.

In AD 679 there arrived in the Balkans a small tribe of Proto-Bulgars under their khan, Asparukh. The Proto-Bulgars were a Turkic people from Central Asia, who had migrated westwards, spending some time in the Kuban and Northern Caucasus. They were a nomadic, cattle-rearing people, skilled in military arts and led by an autocratic ruler, who was at the same time their chief priest. The Proto-Bulgars entered into an alliance with the Slavonic tribes against Byzantium, and a Slavo-Bulgar State[1] was set up, in which, in spite of the numerical superiority of the Slavs, the Proto-Bulgars provided the leadership. This was, no doubt, due to their military prowess and well-disciplined organization which contrasted with the anarchy of the Slavs.

By the end of the reign of Boris I (852–893), the Proto-Bulgars had been completely absorbed by the more numerous Slavs. Their language was lost and little now remains to remind us of them except the name of the country—Bulgaria.

The reign of Boris I saw not only the end of the Proto-Bulgars as a separate people, but also the end of paganism. Christianity became the official religion of Bulgaria in 865 when Boris was baptized according to the Byzantine rites with the Byzantine Emperor standing godfather to him. Boris's motives for adopting Christianity were political rather than religious, and his conversion was accompanied by much bargaining with Rome and Byzantine, as he played off one against the other in the hope of gaining more favourable terms. Above all, Boris wanted his new Church to be independent, and this was not easy to achieve while he had to rely on Greek or Roman clergy. At this point, as if in answer to his prayers, news came that a party of refugee Slavonic clergy had arrived in Belgrade, having been expelled from Moravia.

To understand how this had come about, it is necessary to go back a little in time, and to trace the story of two saints, Cyril and Methodius, whose feast day is still celebrated in Bulgaria as the Day of Culture, Public Education and Slavonic Writing. Though they were born in Salonika, Cyril and Methodius were Slavonic in origin, and while living in a monastery on Mount Olympus, they

[1] The capital of the so-called First Bulgarian Empire was first at Pliska and later at Preslav.

had invented a Slavonic alphabet and had begun to translate the more important Church books into Slavonic. About this time, Prince Rostislav of Moravia, who, for political reasons, wished to rid himself of the Latin-speaking German clergy who staffed his Church, requested the Byzantine Emperor to send him Slavonic-speaking missionaries. Cyril and Methodius were the obvious choice, and for some years they worked successfully in Moravia, preaching to the people in Slavonic, although they had to face bitter opposition from those who believed in the so-called 'Three Languages Theory'. According to this, only the three languages of the inscription on the Cross—Greek, Latin and Hebrew—might be used for cultural and religious purposes. The result was that the mass of the people could not understand the services and the culture of the day was accessible only to a minority. We have Cyril's own answer to those who upheld the Three Languages Theory:

'Does not God send rain equally on all men? Does not the sun also shine on all men? Do we not all breathe the same air? And are you not ashamed to recognize only three languages, and to ordain that all other peoples and tribes shall be blind and deaf?'

After the deaths of Cyril (869) and Methodius (885), Rostislav's successor came to terms with the Germans, the Slavonic clergy were driven out of Moravia, and Latin came back into its own. Then, just when it seemed that the cause of Cyril and Methodius was threatened with extinction, Boris of Bulgaria eagerly welcomed the refugees, and offered them not only sanctuary but every facility to continue their work for Slavonic culture. In this way, Boris obtained his independent Church in the face of violent opposition from the Greek Patriarch, who withheld recognition of the Bulgarian Patriarch until 927.

Thus Bulgaria became the cradle of Slavonic written culture. It was from Bulgaria that the Russians obtained their alphabet and church books when Prince Vladimir of Kiev accepted Christianity in 988, and the Old Bulgarian language remained the literary language of Russia until the eighteenth century.

The adoption of the Slavonic alphabet made possible a great flowering of culture, written in a language accessible to all. Many of the authors of the day expressed in their writings their delight in the new alphabet. Chernorizets Khrabŭr, for example, hotly denied that there was any basis for regarding the so-called Three Languages as God-given, and proudly asserted:

'St Konstantin himself, whom we call Cyril, both created the Slavonic letters and translated the books . . . , therefore the Slavonic letters are more holy and more worthy of honour, because a holy man created them, while the Greek letters were created by pagans . . . If you ask the Greek men of letters who created their alphabet or translated their books, and when this was done, few of them will know. But if you ask the Slavonic men of letters who prepared their alphabet and translated the books, all of them will know and answering will say: "St Konstantin the Philosopher, whom we call Cyril—he made our alphabet and translated the books, he and his brother Methodius, and there are men still alive today who have seen them." '

In actual fact, many scholars now believe that what we today call the Cyrillic alphabet was the work of St Kliment, one of the refugee clergy whom Boris befriended, while St Cyril himself was the inventor of the earlier Glagolithic. But this in no way alters the historic role of Bulgaria as the 'classical land' of Slavonic culture, as Yuri Venelin, the Russian nineteenth-century scholar, called her, and one can readily understand the pride with which Georgi Dimitrov, at the Reichstag Fire Trial more than a thousand years later, repudiated the insinuation of the Nazi court that the Bulgarians were a savage and barbarous people in these words:

'Long before the time when the German Emperor Charles V said that he talked German only to his horse, and when the German nobility and educated people wrote only in Latin and were ashamed of the German language, in "barbarous" Bulgaria, the Apostles Cyril and Methodius had created and spread the use of the old Bulgarian script.'

The reign of Boris's son Simeon (893–927) is known as the Golden Age of Bulgarian literature. It also marked the zenith of Bulgaria's territorial expansion and her frontiers stretched from the Black Sea to the Adriatic, embracing most of Serbia, Albania and Southern Macedonia. The Balkan peninsula was too small to accommodate both the Byzantine and Bulgarian Empires and throughout the Middle Ages there was constant rivalry between them. Numerous wars were fought with now one, now the other gaining the upper hand. Seated in his marble and gold palace, robed in a pearl-sewn mantle, girded with a golden sword and surrounded by the glittering company of his nobles, Simeon dreamed of ruling in Byzantium itself, and fought war after war in a vain attempt to capture the city whose stout walls defied him to the end.

The constant warfare undermined the country's economy, which by now had the characteristic features of feudalism. The magnificence of the court and the cost of the wars was paid for by the unceasing toil of the peasants who lived in utter misery and suffered from frequent conscription and requisitioning. Conditions continued to deteriorate after the death of Simeon until even Presbyter Kozma, the chief apologist for the Establishment, had to admit that the peasants were so loaded with taxes and *angaria* (compulsory unpaid labour) that they had no time to pray. At the same time he noted that the monks and clergy had given themselves up to luxury and riotous living, and that the pastors were less concerned with the welfare of their flock than with grabbing their milk and wool. The answer which some gave to the evils of society was to renounce everything for the ascetic life of a hermit. Such a course was taken by Ivan Rilsky, patron saint of Bulgaria and founder of the celebrated Rila Monastery. Not all could or wanted to follow his example, and popular discontent manifested itself in the Bogomil movement, a dualist heresy which rejected almost all the beliefs and practices of the established Church, and which taught that the world and man's body were created by Satan. While its outward form was that of a religious sect, it was, in essence, a popular revolt against feudalism. The Bogomils believed that he who worked for the Tsar was offensive to God, and regarded the soldier as nothing more than a common assassin. They refused to work for their feudal lords or bear arms, and, as the movement gained in strength, they formed communes, where the land was cultivated in common and the produce shared according to need, and where all but the infirm were expected to perform either mental or physical work. Most of the communes had schools and a high proportion of the Bogomils were literate. Persecution and torture were powerless to eradicate the movement, and it persisted until the Turkish Conquest, dying down in periods of relative prosperity and flaring up again in times of hardship and oppression.

By the end of the tenth century the balance of power between Byzantium and the Bulgarian Empire had altered to such an extent that Byzantium was able to defeat Bulgaria in a series of wars, and by 1018 her victory was complete. For the next century and a half Bulgaria was little more than a Byzantine province. During this period the Greeks, who had never reconciled themselves to the existence of an independent Bulgarian Church, embarked on a policy of hellenization. Bulgarian clergy were replaced by Greeks, Bulgarian schools were closed, the Greek language was introduced into schools and churches, and many Bulgarian literary documents were deliberately destroyed.

The Bulgarians made various attempts to free themselves from Byzantine rule, but not until 1185 were they successful. In this year two noblemen named Petŭr and Asen organized a revolt in Tŭrnovo, as a result of which Bulgaria regained her independence. Since the ancient royal house had died out during the Byzantine yoke, Asen was crowned Tsar. The Archbishop of Tŭrnovo was proclaimed Patriarch of the Bulgarian Church which once more became independent of Byzantium.

During the so-called Second Empire,[1] feudalism in Bulgaria reached the limit of its development and began to fall into decay. The unity of the State and the authority of the Tsar were constantly being menaced by the separatist tendencies of powerful, ambitious nobles, and the economic condition of the peasantry became steadily worse. This time popular discontent took the form of a full-scale peasants' revolt (1277–1280), led by a swineherd named Ivailo, whom the people proclaimed Tsar. So great was the popular support for the revolt that Ivailo entered Tŭrnovo in triumph and married the widow of the previous Tsar, before being finally defeated and slain.

The Second Empire, and in particular the reign of Ivan Alexander (1331–1371), was one of the richest periods of Bulgarian mediaeval culture. Numerous important literary works were produced, and crafts, such as fresco and ikon painting, manuscript illumination, woodcarving, gold and silver work, flourished. One of the most important monuments of the period is the church at Boyana, near Sofia, decorated with unique frescoes executed in 1259. An illuminated copy of the Four Gospels, made for Ivan Alexander, can be seen in the British Museum in London.

On the eve of the Turkish Conquest the Second Bulgarian Empire had split into three more or less independent States: Ivan Shishman (1371–1393) ruled the major part of the Empire with his capital at

[1] The capital of Bulgaria during the Second Empire was Tŭrnovo.

Tŭrnovo, while his half-brother, Ivan Stratsimir, ruled a small state in north-western Bulgaria, and a boyar named Ivanko ruled in the Dobrudzha. This lack of unity within Bulgaria itself was matched by a similar lack of unity among the various Balkan States, so that when, during the fourteenth century, the rising tide of Turkish expansion reached their very doorsteps, they failed to take energetic joint action against the common foe. Step by step in their inexorable march westwards, the Turks were able to overrun the Balkan peninsula. At first they were content to obtain control through alliances, and, where force had to be used, to restore the defeated local rulers as their vassals. But when in 1389 the Battle of Kossovo Field sounded the death knell of Serbian independence, Sultan Bayazid decided to proceed to the next stage of conquest—that of direct rule.

By this time Sofia and almost all southern Bulgaria were in Turkish hands, and only northern Bulgaria retained nominal independence as a vassal state. When the Turkish Army marched on Tŭrnovo, Tsar Ivan Shishman fled to Nikopol, but the capital held out for three months under the courageous leadership of Patriarch Eftimi. Finally the Turks entered Tŭrnovo on July 17, 1393, burning and looting as they came. The leading citizens were gathered together in a church, and a hundred and ten of them who refused to embrace Islam were murdered there. By 1396 Ivan Stratsimir and Ivanko had also been overthrown, and all Bulgaria passed under the Turkish yoke.

CHAPTER II

BULGARIA UNDER
THE TURKISH YOKE

The Continuation of the Turkish Conquest

The conquest of Bulgaria, so fateful and memorable an event in the history of her people, was but an episode in the long chronicle of Turkish expansion, which continued for many years after Bulgaria's fate was sealed.

Shortly after the subjugation of Bulgaria, however, the Turkish Empire entered a period of crisis. This began in 1402 with the victory of Tamerlane's Mongols over Bayazid, who was taken prisoner and died soon after, and it continued during protracted civil wars between Bayazid's three sons from 1403–1413. The Bulgarians tried to take advantage of the opportunity to throw off the new foreign yoke. A rising was organized in 1403, led by Fruzhin, son of Ivan Shishman, and Konstantin, son of Ivan Stratsimir, but it was unsuccessful. Unfortunately none of the Christian powers of Europe made any attempt to exploit the situation created by the civil wars in Turkey, and after 1420 Turkey was able to recommence her conquests in Europe. A Crusade was organized in 1443 by the Polish king, Władysław III, recently elected to the Hungarian throne, but a hard winter forced it to retreat, when it had got as far as present-day Kostenets, en route for Plovdiv. The following year, Władysław prepared a new expedition and travelled down the Danube, reaching Varna, where he awaited Genoese and Venetian ships to transport his army to Constantinople. Before the ships arrived, however, the Turkish Army attacked the Crusaders in the rear and utterly defeated them. After this, apart from Hunyadi's campaigns, little effort was made to dislodge the Turks from the Balkans. Unhindered, the Turks captured Constantinople in 1453, and set up their capital there. Gradually all Greece passed into their hands. The conquest of Serbia was completed in 1459, and Herzegovina in 1467. Albania under Georgi Kastrioti (Skanderbeg) resisted for a time with the help of Rome, Naples and Venice, but on his death, she also was conquered. Her people adopted Mohammedanism, and became zealous supporters of Turkish rule. Rumania retained her autonomy by accepting Turkish suzerainty. The King of Hungary incurred the wrath of the Sultan, Suleiman I (1520–1566), by putting to death the latter's ambassador and the Turks turned their army against Hungary and in 1521 took Belgrade, then in Magyar hands. In 1526 the Sultan invaded Hungary itself and utterly defeated the Magyars at the battle of Mohacs. In 1529 he appeared before the walls of Vienna itself although he did not succeed in taking the city. Apart from these conquests in South-East Europe, the Turks extended their power in Asia Minor and North Africa by taking Baghdad, Rhodes, Morocco, Egypt, Syria, Algiers and Tunis. Thus the Turks became masters in the Mediterranean.

The Effects of the Turkish Conquest in Bulgaria

The Turks conquered the Balkans at a time when feudalism in both Byzantium and Bulgaria was already in decay and its downfall inevitable in the natural course of events. In this case Bulgaria would perhaps have followed the same line of development as in Western Europe where the growth of towns and trade was ushering in a new era of social and economic development. Instead the rise of a Bulgarian merchant class and *bourgeoisie* was prevented by the fact that when the Turks destroyed the Bulgarian feudal nobility and the economic power of the clergy, they did not bring with them a more advanced form of economy, but a new feudalism showing no signs of decay or obsolescence. On the contrary, it was vigorous and efficient, and many years were to pass before it went into decline. Thus, at a time when Western Europe was taking great strides forwards, the Bulgarian people were deprived of the possibility of normal national development and of cultural advance, condemned to a miserably low level of existence, economically, politically and culturally, held back in the Middle Ages by the fetters of a new feudalism and all the accompanying primitive techniques, low productivity, ignorance and poverty. Furthermore, the struggle of the people against feudalism was now complicated by the fact that it had to be waged against a feudal class of foreign invaders, backed by a powerful army fanatically devoted to an alien religion. Even in the field of culture, a long hard battle had to be waged against the Greeks, who by reason of their domination of the Church, gained a stranglehold on Bulgarian culture and even on the Bulgarian lan-

guage. There was thus very little economic or cultural advance until
the end of the eighteenth century, and it is small wonder that until
recently Bulgaria has had to be regarded as a very backward country.

In the past, it has been held that conditions during the first two
hundred years of Turkish rule were relatively good compared with
the misery of the decaying Second Empire. This view has now been
challenged and many historians are now of the opinion that the lot
of the people was worse right from the start. In certain respects
conditions did improve but the improvements were more than
counterbalanced by the new burdens imposed as a result of the
conquest. It is, for example, true that after the initial blood and
violence of the conquest, the peasants were left to till their fields in
more or less uninterrupted peace, since only the Moslems bore
arms, and, after the wars, both civil and foreign, which had been
one of the chief contributing factors to the misery of the people
during the two Empires, this must have been a welcome change.
Furthermore, since the main revenue of the Turkish State came
from the spoils of war, the burden of taxation on the already conquered was not as excessive as it had been in the Second Empire,
and, since the lords were nearly always absentee landlords and did
not supervise the taxation, the peasants were able to keep more
produce for themselves. But against these possible improvements
must be set new and terrible burdens. The Bulgarians had to suffer
national and religious persecution; many were taken into slavery;
women and girls were taken away to Turkish harems; efforts were
made to force individuals to become Moslems, and the Bulgarian
population was chased out of the towns to make room for Turkish
colonists. These aspects will be discussed in more detail below, but
it will be seen that the theory that conditions improved immediately
after the Turkish Conquest is, at best, a very debatable one.

The Turks brought no cultural advances and did little to improve
the towns and villages, though they made certain changes in the
character of the towns to suit themselves. They built mosques with
domes and minarets, and constructed fountains and squares for
markets. They also opened barbers' shops which were the Turks'
favourite places for meeting and conversing. The bells were taken
down from the churches, ikons were burnt, and paintings and murals
were covered over with a thick coat of lime solution. On the whole,
the Turks despised walls and fortresses and pinned their faith in
the bravery of their warriors. Thus little was left of the mediaeval
walls of the cities that surrendered. Their chief innovation was the

construction of *caravanserais*—inns for merchant caravans along the main roads. These were places where travellers might receive lodging and food free for three days. They were square with high stone walls for protection, and had accommodation both for travellers and for their cattle. Apparently these *caravanserais* were sadly lacking in cleanliness, and foreign visitors preferred to spend the night in the humble houses of the Bulgarians. The Turks did make some attempt to improve the roads, and arranged for specified peasants to look after them, but after the middle of the sixteenth century their road-making efforts petered out and many of the peasants responsible for the roads fled.

The southern and eastern parts of Bulgaria which were nearest to Constantinople were thickly colonized by the Turks. The north and north-east regions were much less colonized, while in the centre and south-west, and in Macedonia and Serbia, only the towns and other strategic points were inhabited by Turks. In areas sparsely colonized by the Turks, the old Bulgarian administration was to a large extent left in operation. Tǔrnovo itself lost its status as a capital city, and the Turks made Sofia the centre of their administration in the Balkans, owing to the obvious advantages of its geographical situation. The towns tended to lose their Bulgarian character, owing to the Turks' policy of driving the Bulgarians from the towns, especially after the attempted risings during the quarrels between the sons of Bayazid.

Moslem and 'Raya'

All Bulgarians who did not accept Islam were, like other Christians within the Turkish Empire, reduced to a single social category—the *raya*—i.e. non-Moslem or subject population. Obviously this did not mean that a classless society existed in Bulgaria. The entire Bulgarian people had become the exploitated class in the new feudal society, while the invader had become the ruling class. Those Bulgarians who gave up their religion and embraced Islam *ipso facto* entered the ranks of the ruling class, since the Turks made no division between race or nationality, but only between Moslem and non-Moslem.

Among the Moslems there were theoretically no social divisions, although certainly some were infinitely more wealthy than others. All were considered equal; no Moslem could become a slave, and it was thought degrading for a Moslem to pay taxes, consequently they were not expected to do so.

The alleged superiority of the Moslems was demonstrated by numerous restrictions on the Christian *raya*. Non-Moslems were not permitted to build houses higher than those of Moslems, or to paint them with lime or white, red or green paint. Neither were they permitted to have better horses than the Moslems. Churches had to be lower than the mosques and could not have windows, cupolas or belfries. No bells were permitted and wooden clappers had to be used instead. Religious processions were not allowed outside churches, and at times the building of churches was even forbidden altogether. The *raya* were not allowed to wear bright colours and had to dress in dark clothes.

When the Turks captured a town, they would call the inhabitants together and give them the alternative of embracing Islam or losing all rights and power. Those boyars who refused to change their religion were hunted down, imprisoned, tortured and killed, or sent to Asia Minor. Since the Turkish State was based on religion, it was perfectly possible for renegade Christians to receive posts in the administration, including the highest positions and even the Grand Vizirship.

The Turks were, however, anxious to secure the voluntary co-operation of the conquered people wherever possible, and where villages or individuals might be of use to the Turks, they were given certain privileges in return for services. Where the people had fled to the mountains, they were encouraged by offers of land to come down and till the soil.

Land Tenure

The essential economic feature of the Ottoman Empire was that it was a military feudal state. The backbone of the feudal army were horsemen known as *spahi* who received income from land worked by the subject Christian population, and apportioned to them by the Sultan in return for their service. While the *spahi* estate was the most important form of land tenure, it was by no means the only form. According to Moslem law, all land belongs to Allah, and is held in his name by his 'Shadow upon Earth', the Sultan. In actual fact, the land was divided out in various ways, giving three main forms of land tenure: first *mülk*, which was land held in full private owner-ship; secondly, *miri*, which was held by the State Treasury and was disposed of by the Sultan as he saw fit in the form of feudal estates; and thirdly, *vakif* land, the income from which was held in perpe-tuity for charitable or religious purposes such as the upkeep of mosques, cemeteries, hospitals, dining-rooms for the poor, etc.

Mülk, properly speaking, lay within the village boundaries, but it also included certain land, such as gardens and vineyards, outside the boundaries, but within a radius of one kilometre. Since *mülk* was private property, it might be bought, sold, bequeathed, exchanged or generally disposed of, according to the wish of the owner, whether Christian or Moslem.

Miri was land which was not privately owned, and lay outside the village boundaries. It was composed of fiefs of various sizes, of which some were for the use of the Sultan and his family, and others were given out to individuals in return for services, both civil and military. These people did not become the owners of the fiefs and were not free to dispose of them as they wished, neither did they enjoy administrative immunity within their estates. They merely enjoyed the income from the lands, and even then the revenues from certain taxes were appropriated by the State. For this reason the fiefs were measured not by area but by the income they yielded. There were three types of fief, the *timar* (annual income of up to 20,000 *akché*),[1] the *ziamet* (annual income from 20,000–100,000 *akché*), and the *khas* (annual income over 100,000 *akché*). The latter was generally reserved for the Sultan or members of his family or for the Vizir and other high officials.

A man might not have more than one fief and it was granted to him, not only as a reward for past services, but as an obligation to continue to perform these services, and he could not bequeath or dispose of his fief in any way. The majority of the fiefs were granted to the *spahis* who received the income from the land on the condition that in time of war they appeared in full preparedness at an appointed place, and that they brought with them a given number of horse men also fully armed and prepared, the number ranging from one to nineteen, according to the income from the fief. Defaulters had their land taken away from them, but harder work or greater valour could lead to the granting of estates with higher incomes. This system, while it remained in effective operation, was an important contributing factor to the efficiency of the Turkish Army.

A few estates, known as *gaz-i-mülk*, were awarded by the Sultan in perpetuity to generals with outstanding records. Such estates were hereditary and the recipients might do as they pleased with them.

Before land could become *vakïf* land, i.e. set aside for religious or charitable purposes, the Sultan's permission had to be obtained.

---

[1] Turkish silver coins, each equal to a one one-hundred-and-twentieth part of a piastre.

Only *mülk* or *gaz-i-mülk* might become *vakīf*, and once it had become *vakīf* land, it could never change hands. When lands became *vakīf* documents were prepared by which the bequeather appointed himself and his descendants as the trustees or guardians of the bequest. Since part of the income of the *vakīf* lands was set aside for the guardians it was thus possible for them to ensure an income for themselves and their descendants in perpetuity. People who had received *gaz-i-mülk* and ran the risk of losing it if they fell from favour, were thus able to gain economic security by bequeathing the income from their land to charities, with the proviso that they should become the trustees. Since only *mülk* could become *vakīf* land, the greater part of the latter was concentrated in the villages, apart from former *gaz-i-mülk*. The buildings on *vakīf* land remained the *mülk* or absolute property of their owners, providing rent was paid for the space occupied. *Vakīf* buildings, such as shops, were leased out on a monthly or annual basis. The main income of the *vakīf* lands was derived from the *raya* in the form of taxation, etc.

The *raya*, as the Turks called the Christian population, were not deprived of land. They worked their own holdings which were left to them by the 'mercy' of the conqueror, and also the land on the feudal fiefs. *Miri* land might be given out to the *raya* against the payment of rent. It could be inherited, and, with the consent of the *spahi*, sold, providing tax was paid for the transfer of the *tapia*, or title deed. The land could not, however, remain uncultivated for more than three years. After this time, it was given to someone else. The *raya* were tied to the land, and could not leave one estate for another. If they did, they could be brought back to their original lord, if less than ten years had elapsed. The peasant also had to get the permission of the lord and pay a tax if he wished to plough up a meadow and turn it into a corn field, or cut down a tree, or make other alterations to his holding.

Taxation

In general, the system of taxation existing before the occupation remained in force, with some new additions. Only the non-Moslem population paid taxes. There were about eighty types of taxes and obligations recognized by the Moslem *Sheriat*, or Law, and the main taxes were as follows: a tithe on all agricultural produce, a land tax, a tax on cattle, sheep and pigs, a poll tax on all persons over the age of fifteen, and a levy of Christian children. This latter tax, known as *ispendzh*, was the cruellest tax of all. Every five years, a certain number of the finest Christian children were picked out, taken from their parents and sent to Constantinople. Some were sold as slaves on the way, others entered the households of the Sultan and pashas, and the remainder entered the Corps of Janissaries. These children were brought up to be fanatical Mohammedans and fearless warriors, and they formed the infantry of the Turkish Army, as opposed to the *spahi* who formed the cavalry. The Janissaries were not allowed to marry and, living apart from other sections of the population, they took war as their vocation. This tax fell heaviest upon the poor, since the richer families were able to bribe the collector to pass over their children. The horror of the system was that it was precisely these same Janissaries, imbued with a passionate zeal for their new faith, who were used to quell their own people and subjugate other Christian nations.

The *raya* were expected to provide free hospitality for passing troops and travellers. In time of war, they had to provide free food and transport facilities for passing troops, loans to the State, and money and presents for the pashas and the Commander-in-Chief, etc. The *raya* were also expected to perform *angaria*, repairing bridges, roads and buildings, cutting down forests, and so on. Apart from this, there were all kinds of other taxes such as toll when crossing bridges and fords, an inheritance tax and a tax on the sale of oxen. There were, in addition, special levies in time of catastrophe, such as famine, flood, conflagration, epidemics, destruction by the enemy, locusts and plagues of caterpillars. These levies were made at the discretion of the local governor.

The poll taxes always went straight to the State, and the revenue from other taxes went to the *spahi* or the State, according to the conditions laid down when the former was allotted an estate.

The *raya* on the Sultan's estates enjoyed certain privileges. They were not required to pay State taxes, or perform *angaria*, and no Turk might demand food and such-like from villages belonging to the Sultan or even spend the night there. Peasants on *vakīf* estates were likewise freed from State taxes. The worst burden of taxation, therefore, fell upon the *raya* on the *spahi* estates, which accounted for the largest area of land.

Special Categories of Raya

There were several groups of *raya* who were accorded certain rights and were exempt from certain taxes in recognition of the special services they performed. This was done at the beginning of the occupation in the interests of the Turks themselves to meet their own needs in various fields.

One of the largest groups were the *voinitsi* or *voinugani*, who received land free of tax in return for auxiliary military services, such as digging trenches, building fortifications, arranging transport, going ahead of the Turkish Army to prepare and provision camps. In time of peace, they spent six months of the year on the Sultan's estates in Adrianople and Constantinople, mowing the fields, pasturing the horses, harvesting and cultivating the gardens. They had their own commanders and banner, and at the appointed time they would set out for Constantinople with banners flying and singing songs. Some historians assert that there were no entire villages of *voinitsi*, but merely families, who might form a greater or lesser proportion of the population of any given village. No Turk was permitted to live in these villages, or pass through without the permission of the mayor or *voivoda*. No Turkish child might be born in them, and no dead Turk might be buried there. The *Voinitsi*, unlike other *raya*, were permitted to carry arms and to wear brightly coloured clothing. They were exempt from the Janissary levy, and allowed to keep up to a hundred sheep tax free. Any extra land they might acquire over and above that given to them in return for their services was, however, subject to tax.

The *Dervendzhii* patrolled the mountain passes as a precaution against robbers. The *Korudzhii* patrolled the forests to guard against fire and unauthorized felling. The *Martolozi* performed certain police duties, such as manning the frontier forts, escorting military transports and prisoners, and hunting down criminals and bandits. The *Dogandzhii* trained hawks, falcons and eagles for the use of the Sultan, Vizir, etc. They were excused certain taxes, except when they failed to train the required number of birds. The *Chaltukchii* worked in the rice fields. Rice cultivation was initiated by the State but the fields were given out to the *spahi* and civil servants. The *Chaltukchii* were exempt from certain taxes, but they were tied to the land and were made to work so hard that they lived in virtual slavery. The *Kyumyudzhii* were responsible for providing wood and charcoal for Government departments and the Mint. The *Zhetvari* gave help with the harvest on the estates of the rich Turks.

Apart from these, there were numerous other groups of State servants and skilled artisans who were granted relief from taxation, such as postal workers, and those responsible for maintaining post horses, guides, bridge and ford keepers, boatmen, navigators, architects, master-builders, engineers, builders of aqueducts and fountains, repairmen for fortresses and ditches, men who looked after town clocks, miners and others.

It is very doubtful whether or not these special categories of peasants can be described as 'privileged' since any benefits they might receive were offset by the tasks laid upon them. All that happened, in fact, was that their feudal rent took a different form to that paid by the majority of the population, giving an illusion of superiority and privilege.

In the interests of the national economy, traders were also granted special privileges. The merchants of Dubrovnik, Venice and Genoa who had traded with Bulgaria during the Second Empire and had already been granted certain privileges by its rulers, retained their freedom of movement and trade throughout the Balkans. They were permitted to have shops, workshops, schools and churches, and their apartments were inviolable. In return, they paid high taxes and gave numerous presents to the pashas. Privileges were also granted to subject people who traded within the Empire. On the receipt of a special *firman*, or charter, from the Sultan, the merchants were permitted to move freely about the country, to ride a fine horse, to carry a sword, to smoke tobacco in a long pipe and to do various other things forbidden to the ordinary *raya*. Their houses and shops were likewise inviolable and no one was permitted to demand of them free food and lodging, or the performance of *angaria*. Against all of this they had to pay fairly heavy taxes. Of all the merchants, those of Dubrovnik were the most privileged, together with some Bulgars who turned Roman Catholic and joined the Dubrovnik merchants, who had colonies in many Bulgarian towns.

Administration and Justice

Turkish rule in conquered territory took two separate forms. The first prevailed in the so-called vassal states, such as Transylvania, where there was little interference in the internal administration by the Turks, who contented themselves with receiving tribute and demanded only a general obedience to the principles of Turkish foreign policy. The second form existed where full, direct Turkish administration had been established, and since this form prevailed in the Balkans in general and in Bulgaria in particular, it is this second form that will be outlined here.

The Turkish Empire was an absolute monarchy, headed by the Sultan, who, as the 'Shadow of God on Earth', and Caliph of the

Mohammedans, had unlimited power in both secular and religious matters. The Sultan had a number of helpers and advisers, the most important of whom were the Grand Vizir, chief aide to the Sultan in both State and military matters, keeper of the State Seal and head of the pashas in charge of the various departments; the Sheikh-ul-Islam, or chief Mufti, the spiritual head of the Moslems, interpreter of the Koran and all matters of religious doctrine, which included examining all important Government undertakings and ratifying them if they did not conflict with the Holy Law, and keeper of the Sacred Banner, the unfurling of which was a sign for every Moslem to be prepared to die for the Faith; the three *Defterdari* in charge of finance, and the Reis-Effendi, responsible for relations with foreign courts. The Sultan also had two *Divans*, or Councils. One consisted of the Sultan and his closest associates, and the other consisted of the Sheikh-ul-Islam and the chief pashas. The latter met under the chairmanship of the Grand Vizir, and functioned as the Government. In the nineteenth century, this *Divan* became known to Europeans as the Sublime Porte, the name being derived from the lofty doorway of the palace where the Government worked.

Administratively the Turkish Empire was divided into two parts, one in Asia Minor, and the other in the Balkans, which was known as Rumelia. Constantinople, standing as it does between the two, made a convenient capital for the Empire. These two main areas of the Empire were each ruled by a *beylerbey*. In Rumelia, the seat of Government was first at Plovdiv and later at Sofia. The territory was subdivided into *vilayets*, ruled by a pasha or *vali*. Each *vilayet* was further subdivided into *sanjaks*, and smaller units each headed by an appropriate local governor. The essentially military character of the Turkish feudal state is shown by the fact that the pashas were the military commanders in their own areas, as well as the heads of the administration and economy. They were appointed by the Sultan and paid definite taxes to him, and were subordinated to the Grand Vizir, who had the power to dismiss them at will, if they disobeyed the Sultan's orders. Nevertheless, within their areas they in fact enjoyed almost complete autonomy and unlimited power. They had their own *Divans* but these were only advisory and the pashas did not have to take their advice. In this situation, conditions in any area depended to a large extent on the character of the particular pasha.

In each administrative area, justice was in the hands of a *Kadi*, paid by the State, who together with various helpers, worked closely

1a. The Church at Batak where a large number of people died during the April Rising. Architecturally the church is of interest because it belongs to the period when the Turks placed severe restrictions on the height and style of Christian buildings.

1b. The buckle, or *pafti*, of a Bulgarian woman's costume of the Turkish period. It is made of silver, inlaid with mother-of-pearl and engraved with a Russian Imperial eagle. Buckles of this period were frequently engraved in this way as a symbol of the people's faith that Russia would deliver them from bondage.

(Photograph by Douglas Greene

2b. A fortress-like house at Arbanasi near Tŭrnovo (Seventeenth or eighteenth century)

2a. The Rila Monastery

with the local governor, and judged according to the *Sheriat*, or religious law drawn from the Koran. The *Kadi* dealt not only with the direct dispensation of justice, but also with matters of inheritance and land left without tillers. All agreements and treaties had to be ratified by his signature. He also supervised accounts in the Finance Department, and the prices and quality of goods sold in the markets.

This system of centralized administration through men appointed by the State meant that the feudal lords did not have administrative autonomy within their estates. They had no power to try their own *raya*, since this was done by the central organs. This was in sharp contrast to the Western and Byzantine feudal systems, and even to that which prevailed in Bulgaria before 1393, by which peasants were tried by feudal courts set up by the lord, who had complete power within his estates. This form of administration, together with the system of giving the *spahi* merely the income from an estate and not the estate itself, paralysed separatist tendencies for as long as the State was healthy and capable of controlling both the local governors and the *spahi*.

In the village communes the native administration was often left, and they were ruled by a mayor and village elders who were responsible for collecting the taxes fixed for the village by the local pasha, and in so doing they would take into account the circumstances of each person. The people had the right, on paper at any rate, to complain to the *Kadi* and even to the Sultan against injustice or illegal practices on the part of the local pasha. In their own legal affairs, however, the Bulgars did not usually go to the *Kadi*, but judged crimes according to their old customs, with the elders deciding what punishment should be inflicted. Thieves were led round the village carrying the stolen object, or they might be beaten, or imprisoned, or forced to return what had been stolen or pay for damages. Withholding the sacrament and boycotting by friends and neighbours were also customary punishments. Crimes could be expiated by gifts of wax, oil, etc., to the Church. This could apply even to convicted murderers. The Turks did not regard murder among infidels as a particularly heinous offence, and rarely did anything about it. The Bulgars tended to have a fatalistic attitude towards murder, and unless the relatives of the victim demanded blood for blood (in which case the elders would go to the *Kadi* to seek the punishment of the murderer), often the criminal could be released after giving numerous presents to the Church. Adultery was regarded as a very serious crime, and as a disgrace to the whole family.

B

Chastity, together with piety, were considered the highest virtues, and boys and girls who had pre-marital relations were made to marry immediately. The Bulgars married very young. Boys were often married by fifteen and certainly by eighteen, and one factor which contributed to early marriages was the Janissary levy, since married men were not admitted to the corps. It is interesting to note which sins the Bulgars regarded as being unforgivable. These were: incest, turning one's parents into the street, initiating litigation against one's parents, or attempting to assault them; witchcraft, extortion, plunder and, significantly, betrayal of one's people.[1]

Economy

After the spearhead of the Turkish advance moved beyond the Danube, the peace that prevailed in the Bulgarian lands permitted a revival of the economy. It did not usher in a period of flowering and development, however, because the economy remained feudal in character, and up to the end of the eighteenth century it was predominantly natural economy with primitive technique and little division of labour. The Turks had practically no part in the economic life of the country, being almost exclusively consumers, living on the backs of the *raya*. There was little incentive for the Bulgarian peasants to increase production, and, as a rule, they only cultivated as much land as was necessary to pay the taxes and to provide for the needs of themselves and their families. In this way, much of the land was left uncultivated.

The main occupations of the people remained as they had been under the Tsars: cattlebreeding, agriculture and handicrafts. Grain was still the chief crop, but certain new cultures were introduced by the Turks. Rice was brought from Asia Minor during the fifteenth century and was successfully grown in the Plovdiv and Pazardzhik regions. During the seventeenth century, tobacco and maize were introduced, and from Persia came the oil-bearing rose which is the special pride of Bulgaria. The roses were first planted round Adrianople (present day Edirne, known to the Bulgarians as Odrin) and subsequently in the temperate valleys of the southern slopes of the Stara Planina in the Kazanlük region. As late as the middle of the nineteenth century more of the land was given over to pasturage than to the plough. Sheep, goats, oxen and horses were kept, but pig breeding almost certainly decreased owing to the Moslem ban on pork. Beekeeping retained the importance it had had under the

[1] *Bǔlgaria pod Igo*, N. Stanev, p. 59 (*Bulgaria under the Yoke*), Sofia, 1947.

Tsars and wax was sold to foreign merchants. The villages were more or less self-sufficient, and the peasants went only occasionally to market in town, mainly to obtain agricultural implements.

Owing to the economic importance of metals for the Turks, many miners, though not all, were given certain privileges. Copper and silver were mined as before at Kratovo and Chiprovets. Lead was mined at Kratovo, iron at Chiprovets, Samokov and Etropolé, and gold at Nevrokop and Chiprovets. At Kratovo there was a mint which made silver and copper money. Iron was of particular importance for the needs of the army.

Since the Turks had adopted a policy of expelling the Bulgars from the towns, and displayed little interest in internal trade and the development of the national economy, handicrafts and trade declined, and Bulgaria became one of the most backward countries in Europe. The main handicrafts served the needs of agriculture, the urban population, the ruling class and, of course, the army. They included smithery and the forging of horseshoes, saddlery, the making of horse-blankets and bags from goats' hair, slipper making, pottery, baking, tanning, fur-dressing, weaving, tailoring, tapestry and carpet making and goldsmithery. The artisans practising these trades were organized as before into guilds which only reached their full development during the eighteenth and nineteenth centuries. The craftsmen included both Turks and non-Turks, although it was the former who played the decisive role in the guilds. The craftsmen generally worked by themselves, or with the help of one or two journeymen and apprentices, and disposed of their wares direct without the intervention of middlemen. This led to the restriction of internal trade which was mainly confined to such goods as salt, vegetables, olive oil, rice, seasoning, etc., which were not always obtainable locally.

The Bulgars themselves played a very small part in trade. External trade was largely in the hands of the merchants of Dubrovnik, who exported raw materials such as grain, leather, wax, wool and linen, and imported manufactured goods, including velvets and other luxury textiles, glass, paper and objects for adornment. Genoa and Venice also had trade agreements with Turkey by which the merchants of these cities paid duties amounting to not more than 3 per cent of the value of the goods, were permitted to have their own courts and had the inviolability of their houses guaranteed in return for the payment of a specified tribute. The merchants of Dubrovnik were in a particularly privileged position after 1459 when they were

freed from all payment of duty. They also enjoyed a monopoly in
the export of wool and the import of salt. Internal trade was initially
in the hands of the Greeks and after the sixteenth century the
Spanish Jews began to play an important role. These Jews had been
expelled from Spain in 1492 by Ferdinand and Isabella, and apart
from their activity in trade, many of them made careers as bankers,
doctors and lawyers. The Rumanians took part in trading in the
villages.

Within the Turkish Empire both the Sultan's own coinage and
that of the West European States with which it traded were legal
tender.

The Decline of Turkish Feudalism

Up to the first half of the sixteenth century the Turkish Empire
was in a reasonably healthy condition, and it continued to expand
territorially. The Sultans were capable leaders, and the administration was, in its own way, honest and just. The Empire reached the
height of its power under Suleiman I the Magnificent (1520–1566).
The Turks held all the Balkans, Moldavia, Wallachia, Transylvania,
southern Hungary, Egypt, North Africa, Asia Minor, Syria and Iraq.
There were Turks in the Ukraine, in Podolia and even the Viennese
Emperors had to send missions with rich presents in order to appease
the Sultan and to protect their frontiers. The Sultan also received
presents from Venice, Poland, Rumania and Russia, and, since he
himself seldom sent any, these presents were, in fact, tantamount to
tribute. After Suleiman's death, however, a process of stagnation
and disintegration set in within the Empire, which was accelerated
during the nineteenth century, and ended with the collapse of
Turkey in Europe. While it is true that the Turkish Army had
still many victories to win in the succeeding centuries, it experienced
its first military and diplomatic defeats in the half century after
Suleiman's death. Of these defeats, let it suffice to mention the Battle
of Lepanto (1571) and the war with Austria which ended in the
Treaty of Sitvatorok (1606) by which Austria was released from the
payment of annual tribute to the Turks. In addition the Turks were
obliged to observe the general courtesies of international diplomatic
conduct, instead of treating the Christian rulers with their accustomed
contempt and arrogance. One may also mention the Turko-Persian
war of 1603–1612, as a result of which Turkey lost Tabriz and
Georgia. Although the Turks succeeded in taking Podolia and part
of the Ukraine from Poland in 1672, their two-month siege of Vienna

in 1683 ended in crushing defeat when Jan Sobieski, with a combined Austrian and Polish army, completely routed the Ottoman Army. By the Treaty of Karlovac (1699), Turkey lost almost all Hungary to Austria, and Poland recovered Podolia.

One of the reasons for the decline of the Turkish Empire was the financial crisis which developed as a result of the crippling military expenditure incurred in the ceaseless wars of expansion. After the sixteenth century, Turkey's rivals in Europe were developing trading and manufacturing relations, while Turkey's economy remained on the level of feudalism with its consequently low productivity. With the growth of their financial resources, the European Powers improved their military technique, and Turkey was also obliged to equip herself with artillery, establish arsenals, etc. In order to do this she had to pay dearly for the services of foreign military instructors and engineers. The military expenditure necessitated by Turkey's huge Empire, stretching over three continents, swallowed up the entire revenue and, to make matters worse, when Turkey began to suffer defeats, there was no extra revenue forthcoming in the form of plunder, and she was thrown back on her own internal resources. The Sultans were no longer able to pay the Janissaries or the civil servants who proceeded to make their own living through plunder and corrupt practices. To raise money, the Sultans began to 'sell' posts in the administration, and this opened the door to wholesale corruption and degeneration throughout the political system.

A further reason for the decline of the Turkish Empire was the breakdown of the *spahi* system, in spite of the measures taken to prevent separatism and private ownership of land. The desire of the *spahi* to own land and bequeath it to their children had already manifested itself in the tendency to make land *vakīf*. The *spahi* then began to sell and bequeath land without the Sultan's consent. The military leaders accumulated wealth, and luxury and idleness replaced their former simple, spartan way of life. They no longer had any taste for fighting and took to living in the towns and buying expensive luxury goods from the West which feudal economy could ill afford. During the eighteenth century Holland, France and Great Britain began to receive all kinds of costly goods from newly acquired colonies—chemicals for textiles, drugs, coffee, sugar, precious metals, dyes, etc., and they were manufacturing high quality woollen and cotton products, iron tools, glass and china. A market for all these goods was found not only in Western Europe, but also in

Turkey where they were eagerly bought by officials and ex-army officers who now resided in the towns in high style. In return Turkey exported food to the West where there was an increasing need for food imports. Foreign trade did not bring as much revenue as it might have done, owing to the fact that Turkey signed trade agreements, known as 'capitulations', with France, England and other European States, by which the foreign merchants obtained special privileges. The first of these agreements was made in 1535 with France, with whom Turkey now conducted the major part of her foreign trade. French merchants and pilgrims were accorded the right to travel freely within the Turkish Empire, and other nationalities were often forced to travel under the French flag. The rich Turks were content to make their wealth by exploiting the peasantry and spend it on luxurious living. Thus, in the nineteenth century when the Western Powers began to industrialize and develop along capitalist lines, Turkey did not have the capital accumulation necessary to follow suit. She therefore fell into economic, and consequently political, dependence on the Great Powers, ruined by her own backwardness, and propped up by loans granted by the Great Powers who, in view of the rivalry between them, preferred to do this rather than face the problem of what should replace the Ottoman Empire when it collapsed. All the money spent on luxuries by the rich degenerate Turks was, of course, wrung from the subject peoples, whose standard of living rapidly deteriorated, and who suffered the terrible injustices caused by the corruption that permeated the State machine.

The Sultans themselves contributed to the general decline and collapse of Turkey. They no longer led their troops into battle,[1] and lived soft, degenerate lives, devoted entirely to self-indulgence and unlimited luxury. They helped the spread of corruption within their own administration by selling appointments and they undermined their highly disciplined army—based on the *spahi* system— by giving out lands, not to the most deserving, loyal soldiers, but to worthless flatterers and court favourites. As an example of how the collapse of the feudal system affected the army, the official records show that at the beginning of the seventeenth century an area which was liable to supply a thousand horsemen in fact only supplied fifty. The Sultans were forced to supplement their army with mercenary cavalry which was less efficient and added to the financial difficulties of the State.

[1] Suleiman the Magnificent was the last to do so.

The Janissaries also were becoming a liability rather than an asset. Created in 1330, they had been the bravest, most fanatical fighters, the pride of the Turkish Army, devoted to the Sultan. However, from the fifteenth century onwards, they became an unmanageable powerful force within the country and played the role of a Praetorian Guard, imposing their will on the Sultan and taking part in palace intrigues. As early as 1481, in order to pacify them, the Sultan was forced to give them ten sacks of gold, and in 1515—the head of the Grand Vizir. Between the fifteenth and nineteenth centuries the Janissaries deposed six Sultans and placed five on the throne. The final disintegration of the Janissaries as a fighting force began in the sixteenth century, when Suleiman II allowed Turkish children to join the Corps without going through the stern preparatory training given to the original cadres. This inevitably lowered the standard of the Corps. The next step was to permit them to marry, instead of keeping them segregated from ordinary society so that the maximum attention could be paid to the development of their fighting qualities. After 1638 no more Christians were conscripted. The Janissaries had been dissatisfied with their pay when single, and now that they had families, they began to open shops in garrison towns and to take up trading in order to augment their incomes. The general corruption in the Empire affected the Corps, and it became a repository for those who sought a career and coveted the privileges accorded to Janissaries, i.e. freedom from all taxation, etc. Sons of Janissaries were enrolled in the Corps, and received their pay almost from the day of their birth. People who had never set eyes on a Janissary standard bribed officers to witness that they were members of the Corps and therefore not eligible to pay taxes. The number of Janissaries increased enormously and weighed heavily on the Treasury. The Sultans were unable to pay the Janissaries and the latter found money for themselves in an arbitrary manner. On the death of a Sultan they would take to plunder and pillage, and pledge allegiance to the new Sultan only if he took no action against them. At the beginning of each financial year, they would steal the tax registers and sell them to the highest bidder, who then collected the taxes according to the registers, making sure that he himself made a substantial profit out of it.

Various Sultans attempted to do something about the Janissaries, but without success, until Mahmud II made an all-out attack on them in 1826, and destroyed them utterly, throwing two hundred thousand bodies into the Bosphorus.

From the seventeenth century onwards the internal chaos gave rise to banditry, at first only along the main roads, but later all over the country. Many foreign missions, including the ambassador of Charles II in 1665, have left accounts of the dangers of travel under constant threat of ambush and robbery. One of the worst manifestations of banditry was the Kŭrdzhali movement which began in 1792 and resulted in disorder and the dislocation of all normal life until as late as 1815. It reached such serious proportions that in order to combat it the Turkish Government was even obliged to arm the *raya*, who had hitherto been forbidden to possess weapons.

The Tŭrnovo Rising, 1598

The Bulgarians had never given up hope of liberation, and when the Turkish Empire had passed its zenith and began to decline, the deterioration in conditions and Turkey's defeats gave rise both to increased discontent and increased hopes of throwing off the Ottoman yoke.

The Bulgarians at first looked for help from Turkey's Western rivals. Between the sixteenth and eighteenth centuries, Austria was Turkey's chief enemy, and the Austro-Turkish war which began in 1593 excited great hope, especially when Austria's ally, Michael, *Voivoda* of Rumania, crossed the Danube and brought his army on to Bulgarian soil. Although Michael was forced to withdraw, the Bulgarians prepared to rise against the Turks.

The leaders of the movement were Todor Balina, a leading citizen of Nikopol, and two merchants of Dubrovnik, Pavel Dzhordzich and Peter Sorkočević. The Metropolitan of Tŭrnovo and other members of the upper clergy were also among the organizers. Sigismund Batory, *Voivoda* of Transylvania, who had already revolted against his overlord the Sultan, in alliance with Austria, was invited by Georgič to come and liberate Bulgaria also, and was informed that the people would welcome him with open arms. Later, Sigismund received a similar invitation from Balina. Widespread preparations were made for a rising, embracing such towns as Varna, Shumen, Plovdiv, Rusé, Nikopol and Tŭrnovo. In 1597, Balina and Dzhordzich went to Prague to ask for aid from the Austrian Emperor, Rudolf III, as well. Unfortunately, neither Batory nor the Emperor in fact sent help, but the Bulgars were determined to go through with their rising, and when in 1598 Michael of Rumania, in the course of his war against Turkey, crossed the Danube again, the rising began, with its centre at Tŭrnovo, the ancient capital, and spread over north-eastern

Bulgaria. A descendant of the last Bulgarian royal dynasty was proclaimed Tsar, as Shishman III. The Rumanian troops apparently plundered the country and then retired, leaving the Bulgars to the mercy of the Turks. The rebels were lacking in arms, and, although much organizational work had gone into the preparation of the rising, it was still inadequate. In their enthusiasm, they had seriously underestimated the power which the Turks still possessed. The rising was put down with great cruelty by the Turks, and thousands of Bulgars fled abroad to escape from the Janissaries. Shishman III fled to Russia, but the majority of the other émigrés went to Rumania, where they founded the Bulgarian colony which was to play an important role in the later struggles for liberation.

At the same time as the Tŭrnovo Rising was being prepared, the Archbishop of Okhrid was organizing a similar rising relying on help from Venice and Naples. This help, however, never materialized and the plans collapsed.

Catholic Influence in Bulgaria

While Bulgaria was predominantly Orthodox in religion, there was a certain Roman Catholic element in the country. The Catholic influence came in the first place through the merchants of Dubrovnik who had colonies in most of the chief towns, such as Sofia, Tŭrnovo, Plovdiv, Provadia, Shumen, Razgrad, Varna, Nikopol and Silistra, and in the second place through the Saxon miners of Chiprovets and Kratovo. These Saxons had settled there during the beginning of the fourteenth century, and they had become completely Bulgarianized, although holding to their Catholicism. As a privileged section of the community, living away from the main roads where the Turks passed, the miners and other artisans and traders connected with the iron industry retained an independent and freedom-loving spirit.

For some time, little attention had been paid to the Bulgarian Catholics by the Western Church, but after the Council of Trent (1545–1563) emissaries were sent to investigate the position of the Bulgarian Catholics, together with missionaries to spread the faith. The door to Catholic influence was also opened by treaties signed by Turkey and Austria during the beginning of the seventeenth century, by which the latter was given the protectorate over the Catholics in Bulgaria. Further reasons for Catholic interest in Bulgaria were Austria's desire to gain the support of the local population in her wars against Turkey, and also, in view of her increasing rivalry with Russia, her hopes of using Catholic propaganda as a weapon to

B*

counter Russian influence as exercised through the Orthodox Church.

The centre of Catholic activity was Chiprovets, where in 1595 Franciscan friars arrived from Bosnia and Croatia to act as missionaries, headed by Peter Solinat. In 1601 Solinat was made Catholic Bishop of Sofia but his seat remained at Chiprovets.

The Orthodox Bulgarian families strongly resisted all attempts at converting them to the Roman faith, and would have nothing to do with Solinat and his missionaries. For this reason, the Catholics concentrated their missionary activities on the Bulgar heretics, remnants of the Paulicians and Bogomils, who preserved some of the old Bogomil beliefs, such as the rejection of the Cross, ikons, baptism with water, church buildings and church hierarchy. They lived chiefly in the valley of the river Osŭm, in Nikopol, Svishtov and Lovech, and also in the Plovdiv region. Most of them were poor labourers on the *spahi* estates. Owing to the heretics' hatred of the Orthodox Church, the Catholic missionaries had considerable success among them. Solinat's work resulted in an increase in the number of Catholics in Bulgaria and the founding of four Catholic monasteries and several churches. The total number of Catholics in Bulgaria, however, remained relatively very small and probably did not greatly exceed eight thousand.

Solinat was particularly careful to train native Bulgarians as priests and some were sent to Rome for this purpose. Solinat was succeeded in 1624 as Bishop of Sofia by Iliya Marinov, who was himself born in Chiprovets. Marinov, who had been educated in Rome, paid great attention to educational work in Bulgaria, and opened the first Catholic school in Chiprovets in 1624. Both Latin and Slavonic were used in the Catholic schools and churches. Of the prominent Catholics in Bulgaria, the name of Ivan Lilov should be remembered as a teacher in the Chiprovets school for thirty-two years, 1635–1667. Another prominent Catholic was Petŭr Bogdan, who succeeded Marinov as Bishop of Sofia. Bogdan was also a native of Chiprovets and had studied in Rome. Under him, Sofia was raised to an Archbishopric, and a new Bishopric was established in north-eastern Bulgaria at Martsianopol (near Preslav). Filip Stanislavov, consecrated Bishop of the newly formed See of Nikopol in 1648, was also an educator and prepared the first Bulgarian printed book, the *Abagar* (1651).

Of the eminent Bulgarian clergy, one of the most important was Petŭr Parchevich (1617–1674), also a native of Chiprovets. Parchevich was a well-educated man who received the degree of 'Doctor of Theology and Canon Law' in Rome and became Archbishop of Martsianopol. His greatest activity was not so much in the field of religion as in politics. He was a great patriot, and travelled over Bulgaria as an 'apostle' not merely for the Catholic faith but also for a political awakening among the Bulgarian people. His constant political activity, which absorbed most of his time, was not looked upon favourably by Rome, and he was removed from his See. He was, however, eventually restored and even became a Cardinal. Using his gifts as a linguist and diplomat, Parchevich sought help from the Catholic princes of Europe in order to liberate Bulgaria. The Crown of Bulgaria was offered in the name of both Catholic and Orthodox Bulgars to the Rumanian *voivoda* Matei Basarab, and Parchevich journeyed all over Europe, visiting Warsaw, Vienna and Venice, pleading Bulgaria's cause and seeking military support. From 1646-1674 when he died in Rome, Parchevich toured the Catholic capitals, endeavouring to organize united action for the liberation of his country, but unfortunately nothing materialized. Parchevich eventually became convinced that the Western States had no intention of helping Bulgaria, and, although a Catholic, he began to look to Russia for liberation. He asked the Pope to recognize the title of the Tsar Alexei Mikhailovich whom he called a 'humanitarian and a friend of other peoples', and to send an embassy to Moscow to discuss Russia's participation in the fight against Turkey.

In their efforts to organize an uprising with external help, the Catholics had the support of the Orthodox Christians, and in the common cause, religious differences were, to a large extent, forgotten.

Further Risings

In 1682 war broke out between Austria and Turkey. The Turks laid siege to Vienna itself in the summer of 1683 and captured its outer defences. At the eleventh hour, however, when it seemed that nothing could save Vienna, and with it Western Europe, the Polish King, Jan Sobieski, appeared with an army and inflicted a crushing defeat on the Turks. The latter were forced to retreat, and such was the decisive character of Sobieski's victory that the Turkish offensive against Europe lost its impetus irrevocably. Encouraged by this success, which exploded the myth of Turkish invincibility, the three Catholic powers—Austria, Poland and Venice—formed a Holy Alliance in 1684 and marched south. In 1687 Austria liberated

Hungary by her victory at Harsan near Mohács, and drove the Turks from Slavonia along the Danube and Sava. Venetian troops attacked in Dalmatia and Greece. In 1688 the Austrians took Belgrade, then Niš and Pirot, and some units even reached Dragoman on the present Jugoslav-Bulgarian frontier.

The successes of the Catholic Powers against Turkey stirred the people of the Balkans once again to rise against the Turks. In 1686 Tŭrnovo once more became the centre of preparation for an uprising. Its organizer, Rostislav Stratsimirovitch, who claimed descent from Tsar Ivan Stratsimir, sought support from Russia, who had joined the Holy Alliance and was fighting the Turks in the Crimea. The rising was not successful and Turkish troops devastated Tŭrnovo and massacred a large number of its inhabitants. Rostislav himself escaped and eventually made his way to Moscow.

Even this failure did not make the Bulgarians lose hope of liberation through armed uprising. The defeat of the Turks at Mohács and the capture of Belgrade by the Austrians gave them further encouragement and the situation appeared to them to be favourable for a new attempt. The uprising (1688) was organized by the Catholics of north-west Bulgaria and had its centre in Chiprovets and the surrounding districts. Its leaders were two citizens of Chiprovets, Georgi Peyachevich and Bogdan Marinov, whose armed bands succeeded in breaking through to meet the Austrian forces. The Orthodox Christians, who once again made common cause with the Catholics, appealed to Russia for help. The rising was also cruelly suppressed. The flourishing town of Chiprovets was burnt, and most of its inhabitants slaughtered or enslaved, although some succeeded in escaping to Rumania and Hungary.

As the Austrians advanced into the Balkans, they were received joyfully by the Serbs and Bulgars, who took up arms and joined them. Austrian forces had reached northern Macedonia, when Leopold I was distracted from the Turkish War by the hope of the Spanish succession. This enabled the Turks to recover somewhat. The war continued in the western area of the Balkan peninsula and engendered movements of revolt in Montenegro, Bosnia, Herzegovina and Dubrovnik. Peace was finally concluded between Austria and Turkey at Karlovac in 1699. By this treaty, Turkey lost wide territories in Croatia, Hungary and the Ukraine. Austria returned Belgrade to Turkey. This treaty was an important milestone in the process of disintegration which now seriously affected the Turkish Empire.

Even after the failure of the risings in Tŭrnovo, Chiprovets, etc., the urge of the Bulgarians for freedom was not crushed. During the eighteenth century there were various attempts at revolt—such as the rising in western Bulgaria during the war waged by Austria and Russia against Turkey from 1736 to 1739, when Austrian troops captured Niš.

Bulgarian Colonies Abroad

When the 1736–1739 war ended unsuccessfully for the allies, many Bulgars who had attached themselves to the Austrian troops were forced to retreat with them in order to escape the wrath of the Janissaries. They settled first in the Semograd region and later in the Banat. Serbo-Croat and Bulgarian refugees from previous risings which took place during the Austro-Turkish War of 1682–1699, were already living in Rumania, Transylvania, Hungary and Austria. A large number of the Bulgars settled in Budapest from which the Turkish population had been driven after the liberation of the city. Here the Serbs and the Bulgars set up a South-Slav commune with an elected administration. The Bulgars engaged in peaceful trades such as commerce, handicrafts, vine-growing, agriculture, cattle breeding and gardening. In Rumania they obtained certain rights and privileges from the local Princes, which they retained after part of Rumania had passed under Austrian rule in 1718. Apart from gifts of land, these rights included the right to work and trade, and freedom of worship for the Catholics, who, it will be remembered, played a significant part in the risings. The favourable conditions enjoyed by the émigrés attracted other Bulgars—Orthodox as well as Catholic—who left Bulgaria and joined the colony in Rumania. The émigrés, however, never renounced their nationality, and preserved their folk customs. In the nineteenth century, these émigré colonies were to play a great part in the struggle for liberation and national independence.

The Pomaks

During the period between the fifteenth and seventeenth centuries, there came into being a category of Bulgars known as the *Pomaks*. The name may be derived from *pomagach*—a helper, but probably with the connotation of 'collaborationist', since they were Bulgars who professed the Islamic faith and who therefore sided with the Turks in time of war and insurrection. They assisted the Turks to put down the Greek rising of 1821 and even helped to suppress

Bulgar risings. *Pomak* villages existed in two main areas: in the Rhodope mountains and in the Danubian Plain, north of the Stara Planina. It has been estimated that there were at one time 400,000 *Pomaks*, but after the Treaty of Berlin in 1878 the majority left Bulgaria and settled in Turkey.

Some of the *Pomaks* had been forcibly converted to Islam, while others had accepted it voluntarily for the sake of the benefits thus gained. An account of the forcible conversion of villages in the Chepino district of the Rhodope has been given by a contemporary chronicler, a priest named Methodi Draginov. These Chepino villages were military villages freed from taxes, including those due to the Greek Metropolitan of Plovdiv. In 1657 when Turkish troops were gathering in Plovdiv for the war against Venice, the Metropolitan denounced the villages to the Turks as subversive in revenge for the fact that Chepino paid him no taxes. Vizir Mohammed Küprülü entered the village of Kostandovo with a large number of Janissaries and was about to execute all the priests and village headmen as rebels, when a certain Asan Hodja suggested that their lives should be spared if they accepted Islam. Apparently all of them did. After Mohammed Küprülü left, four Turkish *hodjas* remained behind to complete the Turkicization of the entire population of the villages concerned. The process was facilitated by a famine which was raging in the district at the time. Asan Hodja had grain brought from the State granaries and it was distributed to those households which accepted Islam. The inhabitants were afterwards ordered by the Sultan to assume the status of *raya* and pay the usual taxes. To round off the 'conversion', Asan Hodja had two hundred and nineteen churches and thirty-three monasteries destroyed. However, not all the inhabitants of the ill-fated district bowed to Islam. Of those brave souls who resisted, some were slain and their houses burnt, while others escaped and built new villages elsewhere.

The *Pomaks* are of considerable sociological interest. Unlike the boyars who accepted Islam to preserve their privileges and the Bulgars indoctrinated with Islam in the Corps of Janissaries, they were not absorbed into Turkish society, but remained a closed Bulgar community. They preserved many Bulgarian customs and their Bulgarian speech, and while the latter contains more Turkish words than the Bulgarian spoken elsewhere throughout the country, it also preserves many old Bulgarian words no longer in general use. To this day there are *Pomak* villages in the Rhodope, whose inhabitants retain their Islamic faith.

Apart from such mass 'conversions' as those which occurred in the Rhodope and elsewhere, the Turks also attempted to influence individuals whose good appearance, bravery and other qualities singled them out as worthy candidates for conversion to Islam. One of those selected was Georgi, a goldsmith from Kratovo, who had been forced to leave his home town because the Turks there were trying to convert him. He went to Sofia where he evidently attracted fresh attention, for the *hodjas* tried to woo him with fair words. When, however, he refused to give up his Christian faith, he was arrested for blasphemy. The *Kadi* before whom he appeared also tried to persuade him to embrace Islam. Still Georgi remained obdurate, and when the mob insisted that he be put to death, he was burnt outside the church of St Sofia (1515).

Another case was that of the shoemaker Nikola. He had agreed to become a Moslem after the Turks had deliberately made him drunk, but later he decided to return to Christianity. A learned Moslem tried to persuade him against this course of action, but Nikola remained firm in his resolve. As in the case of Georgi, a Turkish mob intervened, dragged him to court, and after he had again refused to continue in the Moslem faith, he was stoned to death, and his body cut up and burnt (1555).

The Dark Years

For those Bulgars who did not emigrate, the failure of the risings ushered in a period of dreadful repression and virtual slavery. The people called it *Cherno Teglo*, literally the 'black weight'. As the Turkish Empire decayed and passed into decline, corruption pervaded the administration, justice and tolerance were things of the past; taxes and *angaria* were arbitrarily levelled, squeezing the people beyond endurance; the peasants were ruined by usurers and lost their land, some becoming virtual slave labourers on the *spahi* estates and others fleeing to the towns. The villages and special categories of *raya* which had formerly enjoyed certain privileges lost all such rights and became no different from the rest of the subject population. It is not possible to discuss or even list all the outrages committed by the Turks against the subject peoples of the Balkans. The examples below will, however, serve to give an idea of their sufferings.

The existing taxes increased out of all proportion through the corruption of the tax collectors. For instance, a traveller, Lyusyanin, in 1786 describes how a priest complained that *kharach*—the poll-tax on non-Moslems—though legally payable only by persons over the age of sixteen, was levied by the collectors even for babies of eighteen months. Beautiful girls were taken from their homes by force to adorn the Turkish harems, or, together with good-looking boys, to be sold in the slave markets. Such a fate was regarded as a disgrace by the Bulgars, and parents sometimes killed their own children rather than let the Turks have them. The Turkish lords expected to be given all the best produce, such as lambs, chickens, etc., and passing Turks could take what they liked in the way of food, fodder and transport from any village. Refusal or resistance was severely punished. In desperation, whole villages left their homes and settled in desolate inaccessible places to escape from their despoilers. Perhaps the most incredible tax of all was the 'tooth tax'. This outrageous tax was not infrequently levelled on a village by Turks who had eaten and drunk their fill in it, ostensibly for the wear and tear sustained by their teeth during the meal!

Increasing attacks were made on the Christian religion. The Turks forbade the building of new churches and bell towers, and in the existing churches, crosses might not be placed on the roofs, nor might the windows be opened. Apart from these prohibitions, the Turks violated the churches and profaned the ikons.

Worst of all, when the Turks saw the connection between the risings and the wars with the Western Powers, and realized that the raya sympathized with the Empire's enemies, their hatred of the raya knew no bounds. With the vicious cruelty and arrogance masking the uneasy foreboding characteristic of a governing class who feel their throne of power crumbling beneath them, they unleashed a reign of terror on the helpless raya, whose only crime— albeit the one deadly sin in the eyes of the oppressor—was their desire for freedom. That uneasy foreboding led to the raya being forbidden to possess any weapons, and the prohibition was even extended to knives for ordinary domestic uses. Thus the people were left defenceless against wild beasts and robbers.

On every side the Bulgars were humiliated and laden with monstrous indignities. They were not permitted to ride horses in the big towns, but were forced to dismount and lead them. The penalty for disobeying this ordinance was confiscation of the horse and imprisonment for its rider, who might even suffer death if he resisted. If a Bulgar met a Turk on the road, he had to dismount and bow, and in the towns and villages, both men and women had to stand still and show deference to a passing Turk.

Every Bulgar was at the beck and call of the Turks. He could be ordered to hew wood, work in a Turk's garden, clean his lavatory, etc. If a Turk was carrying something in the street, any Bulgar who met him had to take the object from him and convey it to his house. The whole population was reduced to utter slavery. Terrible, savage punishments awaited those who disobeyed, resisted or even displeased the master race. The death penalty was passed on anyone who by accident or design knocked the turban off a Turk's head. Legal investigations were conducted under torture, and both witnesses and accused might be smeared with tar and roasted between two fires, or splinters of wood might be driven under their nails and then set alight, or they might be buried in the earth up to their necks facing the sun. Even Bulgarian women were not spared. Although the Koran forbids the punishment and torture of women, the Turks cunningly got round this difficulty, flouting the spirit of the law, while salving their conscience by obeying its letter. The woman was dressed in baggy trousers in which a cat was placed; the cat was then beaten through the cloth and the terrified animal clawed the flesh of the victim. The end was achieved, yet the Turks could claim that they had not beaten a woman but merely a cat. The traveller Lyusyanin describes how he saw many victims impaled on stakes during his journey through the Empire in 1787.

The Haiduti

To this unbearable oppression and denial of human rights, the Bulgars gave the answer which has been given by so many other tormented peoples before and since. They took up arms and went to the mountains. In Bulgarian they were known as *haiduti*, from a Hungarian word meaning a rebel or one who fights against a foreign invader. 'Guerrilla' or 'partisan' would be the closest equivalent in modern terminology. The *haidut* movement existed alongside and separate from the movements already described, which were, in the main, risings of the upper strata of the former feudal society, the priests and the well-to-do craftsmen and merchants, and were generally armed uprisings in co-operation with one or other of the Western powers, with a view to re-establishing a Bulgarian Kingdom. The *haidut* movement, on the other hand, was entirely popular in character. It had existed since the sixteenth century and consisted mainly of courageous young men, who could no longer tolerate the terrible oppression or stand by and watch their villages plundered and their womenfolk dishonoured or sold into slavery. With muskets and swords they took to the mountains in little bands to avenge the wrongs done to them and their families by their tormentors—both Turks and Bulgarian quislings. They operated in bands varying between ten and twenty in number with a leader, or *voivoda*, and a standard bearer. The bravest and best man in a band was chosen to be the *voivoda*. Sometimes he was elected by contest, such as stone-throwing or marksmanship, and he was deposed only in the event of cowardice or incompetence. His second-in-command was the *bairaktar*, or standard bearer, and the standard was generally green or red. The *haidut* bands operated only while there were leaves on the trees: in summer they lived in the mountain fastnesses, and in winter they returned to their villages to work as shepherds and drovers, etc. They would search out the oppressors of the people and then swoop without warning at night to slay them and burn their houses. They had a high code of behaviour: no *haidut* stole, troubled women or plundered innocent people; no *haidut* ever deserted a wounded comrade, and indeed the fate of a captured *haidut* was a terrible one. He might be impaled on a stake and left to die a slow, agonizing death, or he was torn apart by four horses. If he was dead on falling into Turkish hands, his head was cut off and exhibited in his native village. Sometimes even their relatives were also arrested and tortured. The heroism of the *haiduti* was rewarded by the love and silent help of those who remained in the villages, and the ordinary people risked much to give them food, shelter and information. The Turks retaliated with collective punishment, destroying villages in an area where a Turk had been killed by *haiduti*, and transporting the inhabitants to Asia Minor to be sold or forcibly Turkicized. In spite of the support of the people, the *haiduti* often endured cold, hunger and great hardship in the course of their struggle, yet, notwithstanding the privations they endured and the horrible fate that always hung over them, the *haiduti* by no means lacked a Robin Hood air of romance. They wore the rich, colourful national costumes, ornamented with filigree and braid, that the Turks had forbidden the *raya* to wear, and they were armed with a musket, a chased sword and a brace of pistols. Sometimes during a lull in the struggle, safe in their mountain eyries, the *haidut* bands would gather to rest and make merry and sing the traditional songs of the heroes of old. The *haiduti* themselves were celebrated in many popular songs and ballads, and are the subject of many novels, short stories and poems. The names of some of the almost legendary *haidut* leaders have come down to us—Chavdar of the Rila Mountains, Manush of the Strandzha, Strashil of the Pirin, Kuzman and many others. There were also women *haiduti* who fought side by side with their male comrades as equals. It was even not unknown for a woman to command a *haidut* band. Such a woman was Sirma, who died in 1861. Even as an old woman of eighty, according to Dimiter Miladinov, the collector of Bulgarian folk songs, she kept her pistols under her pillow and her sabre on the wall.

The Phanariot Greeks

The fall of Constantinople brought about the end of the Byzantine Empire, but to the Byzantine Church it brought the fulfilment of one of its most cherished aims—the subjugation of the Bulgarian Church by the Patriarchate of Constantinople. The independent Bulgarian Church fell with the Bulgarian monarchy, but the Greek Patriarch succeeded in winning greater powers, both spiritual and secular, than he had previously held. He obtained from the Sultan a *firman* recognizing him as the representative of all the conquered Christians, thus giving him authority over the Bulgarian, Serbian, Albanian, Walachian and Moldavian Churches. The price of his increased power and privileges was collaboration with the conqueror. The Patriarch was made responsible for seeing that the Christians were loyal, peaceable subjects of the Sultan, and he also assisted the administration by giving information on the numbers of Christians and by co-operating in the fixing of taxes. The Patriarch and the ambitious Greeks around him soon won positions of power and influence under the Turks. The cultural and scientific backwardness of the Turks contributed to the Greek rise to power, because the former were forced to rely on the services of the Greeks as doctors, lawyers, clerks, bankers, translators, drafters of treaties, and so on.

The most powerful Greeks were the Phanariots, so-called after the district of Constantinople in which the lighthouse stood. They grew very rich and acquired enormous influence, both in ecclesiastical and secular matters, by purchasing office from the Sultan. Thus a man might buy the Patriarchate and then sell Bishoprics to the highest bidder, who in their turn accepted bribes from the priests under him. As time went by, the sums required increased enormously. For example, in the fifteenth century, one could become Patriarch for a thousand gold pieces, but the price rose until ultimately a would-be Patriarch had to find a hundred and fifty thousand gold pieces. Sometimes the Greek clergy would depute Bulgarian parish priests to collect the dues for them, and should the Bulgars refuse to do so, or make some mistake in the execution of their task, they were publicly humiliated by the Metropolitans, who beat them with sticks or whips either in the church or in the street.

The Church was not the only ladder to power and riches for the Phanariot Greeks. Some achieved them in secular activities; for example, Michael Cantacuzene, who claimed descent from the old Byzantine royal house. Michael lived during the sixteenth century and through his friendship with the Grand Vizir, his gift for intrigue and his monopoly in the salt trade, he acquired enormous influence and fabulous wealth. The splendour of his palace at Anchialos rivalled that of the Sultan himself, but when his power began to do the same, the Sultan had him arrested. His life was saved by the intervention of his friend the Vizir, and the payment of one hundred and sixty thousand *talers*, but he had not learnt his lesson, and returned to his former pursuit of wealth and power. When these once more passed all limits, the Sultan had him hanged at the gates of his palace at Anchialos.

The Phanariot princes also achieved control of Rumania, where, through Greek trading influence in the Danube and Black Sea ports in the first instance, they were able to infiltrate throughout the Church and administration. They carried out considerable Hellenization in the Rumanian Church and substituted the Greek liturgy for the Slavonic. They took advantage of the civil war between the Prince of Walachia and the Prince of Moldavia during the seventeenth century to entrench themselves still further in the administration. After the death of these two princes, the Phanariot Greeks succeeded in getting themselves elected princes of Walachia and Moldavia, with the support of the Turks, to whom the princedoms had been hostile, and who therefore wished to neutralize these two areas of potential danger. The Greeks then proceeded to suck the country and its resources dry.

It can be readily understood that, as a result of bribery, those who entered the Church were by no means suitable for the calling. They were notoriously ignorant and uneducated. Many monks, if not the majority, were illiterate, and in the seventeenth century there was even a Metropolitan of Odrin (Adrianople) who could neither read nor write. The purchase of an ecclesiastical position was an investment to these grasping, unworthy clergy, an investment from which they drew rich interest in levying fees for all kinds of religious services, such as sprinkling of water, divorce permits and fines for offences against Church laws. Apart from collecting fees and fines, they did a lively trade in false relics, such as pieces of wood treated so as to make it non-inflammable and sold as pieces of the 'True Cross' at exorbitant prices, taking advantage of the simple people's credulity and superstition. Every monastery installed some kind of shrine at which people might obtain all sorts of alleged benefits from heaven—for a consideration—and sent monks through the villages publicizing the shrines. In order to maintain their hold over the people, the Greek priests now and then would 'place curses' on individuals or even on whole communities. These curses were widely regarded as effective, and the people greatly feared them and would do anything to secure deliverance from them.

Thus, what the Turks did not take from the unhappy Bulgars, the grasping, insatiable Greek clergy appropriated by force or cunning.

But that was not the end of the Greek yoke. The Phanariot clergy set out systematically to destroy Bulgarian national consciousness and culture. The Bulgarian language, literature, books, schools, liturgy, songs, customs—all these the Greeks sought to stamp out. Most of the priests were, in fact, Greeks, but even the Bulgarian clergy had to conduct the services in the Greek language, which was foreign to themselves and their congregations. However, the worst feature was not the Greek oppression of the Bulgarian Church, for where there is oppression, so long as an independent spirit burns among the oppressed, the fight for freedom goes on, and all is not lost. The worst feature was that the Greeks succeeded in subverting large sections of Bulgars, and made them believe that Bulgarian was a vulgar, barbarous language fit only for ignorant, boorish shepherds, and that all educated and cultured men spoke Greek and behaved as Greeks. It came about in the following manner. In the second half of the eighteenth century there was a renaissance of Greek national feeling. It was stimulated through the growth of commerce and the contact which the Phanariot merchants had with the enlightened ideas of the newly developed humanism of Western Europe. They saw with shame that Greek culture was admired and studied in Europe but neglected in Greece itself. The result was the opening of Greek schools in many of the chief cities of Europe, including Venice, Padua, Rome, Trieste, Vienna, Bucharest, Moscow and Odessa. The young Greeks who had studied in these schools found on their return home that the schools in Greece were sadly out of date and needed reform, and new ones were opened.

From the time of the Patriarch Samuel (1763) onwards, the patriarchs participated in this movement. The leading Greeks, burning with pride at the rediscovery of their heritage, abandoned the word 'Roman' which had been used to denote a citizen of Byzantium, the East Roman Empire, and reintroduced the classical term 'Hellene'. The rebirth of classicism, however, led first to nationalism and finally to rabid chauvinism. The chief contributory fact was the Russo-Austrian Declaration (1793) that the Byzantine Empire should be revived on the defeat of Turkey. Elated and filled with pride by this prospect, the Greeks set to work in earnest to Hellenize the other Balkan peoples in preparation for the event. The Serbian Patriarchate of Ipek and the Bulgarian Archbishopric of Okhrid were dissolved and brought under the Greek Patriarchate. Church books in Slavonic were no longer imported from Russia but were replaced by Greek ones. Everything possible was done to convince the non-Greek population of the superiority of everything Greek. So well did they succeed that sections of the richer Bulgars in the towns believed them, Hellenized their names, sent their children to Greek schools, used Greek words and expressions in their speech, and called themselves 'New Hellenes'. The stratum most affected by Hellenization was that consisting of the *chorbadzhii*, or wealthy peasants, who had recently moved to the towns in order to take up commerce. While in the towns Turkish was the language of administration, Greek was the language of commerce owing to the leading role played by the Phanariot merchants. In order to get established and accepted in Greek trading circles, and in order to obtain the necessary loans, etc., the *chorbadzhii* ingratiated themselves with the Greeks who were not slow to encourage them in Greek ways. No less affected were the young Bulgars who came to the towns in search of work as apprentices in the Greek workshops, as servants, shop and office workers and the like. Many of these young people did well in their work, married Greek girls, lost their sense of Bulgarian nationality and joined the ranks of the 'New Hellenes'.

Greek propaganda was so successful that the more wealthy urban Bulgars came to despise their own people in the villages who continued to speak their native tongue, and the peasants regarded everybody who wore European dress as a Greek. The Cyrillic alphabet was almost driven from current use, and even people who could not speak Greek wrote Bulgarian in Greek characters. The Russian Slavonic scholar, Grigorovich, travelling through the Slav lands of the Turkish Empire in 1845[1] found no person who could read Slavonic, and Jireček records that as late as the 1880's, he met old people who knew only the Greek alphabet and used it to write Bulgarian.

In their ardour for Hellenization, the Greeks were not content to use only peaceful subversion and economic persuasion. They resorted to appalling acts of vandalism. During the nineteenth century enormous numbers of priceless Slavonic manuscripts were burnt in an attempt to obliterate Slavonic culture. In many monasteries all the Bulgarian books and manuscripts were taken out of the libraries and burnt. Even the ancient library of the Patriarchs of Tŭrnovo was taken out into the Metropolitan's garden and burnt, after the Greek books had been removed to safety.

Thus Bulgaria groaned under the dual weight of Turkish political oppression and Greek cultural oppression. The Bulgarian language disappeared from the towns, but even the Phanariot Greeks could not manage to destroy it altogether. In the villages and mountains, and among the Bulgarian monks in the quiet monasteries, the Bulgarian language and traditions were kept alive until the day when once again Bulgarian national feeling was revived and the people rose to cast off the spiritual yoke of Greece.

Bulgaria and Russia

In order to have a proper understanding of subsequent relations between Russia and Bulgaria, it is essential to realize that, unlike Poland, for example, Bulgaria has a long-standing tradition of friendship with Russia and a feeling of brotherhood towards the Russian people. It is a tradition which was not born of the military alliances of kings and statesmen, nor of short-lived political expediency, but a tradition which has its roots deep down among the ordinary people and which has been maintained often in the face of official disapproval. From very early times there had been cultural links between Russia and Bulgaria. Both peoples were akin ethnically and linguistically. Bulgarian books brought Christian culture to Kiev, and Russia repaid this debt during the Turkish occupation when there was hardly a Bulgarian church or monastery which did not have books sent from Russia. Many Bulgars found sanctuary in Russia. A Bulgar—Kiprian—became Metropolitan of Moscow,

---

[1] Grigorovich's experience does not give an altogether correct impression of the situation at that time, since from 1835 onwards Bulgarian schools using the Slavonic alphabet were being opened.

while his nephew, Georgi Tsamblak, became Metropolitan of Lithuania and Kiev. Some Bulgarian saints such as Ivan Rilsky were adopted into the Russian pantheon and were mentioned in the church services. Biographies of some of them were written by Russian hagiographers: in 1639, for example, Ilya of Pskov wrote a life of Georgi the Goldsmith of Sofia who preferred to die rather than adopt the Islamic faith. But during the period of the Turkish yoke something more than mere cultural affinity developed. For nearly five hundred years, Russia has been affectionately known as *Dyado Ivan*—'Grandfather Ivan'—by the Bulgarian people, and during the long, cruel years of Turkish oppression, they looked towards Moscow with hope and longing, in the unshakable belief that their Russian elder brothers would come and liberate them. Their feeling of affinity with Russia was so strong that for a long time the idea persisted that after their liberation Bulgaria would become part of Russia. As early as 1576 the Venetian Ambassador declared that the Balkan peoples were very much devoted to the Grand Prince of Moscow and were quite ready to take up arms, free themselves from Turkey and become subjects of Moscow. As late as the beginning of the nineteenth century, the outstanding patriot, Sofroni Vrachansky, was also of the opinion that after her liberation Bulgaria should be united with Russia.

The legend of *Dyado Ivan* grew up during the fifteenth and sixteenth centuries. During the early period of the Turkish yoke, many of the Russian princes were vassals of the Golden Horde and not in a position to assist the Balkan Slavs. Those areas not subject to the Tartars were in constant conflict with them, and with the Lithuanians and Poles. During the reign of Ivan III (1462–1505), Moscow established its supremacy over the neighbouring Princedoms of north-east Russia and welded them into a powerful national State. The rise of the Moscow State coincided with the collapse of the Byzantine Empire, and Moscow was then left as the only powerful and independent Orthodox State. Ivan III, who was laying the foundations of autocracy in Russia, regarded himself as the direct successor of the Byzantine Emperors. He had taken the imperial title of Tsar, and further weight, together with some legality, was given to his claim by his marriage in 1472 to Sofia Paleologus, the niece of the last Byzantine emperor. After the marriage, he adopted as the Russian emblem the two-headed eagle of Byzantium. During the reign of Vasili III (1505–1533), the idea, already widespread, of 'Moscow as the Third Rome', received its first literary expression in the works of a monk named Filofei. In brief, this idea expressed the belief that Moscow had succeeded to the moral leadership of the world, first invested in Rome itself, and then in Constantinople, the Second Rome. Moscow was thus the Third Rome, and, according to the theory, there would be no 'Fourth'.

Both Ivan III and Ivan IV the Terrible (1533–1584) were generous in their gifts to monasteries, and wealthy Russians followed suit. Bulgarian monks who went to Russia collecting alms brought back tales of the power and splendour of the Orthodox Tsar in Moscow. Merchants supplemented their stories, and soon the legend of Grandfather Ivan, protector of the Orthodox, enemy of the Turks and Tartars, and future liberator of the Balkan Slavs, spread far and wide among the people. When Ivan the Terrible captured Kazan and Astrakhan from the Tartars, Russia's prestige and the people's hope increased greatly. Ivan's title of Tsar was confirmed and sanctioned by the Patriarch of Constantinople who ordered that the name of the Orthodox Tsar of Moscow be included in the liturgy as that of the Byzantine Emperor had been. The form of the prayer referred to 'Our Tsar Ivan', and the close personal relation of Grandfather Ivan to the Bulgars was further strengthened in popular imagination by the inclusion of 'Prince of the Bulgars' in Ivan's title after the fall of Kazan. The title referred, of course, to the Volga and Kama Bulgars,[1] and had no connection with the Balkan Bulgars, but this fact was completely missed or ignored by the latter, whose attachment to Russia continued to grow.

In 1589 at Constantinople a council of the patriarchs of the Eastern Church, at which Dionisi, Metropolitan of Tŭrnovo, was present, raised the metropolitanate of Moscow to the status of Patriarchate. But even before this the Balkan Christians were looking to Moscow as a power strong enough to protect them. For example, the monks of the Hilendar monastery on Mount Athos wrote to Ivan the Terrible saying that if the Tsar would only send a letter to the Sultan, the monastery would be freed from taxes and their lands restored to them. As early as 1557 in a letter to Ivan the Terrible, the Patriarch of Alexandria, Ioakim, expressed the hope that the Christians now under the yoke of the infidel would be liberated by the Russian Tsar.

As Russia grew in strength and international prestige, so began

[1] When Asparukh migrated westwards, one of his brothers went north and settled near the junction of the Volga and Kama.

the rivalry between her and Austria in the Balkans. Austria had made herself the protector of the Balkan Catholics and Russia then came forward as the protector of the Balkan Orthodox. The history of the relations between the Great Powers will not be discussed in detail in the present volume. It will be sufficient to note certain key dates and developments. The strategic basis of Austro-Russian rivalry was Austria's desire to control the lower Danube and Russia's desire to control the Black Sea Coast for her fleet and to gain access to a warm sea, i.e. the Mediterranean. Both these aims had as their prerequisite, control, or at least controlling influence, in the Balkans. Russia's expansion southwards towards the Black Sea Coast brought her into conflict with the Tartar peoples; in particular, with the Crimean Tartars, who were the vassals of Turkey. Russia's wars with Turkey began in 1677, when Turkey and Poland objected to Russia's annexation of the Ukraine. In 1688, the year of the Chiprovets rising, the Serbian Archimandrite Isaya sent a petition to the Muscovite Regent, the Tsaritsa Sofia, in the name of the Patriarchs of Constantinople and Ipek, and the ruler of Rumania, Shterbin Cantacuzene, asking the Russians to send an Orthodox Russian Army to liberate the Balkan peoples and Constantinople, lest the latter fall into the hands of the Papists. It will be remembered that the Chiprovets rising was organized by Catholics.

The first Russian Tsar to give serious attention to the Balkan Slavs was Peter the Great (1682–1722). He was sufficiently interested in the Bulgars as a people to arrange for a Russian translation to be made of a history of the Slavs, containing a chapter on Bulgaria, by a seventeenth-century abbot of Dubrovnik named Orbini. During the peace negotiations which followed his capture of Azov from the Tartars in 1696, he asked that freedom of religion be accorded to the Balkan Christians, and that the Tsar of Russia should have the right to protect them from excessive taxation. In 1710 Peter again declared war on Turkey and publicly mentioned in a manifesto the names of the Balkan Christian peoples, who languished under the Turkish yoke. Russian agitators were sent to Montenegro, Serbia, Rumania and Bulgaria to rouse the people in revolt, since Russian troops were nearing Bessarabia. Unfortunately, in the following years, the hopes of the Balkan peoples were dashed to the ground, when Peter's army was defeated on the Prut and Russia was forced to sign a treaty with Turkey, which involved the return of Azov to the Turks. Recognition for Russia's right to protect the Balkan Orthodox was finally won by Catherine the Great (1762–

1796) through the Treaty of Kuchuk Kainardji (1774) and was reaffirmed by the Treaty of Jassy (1792).

By the beginning of the eighteenth century, a policy had been formulated by the Western European Powers which was to determine Near Eastern strategy throughout the nineteenth century, i.e. if the alternative to Turkish rule in the Balkans is Russian influence, it is better to keep Turkey in control as long as possible. Although Austria and Russia had been allies in wars against Turkey on three occasions during the eighteenth century, Austria took steps on two occasions to prevent a possible Russian victory over Turkey leading to Russian influence in the Balkans. The first was in 1714 when Russia wished to join in the war between Austria and Turkey, but Austria and Great Britain would not agree to this. Again in 1739 when Russian troops entered Moldavia after costly successes, Austria made a treaty returning Belgrade to Turkey in order to free Turkish troops to fight the Russians. The connection between Russian occupation of Moldavia and Austria's Danube ambitions is obvious.

After the Treaty of Svishtov in 1791, Austria was occupied with Venice, the partitions of Poland and the French Revolution, and her attention was diverted from the Balkans. Russia alone was left to carry on the struggle, and became increasingly popular in the Balkans, both among the merchants and the Church representatives who visited Moscow and among the Bulgarian *raya* who craved for liberation.

Bulgarian Culture under the Turks

The centuries of the Turkish yoke were a very difficult period for Bulgarian culture, but it is not true to say that cultural life ceased entirely. There was, of course, no longer a Bulgarian nobility or court to provide a demand for new literature of the 'official' type, nor was there a national Bulgarian Church with learned theologians translating Greek works and writing their own. Bulgaria, which had stood so high culturally during the Middle Ages, was not able to maintain her advanced position, and at the time of Shakespeare and Milton, she was, as it were, in literary hibernation.

During this time the monasteries, some of which had escaped destruction by reason of their remoteness and others which were rebuilt, played an all-important role in keeping Bulgarian culture alive. Four of the most important centres of Bulgarian culture were the Rila and Bachkovo monasteries in Bulgaria itself and the Zograf and Hilendar monasteries on Mount Athos in Greece. In the monasteries old Bulgarian literature was preserved and carefully copied by the monks, the arts of fresco and ikon painting, woodcarving, etc., were kept alive, and in spite of the Greeks, during the sixteenth, seventeenth and eighteenth centuries more than a hundred monasteries held their services in Slavonic with books imported from Russia. The monasteries, however, were not merely museums of past culture, they also became centres of education and literary activity. Certain monasteries and churches had schools where reading and writing were taught using the Church books as textbooks. Most of the pupils were young monks and candidates for the priesthood, but there were a few lay pupils who subsequently worked as copyists. There were also a few private schools run by priests and monks where parents who could afford a small fee sent their children to learn reading and writing. These were the so-called 'cell' schools which will be described in greater detail in Chapter VI. As a result, most villages had at least one person who was literate. Education for women was absolutely non-existent and the only literate women were among the nuns.

In the absence of printing presses, the copying of existing Bulgarian manuscripts and the translation of foreign ones occupied a very important place in literary activity, but there also appeared new original works, mainly religious in character, such as religious anthologies, prayer books, lives of saints and other didactic works. Works of a more secular character consisted almost entirely of chronicles, but there were other books which gave advice on everyday life, including cures for various ailments, recipes for making colours, rules for ikon painting, etc.

Many of Bulgaria's literary men went abroad to Serbia, Russia and Rumania taking with them many manuscripts and continued their literary work abroad. One such man was Georgi Tsamblak, a native of Tŭrnovo, who had studied under Patriarch Eftimi. After the fall of Tŭrnovo he lived for a time on Mount Athos, then became private secretary to the Patriarch of Constantinople, and later visited Moldavia and Serbia. Eventually he went to Kiev, and after some years he accepted an invitation from Prince Vitold of Lithuania to become Metropolitan of Lithuania and Kiev. He died in 1418, leaving twenty-five literary works, including a panegyric of Patriarch Eftimi of Tŭrnovo, full of hatred for the Turkish conqueror and love for his unhappy people.

Certain important literary landmarks stand out in the dark period of the Turkish yoke. The first Bulgarian printed book, a liturgy, appeared in 1508; not, it is true, in Bulgaria itself, but in the Rumanian town of Târgovişte. A gospel followed in 1512 and by 1605 twenty-four Bulgarian books had been printed in Târgovişte. Bulgarian books were also printed in Venice, where a Psalter was printed in 1560 by Yakov Traikov, a native of Sofia, who later published various other religious books.

In Rome in 1651 there appeared the first Bulgarian printed book with elements of the modern Bulgarian language as opposed to the literary Church Slavonic. This was an apocryphal story about a certain King Abagar, with prayers for special occasions. The author was Filip Stanislavov, a native of the Nikopol region and a fervent patriot, who had been educated in Rome and subsequently became Catholic Bishop of Nikopol in 1648.

In 1714 the first Bulgarian printed book with a purely secular content was published in Vienna. It was the *Stematografia*[1] of Khristofor Zhefarovich.

Within Bulgaria itself much popular oral literature was created, consisting of songs, ballads, stories, riddles, etc., all readily understandable by the ordinary people. Many of the songs were of the exploits of legendary heroes, such as Krali Marko, who rode a winged horse, and performed miraculous deeds. Often these heroes had their origin in actual historical personages, whose real lives, unfortunately, often did not correspond even in spirit, let alone fact, to the heroic defenders of the people celebrated in the song cycles. The discrepancy did not worry the Bulgars at all and they continued to express their will for freedom through their hero epics. Many songs were devoted to the *haiduti*, and again these tended to be somewhat romanticized. One of the most famous characters of the Bulgarian folk tales created during the Turkish yoke was Khitŭr Petŭr, a man whose sharp wits always worsted his rivals, thus demonstrating the Bulgars' contempt for their oppressors.

Architecture was the Cinderella of the arts during the Turkish period, since the restrictions laid down by the Turks regarding Christian houses and churches left little scope for fine building. It is, however, worth remembering that many of the enormous Turkish buildings, such as mosques and *caravanserais*, were, in fact, the work of Bulgarian craftsmen employed by the Turks. Since the Bulgarians were obliged to keep the exteriors of their churches modest in the extreme, they lavished their art on interior decoration.

[1] More details about this book appear in Chapter IV, page 90.

Beautiful frescoes and ikons were produced after the Turks gave permission for the repair of existing churches. Private houses followed the same line of development. Many of them presented forbidding exteriors, with almost windowless ground floors, more reminiscent of a fortress than a dwelling house, while inside, away from the eyes of the Turks, they were comfortable, often well-furnished and decorated wherever possible with exquisite wood carvings. Houses of this type, dating from the sixteenth century, may be seen in the village of Arbanasi, just outside Tŭrnovo. Wood-carving for the interiors of buildings, the making of vessels, candlesticks, etc., of gold, silver, copper and iron, metal and enamelled ornaments for women and embroidery—all these arts continued to flourish.

CHAPTER III

THE ECONOMIC BACKGROUND
TO THE RENAISSANCE

Introduction

The name of 'Renaissance' is given to that period of Bulgarian history which begins in the second half of the eighteenth century and ends with the liberation of 1878. It is one of the most inspiring and stimulating periods of Bulgarian history, the period in which the Bulgarian people began to advance from the stagnation which Turkish rule had forced upon their national development, to do battle for their right to use their own language and to have their own schools and national Church free from the stranglehold of the Greeks, to win recognition for their existence as a separate people, and, finally, to fight for their national independence. It is a period abounding in great names and heroes, in patriots who devoted their lives to the cultural and political advancement of their people, in men who preferred imprisonment and death to aquiescence in their country's slavery.

What we are, in fact, witnessing in the Renaissance is the formation of the Bulgarian nation, and the stimuli to an event of so fundamental a character as this must be sought not on the surface, i.e. in the activities and influence of any individual or group of individuals, but deep down in the economic and social changes that were taking place in the Turkish Empire at the end of the eighteenth and beginning of the nineteenth centuries. The basic, underlying cause of the Renaissance was the development from natural economy to a commodity–money economy and with it the gradual liquidation of the Turkish feudal system in Bulgaria and the growth of a Bulgarian *bourgeoisie* which played the leading role in the Renaissance. The struggle for existence waged by this new class inevitably assumed the character of a nationalist movement since the rising *bourgeoisie* in Bulgaria found its road to power blocked by an alien feudal system and by alien domination in Church and school alike.

It is interesting to note that, initially, Bulgaria's nationalism found expression in bitter struggle, not against the Turks, but against the Greeks, who were the chief rivals of the Bulgarian merchants for markets.

Changes in Agrarian Relations during the End of the Eighteenth and the First Half of the Nineteenth Centuries

Towards the end of the eighteenth century great changes took place in the countryside. The *spahi* system, by which a man was granted the income from an estate in return for military service, began to give way to the *chiflik* system, under which the estate ceased to be a military fief but became the private property of the Turkish lord, with its economy orientated towards production for the market. From the beginning of the eighteenth century onwards there had been attempts on the part of the Turks to avoid military service and to acquire land for themselves and their families in case their fief was taken from them, or in case there was no male heir to undertake the military service in the event of their death. In their thirst for land, the Turks appropriated their demesnes, strips of village land and land belonging to the towns, with the connivance of the local *kadis* and officials in charge of State land. Not only the *spahi*, but also officials, merchants and even Janissary officers and NCO's joined in the scramble for land encouraged by the high prices which agricultural produce was then fetching. Thus ownership of land and military service began to have less and less interconnection. By the end of the eighteenth century, the *spahi* estates themselves were becoming hereditary instead of feudal in character, passing from father to son on payment of a certain sum of money. The Turks turned the land which they had acquired into private farms or *chifliks*, where they lived and sold the produce on the market. Thus a new landowning class had come into being—the *chiflikchii*, composed partly of the former landowning class, the *spahi*, and partly of the other groups who had joined in the rush to gain security through possession of land. Unlike the *spahi* estates, the *chifliks*, or at any rate, part of them, could be bought and sold.

Apart from the *chifliks*, the private ownership of land was expanding in another direction. There was an increase in the form of land tenure known as *mülk*, i.e. privately owned land mainly within the village boundaries, but including gardens and vineyards, etc., in the immediate vicinity. The land attached to towns and villages had increased considerably, owing to the increase in population, at the expense of vacant State land, and in addition, new villages and townlets had grown up in the mountainous districts incorporating fairly considerable amounts of new *mülk* land, all of which could be bought or sold at will. In 1834 the military fief system was legally abolished, and under the reform law all *spahis* who had fulfilled their military obligations were permitted to keep their fief on the basis of private ownership and those whose lands had previously passed to the State through default were given life pensions. The peasants became the owners of their little plots, which could now be bought and sold. Many peasants, however, had insufficient land, or none at all. The Turkish Government continued to collect the same taxes which were formerly received by the *spahi* and increased them yearly in order to pay the compensation to the *spahi* and finance the army. The peasants suffered greatly from abuses which resulted from the Turks' system of selling the right to collect taxes. For example, the stocks of wheat had to be left in the fields until the agent who had the right to collect the wheat tithe had seen the harvest. Often it was as late as October before the Greek, Bulgarian and Turkish merchants had finished their intrigues over who was to have the right of collection and all the time the harvest was spoiling in the fields. The name 'tithe' was by now a euphemism since the so-called tithes amounted to 30 or 40 per cent instead of the correct 10 per cent.

The growing needs of the town population, the garrisons and the army made agriculture a profitable undertaking, and in addition, agricultural produce was exported abroad and to other parts of the Turkish Empire. For example, the American War of Independence led Britain to seek cotton from Turkey, and during the Revolution and the Napoleonic wars France bought grain and other raw materials. Even though the sale of wheat abroad was hampered until 1838 by the existence of a State monopoly by which the Porte obtained grain for the army and the Capital at very low prices, producers preferred to sell their grain to foreign merchants by illegal methods. Apart from the high quality wheat for which Bulgaria was famous and which was mainly grown in the Danube plain and Thrace, and was exported to Constantinople, many other crops, some newly introduced, were grown, including cotton, tobacco, poppies, sesame, anise, peanuts, rice and silk cocoons. This type of produce required improved technique and a certain specialization, with the result that from the middle of the eighteenth century onwards, various regions began to specialize in the cultivation of

C

different crops. Examples of crops and their specialized regions are: rice (Plovdiv and Tatar Pazardzhik regions), hemp (Sofia region), flax (Rhodope), cotton (Plovdiv, Adrianople and Kyustendil regions and Macedonia), tobacco (Ksanti and Enidzhevardar regions), rose oil (Karlovo and Kazanlŭk), silk cocoons and silk spinning (Tŭrnovo, Svishtov, Adrianople, Chirpan, Kazanlŭk, Stara and Nova Zagora, Khaskovo, and by the end of the eighteenth century, Gabrovo), opium (South Macedonia). Cattle rearing remained a very important branch of Bulgarian economy and many cattle were exported to Constantinople and elsewhere. Sheep were kept in large quantities, and Bulgarian wool was considered to be among the best in the Turkish Empire. Dairy and meat products played a large part in Bulgarian agriculture: cheese was sent to Constantinople, and part exported to the Crimea; salted meat was also exported to Constantinople, Anatolia and the Crimea; ox tongues were even sent as far afield as Marseilles; honey and wax were sent to Constantinople for export, and there much was regularly bought by French merchants. Gardening and fruit growing was an important aspect of Bulgarian agriculture especially in areas where there were Turkish garrisons, to meet the requirements of the troops (Shumen, Varna, Rusé, Vidin areas). Wood and charcoal were exported, the latter going in the main to Constantinople.

At the same time as the *chiflik* system of farming developed, new differentiations grew up among the peasants. Rent in kind and money had replaced work rent as the predominant form of rent. *Angaria* was actually forbidden under the reform of 1834, but nevertheless, it did still continue, and there is evidence for its existence as late as 1868. *Angaria* was, of course, no use as an incentive, and the beys and pashas, who often went to live in the towns, gave out land to the peasants on one or other of two systems known respectively as *ispolitsa* and *kesim*. Under *ispolitsa*, the peasant received the land in return for half the harvest. Sometimes such a peasant would have his own plot of land in addition, but since it was inadequate for his needs, he would be obliged to rent further land on the terms just mentioned. Under the *kesim* system, the peasant received a plot of land which he could pass on to his heirs. The lord determined what duties the peasant must perform and what rent he must pay, including work on the lord's land and the provision of lambs and other produce, independent of how large the harvest was. The peasant was obliged to pay all the usual State taxes in addition and was tied to the land, so that this system in effect was a very harsh type of serfdom. *Ispolitsa* was the most widespread system and *kesim* was confined in the main to the south-west part of Bulgaria.

Alongside these feudal labour relations, especially from the second quarter of the nineteenth century onwards, there existed other forms which were already capitalist in character. Some farms were worked by hired labourers known as *momki*, *ratai* or *argati*. These were landless peasants who received wages partly in kind and partly in money and were sometimes given the use of a small plot of land. All taxes on the land used by the hired labourer were paid by the lord, but in return for the wage paid to the man, however, the whole family was expected to work for the lord, the women and children receiving merely their keep. The hired labourers lived either in their own houses or in accommodation provided by the lord. Another form of labour which was already capitalist in character was the seasonal hired labourers such as the mowers, harvesters and threshers. The pay was so poor that peasants were very unwilling to go to work on the *chifliks*, and during the busy times there was often a serious shortage of labour. Therefore the Turkish Government had to order certain regions to send labour at harvest time to the main agricultural areas. For example, the Tŭrnovo district was expected to send 3,000 harvesters a year to the Dobrudzha. The rice fields in the Plovdiv and Pazardzhik regions, partly privately owned and partly State owned but rented to private landlords, were also worked by hired labour sent from the surrounding villages. These seasonal labourers were brutally exploited, badly paid and were often cheated and kept waiting for their wages after the work was done, or made to do work other than that which they had been sent to do.

The *chiflik* system must be seen as a transitional stage between feudalism and capitalism, having features characteristic of both systems. The orientation of *chiflik* farming towards production for sale on the market and the use of hired labour is evidence of the growth of capitalist relations in the countryside, while feudalism lingers on in the relations between certain types of peasant and the landowners.

Apart from the categories of peasant already mentioned, there were a few others. Certain villages existed which were free from land-owners, but in feudal dependence on the State. There were still *vakïf* villages, the income from which supported Moslem religious and charitable institutions, such as Kalofer, which supported the Suleiman Mosque in Constantinople. Apart from these, some of the so-called special categories of peasants who were given certain alleged privileges in return for the performance of special duties still survived, although they accounted for a very small number of peasants.

The *zadruga*, land owned and farmed collectively by several related households, was a characteristic feature of the early nineteenth century among peasants who were not serfs or semi-serfs. Under conditions of natural economy, the *zadrugi* were very large, comprising 100–150 persons, but the growth of capitalist relations, of production for the market and the use of money led to the break-up of the *zadruga*. In the more remote areas of western Bulgaria, the *zadruga* survived until after the liberation of 1878.

The 'Chorbadzhii'

In spite of high taxation, now that rent was paid in kind and money rather than labour, the peasant was able to produce some surplus for the market. Although some Bulgarian peasants fell into debt, lost their land and were ruined, a small number managed to become quite rich through trade. When the Turkish lords found they had accumulated more land than they could conveniently manage, or when they needed money, they would sell part of their farms to these richer Bulgarian peasants, and in the course of time what might be termed a Bulgarian village *bourgeoisie* came into being. This process increased especially after the *Hat-i-Sherif* of 1839 which recognized the right of Christians as well as Moslems to own land, although even before this date some peasants had accumulated appreciable amounts of land. They began to employ hired labour and thus cultivated larger areas of land, and consolidated their economic position by buying watermills from the Turks. They also bought up the land of poorer peasants, or forced them into exchanging good land for worse.

These richer peasants were known as the *chorbadzhii*. The term originally comes from the word *chorba*, meaning soup. The Janissaries called the senior man of a unit, who ladled out the soup, the *chorbadzhi-bashi*, and the Bulgarian *Voinitsi*, or military auxiliaries, who served in close contact with the Janissaries, also adopted the word and took it home to the villages where it was used to denote the headmen of the more or less self-governing Bulgarian communities. Originally the headman or *chorbadzhiya* was elected by the whole village community, but after the 1839 *Hat-i-Sherif* reforms, he was chosen by the leading men of the village. In their original form the *chorbadzhii* existed from the earliest Turkish times as representatives of the Bulgarian population, while in their new form they appeared at the time when commodity production was replacing natural economy, and when the *spahi* estates were being transformed into *chifliks*. In each village there came to be two or three wealthy *chorbadzhii* who came to act as go-betweens for the Turkish authorities and the Bulgarian population, collected the taxes and did everything possible to curry favour with the Turks and win their confidence.

Thus with a few exceptions the *chorbadzhii* came to be hand in glove with the Turkish administration and took little part in the later Bulgarian revolutionary struggle for liberation, often openly siding with the Turks.

Apart from trading, the *chorbadzhii* went in for moneylending on a large scale, since at that time there were no credit organizations in Bulgaria and peasants in financial difficulties had to resort to loans from private people. Some moved to the towns where they formed the richer upper section of the trading *bourgeoisie*. The *chorbadzhii* used their position to pile up wealth as fast as possible. In the villages they soon gained a stranglehold over all the other inhabitants and over village life in general. The *chorbadzhii* of the little town of Elena in the Stara Planina are an excellent example of this. The Elena *chorbadzhii* collected taxes for the Greeks and Turks and added personal taxes for themselves. They forced the peasants to perform *angaria* for them, to provide building materials for their houses, etc., and to give them presents out of their produce, and expected them to double the presents on the occasion of their children's marriages. They obliged the peasants to borrow money from them against interest and to give them their money for safe keeping without interest. They refused to allow merchants into the town and took all the produce themselves at cut prices. Lest one should imagine that the *chorbadzhii* of Elena were a particularly villainous exception, it is also recorded that the *Chorbadzhiya* Stoyancho of Kazanlŭk had control not only over the economic and social life of that town, but also over the private lives of its inhabitants. He married and divorced people, fined and imprisoned them, hanged them or cut them down from the gallows at will. Some *chorbadzhii*, such as Bozhil of Kotel, gained control of the public funds of their town or village. Others gained control of the funds of the church and the school as well.

An important aspect of the activities of some *chorbadzhii* was cattle dealing, which consisted in collecting huge herds of cattle and taking them to Constantinople. In 1844 the chief cattle dealer, or *dzhelep*, was a Bulgarian named Nedyalko Chalŭkov, who was responsible for supplying the capital with sheep. The Chalŭkovs were a very famous *chorbadzhi* family, enormously wealthy and tremendously powerful, which originated in Koprivshtitsa in the Sredna Gora, and moved to Plovdiv where some of their houses are still standing today. Unlike many *chorbadzhi* families, they played an important and beneficial role in the cultural renaissance and the struggle for an independent Bulgarian Church. Other members of the family, in particular, Stoyan Chalŭkov the Elder, were *beglikchii*, i.e. they were responsible for collecting the sheep and goat tax. This was a privileged position, carrying the status of 'Sultan's men', and incidentally a very profitable business. In addition the *beglikchii* were permitted to carry arms. Under them they had a whole army[1] of sheep counters with horses and muskets, who knew the country well, since often the shepherds would conceal their flocks in caves and other hiding-places. Sometimes the shepherds would offer armed resistance and there would be clashes between the tax collectors and the shepherds which might even result in people getting killed. One reason for the clashes was that the *beglikchii* were able to sell for their personal profit all sheep collected over the stipulated number. In the autumn when their work was completed, the tax collectors went home. The lion's share of the profit went to the Chalŭkovs and their chief assistants, but the sheep counters also got a fair return for their labour.

The Growth of Towns and Handicrafts

During the first centuries of Turkish rule, the Bulgarians had been more or less driven out of the towns which were inhabited mainly by Greeks and Turks. During the latter part of the eighteenth century, however, the process began to be reversed, and the populations of the towns began to increase considerably and to consist of fewer Turks and more Bulgars. This growth of the towns was primarily due to the process of division of labour which by the end of the eighteenth century was quite far advanced in the villages, and craftsmen and merchants were beginning to move into the towns. In Plovdiv, for example, Bulgarian names as well as Greek begin to appear in the guild records about this time. The urban population

[1] Chalŭkov is said to have had 3,000 employees and 400 shepherds to look after the sheep.

was further swelled by people who sought refuge in the towns during the *Kŭrdzhali*[1] disorders, and by peasants whose land had been seized by the *spahi*, or who had lost it in one way or another, and were thus driven to seek employment as unskilled labourers in the towns.

During the second half of the eighteenth century handicrafts ceased to be largely a matter of production for domestic use or for bespoke orders, and became geared to the production of commodities for sale all over Bulgaria and other parts of the Turkish Empire. The Turks had little to do with handicrafts, preferring to engage in professions such as barbering or coffee-house keeping, or in work connected with cattle in which they were particularly interested, such as tanning or smithing, and they depended on the Bulgars for handicrafts. It must be borne in mind that the conditions prevailing in the Turkish Empire were extremely unfavourable for the growth of a *bourgeoisie* and for the development towards capitalism, because there was no security of person and property, and it was difficult to accumulate wealth owing to the rapaciousness of the Turks. In the towns the merchants and craftsmen went about modestly dressed and lived in small houses well barricaded against prying eyes in an effort to conceal their wealth. During the eighteenth century it was quite an ordinary thing for rich Bulgars to be murdered and robbed.

Although the old cultural centres such as Tŭrnovo and Okhrid had lost their importance, other towns were expanding. These were the towns situated on the roads leading from Constantinople to the West, such as Plovdiv and Sofia, and the towns of strategic importance such as Varna, Nikopol, Vidin and Niš, where the craftsmen served the needs of the Turkish garrison. Because of the growth of commodity production and exchange, and the increase in the Bulgar population, a whole series of new towns grew up. About twenty of these were new settlements of a town type, such as Popovo, Khaskovo, Lom, Chirpan, Nova Zagora, and Oryakhovo which had a mixed Bulgarian and Turkish population. Another group of new towns appeared in the mountains and foothills, on sites where during the second half of the seventeenth century there had appeared scattered houses or seasonal settlements belonging to drovers, woodcutters, charcoal burners, etc. From about 1730 onwards they began to develop into handicraft centres of between 1,000 and 5,000 inhabitants. To this group belong Kotel, Elena, Gabrovo, Lyaskovets,

[1] Bandits who ravaged Bulgaria at the end of the eighteenth and beginning of the nineteenth centuries. *See* p. 106.

Teteven, Troyan, Vratsa, Berkovitsa, Belogradchik, Orkhanié (Botevgrad), Gorna Dzhumaya, Bansko, Peshtera, Koprivshtitsa, Panagyurishté, Klisura, Karlovo, Kalofer, Sopot and Sliven. Most of these were purely Bulgarian towns, although a few of them such as Vratsa, Karlovo, Berkovitsa and Sliven had a mixed Bulgarian and Turkish population.

Specialization developed in the various handicraft centres and areas. Thus, the working of iron and other metals was the speciality in Malŭk Samokov, Samokov itself and Etropolé, while Sliven and the Gabrovo region were centres for the making of guns, bullets and iron implements of all kinds for use in agriculture, handicrafts and the home. Only a few metal tools, such as vices, anvils and steel files, had to be imported, mainly from Vienna. A German diplomat who visited Gabrovo in 1833 spoke of every house having its forge and resounding with hammer strokes, and described the town as a 'veritable Cyclops village'. Other specialist centres were Kotel and Panagyurishté for carpets; Teteven, Troyan and Bansko for wood-carving, ikon-painting and building; Kalofer, Karlovo and Sopot for woollen braid extensively used in decorating national costumes, and for the printing of material for women's head-dresses; Chepelaré, Peshtera, Batak and Bratsigovo, all in the Rhodope, for wooden building material, firewood and tar. Many master builders were natives of the Rhodope region.

Handicrafts in Bulgaria developed enormously in the second quarter of the nineteenth century when the Turkish regular army was formed. Huge Government orders for cloth and other equipment followed.

Main Branches of Bulgarian Economy

The following were the main branches of Bulgarian economy, other than agriculture:

The cattle industry. This covered the collection of cattle by the *dzhelepi* as described in the section on *chorbadzhii*, fattening, slaughtering and the preserving of meats and fats for sale. This industry was specially well developed in such towns as Gabrovo, Tŭrnovo, and also in towns such as Shumen and Tatar-Pazardzhik which had a predominantly Turkish population. Among the products prepared were dried meat and a type of dried sausage, tallow and edible fats. The richer dealers had their own slaughter-houses, which they would rent to the smaller dealers. Each slaughter-house had between 30 and 35 workers who worked a 13- to 14-hour day.

The textile industry. This was one of the most important branches of Bulgarian handicrafts, especially after the organization of the regular Turkish Army with the ensuing bulk orders for cloth to make uniforms. There were various branches of the textile industry. Cotton was woven mainly in the towns where Turkish troops were stationed, such as Sopot and Tŭrnovo, and where the industry died out when the Turks left the towns. Towels were woven in Sopot, Karlovo and Pirdop. Cotton was also woven by most families for their personal use. Silk was woven in the regions of Tŭrnovo, Gabrovo, Provadiya, Dryanovo and Kharmanli. Bulgarian silk was considered to be the best in the Turkish Empire, but the industry went into decline after the silkworms were stricken by disease in 1865. Linen and hemp were also woven by most families for personal use. The most important branch of the textile industry was the production of *aba*, a heavy woollen cloth which was made all over Bulgaria even before the Turkish invasion. It was made in most towns, but the industry was particularly developed in areas deficient in arable land, but supporting large flocks of sheep, such as Sliven, Koprivshtitsa, Gabrovo, Samokov, Panagyurishté, Kotel, Tryavna, Troyan, Kalofer and the Rhodope. Originally all the work was done in the houses on hand carding combs, spinning wheels and simple wooden looms also worked by hand. In 1834 a loom with a fly shuttle was introduced from abroad in Sliven and Panagyurishté, but its operation was fairly heavy work and its introduction meant that the men were increasingly drawn into the work of making cloth. The family obtained its wool from their own sheep and all the members of the family took part in the work which was done chiefly in the autumn and winter when there was less work to be done outside. Apart from *aba*, a finer woollen cloth known as *shaek* was also made. The making of *gaitan* or braid for decorating costumes was another important and typically Bulgarian branch of the textile industry. It was especially well developed in towns in the foothills of the mountains, such as Sliven, Kazanlŭk, Gabrovo, Karlovo, Kalofer and Pirdop. Woollen carpets were woven in Karlovo, Kalofer, Sliven and Kotel. Another branch of textiles was the making of such articles as horse blankets, belts and sacks out of goats' hair. This trade flourished in towns and villages on both sides of the Stara Planina.

Tailoring. This developed in close connection with the making of *aba* and *shaek* in the textile towns and was especially well developed in towns where troops were stationed. There were also travelling

C*

Bulgar tailors who went from village to village and even went as far
as Asia Minor. Considerable division of labour existed in the tailoring trade and there were tailors who specialized in the making of
individual items of clothing, or in European style clothing. In
Constantinople itself, there was an enormous colony of Bulgarian
tailors: more than 1,000 of them, masters, journeymen and apprentices were housed and worked in the large building known as the
'Hambar'. They all lived together as a community, each bringing
his own meat to be cooked in a common cauldron. They held celebrations on holidays and, because of their usefulness, they enjoyed
certain privileges and were able to do such things as singing *haidut*
songs without the Turks paying too much attention to the matter.

Tanning and leather industry. Tanning was largely in the hands
of the Turks for whose cavalry it was of the utmost importance.
The heads of the guilds concerned in this trade ranked as senior to
those of other guilds. The main centres of tanning were Gabrovo,
Tŭrnovo, Stara Zagora, Kazanlŭk, Tatar-Pazardzhik, Karlovo,
Etropolé, Samokov, Shumen, Khaskovo, Chirpan. In Gabrovo the
trade was largely in Bulgarian hands. Hides imported from Russia
and Rumania were used as well as local ones. Together with tanning,
other allied trades such as saddlery, fur dressing, the making of
pack-saddles and slipper making developed. Various types of slippers
for the Turks were made, as well as peasant sandals. In the course of
time, the making of fur coats lined with rich luxury furs became a
separate branch of furriery.

Mining and metal working. Metals had been worked in various
parts of Bulgaria since very early times, but under the Turks,
mining was weakly developed and very primitive in technique. The
chief mining areas were in the regions of North Macedonia (now part
of Yugoslavia), Kratovo, Kyustendil, Dupnitsa, Samokov and Chiprovets. The metals mined were iron, gold, lead, silver and copper.
The metal industry finally attained considerable development during
the nineteenth century—many different types of products were made:
knives, scissors, swords, daggers, weighing machines for markets,
chains, metal fly-wheels for *gaitan* making, spades, pickaxes,
ploughshares, rifle-barrels and cannon.

As already mentioned, Gabrovo was a great centre for the metal
industry. Both it and Sliven, another metal centre, obtained supplies
of iron from Samokov where, for a time, production increased.
However, in spite of this and in spite of a ban on the export of iron,
the miners of Samokov could not keep pace with the demand. From

the 1840's onwards, iron had to be imported, and as a result mining at Samokov gradually declined. Other centres of the metal industry were Plovdiv, Stanimak, Karlovo and Kazanlŭk. Smithery was largely in the hands of the Turks and the gypsies, and some of the main centres of production for nails and horse shoes were Gabrovo, Sliven, Tatar-Pazardzhik and Plovdiv. Another branch of the metal industry, coppersmithery, was concerned with the production of copper saucepans, dishes and frying-pans, using copper obtained from Trebizond and Constantinople. It was especially highly developed in Kazanlŭk and Karlovo because of the use of copper vessels in the preparation there of attar of roses. Another branch of the metal industry was the making of jewellery, church plate and small objects of copper, zinc and lead such as door knobs, window fastenings, etc., and again Kazanlŭk and Gabrovo were among the centres of this industry.

Other handicrafts were soap and candle making in such towns as Kazanlŭk, Gabrovo, Tŭrnovo, and dye making in Pleven, Sliven, Tŭrnovo, Gabrovo.

Guilds

Guilds had existed in the mediaeval Bulgarian towns of the pre-Turkish era, but they reached a specially high level of development during the second half of the eighteenth and the first half of the nineteenth century as a result of the growth of the towns and the rapid expansion of handicrafts. The basic aim of the guilds was to prevent mutual competition between craftsmen in the same line of business. They divided the big State orders among the workshops, bought raw materials for all the craftsmen, laid down prices and standards and fixed wages.

A valuable source for the organization of the guilds is the *firman* of 1773 issued by Sultan Mustafa III. It is in fact a codification and legal recognition of the trading practices already followed by the guilds. According to this document no man might open a shop with a work bench who was not a 'master' registered with a guild. In order to become a master, one had to be already a journeyman (*kalfa*) with certain experience and qualifications, and in order to become a journeyman, one had to have served as an apprentice (*chirak*) to the satisfaction of a master. Each newly qualified master received a master's belt from the guild according to an ancient ritual, which had to be performed before he could open his own workshop. The apprentice had to work three years without pay, receiving his

keep and a pair of shoes per year, and if he left his own master before
the expiry of the three years, no other master could employ him on
pain of a fine. Most of the first year of his apprenticeship was spent
working in the master's house, or running errands for the master and
journeymen. During the second year, he spent more time in the
workshop learning the trade, and the third year was spent entirely
in the workshop. After three years, the apprentice became a *kalfa* or
journeyman with a small wage fixed by three other masters and
which increased year by year. He had to work for a further period in
order to become an independent master himself and was obliged to
stay at least one year with his original master. The induction cere-
monies for masters were usually held on the day of the guild's patron
saint.

Thus in any small workshop there would be, apart from the master,
a senior journeyman, who acted as the master's deputy, and perhaps
one or two other journeymen and a number of apprentices. There
might also be day labourers who had no fixed place of work and were
paid either by the day or by the piece. Some of these day labourers
were qualified masters who did not have sufficient means to open
their own workshops. While the guild rules decreed that one must
not appear before a master smoking a cigar, they laid down no
limitation of the working day and very long hours were worked.
Fourteen to sixteen hours was the rule, and in some crafts it was
as long as eighteen hours in summer. In the small workshops with two
or three journeymen, the master, journeymen and apprentices all
ate together. The food was usually meagre, consisting mainly of
bread, soup, beans, onions and radishes, and only occasionally was
there meat and bacon. Professor Kosev[1] mentions the existence of
many contemporary anecdotes on the subject of the parsimoniousness
of masters over food.

Guild organization and practice varied from handicraft to handicraft, but the following is broadly true of most guilds of the period.
The highest organ of any guild was the general meeting of masters
known as the *londzha*. The word comes from the Italian *loggia* and
is a relic of the days of the Dubrovnik merchants. Most of the guild
terminology was Turkish, although often parallel Bulgarian terms
also exist. The *londzha* usually met on Sundays and holidays after
church and was responsible for formulating guild rules, running the
guild, punishing members who had transgressed, fixing prices,
controlling the guild's finances, which were often considerable, for

[1] *Lektsii po Nova-Bulgarska Istoriya*, Sofia, 1951, p. 49.

settling disputes, etc. Once or twice a year, the *londzha* chose two or three of its members to act as a kind of executive committee, who were responsible for calling meetings of the *londzha*, collecting guild dues and so on. The executive consisted of the chief master or president of the guild (the *usta-bashiya*), his deputy (the *egidbashiya* or *itbashiya*) and the *chaush*, who acted as messenger between the *usta-bashiya* and the other masters, and, in some guilds, also collected the dues. The two former officials were usually chosen from among the senior masters, while the *chaush* was usually a junior master. The *chaush* was chosen for a year, six months or even only one month. He received no pay for his work and sometimes the job was given to a master as a punishment for some misdemeanour. It was possible to get out of this punishment by a payment to the guild funds. The President held a very responsible position. He saw to the smooth running of the guild, ironed out disputes, and exacted minor penalties from offenders. He was also responsible for ensuring that there was a proper supply of raw materials for the guild members. He kept the account books and was personally responsible to the other masters for guild finances, including seeing that the correct dues were collected, and he had the power to spend guild money, or make loans from it, although he was held responsible for un-repaid loans given without adequate security. Generally the President was unpaid, although occasionally he did receive a salary.

All masters, journeymen and apprentices paid dues to the guild weekly or monthly on a sliding scale according to seniority. Apart from these regular dues, a journeyman paid a considerable sum to the guild on becoming a master, and thereafter he was expected to make a gift to the guild on his own name day, and to donate wax or an equivalent sum of money to provide candles for the service on the day of the patron saint of the guild. A considerable part of the guilds' wealth came from the interest on loans made to masters or private people since there were no credit organizations such as banks. The guilds charged what would seem to be an exorbitant rate of interest, anything between 12 per cent and 50 per cent. It is on record that the *gaitan*-makers' guild of Karlovo actually charged 15 per cent monthly which works out at 180 per cent per annum! Another source of income for a guild was fines imposed on erring members. In addition, it was customary for childless masters to make big donations to the guild funds, and sometimes they would even bequeath all their property to the guild. As a result of all this, the guilds had consider-able wealth at their disposal. They used it for cultural and educational purposes such as the support of schools, churches and monasteries, for mutual aid, such as providing night watchmen for workshops, assistance to orphans and the families of needy masters, etc. They bought raw materials in bulk and distributed it to their members at fixed prices, allowing deferred terms to poorer masters. Many guilds had their own premises where the *londzha* met and where single masters or journeymen or even apprentices could rent rooms, or where visiting merchants could stay. The premises were also used as warehouses for the products of the guild.

The guilds had immense power over their members, who were obliged to obey all the regulations. Breaches of professional etiquette were dealt with in the guild without recourse to the authorities. Such breaches generally consisted of missing a meeting of the *londzha* or arriving late, poaching another master's clients, taking on a journeyman who had deserted his original master, opening his shop on holidays, or selling someone else's goods. Penalties usually consisted of fines, although the *usta-bashiya* also had the power, with the consent of the *londzha*, to close a man's shop, prevent him from carrying on his trade for a given time, or even to have him put in prison without trial. Repeated offences might lead to the offender being expelled from the guild. When a master objected to a penalty or refused to pay a fine, he might be subjected to corporal punishment.

In order to avoid the Turkish courts, people often used to ask the guilds to settle property disputes, or even family quarrels.

From the national point of view, certain guilds such as the tanners, pipemakers and barbers were predominantly or exclusively Turkish. Others were largely Bulgarian and still others were mixed. There is even a record of a Jewish guild in Sofia during the eighteenth century. Within the mixed guilds, all members enjoyed equal rights. During the nineteenth century there was a tendency, especially from the twenties onwards, for the Bulgarians to form their own guilds separate from those of the Greeks and Turks. It was the guilds that first made the Turks conscious of the existence of the Bulgars as a separate nation, since the work of Bulgarian craftsmen was much favoured by the Turks for its good quality and low prices. Previously the Turks had simply regarded all their subject Christian population as a single mass, and ignored all differences of nationality.

Guilds are essentially a feudal form of organization. They played an important role in commodity production at the petty handicraft stage, but after the middle of the nineteenth century, petty handicrafts began to decay and the guilds became an impediment to further economic development, as capitalist relations slowly but surely penetrated the economy of the country. Organized primarily to protect their members against competition, the guilds were unable to continue to do this when faced with cheap imported goods from Western Europe, especially after the Crimean War, and the development of manufacture in Bulgaria itself by trading capital. The coming of the machine spelt death to the guilds, although they persisted right up to the Liberation when Bulgaria was finally freed from the last vestiges of feudalism and became part of the general capitalist economy of Europe.

The Growth of Capitalist Relations

Capitalist relations began to develop at the end of the eighteenth and beginning of the nineteenth centuries in the form of the merchant who went round the villages, bought up raw material, gave it out to be processed by the people in their own homes, and then bought back the finished product. These people were, of course, as much the hired labourers of the merchant as if they had been wage earners in a concentrated enterprise. This form of merchant capital operated mainly in the villages, away from the strong guild organizations of the towns and in industries where guild organization was less highly developed. Seasonal labour, particularly that of women and children, was employed. This system of 'putting out' was especially prevalent in the textile industries, such as the making of *aba*, woollen garments, etc., but it also embraced other trades, such as many of the iron workers in Gabrovo. Examples of such merchant capitalists are Stancho Ivanov of Plovdiv who during the forties of the nineteenth century organized the population of several villages in the Peshtera region to make *aba*, which he exported to Asia Minor, and Atanas Gyumyushgerdan and his son, two Graecomanes from Plovdiv, who exploited the populations of the villages in the Chepelaré area who made *aba* garments, including socks, which the Gyumyush-gerdans sold to the Turkish Army. Hard as was the lot of the apprentices and journeymen, by far the worst exploited were those who worked for these merchant capitalists. Gyumyushgerdan, for example, did not even pay the women whom he employed regularly and honestly, and paid them less than their due on the pretext that they had spoilt the wool. He even obtained the services of Turkish gendarmes who slept during the day and went round the cottages at night to see which cottages were showing lights, in order to find out which women were weaving and knitting and which were sleeping! In the morning the 'lazy' women were scolded, threatened and often even beaten.

As time went by, manufacture developed, i.e. the bringing together of workers producing articles under one roof, though still working by hand as the name implies, and without the large scale mechanization that characterizes the factory stage of industry. Gyumyushgerdan, for example, set up a textile mill and fuller's shop in Plovdiv for which he managed to obtain convict labour and towards 1852 both Tŭrnovo and Sliven each had a textile manufactory. The great demand for cloth led not only to the growth of manufacture, but also to technical progress. As early as 1834 a loom with a fly shuttle was introduced in Sliven where a merchant named Dobri Zhelyazkov had founded the first big textile manufactory the same year. The Turks took a great interest in Zhelyazkov's enterprise. He was called to Constantinople by the Sultan Mahmud who saw samples of the cloth produced and ordered that Zhelyazkov be freed from taxes. A three-year Government contract for material followed and Zhelyazkov was obliged to build a bigger factory which was equipped with weaving machinery from Russia and was run on water power and employed between 400 and 500 workers. The factory resulted in the ruin of the local craftsmen and made enemies for Zhelyazkov among the Turkish population who resented the success of a non-Moslem. After Mahmud's death, Zhelyazkov's enemies succeeded in getting the Government contract cancelled and the factory closed. Another textile factory was also founded in Sliven in 1834 by a Pole and this managed to survive until the Liberation. This factory, like those of Gyumyushgerdan and Zhelyazkov, sold all its produce to the Turkish Government.

Manufacture and mechanization were also advancing in the *gaitan* industry, centred in the towns near the Stara Planina, such as Karlovo, Kazanlŭk and Pirdop. During the eighteenth century *gaitan* was made by hand. At the beginning of the nineteenth century, a wooden fly-wheel was introduced into the *gaitan* industry and during the second quarter of the nineteenth century, the wooden fly-wheels were replaced by iron ones, driven by water power, and doing the work of several workers. These iron ones were expensive, beyond the reach of many small producers and therefore their introduction favoured the bigger producer.

The growth of factories, however, did not proceed very rapidly before the Liberation, and between 1830 and 1878 only twenty large-scale enterprises were started, many of which did not survive long. Most of the factories were connected with the textile industry, although there was also a match factory, a distillery and a glass works.

During the sixties and seventies the first attempts at forming Bulgarian joint stock companies were made. The Bulgarian patriot, Rakovsky, advocated the formation of such companies in order to combat the competition of foreign imports and to develop foreign trade. In 1858 an unsuccessful attempt was made to form a steamship company on the River Maritsa, and altogether about thirty-nine companies were formed in various fields of the economy. Some failed almost immediately, while others survived for shorter or longer periods.

Trade

During the eighteenth and nineteenth centuries Bulgaria itself and the territory immediately adjacent to it, including Macedonia and the Aegean Coast, were the most important part of the Turkish Empire from the point of view of trade. At the beginning of the nineteenth century, although it only represented a twentieth part of the Turkish Empire, it accounted for one-fifth of the Empire's import and export trade. The period saw changes in the countries with which the Turkish Empire had trade relations. During the seventeenth century only France, Holland and Britain had done much trade with the Turkish Empire, but from towards the middle of the eighteenth century onward, trade not only increased with these three States, but in addition another twenty States made trading agreements with Turkey, while Britain, France and Austria established Consulates in several Bulgarian towns in order to assist their merchants in their penetration of the Empire. There was a considerable development of trade with Austria and Russia with a consequent revival of the Danube and Black Sea ports, especially after the Russo-Turkish Treaty of 1774 when the Danube, Black Sea, Dardanelles and Bosphorus were opened to Russian ships and after 1802 when the Black Sea was opened to the merchant ships of all European nations. Bulgaria exported grain, cattle, wool, silk, cotton, tobacco, timber, textiles, skins, opium, wax, red wines (mainly to Russia) and of course the celebrated rose oil, and she imported iron and iron products, non-ferrous metals, olive-oil, salt, dyes, coffee and other groceries, soap, paper, fezes, mirrors, glassware and other luxury goods which were bought almost exclusively by the Turks. From the Danube and Black Sea ports the goods were taken to the inland towns and to the big annual fairs and were distributed in smaller centres by packmen.

During the first centuries of Turkish rule trade, both external and internal, was largely in the hands of foreigners such as the Greeks and merchants from Venice and Dubrovnik, Jews and Armenians, who were granted special privileges and guarantees of inviolability by the Turkish Government. The foreign merchants were, of course, in close touch with the Bulgarian population and certain Bulgars who wished to trade took foreign nationality in order to enjoy the privileges accorded to these foreign merchants. Later on Bulgarian merchants operated under the protection of Austria, France, Russia, etc., often carrying on their trade while employed by foreign merchants as agents, translators, etc. Writing in the middle of the eighteenth century Paisi Hilendarsky speaks of the existence of a considerable body of Bulgar merchants. During the eighteenth century when Turkey's trade relations widened, Bulgarian merchants appeared right outside the Turkish Empire, as far afield as Vienna, Leipzig, Leghorn, Moscow, Bucharest, Odessa and even Basra, Ceylon and Calcutta. By the beginning of the nineteenth century a large part of the export trade with Russia and Austria was in the hands of the Bulgars and they took over the trade of the Dubrovnik merchants, who had been forced to leave the Turkish Empire during the eighteenth century, and regularly appeared at the Leipzig fair in place of them.

At the end of the eighteenth century and the beginning of the nineteenth century trade suffered a considerable set-back as a result of the difficulties and dangers to life and property engendered by the feudal disorders in the Turkish Empire such as the *Kŭrdzhali* movement, the rebellion of Pazvantoglu[1] and the effects of the Napoleonic Wars and the Greek Rising of 1821. For example, during the Napoleonic Wars many Bulgarian merchants who traded in Austria were ruined as a result of a financial crisis in which Austrian paper money suffered a great fall in value. An order went out that the notes must be exchanged, but the Bulgarian merchants were unable to journey to Vienna through Vidin because of Pazvantoglu, and by the time they had made a detour, they were too late to change their money. They therefore made a fire of their now worthless notes in the street in Vienna and brewed coffee over it.

After the end of the Russo-Turkish War of 1828–1829 there was a

[1] See p. 107.

considerable revival of trade throughout the territory of Bulgaria, encouraged by the rapid growth of handicrafts from 1826 onwards. The first merchants who travelled between the towns and the countryside were the *kŭrdzhii*, or packmen, who travelled with all kinds of goods in carts or on horses. Many of them would cover regular routes several times a year and each kept to his own circuit, and did not poach on another man's territory. Often they would travel in groups since even in the nineteenth century the roads were hazardous and travellers were liable to be attacked by robbers. These packmen would set out with various types of goods which they sold direct to the customer, either for money or in exchange for agricultural produce which they then resold at a profit. The packmen did not have shops or warehouses, but eventually some of them accumulated capital and became real merchants. The richer craftsmen also went in for trade and during the second quarter of the nineteenth century, several Bulgarian towns such as Tŭrnovo, Koprivshtitsa, Svishtov, Gabrovo, Plovdiv, etc., became great trading centres with merchants' shops and warehouses beside the craftsmen's workshops. Koprivshtitsa, indeed, had a merchants' guild as early as 1817. Bulgarian trading colonies were established abroad in such towns as Odessa, Bucharest and Constantinople. The merchants became an important element in town life, and were certainly the richest section of the urban population. Since internal trade within the Turkish Empire had been traditionally in the hands of non-Bulgars, such as Greeks, Jews, etc., the first really big Bulgarian merchants appeared in branches of trade to which they were particularly suited and in which they were able to gain complete ascendancy. Such branches were the wholesale supply of cattle to Constantinople (*dzhelepstvo*) and the collection of the sheep and goat tax (*beglikchiistvo*). Some of the *dzhelepi* had their own slaughter-houses and prepared dried meats, fats, etc., for sale on the market. Another significant section of traders were those who obtained from the Turkish Government the right to collect the agricultural tithes.

An important and characteristic feature of trade during the eighteenth and nineteenth centuries were the markets and fairs held in most Bulgarian towns and in the bigger villages. The markets (*pazari*) were held weekly or monthly and had a purely local significance, drawing buyers and sellers from the town in which it took place and from the surrounding villages. The fairs (*panairi*) were much bigger affairs and took place once a year in important economic centres. During the eighteenth century, there was still no single internal market and Bulgaria was divided into three more or less watertight trading areas; the Danube plain with its centres at Rusé, Svishtov and Varna; Thrace with its centres at Plovdiv, Adrianople, Uzundzhovo, with Burgas on the Black Sea and Enos on the navigable Maritsa as its ports, and finally Macedonia and part of southern Bulgaria. In the nineteenth century, however, this regional isolation broke down and with the widening of trade, all Bulgaria formed a single market. The most famous fair was that of Uzundzhovo which took place annually from September 15th to October 15th. Merchants came from all over Europe to Uzundzhovo, even from as far afield as England and Saxony. In 1841 the fair was attended by between 50,000 and 60,000 visitors, and in order to appreciate what a tremendous event the fair was, it must be borne in mind that the normal population of Uzundzhovo was only 2,000. Another important fair was held annually at Sliven from the end of June to the end of July, and this too attracted merchants from all over the Turkish Empire and also from Europe as well. Other fairs, some of them quite large and others with a more local significance were also held in Tatar-Pazardzhik, Nevrokop, Eski-Dzhumaya, Kazanlŭk, Kharmanli, Stara Zagora, Stanimak, etc. The fairs continued until the third quarter of the nineteenth century, when Bulgarian handicrafts began to suffer very badly as a result of the import of cheap goods from Western Europe, and when communications began to improve as a result of road and railway building by the Turkish Government during the sixties then the fairs began to decline and their place was gradually taken by the wide network of importers and exporters who had warehouses in many of the larger towns and ports. Nevertheless, the Uzundzhovo fair kept its significance until as late as 1875, and the Sliven fair till 1850.

Social Groupings in the Towns

On the principle that unity is strength, the Bulgars in the towns began to form general Councils[1] which usually consisted of the *usta-bashii* of the various guilds and the purpose of which was to represent more effectively their common interests before the Turkish authorities. In the course of time these Councils came to have far wider functions than their origin implied. They became communes[2] recognized by the Turks, having certain legal rights and were at the same time responsible to the Turks for the collection of taxes and the apportioning of tax contributions. The communes also undertook various

---

[1] The Bulgarian word is *Sŭvet*.   [2] The Bulgarian word is *obshtina*.

public works such as the building of schools, churches and even bridges and fountains. They were also responsible for appointing and paying the teachers and priests in their area. In general, the communes endeavoured to keep on good terms with the Turks, and this tendency became even more marked when, as might be expected, the leading role in the communes passed to the richest sections of the townsfolk, which included the wealthier craftsmen, the moneylenders, those who had acquired the right to collect taxes, and the large-scale merchants. These people, in fact, did very well for themselves under Turkish rule. They took advantage of the general corruption in the Ottoman Empire to enrich themselves through abuse of their power and by plunder and speculation, and therefore they had no reason to join in the struggle to liberate Bulgaria, but, on the contrary, had every reason to support Turkish rule which made it possible for them to occupy positions of power and profit.

This wealthy town aristocracy by no means had things all their own way. From the thirties of the nineteenth century onwards, they were everywhere being vigorously opposed by the poorer sections of the *bourgeoisie*, including the ordinary craftsmen organized in the guilds, and the really poor proletarian element in the towns, consisting of servants, hired workmen, bath attendants, porters, water-carriers, etc. The opposition also came to include the manufacturers and the importers and exporters, whose economic interests were not bound up with the continuance of Turkish rule; in fact, quite the contrary, for the feudal characteristics of the Turkish Empire gave rise to unfavourable conditions for the development of capitalism, such as the lack of political liberty and security of property, the survival of feudal dues and taxes, and *octrois* (abolished 1874), the high export and low import duties, the existence of State monopolies in such commodities as wool and wheat.[1] Even when reasonably progressive decrees were issued by the Central Government, local authorities frequently ignored or flouted them.

In 1839 the Turkish Government took steps to consolidate the position of their potential allies by instituting the 'election' of Bulgarian representatives from among the leading townsmen. This 'election' was about as democratic as the election of the *chorbadzhii* in the villages, and indeed these town representatives, who always came from the richer sections of the population, also enjoyed the official title of *chorbadzhii*.

[1] These were abolished in 1835 and 1838 respectively.

Western Europe and Turkey's Economy

During the nineteenth century Turkey's weakness and inability to cope with the general decay that beset the Empire by making a really radical transformation of the structure of the State, forced her to seek 'help' from the West in view of the growing threat from Russia, who alone of the Great Powers really wished to accomplish the downfall of the Turkish Empire. The Western countries responded and used their 'aid' as a means of making Turkey dependent on them to an ever-increasing extent. In the period after the Crimean War, especially, her dependence had reached such a degree that she was little more than a semi-colonial country.

For the Western Powers the backward Turkish Empire, still semi-feudal in economy, and lacking industry of its own, was a source of raw materials and, even more important, a market for the products of their own more advanced industry. The flow of cheap foreign goods into Turkey began in earnest after 1838 when Turkey was forced to sign unequal trade agreements with Britain and France by which the Porte agreed to charge very low duties on British and French goods imported into the Empire, only 5 per cent *ad valorem*, as compared to the high duty of 12 per cent on exports by which the Porte hoped to recoup its loss of important revenue. Similar treaties with Russia, the USA and other European countries followed soon after. The effects of this duty policy on Turkish economy were utterly ruinous, so much so that in 1861 new trade agreements were made with the Western capitalist Powers which fixed the import duties at 8 per cent and the export duties at 5 per cent with the rider that they were to be gradually reduced to 1 per cent. This did not, however, help Turkey as much as might be thought, because the international market was already being flooded by vast amounts of Russian and American agricultural produce. Austria and Britain exported goods to Turkey far in excess of the value of the raw materials they imported from her. As a result, Turkey began to have an adverse balance of trade, whereas in her Bulgarian territories at least, she had had a favourable balance of trade during the eighteenth and early nineteenth centuries. As her financial crisis worsened as a result of the Crimean War, she was obliged to obtain loans—ten of them between 1854 and 1870 with increasingly arduous terms—but the financial situation remained desperate and she was obliged to resort to more and more loans in order to pay current interest.

After the Crimean War the Turkish Capital was crowded with foreign capitalists and speculators, all hoping to get concessions from the Turkish Government to build railways and roads, to prospect for coal and metals, to supply drinking water to Constantinople, to open banks, to start insurance companies, etc. etc. The first railway in European Turkey between Cherna Voda and Constanța was opened in 1861, and this was followed by the Varna–Rusé line in 1867. The railways were mainly built by British companies. The granting of concessions for the building of communications helped to open up the country and increase the flood of Western manufactured goods, resulting in the ruin of Bulgarian craftsmen, who could not stand up to this foreign competition. The makers of *aba* and *shaek* fared somewhat better than most other craftsmen, because the durability of Bulgarian *aba* compared favourably with that of Western products, and because the ordinary population continued to dress as they always had done in locally made *shaek*. Bulgarian craftsmen had begun to suffer from Western competition as early as 1845, and after the Crimean War, some Bulgars, including Khristo Botev, opposed the building of railways on the grounds that it would increase the exploitation of Bulgaria by foreign capital. A movement for the boycott of foreign goods was organized during the sixties and seventies which took the form of a campaign against fashions involving the purchase of such goods which were much in vogue among the richer merchant circles. Foreign capital was by no means welcome to the Turkish *bourgeoisie* either, but the Empire was in no state to oppose the wishes of the Western Powers.

CHAPTER IV

THE FIRST 'AWAKENERS'

The Role of Paisi Hilendarsky

About the middle of the eighteenth century, at a time when, as we saw in the previous chapter, great economic changes were taking place in Bulgaria and a Bulgarian *bourgeoisie* was forming in the towns, there appeared the first of the so-called 'Awakeners', men who spoke with a new voice and brought a new message. In 1762 a Bulgarian monk known as Paisi Hilendarsky completed his *Slavonic–Bulgarian History* which was to become one of the most celebrated works of all Bulgarian literature. As a history, Paisi's book had little value: its importance and its appeal lay in its burning patriotism, and its impassioned call to the Bulgarians to be proud of their nationality and their language.

The fame of Father Paisi is such that it is easy to get the wrong perspective when considering his role in the Renaissance. He is sometimes regarded as something quite miraculous, the initiator of the Renaissance, a light shining in darkness, a voice crying in the wilderness. But it is not, in fact, the case that cultural darkness prevailed throughout Bulgaria before the time of Paisi. Cultural life went on, at a slow pace, it is true, and under great difficulties, but nevertheless it was there. Paisi was not even the first Bulgarian whose thoughts turned back to the past. Others before him had given some attention to the history of their people. Neither was he crying in a wilderness, for certain phrases in his *History* indicate that he was consciously addressing people who were already stirring and experiencing the birth of national awareness: 'I have written for you, who love your people and your Bulgarian fatherland, and want to know about your race and people.' The same idea is repeated in other places in the *History* and the people whom Paisi was addressing —though he himself would not have realized it—were the rising Bulgarian *bourgeoisie*. It has already been explained in the previous chapter that the period known as the Bulgarian Renaissance is fundamentally nothing more nor less than the period of the rise and development of the Bulgarian *bourgeoisie* and their struggle for markets and the mastery of their own country which began in the eighteenth century and continued with ever-increasing intensity until the Liberation of 1878 gave them the freedom they desired. It was quite natural that the sword of the new class should first be turned towards their chief rivals in business—the more advanced and well-established Greek *bourgeoisie*—and that their ideology should be one of nationalism. It was the ideology of this new rising class that found its first expression in Paisi's passionately patriotic *History*. This, then, is the role of Paisi: not an isolated phenomenon, not a lonely voice from a remote monastery cell, but the herald and standard bearer, as it were, of a new class which, though weak and rudimentary indeed at the time when Paisi wrote, was nevertheless alive and growing. To assess Paisi in this way, not as an isolated giant but as part of something wider and larger than the individual, in no way diminishes his personal importance, nor the glory of his work. On the contrary it increases and deepens the significance of this most remarkable man because we see him now as the prophet of his age, the first spokesman of the class which was to play the leading role in Bulgarian history for the next hundred years.

Bulgarian Culture before Paisi

There is nothing extraordinary in the fact that the prophet of the Renaissance and of the Bulgarian *bourgeoisie* should be a monk. It was in the monasteries that the written Bulgarian language and its literature were kept alive. In their libraries the precious Old Slavonic manuscripts were preserved and carefully copied by the monks, who also compiled anthologies and composed new works. In the monastery schools monks, aspiring priests and even lay people learnt to read and write in Slavonic, and in the monastery churches the Slavonic liturgy was in regular use. There were about one hundred such monasteries and of these the most important were the Rila monastery in Bulgaria itself and the Zograf and Hilendar monasteries on Mount Athos in Greece. Mount Athos is a peninsula in the Aegean Sea, and at that time constituted a monastic Republic of twenty large monasteries and eleven small ones, with a total population of five or six thousands monks. All the land of Mount Athos belonged to the monasteries who held charters originally granted by the Byzantine Emperors and renewed by the Turkish Sultans. Until 1913 the territory was subject to Turkey to whom the monks paid an annual tax.

Mount Athos was a very important centre of South Slavonic culture, and many manuscripts dating back to the First and Second Bulgarian Empires were preserved there. Since the population of the monasteries consisted of Serbs, Greeks and Russians as well as Bulgars, there was ample opportunity for cultural exchange—and for national rivalry. The Bulgarian monks were considerably influenced by the new national consciousness of the Greeks and Serbs, whose Renaissance began before that of the Bulgars. At the same time, the Bulgarian monks were in no way out of touch with what was going on in their own country, since members of the communities were constantly travelling all over Bulgaria collecting alms and performing other duties. The monks of Rila were, of course, in even closer contact with the people, and every year the monastery was visited by hundreds of pilgrims.

Some of Paisi's eighteenth-century literary predecessors had also been attracted to the theme of Bulgaria's past. One of these was Iosif Bradati, a monk at the Rila monastery who had also travelled extensively, especially in western Bulgaria. He was a writer of fiery sermons and didactic literature of a high moral tone, and his work contains elements of national consciousness and a knowledge of Bulgaria's past. For example, he wrote: 'While we had a pious kingdom, the Greeks did not submit to the Bulgarian Tsar, and the Bulgars did not submit to the Greek Tsar. When God saw their disobedience, he took their kingdom and all their power from them and gave them to the infidels.' Bradati also raised a voice of protest against the troubles suffered by the Bulgars at the hands of the Turks. Another of Paisi's predecessors was Parteni Pavlovich of Silistra who was a fine preacher, writer and collector of antiquities, and wandered about from monastery to monastery. Both he and the third name that must be mentioned, Khristofor Zhefarovich of Doiran, are regarded as belonging equally to Serbian and Bulgarian literature. Zhefarovich is chiefly famous for his book, the *Stematografia*, printed in Vienna in 1714 which contains portraits of Serbian and Bulgarian Tsars and saints, and also fifty-six emblems of various Slav and non-Slav countries, with short comments in verse on the emblems and people of the countries concerned. Among these was the lion emblem of Bulgaria, and the comment that once the Bulgarians had been famous for their power, but now they were slaves to the Turks.

The Life and Work of Paisi Hilendarsky

Very little is known of the life of Paisi Hilendarsky. Even his secular name has not come down to us. He was born about 1722 in the town of Bansko, which nearly two centuries later was to be the birthplace of another patriot and giant of Bulgarian literature—Nikola Vaptsarov. In the days of Paisi, Bansko was a fairly important economic centre with a developing *bourgeoisie*. On his own evidence, Paisi had little education, and when he was twenty-three he was sent to the Hilendar monastery where his elder brother was Abbot. This monastery was supposed to have been founded by the Serbian king, Stephen Nemanya, during the twelfth century, and at the time when Paisi entered it, its community included Serbs, Bulgars, Greeks and Russians. In spite of his sparse education, Paisi had a great love of learning and found much to interest him in the monastery library and to encourage him to write himself. Furthermore, since the monks were in close contact with their own countries through their alms collecting, etc., their discussions reflected life outside the monastery walls and Paisi found himself in the midst of violent controversies on national, cultural and political topics. The awakening of national consciousness shown by the fact that among the subjects round which controversy raged were which Slav country first adopted Christianity and which first had a literature. The relations between the monks from the various countries were not by any means always brotherly and in the heated arguments the Greeks and the Serbs, who had already started their Renaissance, would taunt the Bulgarians that they had no history. Paisi's own reading in the library had led him to the conclusion that this gibe had no foundation and that a great deal of information on the history of Bulgaria did, in fact, exist. He therefore set to work to collect this information together and produce a history of his people. In the spring of 1761 Paisi was sent to the Serbian town of Karlovac to collect the belongings of Gerasim, a former Abbot of the Hilendar monastery who had died there. While he was in Karlovac, Paisi had the opportunity of using the Patriarchal library there. In it he found a history of the Slavs by the seventeenth-century Abbot of Dubrovnik, Mauro Orbini, which had been translated from the Italian into Russian on the orders of Peter the Great and which contained a chapter on Bulgaria. This book, according to Paisi, was one of the most important sources for his own history. Orbini's work was far from scholarly. He made indiscriminate use of all sources available to him, regarding them all as equally reliable, and his History was full of contradictions and faulty chronology. He also counted as Slavs various non-Slav peoples such as the Alans, the Goths, the Avars and the ancient Illyrians. Nevertheless, Orbini wrote with pride of the achievements of the Slavs and their past glory and mentions the creation of the Slavonic alphabet. At first the book was banned by Rome, but later it was revised by a Dominican friar named Ambrasi Guchetich, who expurgated it to the satisfaction of the Papal Curia.

Apart from Orbini's book, Paisi made use of another work—the *Annales Ecclesiastici a Christo nato ad annum* 1198 by Cardinal Cesare Baronius (1538–1607), a Russian translation of which existed in the libraries both at Karlovac and the Hilendar monastery. Like Orbini's History, Baroni's book contains many historical and chronological inaccuracies. While these two books appear to have been the most important sources for his *History*, Paisi also went through the old Bulgarian manuscripts in all the libraries on Mount Athos and also visited many in Bulgaria itself.

Paisi returned from Karlovac to the Hilendar monastery in the summer of 1761 but the constant bickering and rivalries among the monks upset him so much that he was obliged to move to the purely Bulgarian Zograf monastery. Here in spite of ill health with stomach trouble and headaches, he continued to work on his *History* which he finished in 1762. He then either made a fair copy himself or had it done by a monk skilled in this kind of work and set out to popularize his *History* in Bulgaria while ostensibly collecting alms for the monastery. The fair copy has since been lost, but the original rough draft in Paisi's own hand was found in the Zograf monastery in 1906 and was published in 1914 by the Bulgarian Academy of Sciences.

In the winter of 1764–1765 Paisi visited Kotel where he met a young priest named Stoiko Vladislavov, later to become famous as Sofroni, Bishop of Vratsa. Paisi's *History* made a tremendous impression on the young man who immediately copied it and placed it in the church for all to read, adorned with the following stern warning:

'May he who appropriates or steals this book be anathematized and cursed by the Lord God of Sabaoth and by the twelve apostles, by the holy fathers and the four evangelists. May hail, iron and stone fall on him and may he perish for ever.'

Nearly fifty other manuscript copies and reworked versions of the *History* have come down to us, and this is, in itself, ample evidence of its popularity. All these copies are dated prior to 1845 and no copies appear to have been made subsequently. The main reason for this is that a version of it was published as a printed book in Budapest by Khristaki Pavlovich in 1845.

After 1765, the year of his meeting with the future Sofroni Vrachansky, nothing is known of Paisi's life. We do not even know where and when he died.

Paisi's History

The full title on the original rough copy is *A Slavonic–Bulgarian History of the people, Tsars and saints, and of all their deeds and the Bulgarian way of life. Assembled and set out by the Ieromonakh Paisi who dwelt in the Holy Mountain of Athos, having come from the diocese of Samokov in 1745, and who assembled this history in the year 1762 for the benefit of the Bulgarian people.* Though based on Church Slavonic, the language in which the *History* is written is simple, vital and direct as befits a theme of popular appeal. It also contains various Russicisms and Serbisms and a sprinkling of idioms from the West Bulgarian dialect. The interesting feature of Paisi's *History* is that its value depends not on its worth as a piece of scientific scholarship, but on the message which the author is trying to convey often to the detriment of the facts. It has already been pointed out that his two main sources, the Histories of Orbini and Baroni, were far from reliable, and that their authors made indiscriminate use of sources. Paisi did much the same, and, moreover, in order to achieve his purpose he idealized and romanticized Bulgaria's past, eulogized all her Tsars and dwelt almost exclusively on their glories and victories. Yet all this, which would normally divest such a book of any value, does not affect the significance of Paisi's *History*. His basic aim was not to teach the facts of history, but to rouse his people's national consciousness and make them proud to be Bulgars. In order to do this he made use of history to demonstrate that the Bulgars were a people in their own right, that they had glorious traditions and something of which to be proud. Above all, his attack was directed against those who had abandoned the Bulgarian language and customs for those of the Greeks, whom they thought to be superior and more cultured:

'And some there be that do not want to know about their own Bulgarian people, but have turned to a foreign culture and a foreign language and do not care for their own Bulgarian language but

learned to read and speak in Greek and are ashamed to call themselves Bulgars—O you senseless and foolish people! Why are you
ashamed to call yourselves Bulgars and why do you not read and
speak your own language?'

Paisi pointed out that the Bulgars once had their own Kingdom,
that they were celebrated throughout the world, and that more than
once they had exacted tribute from the 'powerful Romans and wise
Greeks'. He reminded them that among the Slavs, the Bulgars were
the first to have their own Tsar and Patriarch and they were the
first to be baptized. 'Why then', he asks, 'are you ashamed of your
origin and why do you cling to a foreign people?' He also indignantly
countered the argument that since the Greeks were wiser and more
cultured than the Bulgars, who were simple and uneducated, it was
better to ape the Greeks. He pointed out that there were other
peoples wiser and more cultured than the Greeks, but no Greek
ever thought of abandoning his language and nationality for this
reason. To clinch the matter, he argued that even if there were few
merchants, scholars and experts among the Bulgars, even if the
majority of their people were simple ploughmen, shepherds and
artisans, so also were the great men of the Bible, among whom there
were no merchants or learned men. But, Paisi says, his *History* was
not intended for those who blasphemed their fathers and had no
love for their own people and language, but for those who were
proud of them, that they should know that their Tsar and churchmen did have their own Chronicles and Histories like other nations,
but that these were unfortunately destroyed during the Turkish
Conquest.

The *History* begins with an introductory article on the use of
history, taken almost entirely from the Russian preface to Baroni's
book. Briefly, the purpose of history as set out in this preface is to
gain wisdom so that one may not be at a loss to answer the questions
of children and simple folk, so that one may better understand the
world without the fatigue and danger of having to travel to see for
oneself, and, in the case of rulers, that they may be helped in their
task by knowledge of the past. The study of history was, in Paisi's
view, particularly helpful to enslaved people, since it would show
them how they might resurrect themselves. Paisi's own philosophy of
history was, of course, an essentially religious one, in which everything was ordered and directed by God. After the first Preface
comes the title of the book as given above, and then there follows the

second Preface which is really the most important part of the book, since it contains his call to the Bulgarians to be proud of their nationality and their language, and the material and arguments referred to in the previous paragraphs on Paisi's purpose in writing the *History*. The next chapter gives a brief outline of Bulgarian history up to the time of Ivailo, i.e. 1278. The outline begins in the manner of the chronicles with the story of the Flood and the traditional division of the earth among the sons of Noah. The history of Bulgaria itself is written in such a way as to stress the positive qualities of the Bulgarian people and their Tsars to the exclusion of all else. He writes of their lion-like courage, their strength, their military victories and their goodness, and even stated that weak and dishonourable Tsars were not tolerated by the people, who made a practice of dethroning such rulers. The fourth section of the book is devoted to a brief and very selective survey of the Tsars of Serbia, and is intended to show that the Bulgars had a much more glorious past than the Serbs. The fifth section deals with the history of Bulgaria from Ivailo to the Turkish Conquest, with pride of place once more going to Bulgarian victories, real and imagined. Paisi apportioned the chief blame for the enslavement of the Christian States by the Turks to the Greek Emperor, Manuel, who first encouraged the Turks to attack Bulgaria, although he also mentions the divisions between the various Christian rulers. The sixth section consists of a list of the Bulgarian Tsars, and the seventh—of brief characterizations of the most important of them. The eighth section is devoted to the saints, Cyril and Methodius, and their work for Slavonic culture. In it, Paisi declares with pride that of all the Slavonic peoples the Bulgars were the first to have their own written language, whatever anybody else might say to the contrary. In this section also, Paisi outlines the history of the Bulgarian Church and describes its position under the Greek Patriarchate, pointing out that Greeks and not Bulgars were chosen as bishops and that Bulgarian schools and teaching were replaced by Greek. In the ninth section Paisi recounts the life and work of saints who were Bulgarian in origin. The *History* ends with an Epilogue which describes the circumstances in which the *History* was compiled, and gives us some autobiographical information about the author.

Paisi's own efforts at making his *History* known have already been described. He was, however, very much of a forerunner, and lived and wrote at a time when the *bourgeoisie*, which was to be the driving force behind the Renaissance, was at a very elementary stage of development and was still largely inarticulate. The growth of new ideas and new consciousness proceeded very slowly and nearly sixty years passed before a mass movement appeared, fired by the same ideas that had inspired Paisi in the writing of his *History*. Most of the copies of the *History* belong to the nineteenth century, that is, at least thirty years after Paisi set out on his journey to popularize it. In the thirties and forties when the movement for national culture and national schools swept the country, Paisi's *History* came into its own. The printed version, edited by Khristaki Pavlovich, which appeared in 1845, was used as a history textbook in the new Bulgarian schools. An example of the kind of impression that Paisi's *History* made on his fellow countrymen is the evidence of Petko Slaveikov, the great writer and public figure, who declared that as a boy he had intended to enter a monastery, but after he had read Paisi's *History* in a manuscript copy, he no longer thought of how he could save his own soul, but rather of how he could save his people.

Other Histories

Another history actually called *A Brief History of the Bulgar Slav People*, but generally known as the *Zograf History*, has been found in manuscript form in the library of the Zograf monastery. Its author was a Bulgarian monk whose name is not known, and it is considered possible that this history was finished in 1761, i.e. just before that of Paisi. It is very probable, though there is no actual evidence to support this view, that Paisi and the unknown monk knew each other and assisted in each other's research.

A further History with a similar title to that of the unknown monk was written some thirty years later in 1792 by a monk called Spiridon. He was a native of Gabrovo, and at the time he wrote, he was living in the Nyamtsu monastery near Jassy in Rumania. Some consider that he was at one time a pupil of Paisi Hilendarsky, while others believe that he was only indirectly influenced by Paisi through reading a copy of his *History*.

Neither of these works had the merit nor the wide appeal of that of Paisi. The *Zograf History* is the less interesting of the two, being somewhat dry, phlegmatic and similar in style to the old Chronicles. Spiridon's *History* is a little more animated than the *Zograf*, but although he does point with pride to the fact that Bulgaria was the oldest Slavonic kingdom and the first to accept Christianity, his *History* lacks the burning, militant patriotism of Paisi. While the latter wrote mainly of the past of the Bulgarian people, Spiridon

3. The inner courtyard of the Rila Monastery

(Photograph by J. Allan Cash)

4a.

Kableshkov's house in Koprivshtitsa (nineteenth century). View from the street showing the high garden wall and windowless ground floor typical of this period

(Photograph by J. Allan Cash)

4b.

A typical house in Koprivshtitsa (nineteenth century)

devoted more space to the Greeks and Roman Emperors and the Turkish Sultans than the Bulgarian Tsars. Moreover, while Paisi frequently referred to the Bulgarian people, Spiridon confined himself to the doings of the Tsars and the saints. The ideological and propagandist element was also lacking in Spiridon's *History*. For all these reasons, it never attained the same popularity or played the same political role as that of Paisi, and only one copy has been found. This was made in 1819 by one Petko Pop Manov of Gabrovo.

Sofroni Vrachansky, 1739–1814

Sofroni Vrachansky, or, to give him his secular name, Stoiko Vladislavov, was one of the great figures of the Bulgarian Renaissance who drew his inspiration from Paisi. We have already heard of his personal meeting with Paisi in Kotel in 1765 and his subsequent copying of Paisi's *History*. This meeting was a great turning-point in his life, for the *History* made such an impression upon him that from that day on he devoted his life to the service of his people. The lasting impression that Paisi's *History* had on him is shown by the fact that considerably later, in 1781, he made a second copy for his own use.

Stoiko Vladislavov was born in 1739 at Kotel, then one of the most flourishing centres for trade and handicrafts in Bulgaria. His father and uncle were *dzhelepi*, i.e. cattle dealers who supplied Constantinople with meat. In his autobiography, entitled, *The Life and Suffering of Sinful Sofroni*, Stoiko tells us that he had been too sickly to commence his education until he was nine. Learning came easily to him and he soon learned to read, although all the education was conducted in Greek. In 1750 his father died of plague in Constantinople and he was adopted by his uncle. At the age of eleven he was apprenticed to a trade, and in 1762 he was ordained as a priest. It is a commentary on the standard of education then prevailing in the priesthood that Stoiko with his meagre two years attendance at school was considered the most erudite among his fellow priests, who hated him for his learning. Three years later came the historic meeting with Paisi. During the Russo-Turkish War of 1768–1774, Stoiko and all the inhabitants of the Kotel area suffered greatly at the hands of passing Turkish troops, who devastated the Christian villages and murdered at will. Sometime between 1770 and 1774 he visited Mount Athos and spent six months there. On his return, as well as acting as priest, he began teaching the children to read, and, following the exhortation of Paisi, he gradually

D

introduced the use of Bulgarian in place of Greek in his little school, and taught in Kotel for twenty years. On a visit to Osman-Pazar where he had gone in order to intercede on behalf of the people of Kotel over the fixing of taxes, he was imprisoned by one of the Turkish lords who were then engaged in civil war. Here, according to his autobiography, he was ill-treated, reviled and fed on bad food, and as a result, all his hair fell out.

When he gained his freedom, he was afflicted by new tribulations. He had developed a nervous disease and had to go to Constantinople for treatment. Apart from that he was persecuted by creditors and by the Greek clergy, and since the Greek bishop would not let him take services for six whole years, the unfortunate Stoiko had to live on charity. He also managed to fall foul of the local Bulgarian notables, and in the end he was obliged to leave Kotel and become priest at Karnobat. Here, however, he once more earned the hostility of the powers-that-be, and was persecuted, beaten and threatened with death. He fled to the village of Shikhlari where he narrowly escaped being hanged by the Sultan for officiating at the wedding of a Bulgarian girl whom the Sultan had wished to marry. Let us hear part of the story in Stoiko's own vivid words:

'He [the Sultan] already had a wife, a Khan's daughter. This Sultan fell in love with a Christian girl from that village, the daughter of *Chorbadzhiya* Yuvan who called himself Kovandzhi Ulu, and intended to take her as his second wife. But the Khan's daughter would not give him leave to take a second wife. And so he kept the girl waiting four or five years, neither marrying her nor giving her leave to marry. And one day I was called to Karnobat to officiate at a wedding, and I asked "Who is the girl?" And they told me who the girl was, and that the Sultan had wanted to take her for his second wife, but had now given her permission to get married herself, and so they had brought her there. And I believed them and married them. Three days later I heard that the Sultan had been pursuing her father with the intention of killing him, but that he had escaped, and that the Sultan had seized her brother, beaten him a great deal and fined him. Whereupon I became alarmed and had grave doubts. . . .' Not long after, Stoiko actually met the Sultan, who asked him if he was the village priest. On hearing that he was, the Sultan asked if he had officiated at the wedding of Kovandzhi's daughter at Karnobat: 'I replied: "I am a stranger in these parts, I've only just come here and I didn't know who Kovandzhi's daughter was." But he immediately lifted his rifle and struck me twice across the shoulders with it . . . and then drew his pistol at me. But since I was close to him, I seized his pistol and he shouted to his servant: "Give me a rope quickly so I can hang this pimp!" And the servant came and took my horse's halter . . . and put it round my neck. And there was a willow tree there and immediately he climbed into it and dragged me up by the halter. But since my hands were not bound, I seized the halter and pulled him down, and begged the Sultan to have mercy on me. But he just sat on his horse and shouted at Milosh [Stoiko's companion] in a great rage, saying: "Come and lift up this pimp". But Milosh began to intercede with him on my behalf, and the Sultan struck him in the face with the rifle and his forehead was badly cut. Then the Sultan turned his gaze back to the willow and pointed his rifle at his servant and shouted: "Why don't you pull that rope, eh? I'll bring you off that willow in a minute!" The servant pulled up, while I pulled down, since my hands were not tied. But while the Sultan was gazing up, my comrade, Milosh, ran off and there was nobody to lift me up. Then the Sultan said to his servant: "Come down and we'll go into the village and hang him there for everybody to see!" And they gave me my horse to lead by the bridle, and dragged me along by the rope round my neck. . . . And the Sultan came behind me, cursing me and saying: "If I don't kill you, whom shall I kill? You've been and married my wife to a giaour!" ' . . .

In the end, the wretched Stoiko escaped with his life by promising to give the girl a divorce. He saddled his horse and fled to the village of Sigmen where, in his own words, he 'quickly drank down three or four glasses of potent rakia' and trembled all over.

A year later he went to Karabunar where he actually spent a whole year in peace, and then moved to Arbanasi near Tŭrnovo. Here in 1794 he was consecrated Bishop of Vratsa and took the name of Sofroni. About this time, Turkey passed into a period of violent feudal disorders and anarchy. Robber bands known as the *Kŭrdzhali* roamed Bulgaria pillaging and burning, and in Vidin, Osman Pazvantoglu set himself up as an independent ruler, defying all attempts on the part of the Sultan to regain control of the area. Vratsa itself was in the area terrorized by the *Kŭrdzhali* and the bands of Osman Pazvantoglu, and Sofroni was probably given the diocese because no Greek candidate would venture into such a trouble spot. Apart from that, the diocese was a very poor one and held little attraction for the greedy Greek clergy. Undaunted as ever,

Sofroni set out for Vratsa, and, in spite of facing robbery and death at every step, he eventually arrived at the centre of his diocese to the great joy and amazement of his flock. In Vratsa he taught his congregation in the Bulgarian language which apparently caused a sensation since no previous Bishop had ever done such a thing, Greek being the rule. From 1795 onwards the disorders grew worse and worse. Villages were plundered and burnt and on two occasions, in 1796 and 1797, Vratsa itself was besieged, once by the Sultan's troops, and once by Pazvantoglu's men. In such conditions, Sofroni could not collect the Church taxes and his debts mounted up. During these troubled times, poor Sofroni frequently had to leave Vratsa to hide, but his strong sense of duty led him to return to Vratsa whenever he could. One January he spent twenty days hiding in a shepherd's hut. He had to flee from village to village. He hid in caves and on one occasion he even took refuge in a harem. He suffered hunger and privation, and he writes of the shame that he felt when he saw naked children in Svishtov but had no money with which to buy them clothes. Finally, he was tricked into going to Vidin itself by a wily Greek monk named Kalinik, and was virtually imprisoned there for three years, suffering many humiliations. During his detention in Vidin, since he could not fulfil his normal duties towards his flock at Vratsa, he devoted himself to literary activity, mainly translations from the Greek, and compiled two anthologies of very mixed content, containing such items as translations of Aesop's fables, material from mediaeval Bulgarian literature put into simple modern language understandable to all his readers, moral stories, discourses, etc.

At the end of three years Sofroni was released but the continuation of the *Kŭrdzhali* disorders made any return to Vratsa impossible and he went first to Kraiova and then to Bucharest in 1803, where his two nephews, Stefan and Atanas Bogoridi, were studying at a Phanariot academy. In Bucharest he was received very hospitably by the Metropolitan Dositei, and his sufferings and privations were at last at an end. Nevertheless, he felt very badly about having left the people entrusted to his care, although, as he says, he did not run away for the sake of peace and quiet, but because necessity and heavy debts compelled him to leave. To ease his conscience towards his flock and to continue to serve his people though in exile, he turned again to literary activity. 'Therefore, I am working day and night to write a few books in our Bulgarian language, so that if I, a sinner, cannot speak to them verbally for them to learn from me, then they can read my writings and benefit from them and pray to God for me, unworthy one, that he should correct my ignorance.' Sofroni revised one of the anthologies which he had compiled in Vidin, and with the financial assistance of Bulgarian merchants in Rumania, he had it printed in Rimnik during 1806 under the new title of *Kyriakodromion or Nedelnik* (Sunday). It consisted of a preface and various sermons or homilies for Sundays and saints' days which not only dealt with theology but also with practical Christianity in everyday family and social life. This book became enormously popular and the people called it the *Sofronié* after its author. It is considered to be the first Bulgarian printed book of modern times, since the only two books printed previously, the *Gospel* of 1512 and the *Abagar* of 1651, belong by reason of their content and language to old Bulgarian literature. In 1805 Sofroni compiled an anthology under the title of *A Confession of Orthodox Faith*, which includes his famous autobiography. This is the first realistic work of Bulgarian literature, and, as the reader can observe from the extracts quoted above, it is written in a popular, racy style, with an immediate appeal to the widest possible reading public. Sofroni's last work, written in 1809, is *Theatron Politikon*, a complete translation of the *Theatrum Historicum* by the Protestant writer Wilhelm Strateman, which Sofroni knew in a Greek translation, and certain excerpts from which he had previously included in one of the anthologies he had prepared in Vidin. This book was full of the ideas of liberty and humanism which arose with the Western European Renaissance. Its chief theme was the correct relations between lords and their subjects, and between authority in general and the people.

Sofroni wrote in a preface:

'I, humble in zealousness for my people, have worked and translated from Greek into Bulgarian, because this book is very useful and necessary to men. And not only to the rulers who are in power, in that it will teach them gently how to rule their States and subjects justly and honourably, but it is also necessary and useful to everyone.'

Sofroni is therefore a most important figure in Bulgarian literature. Apart from being the author of the first modern printed Bulgarian book and the first realistic, almost secular work, he is important because of his insistence that books be written in simple popular speech so that everybody can understand, and not in the fossilized

literary Church Slavonic. In his appeal to the merchants to finance
the printing of the *Nedelnik*, he wrote: 'Up till now there has been
no such book in popular Bulgarian speech in the world, but the
Greeks, Serbs and Rumanians, and the Russians, and people of
other faiths have such books; only our poor Bulgars lack such a gift.
Therefore they are darkened by ignorance.' Sofroni's language
cannot, however, be considered to be entirely similar to the spoken
Bulgarian, for while it contains many popular forms, it does also
still contain some Old Bulgarian forms.

Though a bishop, Sofroni held remarkably advanced and enlightened views on many vital subjects, and was obviously influenced
by the humanist ideas born in Western Europe of the Age of Reason
and the French Revolution. He saw knowledge and education as
being of paramount importance in the resurrection of the Bulgarian
people. He even upbraided his fellow-countrymen for giving money
to monasteries where the monks spent their time in idleness, eating
and drinking, instead of giving it to finance schools and teachers to
educate their children. He saw clearly the need for new secular
schools with a modern syllabus as in Western European countries,
and pointed out the power and wealth that these nations had gained
through education. Like Paisi, Sofroni was a man of great vision
and understanding, who saw the necessity for certain measures
long before these became the demands of a mass movement, and in
his views on education he was the forerunner of the great movement
for Bulgarian schools which began in the thirties and forties of the
nineteenth century.

A further aspect of his labour on behalf of his people was his
political activity during the Russo-Turkish War of 1806–1812,
when he emerged as the representative spokesman of the Bulgarian
people and was recognized by the Russians as such. In his *Appeal
to the Bulgarian People,* he urged the Bulgars to welcome and assist
the Russian troops as brothers and liberators. This aspect of his
work will be dealt with in greater detail in the section on the Russo-
Turkish War in Chapter V.

Though so much is known of the details of Sofroni's life from his
Autobiography and other sources, and though we have a portrait
of him believed to be a self-portrait (for Sofroni was both a fine
artist and caligrapher), we know nothing of his death. Since nothing
more is heard of him after 1813, we must assume that he died about
this time, although when he died and where he lies buried remains
a mystery.

CHAPTER V

POLITICAL EVENTS
IN TURKEY 1768-1839

The Russo-Turkish War, 1768-1774

Starting in the second half of the eighteenth century, a new series of wars began between Russia and Turkey in which the Bulgarians took an energetic and enthusiastic part, hoping that at last the hour of liberation had struck. Unfortunately, although Russian troops often entered Bulgarian territory and although the Serbs, Rumanians and Greeks eventually won their independence, the Bulgars gained nothing and indeed suffered terribly from Turkish reprisals when the Russian troops withdrew again.

The first Russo-Turkish War of the series began in 1768. Catherine the Great's expansionist policy, aimed at gaining control of the Black Sea coast and Crimea from the Turks, and thus acquiring for Russia a much needed outlet to a warm sea, aroused not only the natural opposition of Turkey but also that of France, who objected to the increase of Russian influence in that part of the world. France successfully encouraged the Sultan to declare war on Russia in 1768. From Russia's point of view, the war came at a very bad moment, when she was involved in both internal and external difficulties. In order to divert Turkey's attention and to lessen the striking power that could be used against the Russian armies, Catherine decided to rouse the Balkan people to revolt. She sent agents to Bulgaria including a Bulgar named Korazin who was serving as a colonel in the Russian Army, to encourage the people in the belief that liberation would be theirs if they would rise in support of the Russian troops. When, after a series of victories, Russian troops entered Bulgarian territory by way of the Dobrudzha during 1773 and 1774, hundreds of Bulgars fought beside the Russians in volunteer detachments and partisan units. In 1774 a rising was organized in Vidin, but the plot was discovered and the rising was crushed by the Turks in its initial stages. In the same year, the Turks surrendered to the Russians, and the war ended with the Treaty of Kuchuk-

Kainardji which, however, left the Bulgarian people still unliberated, although certain other territories of the Turkish Empire passed into Russian hands and the Russians gained the right to act as protectors of the Balkan Christians. Infuriated by the active sympathy of the Bulgars for the Russians, the Turks prepared 'black lists' of Bulgars known to have participated in the war on the Russian side, with the intention of wreaking vengeance on them. Because of this many Bulgars emigrated across the Danube to Walachia, Moldavia and Bessarabia, while the members of some units who preferred to remain in Bulgaria took to the mountains and re-grouped as *haidut* bands.

In spite of the fact that the war did not end in Bulgaria's liberation as many had hoped, the Bulgars nevertheless kept their hope that it would be Russia who would liberate them, a hope they retained even though subsequent Russo-Turkish wars brought liberation to their neighbours but not to them, and even though they had to wait more than a hundred years before their turn came.

The Russo-Turkish War, 1787–1791

In 1787, encouraged this time by Great Britain, the Sultan again made war on Russia, hoping to regain the Crimea. Austria was Russia's ally in this new war, but in 1790 she made a separate peace at Svishtov, leaving Russia to carry on the war alone. Nevertheless, Russian troops under their brilliant general, Suvorov, who has the distinction of never having been defeated and under whose command Bulgarian units had served in the war of 1768-1774, won new victories in Moldavia, and Turkey, threatened from the sea as well by the Russian Black Sea Fleet under Admiral Ushakov, was once again forced to ask for peace. Under the Treaty of Jassy in 1791, Russia gained the whole of the north Black Sea coast from the Kuban to the area between the Bug and Dnestr, and her merchant navy won the right to visit Turkish Black Sea and Danube ports. Walachia and Moldavia became semi-independent princedoms under Russian protection. Again the Bulgars were no better off, but they still kept their optimism and believed that their turn would soon come, although they were mercilessly plundered by the Turkish troops who were embittered by defeat and lack of booty, and by other marauding Turks who cared nothing for law and order.

Reforms in Turkey

The two wars against Russia which had been unsuccessful in spite of the backing of the Western Powers, had shown up more than ever the growing decay and chaos within the Turkish Empire. The brilliant war machine of *spahi* horsemen and Janissary infantry which in previous centuries had carried all before it, was now in a sorry state. About two-thirds of the so-called *spahi* no longer appeared for military service, but were in fact ordinary citizens who had acquired, by one means or another, small pieces of land from *spahi* estates which were too small to support them, thus these *spahi* represented a discontented, lawless element. The degeneration of the Janissaries as a fighting force has been described in a previous chapter.

The finances of the Empire were also in a parlous state, undermined by the corruption of the local officials who misappropriated the State taxes for which they were supposed to be responsible and collected extra taxes on their own account from the long-suffering population, thus making themselves *de facto*, if not *de jure*, independent of the central administration. The financial situation was not improved by the loss of Turkish territory to the Russians.

After the Treaty of Jassy, marauding bands of demobilized soldiers, lawless Janissaries and discontented minor *spahi*, known as the *Kŭrdzhali* or *daalii*, began to form all over the Balkans, and both there and in Anatolia rebellions against the central authority began to take place.

Faced with this terrible situation, the Sultan, Selim III (1789–1807), began in 1791 to introduce a series of reforms by which he hoped to reimpose the power of the central authority all over the Empire, strengthen the economy and provide adequate armed forces of a kind capable of defending the Empire. In this project he was greatly encouraged by France and Great Britain, who feared that Russia would step in, should the Empire collapse entirely. As a first step, old taxes were increased and new ones were introduced on such things as spirits, coffee, tobacco, silk, etc. Then the Government turned its attention to the now rotten *spahi* system with the aim of evicting all those who were not proper *spahi*, and of creating by degrees a new regular army on Western lines with French instructors. The Sultan also envisaged certain governmental reforms with the aim of making Turkey into a centralized, absolute monarchy. These reforms were to include restaffing the provincial administration with nominees paid by the Government, limiting the power of the Vizir and replacing the *Divan* which had become a mere tool of the Janissaries and feudal aristocracy by a Council under the personal direction of the Sultan.

D*

In these reforms the Sultan had the support of a handful of feudal lords and officers, but the vast majority of the feudal class, as well as the local governors and the religious leaders, were utterly opposed to them. In various areas of Asia Minor and the Balkans, the local governors refused to obey the central authority and began to function as independent rulers and fought civil wars with each other, adding to the general confusion.

The Kŭrdzhali Movement

Apart from the independent pashas and their wars, Bulgaria was plagued from 1792 until as late as 1815 by armed bands, known as the *Kŭrdzhali*, who lived by plunder. These were composed of discontented mutinous Janissaries who saw the proposed army reforms as the end of their power, petty feudal lords, town officials and demobilized Turkish soldiers who had no land to which to return. With the Central Government powerless to say them nay, the *Kŭrdzhali* ran riot throughout Bulgaria, burning and plundering, and they terrorized the country, interfering with normal work and depopulating whole areas, the inhabitants of which emigrated in thousands or sought refuge in the towns. In order to combat them, the Turkish Government for the first time took the serious step of arming the Bulgarian and Serbian Christian population, hitherto forbidden to possess arms. Although the Sultan's edicts referred to the *Kŭrdzhali* as 'revolutionaries', they were, of course, reactionary in character, since the movement originated in the opposition of the old Janissary military organization and other discontented feudal elements to the reforms of Selim III, and the *Kŭrdzhali* had the tacit support of the anti-reformist *mullahs* and the most reactionary elements in Turkish society. Selim III was finally driven from his throne and killed by the Janissaries with the support of the religious leaders.

Sometimes the *Kŭrdzhali* raids would take the following form: the *Kŭrdzhali* would descend on a village and the leader would commandeer the finest house for his own use. In the absence of a suitable one, he would pitch his tent in the best site, near a fountain or spring, and would call the inhabitants together. He would then demand furnishings from them and when he was luxuriously installed he would order them to bring him all their possessions, which he and his band would divide between themselves. Then the wretched villagers were expected to provide free fodder for the horses and food for the bandits. Anyone who was so rash as to conceal any wealth from them was roasted between two fires, or bound with red-hot chains.

The *Kŭrdzhali* wore distinctive, gaily-coloured clothes; their horses were beautifully accoutred and their weapons were wrought with gold and silver. On their expeditions they were accompanied by female slaves, who waited by their lords' horses in time of battle and entertained them in time of rest.

There were, in fact, some Bulgars in the ranks of the *Kŭrdzhali*, an example being Indzhé, an historical figure celebrated in a famous short story of the same name by Yordan Yovkov. Indzhé, a former *haidut*, joined the *Kŭrdzhali* with a band of approximately five hundred Bulgars and is known to have attacked and burnt Kalofer in 1799 after the local *chorbadzhiya* refused to pay him the sum he demanded. It would appear, however, that the Bulgarian *Kŭrdzhali* had different aims and motives to those of the Turks, and the former probably thought, owing to the lack of political understanding which characterized the *haiduti*, that by taking part in the *Kŭrdzhali* rebellion against the Sultan, that they themselves could strike a blow for Bulgarian freedom. Later on, after 1802, Indzhé, together with his band broke away from the other *Kŭrdzhali* and henceforward appeared as the defender of the Bulgarian population in the southeast part of the country where he operated.

It remains true, however, that the vast majority of the Bulgarian people were utterly opposed to the *Kŭrdzhali* and played the leading role in combating them. The citizens of Kotel, for example, made their own guns, pistols, knives and gunpowder for their defence, and other towns did the same. In the countryside, the Bulgars guarded the mountain passes, organized elaborate defence systems for the villages and even met the *Kŭrdzhali* bands in open battle. An important part in the fight against the *Kŭrdzhali* was played by the Bulgarian *haiduti*. The *Kŭrdzhali* movement gradually subsided with some of its members killed and others grown weary of bandit life, and it finally came to an end in 1815.

Osman Pazvantoglu

One of the most famous feudal lords who rebelled against the Turkish Government in the reaction against the reforms was Osman Pazvantoglu. His father had been pasha at Vidin, and had been executed on suspicion of preparing a rising against the Sultan. Osman himself had somewhat redeemed the family honour by participating in the war against Austria in 1789 and, as a reward,

had received back part of his father's land which had been confiscated, and had been made responsible for collecting certain taxes
in the Vidin and Svishtov areas. Pazvantoglu's career as a loyal
subject of the Sultan was, however, short-lived. In about 1792 he
collected together a band of cut-throats and took to plunder.
Making use of the widespread opposition to the reforms, he organized
a revolt and in 1794 he captured Vidin where he set himself up as an
independent ruler. He skilfully won widespread support for his
revolt by promising all things to all men. To the Bulgarian peasants
he promised that they would be freed from Government taxes, and
to the vast mercenary army of *Kŭrdzhali* which he collected round
himself, he promised land and booty. The *Kŭrdzhali* certainly got
their booty, but the duped Bulgars got no tax relief; in fact, the
taxes became heavier and heavier, and in addition, they had to
endure fire and plunder at the hands of Pazvantoglu's ruffians, and
feudal exploitation at the hands of Osman's henchmen who were
given estates in the areas he controlled. The Bulgarians soon discovered how they had been deceived and they gave their answer to
Pazvantoglu in no uncertain way: they left their villages and either
crossed the Danube into Rumania, or hid themselves in the mountains. As a result, the whole of north Bulgaria from Vidin to Tŭrnovo
became a wasteland. This was, in the end, to prove the undoing of
Pazvantoglu. In the meantime, however, he lorded it in Vidin, and
even attempted to pursue an independent foreign policy. He entered
into negotiations with the French *Directoire* about joint action
against the Porte, and suggested to Tsar Alexander I that he, Osman,
should become a Russian subject! He avoided meeting the armies
sent against him on various occasions by the Sultan, preferring to
remain within the fortress at Vidin, which had not long before been
rebuilt and modernized by Polish engineers. One of the main reasons
for this was the difficulty of provisioning an army in the field in
the depopulated, uncultivated countryside. The same difficulty
beset the Sultan's troops sent against him, and in addition, the Porte's
attention was diverted by the French invasion of Egypt, so Osman
remained undefeated and entrenched in Vidin.

From the turn of the century onwards, however, Osman's little
Empire began to totter. Many of the local feudal lords woke up to
the fact that the economic results of the cessation of agriculture and
exports along the Danube were disastrous. Their estates were of
little value without peasants to work them, and, moreover, they
were in danger of losing their land to Pazvantoglu's henchmen, and

a movement against Osman began. He was obliged to stop giving land to his *Kŭrdzhali* and since he could no longer feed and maintain them, he was obliged to disband them. Left with his own little band, he was defeated by the lords of Kladovo in 1805, and was obliged to retire to Vidin, where he died in 1807.

The Russo-Turkish War, 1806–1812

In 1806 Turkey again went to war with Russia, encouraged by Napoleon, who planned to facilitate in this way his own projected war against Russia, and spurred on by the hope of regaining the territories of the north Black Sea coast which she had lost to Russia in the previous wars. The war ended as the two preceding ones had done, in a Russian victory and a treaty which stripped the Porte of its power over still more territory and no obvious gains for the Bulgars, though in this connection it must be borne in mind that Russia's style was cramped by Napoleon's invasion. By the Treaty of Bucharest in 1812, Russia gained Bessarabia, together with all the fortresses in the Danube Delta and along the Black Sea coast, while Walachia and Moldavia won a greater degree of independence, still within the Turkish Empire, but under Russian protection, and Serbia won internal autonomy.

The period of the war is notable for the progress in Russo-Bulgarian relations which took place immediately before and during the hostilities. The feudal disorders, especially Pazvantoglu's revolt, had not only given the Bulgars experience in warfare, but had shown them the chronic weakness of the Turkish Empire, and thus raised their hopes of speedy liberation. Since about 1800, when Pazvantoglu was still very much in power, eminent citizens of Vratsa, Teteven and other towns in north-west Bulgaria had been in contact with Russian observers in Rumania, hoping to get Russian aid. There was a further step forward in 1804 when the Serbian Rising[1] took place, and a Serbian delegation went to St. Petersburg. Two Bulgars, Ivan Zambin of Vratsa and Atanas Nikolaev of Teteven, who had moved to Bucharest for the sake of closer contact with the Russians, also went to Russia with the support of the Bulgarian émigrés in Rumania, and the authority of Sofroni, Bishop of Vratsa. In 1804, however, the international situation and in particular Russia's relations with Turkey did not create a very favourable atmosphere

---

[1] Bulgarian detachments took part in the Serbian Rising, hoping that as a result of the rising, Bulgaria would also be liberated.

for the presentation of the Bulgars' political demands, and the little delegation was obliged to wait until 1806 when relations between Russia and Turkey again became strained. Shortly before the war broke out, they presented their case to the Russian Minister for Foreign Affairs, and after the war had actually started the Russian Government made a grant of money to the Bulgars. Nikolaev then returned to Rumania, while Zambin remained in St Petersburg. Not long afterwards, Zambin received a letter from Sofroni in which he spoke of the close ties of blood and religion which existed between the Russians and Bulgars, and offered Russia the help of the whole Bulgarian people in the war, speaking of their earnest desire to be liberated and to become part of the Russian Empire. Zambin then wrote a similar letter to the Minister for Foreign Affairs, repeating that the desire of the Bulgars was to be united with Russia and begging the Minister to intercede with the Tsar on their behalf. It is indicative of the tremendous enthusiasm for *Dyado Ivan* and of the great consciousness of kinship with the Russians felt by the Bulgars, that at this stage they saw the immediate result of their liberation as union with Russia. Although Zambin died of tuberculosis soon after presenting his case to the Minister, the work of the Bulgars bore fruit, for the requests of Zambin and Sofroni were in fact laid before the Tsar, and in the following year, 1807, three infantry and three cavalry units were formed, composed of Serbs, Rumanians and about six hundred Bulgars. In 1810 a purely Bulgarian unit was formed in Rumania under the command of a man named Captain Batikioti, and it was known officially as the *Zemskoe Bolgarskoe Voisko*. It was formed from a nucleus of those who had volunteered in 1807, and had its own seal and standard. The Russian commanders kept in contact with Sofroni and the latter's promise of help to the Russians was well kept. Information on Turkish troop movements was collected by a group of Bulgarian émigrés who maintained contact with several towns inside Bulgaria, and when the Russian troops eventually crossed the Danube, the Bulgarian people responded to an impassioned call from Sofroni declaring that the hour of liberation had come and urging them to help the Russians in every way, and they gave the Russians a great welcome. Silistra, Dobrich, Rusé, Nikopol, Pleven, Lovech and Sevlievo all fell to the Russians, and many Bulgars left their homes and fought alongside the Russian troops whose Commander-in-Chief was General Kutuzov, shortly to become famous for his defeat of Napoleon. But the hour of liberation had not yet come, and at the end of the war three thousand Bulgarian families left with the Russian troops to avoid the wrath of the Turks.

The Greek Rising, 1821

The suffering which they endured when time after time their hopes of liberation were disappointed, did not deter the Bulgarians from further attempts to free themselves. As they had taken part in the Serbian Rising, so also they joined with the Greeks in preparing and carrying through the latter's attempt at winning liberation from Turkish rule. In all the main towns in Rumania and Bulgaria, as well as in Greece itself, the Greeks organized secret societies known as *Heteriai* (sing. *heteria*) to prepare for the rising. Throughout Bulgaria, Bulgars participated in the work of the *heteriai* and donated large sums of money to the cause. Most of the Bulgars involved were merchants and artisans who were closely connected with the Greek *bourgeoisie* economically and socially, and often even dependent on them. Co-operation between the two nationalities was still possible at this period because both suffered equally from the fetters which the continued existence of feudalism in Turkey placed on economic progress, from the absence of security of person and property, and the losses and difficulties caused by the feudal disorders. The Bulgarian *bourgeoisie*, though steadily developing, was still too weak to play an independent political role and the fierce rivalry between Bulgarian and Greek merchants for markets which characterized later periods had not yet developed to any great extent. The *heteriai* were secretly encouraged by the Russian Government who hoped that in the event of the collapse of the Turkish Empire a new Greek Kingdom might be set up in which Russia would have considerable influence.

The Greek Rising first broke out in Rumania under the leadership of Alexander Ipsilanti, and many Bulgarian émigrés as well as volunteers from Bulgaria itself formed detachments and fought alongside the Greeks. One of the leading Bulgarian commanders was Sava Binbashi, a native of Sliven, where the *heteria* movement was particularly highly developed. So involved were the inhabitants of Sliven that in 1821 the annual fair, which was second in importance only to that of Uzundzhovo, did not take place. It is even widely held that Indzhé, the one time *Kŭrdzhal* commander, also took part in the rising. When the rising was cruelly put down, many Bulgars were killed by the Turks or committed suicide. Even then the Bulgars did not lose heart, for when the rising broke out in

Greece itself, volunteers from Macedonia, southern Bulgaria and even northern Bulgaria hastened to join the Greeks in the struggle. The effect of this joint effort on Bulgar–Greek relations was not altogether what might have been expected. The Greeks attempted to make use of the Bulgars instead of treating them as equals who also sought freedom for their country and people. As a result the Bulgars became somewhat disillusioned with the prospects of achieving their aims in alliance with the Greeks, and subsequently tended to develop their own independent struggle.

The Russo-Turkish War, 1828–1829

This war was the first fought by the newly reformed Turkish Army. The Greek Rising had further demonstrated the weakness of Turkey and the uselessness of the Janissaries as a fighting force. The Janissaries had long been more of a menace than an asset and the Sultan Mahmud II decided to carry through part of the unfulfilled plans of his predecessor, Sultan Selim. The Janissaries were annihilated in 1826 and a new regular army on the Western pattern with French and Prussian instructors was set up. This drastic reform gave Turkey a new lease of life and made the Bulgars' struggle henceforward considerably more difficult, but at the time of the 1828 War insufficient time had elapsed for the full effect of the reform to be felt.

The news of the war and of the approach of the Russian Army filled the Bulgars with new hopes of liberation and two Bulgarian detachments were formed to fight with the Russian Army, one composed of about nine hundred émigrés in Rumania, Bessarabia and Moldavia under the command of a Russian officer named Liprandi, and another organized by Georgi Mamarchev Buyukli, a native of Kotel, who had been a member of the *Zemskoe Bolgarskoe Voisko* in 1810. Evidently hopes of liberation were very high indeed this time, because a Bulgarian Committee was set up in Bucharest to deal with the whole question of liberation. This committee mandated Alexander P. Nakovich to be their representative before the Russian High Command, to whom he presented a *mémoire* in which the Bulgars expressed their belief that only from Russia could they hope for protection and salvation, and asked that they too might have the same rights as Serbia, Walachia, Moldavia and Greece. The *mémoire* was also presented to Tsar Nicholas I when he arrived in Varna in September 1828. The Tsar took a very favourable view of the Bulgarian requests and a plan for a liberated Bulgaria was prepared. Bulgaria was to be an independent princedom with her own prince, administration, schools, clergy, etc., while the army was to be staffed with Russians officers.

In 1829 the Russian Army, in a series of brilliant victories, took Silistra, in the siege of which Georgi Mamarchev's detachment distinguished itself by its bravery, captured Adrianople and was ready to pursue the Turks to Constantinople itself. Again, however, the Bulgars were doomed to disappointment. The Russian advance was menaced by epidemics among the troops, strained lines of communication and, above all, by the threat of intervention on the part of Britain and Austria, who were not prepared to see Russia establish herself on the ruins of the Turkish Empire. Russia was therefore forced to abandon the idea of liberating Bulgaria for the present, and the war was brought to a close by the Treaty of Adrianople by which Greece gained her independence, the autonomy of Walachia, Moldavia and Serbia was extended and guaranteed, and Russia gained further Black Sea territory from Turkey and the right to sail her ships through the Dardanelles. Russia undertook to withdraw from Bulgarian territory with the exception of Silistra which remained in Russian hands as a guarantee for Turkey's unpaid reparations. As usual, when the Russians left, many Bulgars emigrated to Russia, Rumania and Bessarabia to avoid Turkish reprisals.

Mamarchev's Rising

The terms of the Treaty of Adrianople, which gave no concessions at all to Bulgaria, evoked great discontent and disappointment throughout the country. One of the most dissatisfied people was Georgi Mamarchev who had commanded the Bulgarian detachment during the war. He would not accept Bulgaria's continued slavery and began to prepare a rising in Sliven where the people had robbed the Turkish barracks during the war and had acquired a considerable amount of arms. The plot, however, came to an abrupt end when the Russian Commander-in-Chief, General Dibich, sent two hundred Cossacks to arrest Mamarchev, lest a rising should involve Russia in international difficulties. A Bulgarian delegation then went to General Dibich and asked that Mamarchev should be freed. He refused and explained to them how the delicate international situation forced the Russians to act in this manner.

The Treaty of Unkiar Iskelesi, 1833

The Treaty of Adrianople had left Turkey very much dependent on Russia. Russian troops were stationed just across the Danube in

Rumania and Moldavia, and even had a foothold south of the river in Silistra. In 1833 the Governor of Egypt, Mehmed Ali, and his son Ibrahim, revolted against the Turkish Government and began to march through Asia Minor towards Constantinople. The Porte could not get help from any of the Western Powers and being too weak to oppose Mehmed Ali alone, it was obliged to seek aid from its old enemy, Russia. As the Sultan himself remarked: 'When you are drowning, you clutch even at a serpent.' A Russian fleet was duly sent, Russian troops were landed on the shores of the Bosphorus and the Sultan concluded the Treaty of Unkiar Iskelesi with the Russians who won the right to bring their troops on to Turkish territory.

The Velcho Zavera,[1] 1835

Mamarchev was subsequently made Mayor of Silistra, the Bulgarian town which the Russians still occupied as security for Turkey's reparations, but he had by no means lost his taste for revolt, and entered into conspiratorial relations with various Bulgars, mainly merchants and craftsmen, in other towns. Among these was Velcho Atanasov Dzhamdzhiyata, a merchant of Tŭrnovo, from whom the subsequent rising took its name. The centre of the conspiracy was Tŭrnovo, but merchants and craftsmen in Elena, Tryavna, Vratsa and other towns were also in the plot. The conspirators met in a monastery near the village of Plakovo, where the Abbot Sergei shared their ideas. The plan was to take Tŭrnovo and proclaim Velcho its prince. Both Velcho and Mamarchev hoped that the rising would result in Russian intervention and the subsequent liberation of Bulgaria. The forces necessary for the rising were to be gathered in a most ingenious way: Dimiter Sofiyaliyata, a master craftsman, had been ordered by the Turks to assemble about two thousand workers to repair the fortress at Varna, and using this as a cover the conspirators hoped to assemble a large rebel army without arousing the suspicions of the Turks. Unfortunately the plot was betrayed by a *chorbadzhiya* from Elena, named Yordan Kisyov. The Turks arrested Mamarchev and the Abbot Sergei at the Plakovo monastery, while the other leading conspirators, including Velcho and Dimiter, were taken in Tŭrnovo and Elena. The arrested men were tortured but refused to betray any more. Velcho and Dimiter

---

[1] The word *Zavera* is derived from a Persian word meaning a 'rising'. It is also used of the Greek Rising of 1821 and in general of Christian risings against the Turks.

and some others were finally hanged, while Father Sergei was imprisoned and died from the effects of torture. Mamarchev, who was considered to be a Russian subject, was imprisoned first in Asia Minor, then in Samos, where he died in 1846. And, as if the treachery of the *chorbadzhiya* Kisyov was not enough, the Governor of the island, a Bulgarian named Stefan Bogoridi, who had risen high in the Turkish administration, shamefully ill-treated his prisoner throughout his captivity. This well illustrates the fact that while the majority of the Bulgarian people earnestly desired liberation and were ready to lay down their lives in order to gain it, there was also a section of Bulgars whose wealth and position so bound them up with the Turks that they took the side of the oppressor against their own people.

The Gyulkhan Hat-i-Sherif, 1839

The army reforms of 1826 still left Turkish feudalism in a very grave state of crisis. It was obvious that something radical would have to be done to preserve the Turkish Empire from disintegration. In 1834 as a continuation, as it were, of the 1826 reform, a land reform was promulgated with the intention of putting an end to the whole *spahi* system of land tenure, and the legal existence of the *chifliks* was recognized. In 1839, however, Mehmed Ali once more threatened the Porte, having defeated the Turkish Army and Navy. The Western Powers, fearing Russian intervention under the Treaty of Unkiar Iskelesi, urged the Porte to introduce new reforms. The main idea behind these reforms was to remove the worst inequalities which gave the subject peoples cause for grievance and in this way to avoid giving Russia pretexts for intervention in their defence. The reforms, known as the *Gyulkhan Hat-i-Sherif*, were ceremoniously proclaimed in the Pavillion of Roses (*Gyulkhan*) by Sultan Abdul Medzhid, in the presence of the representatives of all the Christian Churches within the Empire. The new law proclaimed the inviolability of the life, honour and possessions of all Turkish subjects whether Moslem or Christian; promised reforms in the fixing and collection of taxes; declared that the army was to be recruited in future on a regular basis from Moslem and Christian alike, and included various other items which were intended to give the Turkish Empire the illusory appearance of being a civilized State on the Western European model.

The reforms evoked fierce opposition within the Turkish Empire. The officials enjoyed the corruption which prevailed in the administration and made a good living out of it. The whole conception of equality for the Christians was abhorrent to the pious Moslems.

Even the small and weak Turkish *bourgeoisie* whose interests ran counter to the continued existence of elements of feudalism within the Empire and whose representative, Reshid Pasha, as Grand Vizir, took part in the promulgation of the reforms, found cause for complaint in the clauses which gave equal rights to the Christian rivals in trade. Even the Porte was unenthusiastic but had to submit to Western pressure. The result, of course, was that the much boosted reforms remained largely on paper, and nothing much changed. The Government did not press its local organs to carry them into practice and these local organs went through the formality of announcing the reforms and left it at that, without even having the text of the laws translated into Bulgarian. The Bulgars, however, took the *Hat-i-Sherif* very seriously. The émigrés in Bucharest had it translated in two editions, one in 1839 and a second in 1841, and it was circulated throughout the country. They regarded it as a charter of liberties on which they took their stand and which they quoted in support of their demands. The local authorities even tried denying that the *Hat-i-Sherif* was still in force, but protests poured into the Government which had to reaffirm in 1843 and 1845 that it was still in force, and the Sultan himself toured a number of Bulgarian towns reassuring the people that such was the case. The final result of the reforms turned out to be the opposite from that which the Western Powers had intended when they pressed the Porte to announce them. Far from pacifying the subject people, the *Hat-i-Sherif* acted as a spur to increased agitation and struggle on the part of the Bulgars.

CHAPTER VI

THE STRUGGLE FOR
CULTURAL INDEPENDENCE

Cell Schools

For centuries before the great movement in the thirties to create schools of a new type, the sole medium of Bulgarian education was the so-called 'cell' school. From the description given below it will be seen how great was the need for a revolution in education, and how right Sofroni Vrachansky was to call his fellow countrymen's attention to the need for proper education. The cell schools were generally organized in monasteries, or on church premises, but when the demand for education increased, they were organized in private houses as well. The teachers were usually monks or parish priests, but some of them were lay people, such as cripples and old people, who were unable to undertake any heavy work. The school premises were usually very unsatisfactory, often cramped, cold and damp. The pupils, who were all taught together regardless of age or knowledge, sat on the floor or on boards brought from home. The teachers were maintained by the parents and were very poorly paid. Sometimes, if they were craftsmen, they would carry on with some handicraft while the pupils were reciting by heart. The pupils were expected to do little jobs for the teacher such as cutting wood and fetching water. The syllabus in the cell schools was little better than mediaeval. It consisted of learning the Church Slavonic alphabet, and then words which were written out by the teacher for each pupil on a special board called a *pinakida*. Then they learnt the Prayer Book and the Psalter by heart. Some children never got farther than the Prayer Book and the Psalter was considered almost as higher education. Those who reached this height of education might even tackle the Acts of the Apostles and the Gospels. All these books were, of course, written in the obsolete Church Slavonic, which is infinitely farther removed from ordinary Bulgarian speech than the language of the English Bible is from spoken English. Some pupils tended merely to learn by heart, in the manner of schoolboys studying set Latin texts, and left school unable to read or write their own names. Some schools were, of course, better than others, and a great deal depended on the individual teacher. Sofroni Vrachansky, for example, did attempt to broaden the syllabus in the school where he acted as teacher by introducing his pupils to Paisi's *History*.

Somewhat better cell schools appeared, run by the communes instead of private individuals, but the syllabus remained predominantly religious as before. One of the chief purposes of the schools was to train people for the priesthood and often the syllabus would include chanting and the order of service, and in the absence of printing, special attention was paid to teaching children how to copy Church books. In 1750 there were only twenty-one cell schools, by 1800 there were forty-eight, and by 1843 there were one hundred and eighty-nine.

The greatest drawback of these schools was that when all was said and done, the sum total of learning to be gained at them was reading and writing. For the rising *bourgeoisie* and merchant class this type of education was totally inadequate. They needed schools where children could learn arithmetic, geography and other subjects necessary for the pursuit of commerce. Thus, as the *bourgeoisie* grew in size and strength, so did the movement for better and more modern schools.

The Helleno-Bulgarian Schools

The Greek *bourgeoisie* was considerably more advanced in development than the Bulgarian *bourgeoisie*. Being a maritime State, Greece was drawn into trade earlier than the other Balkan States and had considerable contact with Western Europe. Greek cell schools had long existed all over Bulgaria wherever there were Greek colonies. These schools were not much different from the Bulgarian cell schools, but they were dangerous centres of Greek influence in Bulgaria, because of the economic advantages of knowing Greek, which was the *lingua franca* of trade in the Balkans, and because of the misplaced snobbishness of certain wealthy Bulgars who considered it 'cultured' and 'educated' to speak Greek and live like Greeks. The Greek *bourgeoisie* soon became aware of the inadequacy of the cell schools and began to set up new secular schools on the European model using the monitorial method of teaching of Bell and Lancaster[1] practised in Western Europe since the end of the

---

[1] Joseph Lancaster, 1778–1838, and Andrew Bell, 1753–1832, were English educationalists who, independently of each other, used this method, the former in England, the latter in Calcutta as well as England.

eighteenth century. The essence of the method was that one teacher could teach many pupils by enlisting the aid of the more advanced pupils. This method could be employed to great advantage in backward countries where there was a shortage of teachers.

Such schools were opened in Constantinople, Smyrna, Corfu, Janina, on the islands of Andros and Chios, and at other places. The syllabus included classical languages, French, mathematics, physics, chemistry, history, geography and other subjects, and represented an immeasurable advance on the old cell school course.

The Bulgarian *bourgeoisie* was as yet not sufficiently well organized to set up similar Bulgarian schools, although they felt the need for a new type of education, and as a result, the children of the Bulgarian *bourgeoisie* were sent to the new Greek schools. This led to a certain extension of Greek influence among the Bulgars but it also had another somewhat different effect. The Greek schools were filled with the spirit of Greek nationalism and the new liberal ideas preached by the French Revolution. Many of the teachers were devoted patriots and liberals who taught their pupils accordingly. Such men were Adamanti Korais and Theophil Kairis. The Greeks preached the idea of 'Greater Greece' and sought to influence the Bulgars and make them Greek, but many Bulgars did not entirely succumb to Hellenization and the inspiration of the Greek patriotic teaching made them consider the plight of their own people and how they too could be 'awakened'. For example, some of the Bulgarian pupils at Kairis's schools on Andros formed a secret 'Slavo-Bulgarian Philosophical Society' for the purpose of educating the Bulgarian people. When Kairis's school was closed in 1839, some of the pupils moved to Athens where in 1841 they set up a revolutionary society with the aim of preparing a Bulgarian rising to take place simultaneously with the Greek risings in Crete and Thessaly. Many of the future leaders of the Bulgarian Renaissance, such as Aprilov, Bozveli and Rakovsky, were educated in these Greek schools.

Many Greek-educated Bulgars, nevertheless, came to believe that the Bulgars could not develop culturally independently from the Greeks and that the study of Greek literature was necessary for Bulgaria's advance, i.e. they had been won over to the idea that Greek culture was superior to their own and that Bulgaria's future lay in learning from the Greeks. As a result, the Greek-educated Bulgars began to open similar schools in Bulgaria, known variously as 'Helleno-Slav' or 'Helleno-Bulgarian' schools. Here the teaching was conducted in Greek and the syllabus included ancient and modern

Greek as well as Slavonic. Helleno-Bulgarian schools were set up by Emanuil Vaskidovich in Svishtov, 1815; by Khristaki Pavlovich, also in Svishtov in 1830; by Raino Popovich in Kotel, 1819, and in Karlovo, 1826; by Sava Dobroplodni in Shumen; by Konstantin Fotinov in Smyrna, etc. etc.

The Helleno-Bulgarian schools were, of course, much better than the old cell schools, but they perpetuated Greek influence and did not meet the need of the Bulgarian people to receive modern education in their own language. The leadership in educational reform now passed to the Bulgarian emigrants in Rumania and Russia, where, unlike the richer *bourgeoisie* at home, they were relatively free of Graecomania.

Petŭr Beron

Unlike all previous Bulgarian literary men, Petŭr Beron was a layman and wrote the first wholly secular literary work. He was born in Kotel in 1795 or 1797, the son of a wealthy family of *aba* weavers who were ruined in the Russo-Turkish War of 1812. He began his education at a cell school in Kotel and was then apprenticed to an *aba* weaver in Varna. From here he managed to emigrate to Rumania where he entered a secular Greek school in Bucharest, and then became a teacher in a rich Bulgarian family in Braşov, Transylvania. After this he went abroad and studied medicine in Heidelburg and Munich, and qualified as a doctor in 1831, writing his thesis in Latin. He returned to Rumania and for a time practised as a doctor. Then he took up trading, made quite a considerable amount of money and gave generous donations to further Bulgarian education. He did not stay in Rumania, however, but returned to Western Europe and visited England and France. He spent most of his time in Paris where he occupied himself with studies connected with physics, mathematics and philosophy. He mastered numerous languages and was able to write scientific and philosophical monographs in French, German, Latin and Greek. He was tragically killed in Kraiovo in 1871 by people who were robbing him. Petŭr Beron reached a height of scholarship and learning rare, if not unique, among Bulgars of his day. Like Sofroni, he saw the great advantages that Western Europe enjoyed in matters of education and was deeply conscious of the backwardness of his own people.

Curiously enough, the book for which he is particularly remembered was written very early on in his life when he was a teacher in Braşov, and before he had travelled to Western Europe. Even at this time he was deeply conscious of the shortcomings of Bulgarian education and the total inadequacy of a syllabus, the sole reading matter of which was the Psalter and other ecclesiastical books in archaic language. Beron's book, published in Braşov in 1824, was known as *Riben Bukvar* (*The Fish ABC*) because of a picture of a dolphin on the back cover. It was not at all what we understand by an ABC today, but was more like a little encyclopaedia. It consisted of eight sections. The first dealt with the letters of the alphabet and the parts of speech. Beron did not attempt definitions of the latter but merely gave examples. The second section contained various prayers with directions for when to say what, but no passages from the Bible, since Beron did not consider it suitable for children. The third section contained proverbs and sayings intended to teach practical guild and Christian morality. The fourth section consisted of wise answers made by ancient Greek philosophers such as Socrates, Aristotle, Plato, Diogenes, and Aesop. The fifth section was devoted to 'Fables' and the sixth to 'Miscellaneous Stories', all of which, like the sayings of the fourth section, were aimed at the moral education of the child and at acquainting him with the wisdom of the past. The seventh chapter contained an account of some aspects of nature, including substances and plants such as coffee, salt, tobacco, cotton and sugar, and animals such as the elephant, the whale, the monkey, the beaver, the dolphin and man himself. Beron gave special attention to creatures such as the ant and the bee which have some sort of social organization, that his readers might learn civic duty alongside natural history. The eighth section of the *ABC* was devoted to arithmetic, again without definitions and theoretical explanations, and the book ended with pictures of some of the beasts described in the seventh section, including the famous dolphin.

An important literary feature of the *ABC* is that although for technical reasons it was printed in the Old Church Slavonic letters, its language is the popular speech of eastern Bulgaria without any of the old forms which crept into Sofroni's writings. The *ABC* is therefore the first Bulgarian book written in the spoken language. Moreover, the eastern dialect is today considered to be the literary language of Bulgaria, while before Beron the vast majority of books produced, including those by Sofroni himself, tended to be in the western dialect. It is thus doubly historic from the literary point of view.

As an educational reformer Beron desired to make Bulgarian education suited to the practical needs of life and he had a strong sense of moral and social duty which he felt must be encouraged in the young. He was himself a supporter of the Bell–Lancaster 'monitorial' method of teaching. Among his innovations was the introduction of a new method of learning the letters of the alphabet, by their sounds instead of their traditional names, and he also introduced very varied subjects as reading matter in place of the eternal Church books. He believed in the intuitive method of teaching, in taking pupils out into the fields, and in teaching them dancing and singing.

Beron felt it to be of the utmost importance that the teacher should be a person of the highest moral integrity and for him to set a good example to his pupils in every way. To him, teaching was a 'sacred cause', not to be undertaken by civil servants or artisans, or people whose first consideration was financial reward. It may be noted here that Petŭr Beron's high ideals were in no way betrayed by the long line of Bulgarian teachers of the Renaissance who followed him. They included many great patriots who devoted their lives to the resurrection of the country and people, and it was not for nothing that Ivan Vasov, author of the great novel *Under the Yoke*, made his hero, Ognyanov, a teacher by profession.

Beron's other works were mainly scientific and were written during his sojourn in Western Europe. They include *Système d'atmospherologie* published in Paris in 1846; *Système de Geologie et Origine des Comètes ou très court résumé du deuxième volume d'Atmospherologie*, which was a continuation of the previous volume in 1847; *La Déluge, sa cause, ses actions et ses effets . . .*, 1857, and a further work on this subject in 1858; *The origin of the physical, natural, metaphysical and moral sciences* and *Text for the cosmobiographical Atlas* also in 1858; the Atlas itself in 1859 and *Meteorological Atlas* in 1860. In 1861 in Paris he produced the first volume of a monumental seven-volume work on a single science which he called *Panépistème*, and which in his own words embraced 'everything which exists in the world and everything which proceeds from the mind of man'. Previously, in 1855, he had published in Prague in German a work called *Slavonic Philosophy*, which had already raised some of the ideas which he developed in greater detail in his *Panépistème*.

This list gives a very good impression of Beron's enthusiasm for science and enlightenment, and his encyclopaedic breadth of interest. The *Fish ABC*, however, remains the work for which he is chiefly remembered by his fellow countrymen and which had the greatest influence on the course of the Bulgarian Renaissance. It was received with enormous interest at the time of its publication, but its immediate effect on Bulgarian education was very disappointing. The Bulgarian *bourgeoisie* was either not yet prepared to make the effort to change the educational system, or lacked the means to do so, and, in spite of Beron's high hopes, the *ABC* was not immediately adopted as a textbook, and, in general, the cell schools continued as before. Ten years were to pass before Beron's ideas were finally put into practice. It came with the opening of the first modern Bulgarian school in Gabrovo in 1835 by Vasil Aprilov, who had been inspired in his work by a man named Yuri Venelin.

Yuri Ivanovich Venelin, 1802–1839

Yuri Venelin, who devoted his life to studying Bulgaria and her people, was not himself a Bulgar. He was a Carpathian Russian, born in the village of Velika Tibava where his father was the priest. In spite of being left an orphan, he managed to have a good education, and in 1823 he went to Kishinev where he was well received by the Governor, General Inzov, and was given a post as teacher in the seminary there. General Inzov, incidentally, also befriended the Russian poet Pushkin who was in Kishinev at the same time. During his stay in Kishinev, Venelin met many Bulgarian refugees who had left their country as a result of the Russo-Turkish wars and had settled in Bessarabia. He was already interested in Slavonic history and had studied history at Lvov University, and now, as a result of his contact with the émigré Bulgars, he began to do research on Bulgarian history. In 1825 he went to Moscow and entered the medical faculty there, but he still maintained his interest in Bulgarian history, and in 1829 he published his *History of the Ancient and Present-day Bulgars* with the financial backing of Professor Pogodin, editor of the *Moscow Journal* (*Moskovskii Vestnik*) who had encouraged him to write it. Just before the book was published, he wrote an article in the *Moscow Journal* in which he reproached the Slavs, in particular the Russians, for having forgotten the Bulgars from whom they had received baptism and the alphabet. 'In their language we conduct our services today, and in that language we wrote almost up to the time of Lomonosov[1]—the cradle of the Bulgars is indivisibly linked with the cradle of the Russian people.' He goes on to point out that the Bulgars have lived five hundred years in slavery. In his *History* Venelin also reproached the Russians

[1] 1711–1765. He advocated limiting the use of Church Slavonic words in literature and increasing the use of the living language.

and also the West Europeans for bewailing the fate of Greece and forgetting that of Bulgaria. 'While they moan over the fate of the Greeks, while they discuss whether or not the eagle of Byzantium should rise again—they do not remember the Bulgars; not even one Slav has wept over the body of the dead lion. Why is this? His huge body is cast over the Balkan, Macedonian and Rumelian mountains. There the two-horned monster from the deserts of Arabia feeds on him, while the feathers of the eagle are dispersed all over the world.'

Like Paisi, Venelin saw the important role a knowledge of the past could play in the resurrection of the Bulgarian people, and though, like Paisi, his facts were not always correct, his book was spirited, impassioned and polemical, and it was rapturously received by the Bulgarian émigrés in Rumania and Russia, and was also welcomed by the Russian Slavophils.

In 1830, with the help of Pogodin and the Slavophil Aksakov, he achieved his great wish—to visit Bulgaria which he called the 'classical land' as far as Russia was concerned. He did not, however, get any farther than Varna and the Dobrudzha because the Russian troops, still in occupation since the war of 1828–1829, soon withdrew and Venelin had to leave with them for Rumania. Nevertheless he did manage to collect a certain amount of material on folklore during his stay in Bulgaria and continued his collection among the Bulgarian émigrés in Russia. He urged all the Bulgars he met to collect folk songs, which often contained stories of Bulgaria's past, and to preserve other documents which might shed light on her history. It appears from a letter which Venelin wrote to Aprilov in 1837 that many of the Bulgars whom he met were apathetic about their own national heritage and did not reply to his letters asking for historical and ethnographical material and this was a source of much sorrow and discouragement to him. Nevertheless, in 1835, Venelin published a book on the character of the folk songs of the Balkan Slavs, mainly, it must be admitted, based on Serbian songs. This book is the first serious attempt to study national character and 'soul' through the study of folk-song. He also prepared a modern Bulgarian grammar, the manuscript of which was sent to the Russian Academy in 1835, but it was never published owing to the fact that it earned the disapproval of the leading philologist, Vostokov. It remains, nevertheless, important as the first attempt at compiling a scholarly grammar of the Bulgarian language. To appreciate the work of Venelin in this respect, it must be realized that prior to Venelin, European scholars knew little about the Bulgarian people and their language. In 1814, for example, Joseph Dobrovský, one of the first Slavonic scholars, even considered that the Bulgarian language was merely a dialect of Serbian. Vuk Karadjić, the Serbian poet and patriot, writing in 1822, was the first to describe the peculiarities of Bulgarian as a separate language of the Slav family.

Among Venelin's other works was a work on the Proto-Bulgars published posthumously in Moscow in 1849. Venelin believed—erroneously, but due no doubt to his enthusiasm to show the insoluble links between the Russian and Bulgarian peoples—that even the Proto-Bulgars were Slavs and had taken their name from the Volga river. In 1853 this book appeared in a Bulgarian translation made by Botyu Petkov, the father of Khristo Botev.

Venelin died in 1839 while still quite a young man. Two years later, the Bulgarian colony in Odessa erected a monument over his tomb in Moscow with the inscription:

'To Yuri Iv. Venelin—the Odessa Bulgars 1841. Born 1802, died 1839. He reminded the world of the forgotten but once glorious and powerful Bulgarian people and ardently longed to see their Renaissance. Almighty God, hear Thy servant's prayer!'

Aprilov and the First Bulgarian Schools

One of the men who was most profoundly influenced by Venelin's *History of Bulgaria* was Vasil Evstatiev Aprilov, who was born in Gabrovo in 1789. He spent the first ten years of his life in his home town and attended a cell school there. He was orphaned at an early age and his brothers, who were merchants operating in Russia, took him to Moscow where they sent him to a Greek school. Having completed the course there, he was sent to Transylvania where he spent five years at a German gymnasium in Braşov. He then went to study medicine in Vienna, but was obliged to give up the course owing to bad health and his brothers' financial difficulties, and he went back to Moscow. In 1811 he moved to Odessa and became a merchant himself. He went into partnership with a Greek named Todoridi and became quite wealthy, but ill health once more obliged him to stop work and he went to Constantinople for treatment, returning to Odessa in 1831. This date was the turning-point in Aprilov's life. Up to 1831 he was definitely a Graecophil in sympathy and, indeed, he regarded himself as a Greek and not a Bulgar. He lived among the Greek colony in Odessa and being an enlightened man, influenced by the progressive ideas of Western Europe, he assisted the Greek revolutionaries and helped to support Greek education in Odessa. On his return from Constantinople, Aprilov by chance came across the first volume of Venelin's *History* and read it. It was for him a revelation. From that moment on he became infused with patriotism, ceased to be a Graecophil and devoted himself to the education of his own people.

Aprilov determined to set up a modern Bulgarian school on European lines, the very first of its kind, in his native Gabrovo. Gabrovo was an ideal town for this pioneer scheme, for it was one of the most prosperous and economically developed towns in the country and had a purely Bulgarian population. Aprilov enlisted the financial aid of Nikolai Palauzov, another Bulgarian merchant in Odessa, who was also a native of Gabrovo, and Palauzov promised to guarantee an annual sum towards the maintenance of the school. Aprilov also sounded the wealthy men of Gabrovo itself, but they refused to help, feeling that it would be good money thrown away. The Bulgarian émigrés in Bucharest were more enlightened and responded to his appeal.

If the rich men of Gabrovo were not interested in the school, the poor were. They carted building materials and worked without pay to erect it. The man chosen as teacher for the new school was a monk named Neofit Rilsky, and during the building of the school, he was sent to Bucharest to learn the Bell–Lancaster method of teaching and to prepare textbooks, since Aprilov had set his heart on the school being really modern and a complete break with the old cell schools. Finally everything was ready and on January 2, 1835, the school was opened. Neofit Rilsky taught according to the new method and in Bulgarian, although the Metropolitan of Tŭrnovo had insisted that the teaching must be in Greek. Tuition in the new school was free and open to all, and the teacher was paid an annual salary.

Though a great patriot and lover of his people, Aprilov was in no way a revolutionary. He was, in fact, opposed to the revolutionaries and condemned Rakovsky's Braila conspiracy.[1] For him, the key to Bulgaria's national revival was education, backed by such governmental reforms as the *Hat-i-Sherif* of which he had great hopes. Though violently opposed to the use of Greek in church and for teaching in schools, he did not suggest that Greek should not be learnt at all by Bulgars, because, as a merchant, he was fully aware of its importance in trade. He merely advocated that children

[1] *See* p. 174.

should have a solid grounding in their own language first, and only then proceed to foreign languages, including Greek.

Aprilov was the author of several books, mainly on educational matters, but also on historical and literary subjects. Most of his works were written in Russian. He also wrote a polemical article answering a Serb who had claimed that Saint Cyril was in fact a Serb. Like Venelin, he collected ethnographical material and made a collection of Bulgarian folk songs which was the first attempt of its kind. The collection was, however, never published.

In 1845 he wrote an appeal to young people which clearly reflects his burning patriotism and love of his people:

'Hold it your sacred duty to love your country, as you will see all other Europeans love theirs, and assist it in every way, and when you have finished your studies, return home[1] and minister to its wants and needs as the other nations do. Do not abandon this idea, because you will otherwise be called not benefactors, but traitors to your people. The people's curse will find you out wherever you are. The voice of the people is the voice of God; your conscience will torture you, you will endure great hardships and, reduced to poverty, you will breathe your last breath forgotten, despised and forsaken by all. An eternal curse will lie on your soul, and eternal shame will follow your relatives in your motherland.'

The Growth of Bulgarian Education

The effect of the opening of the pioneer school at Gabrovo was immediate and far-reaching. Its fame soon spread and similar schools were set up in many towns. As early as 1836 new schools were opened in Kazanlŭk and Koprivshtitsa, and Khristaki Pavlovich, influenced by the example of Gabrovo, turned his Helleno-Bulgar school into a purely Bulgar one. Svishtov, Kalofer, Tryavna, Elena, Panagyurishté, Sopot, Sofia, Kotel and other towns also opened schools and by 1840 there were in all thirteen new schools, while by the 1850's most towns and larger villages had schools.

The celebrated teacher of Gabrovo received several invitations to go and teach in other towns and he accepted an invitation from the *chorbadzhii* of Plovdiv to go and found a school there. The school was to be a national one with two pupils from every town in the country, but the scheme met with the violent opposition of the

---

[1] Aprilov had in mind those who completed their education abroad in the absence of suitable establishments in Bulgaria.

Greek bishop and local Graecomanes, whereupon the *chorbadzhii* who had originally made the proposal capitulated and gave up the idea. Neofit Rilsky went instead to Koprivshtitsa.

During the 1840's progress was also made in women's education. This had previously been non-existent, for the mediaeval attitude that women were inferior beings was reinforced and given a new lease of life by the influence of the Moslem view, and it was considered shameful for a girl to attend school. There is some evidence that during the 1820's this attitude was beginning to break down, and a few girls were attending cell schools. The redoubtable Baba Tonka,[1] of whom more will be heard in a later chapter, once began to attend a cell school but gave it up after two or three days because her girl friends ridiculed her continuously. In 1820 a cell school for boys and girls was opened in Kotel, but no girls ever appeared for tuition. It was in Pleven in 1840 that the first regular school for girls was opened. The teacher was Anastasia Dimitrova, who had herself been taught at the Kalofer convent. Nothing is known of the syllabus, but it was probably similar to that of the cell schools with some secular elements, and was not really modern at all. Nevertheless, a start had been made and other girls' schools were opened by Anastasia Dimitrova's pupils in Vratsa in 1843 and in Svishtov in 1845. Progress was slow, and even by the middle of the century the education of girls lagged behind and was inferior to that provided for men, but it must be remembered that even the principle of educating girls was something new and revolutionary.

The successful establishment of the new secular Bulgarian schools was an immense step forward, but it was only a first step. Much remained to be done. The new schools provided only elementary education, and anybody who required secondary or higher education had to attend Greek schools or go abroad. The problem of getting teachers was also very great as the Bulgars had no facilities for training teachers. All their teachers had been to Greek schools, but the growing antagonism between the Bulgarian and Greek *bourgeoisie* as well as the rampant chauvinism of the Greeks made patriotic young Bulgars very unwilling to study at the Greek higher educational establishments. The Bulgars now began to turn to Russia with whom they had so much in common culturally, and by whom they hoped to be liberated. Aprilov played a leading role in

[1] Baba Tonka and all her children took an active part in the revolutionary movement in Rusé during the sixties and seventies of the nineteenth century.

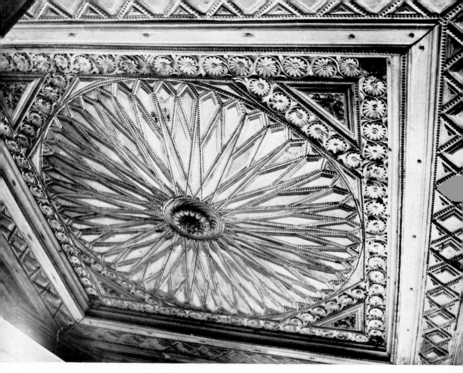

5a. A carved wooden ceiling in the Daskalov house in Tryavna, 1808

5b. The carved wooden ceiling of a house in Sliven

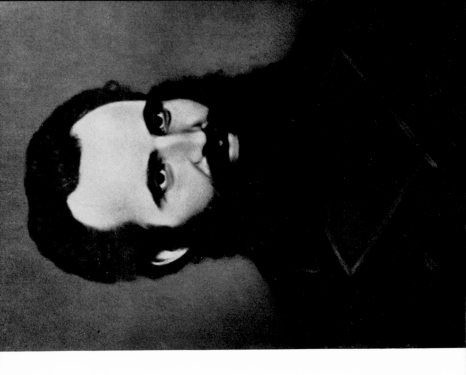

6a.
(*Left*)
Georgi
Rakovsky

6b.
(*Right*)
Lyuben
Karavelov

reorientating Bulgarian education towards Russia. He managed to persuade the Russian Government to provide a number of grants for Bulgars to study in Russia, and himself bequeathed money in his will to send Bulgars to Russia, on the condition that they took up educational work on their return. He was warmly supported by another leading Bulgar, Seliminsky, who suggested that the Bulgars should themselves collect money to send pupils to Russia. Some girls also went to study in Russia. To hide the fact from the Turks they made the journey on horseback dressed as boys. The first girl to finish her education in Odessa was Anastasia Tosheva, who later became headmistress of a girls' school in Stara Zagora, her home town.

By the 1850's the first of the Russian-trained teachers were returning home and Bulgarian education entered a new phase—that of the establishment of schools with various classes, which could provide secondary education. The first such school was founded by Naiden Gerov in Koprivshtitsa in 1846. Gerov had himself studied under Neofit Rilsky at the 'monitorial' school in Koprivshtitsa and also in Russia. The new school was modelled on Russian lines, and began with two classes and subsequently added a third. The subjects taught were Bulgarian grammar, catechism, universal history, algebra, geometry, arithmetic, physics, ecclesiastical history, geography, singing, painting and physical culture. About the same time, Botyu Petkov opened a class school in Kalofer, and soon other class schools appeared in Sofia, Elena, Gabrovo, Karlovo, Sopot, Pazardzhik and other towns. In 1850 Naiden Gerov founded a second school, this time in Plovdiv, a town with a considerable Greek population and a stronghold of Hellenism. The school had several classes and the education was such that pupils completing the course were able to proceed directly to a University. The teaching of physical culture caused some trouble, since the Greek Bishop complained to the Patriarch that some Muscovite was teaching the Bulgarians military drill and the Turks immediately pricked up their ears. They were finally pacified by Stoyan Chalŭkov, the influential *chorbadzhiya* who had invited Gerov to Plovdiv in the first place. The Chalŭkov family were an exception to the rule that the *chorbadzhii* tended to be Graecomanes and pro-Turkish. They played a leading role in the fight against Greek influence and in the Renaissance as a whole.

Gerov called his school after the Saints Cyril and Methodius and in 1851, on his initiative the Saints' Day, May 11th (24th new

E

style), was celebrated in Plovdiv as the Festival of Bulgarian education. By degrees this custom was adopted by all the schools in Bulgaria and by the whole Bulgarian people.

Apart from the schools already mentioned, two Turkish schools must also be included in the list since a few Bulgars attended them. One was a military medical school founded by the Sultan in 1840 to provide doctors for the Turkish Army. It had French teachers and was run on European lines with the teaching conducted in French. The other school was the Sultan's *lycée*, founded in 1858 to train personnel for diplomatic and State service. Here also the teaching was in French and it was staffed by French professors sent by Napoleon III.

Neofit Rilsky

Nikola Petkov, better known under his Church name of Neofit Rilsky, the first teacher in the first Bulgarian school at Gabrovo, was born in Bansko in 1793. His father was a priest and wanted him to learn ikon painting. He therefore went to the Rila monastery in 1808 and became a monk in 1811 taking the name of Neofit. About 1818 he visited Sofia and Pirot and was ordained a priest. In Sofia he met a learned Greek who taught him the Greek language and he then continued his studies for four years under a famous teacher in the Greek school at Melnik. He mastered classical and modern Greek and obtained a knowledge of Greek literature. In 1827 Bishop Ignati invited him to teach in Samokov, but in 1829 the Bishop was murdered and by 1831 Neofit found things so unpleasant in Samokov that he withdrew into a monastery. In 1833 the monastery was burnt down and Neofit went to Kazanlŭk to collect money for its rebuilding, and was appointed Confessor at the monastery church there. Kazanlŭk was part of the diocese of Tŭrnovo and in this way Neofit became acquainted with Ilarion, Metropolitan of Tŭrnovo, who recommended to the founders of the Gabrovo school that Neofit should be its first teacher. He moved to Koprivshtitsa in 1837 and then taught for a time at the Rila monastery. After 1846 he taught in Stara Zagora and then on the island of Halki, near Constantinople, where he taught Slavonic in the Greek theological college. In 1852 he returned to the Rila monastery where he was Abbot from 1860–1864. He remained in the monastery until his death in 1881, having lived to see the liberation of his country by Russia, of whom he wrote the following lines during his stay in Koprivshtitsa:

'No other hope remains for Bulgaria,
Sadly she makes this entreaty to Russia:
"O Russia, my dear sister of one blood!
Why have you forgotten me for so many centuries?" '

Like Sofroni, Neofit Rilsky believed that education should be the first consideration of all Bulgars and taught that schools were more necessary than churches, since, as he pointed out, one could pray anywhere, but one could learn only in schools. He was the quietest and most peaceable of men, much loved and respected by his contemporaries, and though in recognition of his high qualities he was offered various Bishoprics, he refused them all, preferring to work humbly in schools and libraries. He had an extensive library of his own, composed of Greek, Serbian, Russian and Bulgarian books, and he had a special building erected by St Luke's chapel at the Rila monastery where he could keep his books and work undisturbed. For him, as for Aprilov, the way ahead for the Bulgarian people lay through education and he took no part in political struggles nor in the fight for an independent Bulgarian Church. He was, in his own quiet way, a devoted patriot, filled with love for his people. He wrote: 'It is the duty of every true son of the Motherland to sacrifice for the happiness of the people everything that he holds most honourable and most precious . . . and the last drop of his blood', and 'there is nothing dearer than one's country', declaring that a man cannot shut himself up in his own personal life, because he is part of a great body, part of the people. Yet Neofit Rilsky remained a great admirer of Greek culture. He was well versed in Greek literature and wrote a Greek grammar and embarked on a huge Bulgarian–Greek dictionary which was never finished. He believed that every Bulgar should first learn his own language and accordingly taught in Bulgarian despite all opposition, yet he believed that a knowledge of Greek would help his fellow countrymen to share in the culture of Europe. Apart from the works already mentioned, Neofit Rilsky wrote for the school at Gabrovo various textbooks including a Bulgarian grammar, which were published in Kragujevac in Serbia in 1838. He also translated the New Testament from Slavonic into Bulgarian (published in Smyrna, 1840).

Neofit Bozveli, 1785–1848

Another teacher and writer of textbooks who lived at the same time as Neofit Rilsky was Neofit Bozveli. He was born in Kotel in 1785 and as a young man he became a monk in the Hilendar monastery on Mount Athos. About 1813 he went to the monastery at Svishtov but soon severed his connections with the brotherhood and became a teacher. He taught in Svishtov for twenty-five years, and like Beron and Aprilov, he was inspired by the idea of creating a truly national system of education. In 1835 he published a number of textbooks, the most important of which was a pedagogical encyclopaedia, written in collaboration with Emanuil Vaskidovich and called *Slavenobolgarskoe Detovodstvo* which could be translated *A Slavo-Bulgarian manual for bringing up children*. It was in six parts and contained information on the alphabet, spelling, grammar, arithmetic, geography, guidance on how to write letters correctly according to the circumstances, and various stories such as fables from Aesop and other moral teachings. The section on letter writing is an interesting indication of how Bulgarian education was responding to the demands of the rising *bourgeoisie*, in that it reflected the growing need of the merchants and craftsmen to write business letters, etc. The geographical section is also interesting in that it gives a description of the Bulgaria of those days, and in that Neofit made use of the opportunity to point out the glories of Bulgaria's past and to instil patriotic sentiments into his readers.

Neofit Bozveli felt very strongly about the need for proper education in Bulgaria and supported the establishment of the new secular schools. In other ways, however, his views differed considerably from those of his contemporaries in the educational field, Aprilov and Neofit Rilsky. Bozveli was violently anti-Greek and did not consider it advisable to learn Greek. He believed that Bulgaria's present unhappiness was caused mainly by the Phanariot Greeks and the Bulgarian Graecomane *chorbadzhii* whom he regarded as the enemies of Bulgaria. He wrote four dialogues on this theme, which were published after his death. The first, written in 1842, is between Mother Bulgaria, her son and an educated European who is his teacher, and it takes place on the banks of the Yantra beside the ruins of Tŭrnovo and describes the piteous plight of the Bulgars under the Phanariot yoke. The last of these dialogues, *Mother Bulgaria*, is considered to be the best and most mature of the four. In it Bozveli makes the first call of the new period to oppose these enemies of Bulgaria and to fight against them. In this too, Bozveli differed from Aprilov and Neofit Rilsky, who were opposed to revolutionary action and confined their activities purely to education. Bozveli waged open struggle against the Greek clergy and his activities in this field will be described in the next chapter. For the present suffice it to say that because of his fearless opposition to the Greek clergy, he ended his life chained in a damp dungeon. That was in 1848, and his last words were 'Bulgaria, dear mother'.

Here we must note that in common with many of the figures of the cultural movement, Bozveli saw the Greeks and not the Turks as the chief enemy of Bulgaria. In one of his dialogues, probably influenced by the announcement of the *Hat-i-Sherif*, Bozveli even spoke of the mercy of the Sultan whom he referred to as the legitimate ruler, but he did not really see much hope for Bulgaria from that quarter owing to the corruption of the Turkish administration and the influence of the Phanariot Greeks there also. The fight against the Turks became the focal point of Bulgaria's struggles considerably later when the fight against the Greeks and the cultural struggle had been taken as far as possible.

Other Eminent Teachers

It will already have been noticed that the men in the forefront of the movement for a new educational system in Bulgaria were by no means agreed on the merits of Greek culture and its place in Bulgarian education. Among the famous teachers of the period who felt that it was necessary for Bulgars to know Greek were Raino Popovich, Khristaki Pavlovich and Emanuil Vaskdovich. All these men had founded Helleno-Bulgarian schools. Popovich taught in Kotel and Karlovo and used mainly Greek, but under the influence of Aprilov, he became considerably less of a Graecophil and came to agree with the necessity of having books in Bulgarian, of using Bulgarian as a medium for teaching, and of Bulgars being able to read and write their own language. Among those of his pupils who were later to achieve fame as patriots were Georgi Rakovsky and Botyu Petkov.

Khristaki Pavlovich was born in Dupnitsa in 1804 and studied at the Rila monastery and at two famous Greek schools. He returned to Rila and in 1831 he went to Svishtov at the invitation of the citizens of that town, and set up a Helleno-Bulgarian school there with the help of Emanuil Vaskidovich. In 1836, influenced by the example of the Gabrovo school, Khristaki Pavlovich turned his school into a purely Bulgarian one. Later he opened a Bulgarian class school and a girls' school. He did, however, believe that Bulgarian children should learn Greek as well as their own language. Pavlovich was the author of a number of textbooks, including a book on arithmetic (1833), a phrase book for Bulgars wishing to learn Greek (1835), a Bulgarian grammar (1836, second edition 1845) and a version of Paisi's *History* pruned of much of its lyricism but retaining Paisi's basic message (1844). This was the first printed version of Paisi's *History* and in this way Pavlovich did much to popularize the *History* among a wide circle of readers. He died at a comparatively early age, of cholera, in 1848.

Pavlovich's one time colleague, Emanuil Vaskidovich, is very interesting in so far as he is a rare example of a person of Greek origin who sympathized with Bulgaria's national cultural aspirations. He urged the Bulgars to study their own language and expressed Bulgarian national sentiments in the textbooks which he wrote. He taught for thirty years in Svishtov and for ten in Pleven, including Bulgarian grammar in his school syllabus. He was even able to collaborate with the violently anti-Greek Bozveli in the writing of his *Detovodstvo*, and among his pupils in Svishtov was Petko Slaveikov, the future poet and patriot.

Another foreigner who espoused Bulgaria's cause was the Serb, Konstantin Ognyanovich, who was for a time a teacher in Vratsa. He also took part in founding the first Bulgarian printing press in Constantinople, known as the 'Industrious Bee', which printed a number of books during 1842 and 1843.

While most of Bulgaria's men of letters were teachers and while most of the literature written consisted of textbooks for the new schools and works on education, some Bulgarian writers were already trying their hand at poetry. Some of the textbooks had verses in them, and Ognyanovich's most famous work, a life of St Alexei, was written in syllabic verse (verse with a set number of syllables in each line regardless of stress). The early attempts at poetry were full of patriotic feeling, but were very artificial and had little artistic merit. The founders of modern Bulgarian tonic poetry (poetry with a rhythm based on stress) were Naiden Gerov and Dobri Chintulov (1822–1886), and the first great poet was Petko Slaveikov.

Greek Opposition to the Schools

The path towards creating a modern educational system was by no means an easy one. All the expenses connected with school building and maintenance had to be met after the Bulgars had paid very heavy taxes to the Turkish Government and to the Greek clergy, and the main financial burden fell on the young Bulgarian *bourgeoisie*.

Some of the rich *chorbadzhii* helped the schools, but the educational activities of some of them often amounted to wrecking, for they misappropriated funds, interfered in the running of the school and made the teachers' lives unbearable. Other *chorbadzhii* were frankly against the Bulgarian schools and supported the Greek ones. As for the Greeks themselves, the Bulgarian educational movement ran counter to their chauvinistic dreams of a Greater Greece embracing Bulgaria as well, and in many towns, especially in those with a large Greek colony, the new schools were fiercely opposed by the Greeks. We have already mentioned how the Greeks prevented the setting up of a Bulgarian school in Plovdiv with Neofit Rilsky as its teacher, and indeed on at least two other occasions they prevented Rilsky from taking up teaching posts, once in Kazanlŭk and once in Stara Zagora. Worse was to follow. In Khaskovo the establishment of a Bulgarian school met with violent opposition on the part of the Greeks and the Graecomane *chorbadzhii*, culminating in the murder of the energetic and devoted Bulgarian teacher, Atanas Cholakov Dup-chanin, in 1852. The Greek Metropolitan Khrisant then closed the Bulgarian school in Khaskovo and prohibited the holding of services in Church Slavonic in the church at Pazardzhik. One of the chief methods by which the Greeks attacked the Bulgarian schools was to denounce the teachers to the Turks as subversive, and in view of the Turks' fear of anything Russian, this was particularly effective when the Bulgars who had studied in Russia returned home to teach.

In Macedonia the struggle between the Greeks and the Bulgars was even more bitter owing to its proximity to the centre of Greek culture. For example, Yordan Konstantinov Dzhinot of Veles, who in 1840 opened the first Bulgarian 'monitorial' school in Macedonia, was constantly in conflict with the Greeks and suffered much perse-cution at their hands. Because of their slanders and intrigues, Dzhinot was chased from pillar to post and was frequently arrested. In 1861 he was denounced by a Greeks bishop, brutally beaten and imprisoned in the fortress of Gyuzel Khisar. Both the Miladinov brothers, famous for their collection of Bulgarian folk songs and for their leading role in the national movement in Macedonia, died in prison, denounced by the Greek clergy.

From these few examples, it will be clear how much hard work, heroism and self-sacrifice were necessary before the Bulgars estab-lished their right to have their own schools and to be taught in their own language.

The Development of Bulgarian Printing

It has already been mentioned that up till 1806 when Sofroni Vrachanski's *Nedelnik* was published, all Bulgarian books were copied by hand. Even after 1806, Bulgarian books had to be printed abroad in such towns as Belgrade, Budapest, Bucharest, Braşov, Kragujevac, etc., since there were no facilities inside Bulgaria itself. Books were therefore rare and costly things, and before 1835 not more than four Bulgarian books were published in any one year, and there were eight years between 1806 and 1835 in which no books were published at all. The great educational movement and the ever-increasing number of new readers made the provision of cheap, plentiful books a problem of immediate importance. Aprilov and Palauzov, the founders of the Gabrovo school, had hoped to set up a printing press at Gabrovo to publish textbooks, but were not allowed to do so. Neofit Rilsky and Raino Popovich were also interested in the possibility of setting up a press but nothing came of it. Rilsky even entered into a correspondence on the subject with Nikola Karastoyanov of Samokov, who printed and bought books in Serbia, and who had in 1828 installed a secret hand press in the cellar of his house in Samokov for printing ikons and church pictures. In 1835 Karastoyanov obtained metal type from Budapest, but it appears that he was not able to print any books with it until 1846 when he secretly printed a book about Mount Athos. He continued to print books in Serbia until 1846 when he at last obtained permission from the Metropolitan of Samokov to print his own books and published a number of religious books.

The first officially recognized Bulgarian press was opened in 1838 in Salonika, the birthplace of Saints Cyril and Methodius. Its founder, Hadzhi Teodosi Sinaitsky was born in the Macedonian town of Doiran which was also the birthplace of Khristofor Zhefarovich. He had studied in Constantinople and had then returned home and became a priest. After the death of his wife he travelled in Macedonia intending to enter a monastery, and became firm friends with Kiril Peichinovich, Abbot of the Leshok monastery. In 1827 he entered the Sinai monastery, became a monk and soon reached the rank of Archimandrite. He conducted services in Slavonic and translated various prayers into Slavonic, and in 1831 he was invited to become priest at the Church of Saint Mina in the Bulgarian quarter of Salonika. As a result of his contact with the Bulgarian guildsmen, merchants and intellectuals in Salonika and in other towns, he determined to set up a printing press to print books for the Bulgarian churches and schools. Tradition has it that Teodosi was much influenced in his decision by a teacher named Kamché, who was teacher in the village of Vatosha. Be this as it may, it was Kamché who, financed by Teodosi and a rich man named Iovko Markov, obtained type from Belgrade and set it up in his own house. When the Greek bishop heard about the press, he forbade Kamché to teach in the village. Teodosi, however, was on very good terms with the Greek Church authorities in Salonika and obtained their permission to open a Bulgarian press in that city in 1838. Unfortunately, the press was destroyed by fire in 1839, but it was set up again with the financial help of Kiril Peichinovich. In 1841 it was again destroyed by fire, though on this occasion it was arson on the part of the Phanariots. The new disaster made Teodosi lose heart and he returned to Doiran where his sons ran a mill. He was seriously injured when part of the mill collapsed under the weight of heavy snow and died soon after (about 1843).

In 1840 a Greek printer named Damiani who owned a press in Smyrna furnished it with Slavonic type from the USA at the request of the British and Foreign Bible Society, a Protestant missionary body working in Bulgaria. This press printed Neofit Rilsky's translation of the New Testament which had been commissioned by the Bible Society.[1] Damiani's press also printed the first Bulgarian periodical *Lyuboslovie* which will be described in greater detail in the next section.

In 1847 with the help of Bulgarian merchants and craftsmen, Ivan Bogorov opened a Bulgarian press in Constantinople where the Bulgarian colony was numerically larger than the population of any town in Bulgaria itself. The early attempts of the Bulgars to set up presses were much hampered both by the opposition of the Phanariot Greeks to the development of an independent Bulgarian culture, and by the Turkish Censorship which forbade the publication of political books and even certain literary ones. The Turks particularly objected to Russian books which they regarded as dangerous and subversive.

The Development of the Periodical Press

As the national movement developed, so also did the need for newspapers and periodicals in which the topics of the day could be

[1] The Protestant missionaries met with very little success in Bulgaria. They went to the Balkans in 1821 and it was 1852 before they succeeded in making a Bulgar convert. In 1860 they founded the first mission school in Plovdiv.

E*

discussed and through which information could be disseminated. Newspapers appeared in Bulgaria very much later than in other European countries. Germany had a daily paper as early as 1660. Nearer home, the Serbs in Austria began publishing a journal in Vienna in 1791, but it was not until 1834 that the first journal appeared in Serbia itself. The first Greek journal appeared in Vienna in 1793. The Bulgarian merchant class were acquainted with journals and newspapers by reading those of their neighbours, but it was only in 1844 that the first Bulgarian periodical appeared, published in Smyrna by Konstantin Fotinov. In 1846 another Bulgarian journal appeared in Leipzig—Ivan Bogorov's *Bŭlgarski Orel* (*Bulgarian Eagle*), later renamed *Bŭlgarski Naroden Izvestnik* (*Bulgarian National News*). Fotinov and Bogorov are the two great names of the early days of the Bulgarian Press.

Fotinov was born about 1800 in Samokov. He went to a cell school and then to a Greek school in Plovdiv and later to Greece itself for higher education. He was thus well acquainted with Greek culture. On the other hand he spent his early years in a district rich in legends of Bulgaria's past greatness. A third influence came from his grandmother who brought him up and who was a strict and deeply religious woman and taught him accordingly. In 1825 Fotinov went to live in Smyrna, where he traded in figs and other fruit. Smyrna at that time was a flourishing centre of trade and culture with a Greek school. It also had a fairly large Bulgarian merchant colony and church premises where services were conducted in Church Slavonic. Fotinov was not very successful as a trader and in 1828 he opened a private school based on the 'monitorial' method. His pupils included both Greeks and Bulgars and he used both languages for teaching. The subjects he taught were fundamentally ecclesiastical: Christ's teachings, caligraphy and music. He soon became celebrated as a teacher of Church music and monks came from as far afield as the Rila monastery to study under him.

In Smyrna Fotinov became acutely aware of the fact that most other peoples had their own papers and periodicals while the Bulgars merely had a few books of limited subject-matter. It so happened that owing to the publication of the Bulgarian New Testament by the Bible Society, Slavonic type was available at Damiani's press in Smyrna, and, in 1844, using this type, Fotinov began regular publication of the first Bulgarian periodical *Lyuboslovie*. Already in 1842 Fotinov had brought out a trial copy which began with a kind of editorial describing the virtues of having periodicals and an account of the subjects which *Lyuboslovie* would deal with (these covered a very wide range). It also had a coloured plate of the two hemispheres, a description of Asia, a story about the Japanese, an article on agriculture, information on modern bone fertilizers, a story about the Ancient Greeks, and an article on the origin of the Slavs. After he had brought out this trial copy, Fotinov toured Bulgaria getting subscriptions for *Lyuboslovie* and for a geography book, part translated from the Greek and part written by himself. Eighteen hundred people subscribed to this book. Geography was very popular during the period of the Renaissance, no doubt because the Bulgars' growing feelings of nationalism made them conscious of the existence of different countries and led them to desire information, especially about their own. Fotinov's geography was illustrated and contained many references to Bulgaria's past glory, her Tsars, Patriarchs, etc. It was printed on Damiani's press and appeared in 1843.

Starting from 1844 *Lyuboslovie* came out regularly for two years. It continued to have a very wide range of subject-matter, embracing practically any knowledge which could be imparted through the medium of words. History and geography were favourite topics of Fotinov's, and he also discussed religion, teaching, agriculture, hygiene, trade, morals and literature. In addition he included topical information mostly of a semi-scientific nature, such as the story of an old nun who grew new teeth, notes on railways, aqueducts, steamships, crop rotation, artificial fertilizers, the structure of the brain, etc. *Lyuboslovie* was very well received at first, but later support for it began to slacken, partly because of the excessive length of the articles, some of which ran as serials for almost the whole two years of its existence. The journal's financial backer, a rich merchant from Shumen, finally withdrew his support and it could no longer be produced. After it closed down, Fotinov continued to teach and trade and wrote books, including Bulgarian translations of Old Testament books and an unfinished Russian–Bulgarian–Greek dictionary. He died of tuberculosis in 1858.

Fotinov followed in the tradition of Aprilov and Rilsky and took no part in politics which, incidentally, had little place in his *Lyuboslovie*. He tried to rouse the patriotic sentiments of his fellow countrymen by every legal means, but he steered clear of all revolutionary activity. He was, however, a great believer in women's education because he saw the tremendous role that women played in shaping family and social life. In this respect he considered them to be as important and influential as priests and teachers.

Although *Lyuboslovie* had died, Ivan Bogorov took up the torch, and in April 1846 he published the first number of *Bŭlgarski Orel* which is regarded as the first Bulgarian newspaper. Ivan Bogorov was born in Karlovo in 1818. He studied first under Raino Popovich, then in Constantinople, where he became friends with Rakovsky, and finally in Odessa where under the influence of the local Bulgarian colony he developed strong patriotic feelings. In 1840 he published the lithographs of the Bulgarian lion emblem and the portraits of Ivan Asen and Ivan Shishman from Zhefarovich's *Stematografia*. Later he travelled widely in Bulgaria, trying to persuade his fellow countrymen to stop regarding themselves as Greek, and then taught for a time in Stara Zagora during 1843. He wrote various books, including a translation of V. Bardovsky's *Mathematical Geography* (Odessa, 1842), a collection of Bulgarian national songs and proverbs (Pest, 1842), a geography for children (Belgrade, 1843), and a Bulgarian grammar (Bucharest, 1844). This last book is important because it helped to establish the living Bulgarian spoken language as the language of literature. In 1845 Bogorov went to Leipzig to continue his studies and it was there that he began the publication of *Bŭlgarski Orel* in April of the same year. The second number appeared in September under the name of *Bŭlgarski Naroden Izvestnik*, and the third number appeared in January 1847, once more as *Bŭlgarski Orel*. Bogorov's motive in producing the paper was to assert Bulgaria's right to equality with the other nations of Europe, who all had their own newspapers and the benefits that went with them. In his paper, Bogorov proposed to give 'public news from everywhere', to describe interesting places and people in Bulgaria and in Europe, to discuss Bulgarian schools and the educational system with a view to improving them, to help merchants and craftsmen to reach economic prosperity comparable to that of other European peoples, to print stories, fables and poetry, and to review all new Bulgarian books. Unfortunately, the paper came to a premature end after the third issue owing to financial difficulties. Bogorov then left Leipzig and went to Constantinople. There he obtained the permission of the Turkish Government to publish a Bulgarian newspaper and on January 1, 1848, he produced the first number of *Tsarigradski Vestnik*, which survived until 1861, and played a very important role in Bulgarian cultural and educational life, having among its contributors the foremost Bulgarian teachers and literary men of the day. Bogorov himself got into new financial difficulties and fled to Rumania in 1851, and his creditors sold the press to Alexander Eksarkh who continued to produce the paper until 1861. During the great battles between the Bulgars and the Greek Patriarchate, the paper took a very moderate standpoint since it was subsidized by the Russian Government, who for some time opposed the setting up of an independent Bulgarian Church.

After leaving Constantinople Bogorov published *A Short Mathematical, Physical and Political Geography* (Bucharest, 1851), which contains much interesting information about Bulgaria of the time. Later he went to Paris to study medicine, and then returned to Constantinople where for a year he edited *Bŭlgarski Knizhitsi* (*Bulgarian Papers*) with the avowed aim of concentrating people's thoughts on science, commerce, handicrafts and agriculture. He regarded material improvement and economic advance as vital to Bulgaria's future, and even when he took up a post as town doctor in Plovdiv, he felt that the people had more need of industry than of medicine, and in 1862 he founded a periodical called *Journal of Science, Handicrafts and Commerce*, which came to an end after its third issue. Later he visited Russia and had the distinction of being the first Bulgar who was a Turkish subject to be received by the Tsar. Space does not permit more than a brief mention of the remainder of his life. He continued to work as a journalist, editing various journals, in Constantinople in 1873 and in Prague 1874–1875. Among his later books were a *Bulgarian–French, French–Bulgarian Dictionary* (Vienna, 1869, second edition 1872), and various works on language, advocating the use of the spoken language in literature and the elimination of foreign words. He died in Sofia in 1892.

After the pioneer papers of Fotinov and Bogorov many others followed. In Vienna in 1850 there appeared *Mirozrenie* (*World View*) edited by the Slavophil Ivan Dobrovsky from Sliven. His aim was to promote the unity of the Slav peoples through mutual understanding and knowledge of each other and through drawing them closer together culturally. Only five issues of *Mirozrenie* appeared. In 1857 Georgi Rakovsky began his career as an editor, with *Bŭlgarski Dnevnitsa* (*Bulgarian Diary*) published in Novi Sa. In 1859 Dragan Tsankov's *Bŭlgaria* appeared in Constantinople and in 1860 two more papers appeared: *Bratski Trud* (*Brotherly Labour*) in Moscow and *Dunavski Lebed* (*Danube Swan*) in Belgrade. In 1863 Petko Slaveikov started *Gaida* (*Bagpipes*) in Constantinople, and another called *Makedonia*. The story of some of these and subsequent papers and journals and their role in the national movement will be told in a later chapter. Up to the Liberation, seventy Bulgarian newspapers and thirty-seven journals were started, some very short-lived. The Press in Bulgaria during this time played a very important part in the victorious struggle for an independent Church and in organizing the people for revolutionary action for political freedom. The Press developed particularly after the Crimean War, when such men as Rakovsky, Karavelov and Botev were active as editors, and the various trends and ideological struggles within Bulgarian society found their reflection in the newspapers and journals of the period.

A feature of the development of the Press in Bulgaria was the formation of literary societies the aim of which was to facilitate the publication of journals, etc. In 1852 a society called *Bŭlgarski Knizhnina* (*Bulgarian Letters*) was formed in Constantinople to publish *Bŭlgarski Knizhitsi*, of which Bogorov was the editor. In 1860 a society called *Bratski Trud* was set up in Moscow to publish the journal of the same name, and in 1870 *Bŭlgarsko Knizhovno Druzhestvo* (*Bulgarian Literary Society*) was formed in Braila. The latter society was the ancestor of the present-day Bulgarian Academy of Sciences.

CHAPTER VII

THE STRUGGLE FOR
THE INDEPENDENCE OF
THE BULGARIAN CHURCH

Introduction

The origin of the Church struggle goes back to 1393 when the national Bulgarian Church founded by Boris I lost its independence and became subject to the Greek Patriarchate. Some Bulgarian territory, it is true, remained under the Archbishop of Okhrid and the Serbian Patriarchate of Ipek, but these were dissolved in 1766 and 1767 respectively and henceforward all Bulgaria came under the Greek Church. The activities of the Phanariot Greeks have been described in a previous chapter and it will be sufficient here simply to recall a few outstanding facts about the Greek clergy. The Patriarch of Constantinople was granted certain privileges by the Turks in return for co-operation with the conqueror. To give a small example, the laws prohibiting Christians from riding horses and from wearing rich apparel did not apply to the Patriarch. To begin with the Greek clergy received the same Church taxes as the Bulgarian clergy had done, but soon they were demanding more and more. After the introduction of the custom of selling the Patriarchate and other Church appointments to the highest bidder, the need for higher Church taxes increased and the situation was made worse by the Turks who encouraged frequent changes of Patriarch in the interests of the Treasury. Moreover, the Bishops and their suites had to be entertained free when they travelled just as though they were the Sultan's officials. The selling of Church appointments meant that the Church was full of greedy, ignorant people, out for what they could get, totally unworthy to be the people's spiritual leaders and often even illiterate. Those who could not or would not pay the Bishop's tax were liable to have their household goods confiscated and sold. Sometimes as a collective punishment on a village, the churches might be closed by order of the Bishop and all sacraments discontinued. It was the economic burden which the

Greek clergy imposed upon their Bulgarian flocks that first provoked discontent and revolt. Soon the chauvinism which forced the Bulgarians to listen to services in Greek conducted by Greek priests, and sought to stifle all Bulgarian national consciousness also provoked a public outcry. The reaction against Greek domination in the Church initially expressed itself in the relatively modest demand that predominantly Bulgarian dioceses should have Bulgarian Bishops, but it grew into the demand for a complete break with the Greek Patriarchate and the setting up of an independent Bulgarian Church. The Church struggles were sharpest in the most economically developed towns owing to the leading role of the Bulgarian *bourgeoisie* in the nationalist movement.

The Beginning of the Struggle

The first major struggles against the domination of the Greek clergy took place in the 1820's. In 1824 the people of Vratsa, led by the *chorbadzhiya*, Dimitraki Kh. Toshev, refused to pay an extra tax which the Greek Bishop Methodius was collecting on the instructions of the Metropolitan of Tŭrnovo, Ilarion the Cretan. This Metropolitan, incidentally, had originally been chased out of Austria and Rumania for theft and banditry. While Metropolitan, he made his groom a Bishop, and when he died in 1838, he left a vast sum in gold to his relatives and to support Greek schools. As well as opposing the new tax, Toshev and his confederates also demanded that Bishop Methodius be replaced by a Bulgar, the Archimandrite Gavril Bistrichanin, who was then in Bucharest. The Metropolitan, however, continued to support Methodius and enlisted the aid of the Turks who arrested the leading citizens of Vratsa. The revolt came to an end in 1827 when Toshev was executed as a rebel in Vidin, but fresh struggles were beginning in other towns such as Stara Zagora, Tŭrnovo, Samokov and the Macedonian town of Skoplje, all aimed at driving out the Greek clergy. In Stara and Nova Zagora in 1836, the Bulgars actually succeeded in ridding themselves of the Greek Bishop and in getting the Bulgar, Onufri Popovich, appointed in his place.

Neofit Bozveli and the Metropolitans of Tŭrnovo

On the death of the Metropolitan of Tŭrnovo, Ilarion the Cretan, a Greek named Panaret was appointed as his successor. This Panaret, who had originally been a circus fighter, was uneducated and boorish, and was said to be mad into the bargain. It was natural that the appointment of this most unsuitable candidate should arouse great indignation among the Bulgars, who in any case wanted a Bulgarian Metropolitan. A great agitational campaign developed against Panaret led by Neofit Bozveli, who before 1838 had been primarily a teacher and whose early life and educational activities were described in the previous chapter. In 1839 Bozveli went to Constantinople to seek the support of the Bulgarian colony there, and in 1840 a delegation followed, with a unanimous mandate from all the sixteen districts of the Tŭrnovo diocese to present a petition to the Porte and to the Patriarchate, demanding that Panaret be removed and that Neofit Bozveli should take his place as Metropolitan of Tŭrnovo. The Bulgars had been goaded into sending this delegation because Panaret, laying on the proverbial last straw, had denounced the Bulgars to the Turks as rebels. Even the Turks now agreed that Panaret was quite unbearable and told the Patriarch to agree to the Bulgarian demands. The Patriarch was utterly opposed to the appointment of so fervent a Bulgarian nationalist as Bozveli, and he managed to prevent the development of this dangerous situation by bribing a section of the delegation to agree to the appointment of another Greek, Neofit Byzantios. As a sop to the Bulgars as a whole, the Patriarch appointed Neofit Bozveli as assistant and *protosingel* to the new Metropolitan with a vague promise that he should later be made Bishop of Lovech. The Bulgars regarded the appointment of Neofit Byzantios as an insult, more especially as he was only twenty-five, and therefore too young to hold so important a post in the Church hierarchy. It was impossible for Neofit Bozveli to work with him and he therefore resigned in order to be free to continue the campaign against the Metropolitan. It was, incidentally, the Metropolitan's secretary who gave him the name of Bozveli after a *Kŭrdzhal* bandit in Yambol. Bozveli turned the intended insult into a matter of pride, rejoicing in his nickname because it indicated how much the Greeks feared and hated him. Soon the Metropolitan took steps to rid himself of his enemy and had Bozveli arrested and sent in chains to Constantinople. The Patriarch then had him imprisoned without trial in the Hilendar monastery for four years, but in 1844 he escaped and returned to Constantinople to continue the fight.

Ilarion Makariopolsky

When Bozveli came to Constantinople in 1839 he met Ilarion Stoyanovitch Mikhailovski, the man who was to be the second great leader in the struggle against the Greek clergy, and the two patriots became friends and comrades in the fight. Better known to history as Ilarion Makariopolsky, he was born in Elena in 1812. At the age of nineteen he became a monk in the Hilendar monastery and attended the school on the island of Andros run by the famous Greek teacher, Kairis. The atmosphere at the school was one of violent Greek nationalism and the Bulgarian pupils were despised as being no better than gypsies. Kairis had invented a new religion which, among other things, taught contempt for the 'Jewish' Christ and for non-Greek nations, and the Patriarch intervened and closed the school. The nationalism of the Greek pupils did not make the Bulgarian pupils Graecophils, but, on the contrary, it made them Bulgarian nationalists, and since the Greeks formed a patriotic society, the Bulgars did likewise and Ilarion became its chairman. After the closing of Kairis's school, Ilarion studied at the Patriarch's school at Kuru-Chesmé and at Athens. Aprilov had secured a scholarship for him to study in Russia, but the Patriarch would not allow him to go. Ilarion returned to Constantinople from Athens in 1843, and met Neofit Bozveli again on his return from prison in 1844. These two men, Ilarion and Neofit Bozveli, now became the recognized leaders of the Bulgarian people, and in 1845 they received a mandate from the Bulgarians in Constantinople to represent them before the Porte and the Patriarchate.

Bozveli and Ilarion in Constantinople

The centre of the Church struggle now shifted to Constantinople with its large Bulgarian colony. During his previous sojourn in Constantinople from 1839 onwards, Bozveli had found fertile ground for his agitational activity among the Bulgarian guildsmen who were already conscious of being Bulgarian and not Greek. He acted as confessor in the 'Hambar', the huge barrack-like building where a thousand Bulgarian craftsmen lived and worked, and he conducted services in Slavonic for them. His activities were very unwelcome to the Patriarch, who had him arrested at night and conveyed by Greek boat to Athos where he was imprisoned for a time, until the Bulgarians secured his release. Bozveli also conducted the liturgy in Slavonic for the *chorbadzhiya* Chalŭkov in a room in his house near Constantinople, and gradually the Bulgarians began to feel the need for a church of their own in Constantinople.

This demand found public expression in 1845 when Ilarion and Bozveli, now both in the capital again and newly mandated to represent the Bulgarian people before the Porte and the Patriarchate, presented a declaration to the Porte making certain demands on behalf of the Bulgarians. The significance of the demands was that they, in fact, required that the Turks should recognize the Bulgarian people as a separate national group within the Empire. The declaration asked that Bulgarian Bishops be appointed to Bulgarian dioceses, that the Bishops be elected by the people, and replaced if the people so desired, that the Bishops be paid a fixed salary; that the Bulgars should have their own representatives before the Porte, and that the Bulgars in Constantinople be allowed to build a church of their own with a Bulgarian Bishop attached to it, and be allowed to publish a Bulgarian newspaper.[1] It must be mentioned that the announcement of the *Hat-i-Sherif* reforms in 1839 and their reaffirmation in 1843 and 1845 greatly encouraged the Bulgarian national movement. While little came of the promised era of reforms, though some leading Bulgars, including Neofit Rilsky, had greeted the *Hat-i-Sherif* with enthusiasm, at least the principle of equal rights for all peoples within the Turkish Empire had been conceded and could be quoted to support the Bulgarian demands.

Neofit Bozveli realized that it was necessary to have the support of the Turkish Government in the fight against the Patriarch, and after his return to Constantinople in 1844 he succeeded in obtaining the protection of certain high-ranking Turkish officials, in particular a Polish émigré named Mikhail Czaikowski, who also came to be known as Sadĭk Pasha. Czaikowski was one of the numerous Poles who had fled to Turkey after the suppression of the 1831 Polish Rising by the Russians in order to continue their anti-Russian activities. In Turkey, of course, the enemies of Russia were very welcome. Czaikowski was interested in building up an anti-Russian coalition and advised the Porte to grant the Bulgarian demands in the hope of drawing the Bulgars closer to the Turks and thus away from Russia. For their part, the Turks considered it advantageous to encourage enmity between the Greeks and Bulgars, and welcomed any rift in the Orthodox Church, which formed a strong link between the Balkan Christians and the Russians. Believing that divisions among the Christians would lessen Russian influence in the Balkans, the Turks were inclined to take a favourable view of the Bulgarian demands, and indeed throughout the Church struggle they gave certain support to the Bulgarian cause for this reason. Russia was,

[1] This demand was achieved in 1848 when Bogorov received permission to publish *Tsarigradski Vestnik*.

of course, interested in maintaining the unity of the Orthodox Church, and when the Porte suggested to the Patriarch that the Bulgarian demands be granted, the Patriarch made skilful use of Russia's interest, in order to avoid granting the demands. He convinced the Russians that Bozveli and Ilarion aimed at splitting the Orthodox Church, which was quite untrue at that stage, and insinuated that the two men were tools of Roman Catholic propaganda because of their association with the Polish émigrés, which was also quite untrue. He also accused Ilarion of holding the heretical religious views of his former teacher, Kairis. Then, relying on Russian support, since Russia had wielded considerable influence in the Turkish Empire subsequent to the Treaty of Adrianople, the Patriarch attempted to deprive the Bulgarian movement of its leadership by arresting Neofit Bozveli and Ilarion without obtaining the permission of the Turkish Government. The two men were taken in chains to Prinkipo, but the Bulgarian guilds sent fifty young men there to look for their leaders, and the Patriarch, fearing they might be liberated, had to call in the Turkish police. The priests were then taken to Mount Athos and imprisoned in a monastery. The Bulgars protested strongly to the Turkish Government, which was quite willing to have them released, but the Russians, still believing that the Bulgars were out to split the Orthodox Church, supported the Patriarch and the men remained in prison.

The Bulgars, however, continued to protest and in 1846 when the Sultan, Abdul Medzhid, was touring Bulgaria, he was greeted in every town with petitions, complaining about the Greek clergy and demanding that Bozveli and Ilarion be released. The Sultan ordered the Patriarch to remove Neofit Byzantios, whose appointment as Metropolitan of Tŭrnovo had so angered the Bulgars, but another Greek, Anastasi, was appointed in his place. He soon followed the time-honoured custom of Greek Bishops and accused the citizens of Tŭrnovo of sedition. This time, however, the Turks were not taken in, and the Pasha of Vidin took stern measures to deal with the nuisance. He called the leading Bulgars together and asked Anastasi to point out exactly which of them were preparing a rebellion. The unhappy Metropolitan asked for twenty-four hours' grace, and then threw himself into a well and was drowned.

Unfortunately the Bulgars were not able to secure the release of Bozveli, who died in prison in 1848, but Ilarion was released in 1850 on the intervention of Andrei Muraviev, the Russian scholar and traveller, and he returned to Constantinople.

The First Bulgarian Church in Constantinople

After the imprisonment of their leaders, the Bulgars concentrated on building a Bulgarian Church in Constantinople, and twenty-four guilds gave a written mandate to Nikola Sapunov, a master *aba* weaver, to take the necessary steps. Permission from the Turkish Government was essential and Alexander Eksarkh was authorized to negotiate for a *firman* granting permission. Alexander Eksarkh, a native of Stara Zagora, had returned to Constantinople in 1847 having worked on behalf of his people in Paris, London and St Petersburg, and he was given the task of obtaining the *firman* because he had connections with the Turkish Government. Alexander Eksarkh had intended to purchase a site for the church with funds from Russia, but Stefan Bogoridi (Stefanaki Bey) stepped in and offered a house and a large courtyard suitable for conversion in the Phanar district of Constantinople. Bogoridi was a native of Kotel and the nephew of Sofroni Vrachansky. He had risen high in the Turkish administration and was made Governor of the Island of Samos in 1832. He also acted as counsellor to the Sultan, being the first Bulgar to hold such a post, and the Sultan even attended his daughter's wedding. This was the first time a Sultan had been present at a Christian wedding. Although he spoke in Turkish to his fellow countrymen and although his family had succumbed to Greek influence to the extent that he himself was regarded as a Phanariot by the Patriarch, with whom he had considerable influence, Bogoridi himself recognized that he was a Bulgar, and indeed his old mother still spoke only Bulgarian, continued to wear the traditional costume of Kotel and received visitors from her home town, who were helped by Bogoridi. His offer of premises appears to have been motivated by a desire to prevent Alexander Eksarkh from gaining too great an influence over the Bulgarian popular movement. Alexander Eksarkh, for his part, opposed the acceptance of Bogoridi's offer, fearing lest his position as a high Turkish official should adversely affect the independent and progressive character of the movement. In the end, Alexander Eksarkh and his supporters found themselves in the minority and Bogoridi's gift was accepted, and in 1849 the *firman* for the building of the church was granted by the Turkish Government. This *firman* was of historic importance not only because of the church, but also because it was the first Turkish document to refer to the *Bulgarmiletani*—the Bulgarian people, thus recognizing officially a difference between the Bulgars and Greeks. After much discussion the church was dedicated to St Stephen in honour of its benefactor and opened on October 9, 1849. It was consecrated by a Bishop who knew Bulgarian and all the services there were conducted in Slavonic. A large church building was subsequently built to accommodate visiting Bulgarians from the provinces and a Church Charter was drawn up, declaring the church to be the property of all Bulgars and providing for it to be administered by an elected council of twenty, presided over by a Bulgarian Bishop. Thus a Bulgarian Church Commune, led by the merchants and guildsmen, was established in Constantinople and became the centre of the movement for a national Bulgarian Church.

At first the Bulgars had no Bishop of their own in Constantinople, although the church was visited by Greek Bishops and Metropolitans and even by the Patriarch himself. They were determined to have a Bishop and the man they wanted was their old leader, Ilarion. He was released from prison in 1850 but the Russian Envoy, still suspecting him of being in league with the Poles, insisted that the Russian educated Serbian Archimandrite, Stefan Kovachevich, be consecrated Bishop of the Bulgarian Church. This arrangement proved to be only a temporary one, since the appointment of a Serb did not satisfy Bulgarian national feeling, and since the new Bishop himself was far from suitable.

The Effects of the Crimean War

The Crimean War of 1853–1856 ended in Russia's defeat at the hands of Britain and France. Russia lost Bessarabia and the right to keep a Fleet in the Black Sea, and as a result of her defeat, her influence over the Turkish Empire, which had been considerable since the Treaty of Adrianople in 1829, now declined and the influence of the Western Powers increased. The economic aspects of this influence and the opening up of Turkey to Western investments have already been outlined in Chapter III. On the political front, the Western Powers once more urged the Turkish Government to introduce reforms, hoping as before to lessen Russian influence among the Balkan Christians and to prevent the break-up of the Turkish Empire. In 1856 the so-called *Hat-i-Humayun* was announced. This confirmed the earlier *Hat-i-Sherif* and gave new promises of equality between Christians and Moslems within the Empire. Heavy taxes were to be rescinded, there were to be no executions without trial, Christians were to be allowed to serve in the army and the Civil Service, peasants were to be allowed to buy land from the *agas'* estates and all people were to have freedom of religion. It also proposed certain Church reforms: that Bishops should receive a set salary and that the Bishops' Tax be abolished, that each Christian community be governed by a Council of lay and clerical persons. The paragraph in the *Hat-i-Humayun* which dealt with freedom of religion greatly encouraged the Bulgars in the struggle with the Greek clergy and made them feel that the law was on their side. After the Crimean War the struggle entered a new stage in which the Bulgars gradually advanced from merely seeking Bulgarian Bishops for Bulgarian dioceses to demanding a complete break with the Patriarchate and the formation of an independent Bulgarian Church.

The Bulgars were, however, not completely united, and after the Crimean War, two separate groupings emerged—the moderates and the extremists. The moderate section consisted of the big merchant and money-lending *bourgeoisie* and the industrialists, who did not want to advance beyond the original pre-war demands, i.e. the right to use the Bulgarian language in the churches and the appointment of Bulgarian Bishops for Bulgarian dioceses. The moderates were further subdivided into the Russophils who supported the Russians in their desire to maintain the unity of the Orthodox Church in Turkey under the Patriarch of Constantinople, and the Turkophils who sought the support of the Turkish Government and proposed to act in conjunction with it. The extremist section embraced the guildsmen, minor traders and the petty *bourgeoisie*, and their declared aim was the creation of an independent Bulgarian Church with its own head elected by the people. The two parties became known respectively as the 'Old' and the 'Young'. The leader of the 'Old' or moderate party was Gavril Krŭstevich, while the leader of the 'Young' or extreme party was Petko R. Slaveikov.

The Church Council of 1858

In the spring of 1856, encouraged by the terms of the *Hat-i-Humayun* and led by the 'Young' group, the Bulgars in Constantinople sent a petition to the Sultan in the name of 6,400,000 Bulgars asking for permission to elect a supreme Bulgarian Church leader in whose work neither Christian nor non-Christian should interfere, and a supreme civil leader who would assist the Sultan to choose suitable Bulgars to act as judges, officials, etc., in Bulgaria. In other words, the Bulgars were demanding not only religious but also political autonomy within the Turkish Empire. These demands met with an unfavourable reception from all sides. The Russians saw them as an attempt to split the Orthodox Church, while the Western Powers suspected that all agitation on the part of the Bulgars was instigated by the Russians. The Greeks encouraged the Porte to regard the petition as Russian inspired, and the Porte in fact ignored it. Later in the same year, 1856, on the instigation of the Constantinople Bulgarian Commune, many of the chief towns of Bulgaria either sent representatives to Constantinople, or mandated Bulgars resident there to act for them, and in 1857 these representatives presented the Porte with sixty separate petitions demanding an independent Bulgarian Church. Still the Porte took no notice and the delegates gradually dispersed, since they had insufficient funds to enable them to remain in Constantinople indefinitely. By the beginning of 1858, however, the Porte seemed to have become convinced that the agitation among the Bulgars was not foreign inspired, but the Turks maintained that it was not for them but for the Patriarchate to take action in religious matters. Accordingly, the Patriarch was ordered to summon a council to consider certain aspects of Church administration, such as the appointment of clergy and the fixing of salaries and Church taxes. Although the agenda precluded any proper discussion of Bulgarian national aspirations and although the Bulgars were only allowed four delegates out of a total of forty-five, the 'Old' party decided that it was worth while to take part and advanced the following demands: that the Bishops be elected by the dioceses, that they should be acquainted with the language of the local population and that they should be paid fixed salaries.

The Council sat from October 1858 to February 1860 and refused to grant even the modest demands of the 'Old' Party. The results of the Council made it quite clear to most of the Bulgars that nothing was to be gained by discussion with the Patriarch and that the way forward must lie through joining battle with it. Even some of the leaders of the 'Old' Party realized the impossibility of coming to an understanding with the Patriarchate, and after the Church Council, the 'Young' Party became dominant in the Church movement and the establishment of an independent Bulgarian Church became its primary aim.

Although the outcome of the Council was entirely negative, the Bulgarians were able to boast of certain successes during the years of its sitting. In 1858 on the suggestion of the Constantinople Church Commune, May 11th (24th new style), the Festival of St Cyril and St Methodius, was celebrated for the first time as a general national holiday. In 1858 also the Serb who had been appointed Bishop of St Stefan's Church was imprisoned by the Patriarch for leading a life of vice and, through the good offices of Bogoridi, the Patriarch finally agreed to the appointment of Ilarion as his successor providing he did not ask for a diocese or ask to be made a Metropolitan. Ilarion was consecrated a Bishop in September 1858, taking the name of Makariopolsky, and was received by the Bulgars with great joy.

After services had been held for some years in Bogoridi's converted house, the Commune decided to erect a fine new church in Constantinople and in 1859 the foundation stone was laid in the presence of the Patriarch and the whole Synod, the Patriarchs from the Middle East who were in Constantinople for the Church Council, the Rector of the Greek theological college at Halki, Russian, Serbian and Turkish representatives, and, of course, many leading Bulgars, including Bogoridi and Antim, who was to become the first Exarch of Bulgaria in 1871 when the Church struggle ended in final victory for the Bulgarians.

The Struggle in Plovdiv and other Towns

While the centre of the Church struggle had now shifted to Constantinople, activity directed against the Greek Bishops continued with increased vigour in Bulgaria itself in such towns as Tŭrnovo, Sofia, Samokov, Vidin, Lovech and Plovdiv. In Plovdiv the struggle was particularly violent, not to say spectacular. It will be remembered that Plovdiv had long been considered a Greek stronghold and that its Metropolitan, Khrisant, was a particularly vicious opponent of the Bulgarian national movement. At the same time the Bulgarian guilds had grown very powerful, and had gained control of all the crafts and the extensive horticulture which went on in the fertile surrounding countryside. Moreover, the leading Bulgarian *chorbadzhii* were an exception to the general rule that most *chorbadzhii* tended to be Graecomanes. The leading *chorbadzhii* of Plovdiv were members of the Chalŭkov family who had moved there from the purely Bulgarian town of Koprivshtitsa and had kept their Bulgarian national consciousness. Stoyan Chalŭkov was able to force the Metropolitan to build a Bulgarian church in Plovdiv in 1847 and various schools were started in the area including the one at which Naiden Gerov became teacher in 1850. All this activity met with fierce opposition from the Greeks who accused the Bulgars of using the schools for political aims and for propagating panslavism.

The Metropolitan himself slanderously accused the Bulgars of preparing a rebellion against the Turks, but as in the case of Anastasi of Tŭrnovo, the Turks found no evidence to support the charge. Legal proceedings were taken against the Metropolitan, and the Patriarch was obliged to remove him and send him to Asia Minor. His successor, Paisi, was, like Chalŭkov, an exception to the rule. Unlike most Greek Bishops, he was an educated man, and just in his dealings. Later on, he was proved an even more remarkable exception: he sided with the Bulgarians against the Patriarch and suffered imprisonment because of his action.

The Bulgars asked that they should have the Bogoroditsa church in which to hold Bulgarian services. This request was in fact perfectly reasonable, since the church was built by Bulgarian craftsmen and financed by Bulgars. The Greeks opposed the idea and appealed to the Metropolitan Paisi, who, however, passed the matter on to the Patriarch, no doubt to avoid having to make the decision himself and run the risk of offending either side. The Patriarch made no reply and the Bulgars, who were not prepared to wait indefinitely, decided to take the bull by the horns. One Sunday in 1859 a pupil from a Bulgarian school rose during a service and began to read the Gospel in Slavonic. For his courage he was nearly beaten to death by the Greeks. On the following Sunday all the Bulgarian guildsmen and gardeners from the outlying districts gathered in force and a fight between the Greeks and Bulgars broke out in the middle of the service, with ikons, candles and candlesticks, etc., used as weapons. The Bulgars were victorious and took possession of the Bogoroditsa church.

In other towns storms arose over Church taxes and reached such proportions that the Patriarch became alarmed and began to allow the consecration of Bulgarian Bishops and gave permission for occasional services to be held in Bulgarian in the Greek churches of the larger towns. In Tŭrnovo the conservative Graecomane *chorbadzhii* managed to secure the reinstatement of Neofit Byzantios as Metropolitan, and although he did try to placate the Bulgars by consecrating some Bulgarian Bishops, he had not really changed and in 1857 public opposition forced the Patriarch to replace him.

Bitter struggles also took place in Macedonia and the people of Kukush, enraged by the Patriarch's refusal to grant them the Bulgar, Parteni Zografsky, as Bishop in place of the hated Greek, Meleti, sought a Uniat with the Church of Rome in 1859. Ilarion Makariopolsky managed to dissuade most of them from leaving the Orthodox

Church and when they had repudiated the Uniat, the Patriarch finally appointed their chosen candidate Parteni to succeed Meleti. Meleti was also opposed by the people of Okhrid who collected nine thousand signatures to a petition opposing his appointment. The great patriot and collector of folk songs, Dimiter Miladinov, was denounced by Meleti, and as a result was imprisoned in Constantinople. In 1862 popular agitation secured an order for the release of both him and his brother who was also in prison for his patriotic activities, but they were found to be dead.

The Bulgars not only opposed the Greek Bishops but also certain Bulgarian Bishops such as Dorotei of Vratsa and Ilarion of Lovech who had been appointed by the Patriarch and who were regarded as renegades and tools of the Phanariots.

Easter Day, 1860

The unsatisfactory conclusion of the Church Council convinced the leaders of the Church movement that resolute action was necessary if any progress was to be made. Moreover, such action must be speedy, since there was a growing danger that those Bulgars who were losing all patience with the Patriarch might seek a Uniat with Rome like the people of Kukush. Accordingly, the Bulgarian Commune of Constantinople held a meeting at which it was decided with the support of the 'Young' Party and certain members of the 'Old' Party, that the Bulgars should publicly declare that they would no longer recognize the Patriarch by omitting his name from the Liturgy. This was first done by Ilarion Makariopolsky in the crowded church of St Stefan on Easter Sunday, 1860. The Sultan, however, was mentioned and, with the intention of winning the support of the Turks and of demonstrating that the Church movement was not subversive, a special hymn of praise to the Sultan was sung at the end of the Liturgy, and this same hymn was sung throughout the following day from the balcony of the church. A petition signed by a thousand Bulgars, asking the Turks to recognize the separation of the Bulgarian Church from the Greek Patriarchate, was presented to the Porte. The Turks were by now quite convinced that the Church movement had its roots in Bulgaria itself and was in no way instigated from outside, but they were anxious to prolong the struggle in order to lessen Russian influence and to divert the Bulgars' national feeling from political and revolutionary activity. They therefore gave certain encouragement to the Bulgars but avoided taking much positive action, in spite of continued Bulgarian representations to the Porte asking that Ilarion be recognized as the head of a separate Bulgarian Church.

Ilarion's action on Easter Day was greeted with enthusiasm throughout Bulgaria. He received many messages of support, and on St Cyril and St Methodius's Day in 1860, the Patriarch's name was omitted from the Liturgy in about thirty Bulgarian towns, while that of Ilarion was included. As a result the struggle became much sharper. More and more Bulgarian communities disowned their Greek Metropolitans and informed the Porte and Ilarion of the fact. Fights occurred in several churches. People were arrested. Three Bishops in Bulgaria itself, Gedeon, Avksenti Veleshki and Paisi of Plovdiv, came out openly in support of Ilarion, and the remarkable thing was that both Gedeon and Paisi were themselves Greeks. Thus by 1860 the Church movement had swelled to a flood and had become nation wide.

The Church Council, 1861

A second Church Council was summoned by the Patriarch in 1861. It was attended by twenty-seven Bishops including four Bulgars, and the Patriarchs of Constantinople, Jerusalem, Alexandria and Antioch. The four Bulgarian Bishops were, however, faithful supporters of the Greek Church. The Council condemned Ilarion and Avksenti, and anathematized all those who associated with them. With tragic irony, the Greek Bishop of Plovdiv, Paisi, who had taken the Bulgarian side, was also included in the condemnation on the insistence of the Graecomane Bulgarian Bishop, Dorotei. The strength of the Bulgarian Church movement had, however, alarmed the Patriarch sufficiently to induce him to make a few token concessions. He agreed that teaching might be conducted in Bulgarian providing the syllabus was approved by himself; that Bulgars or Bulgarian-speaking Greeks might be appointed in purely Bulgarian areas, and that Bulgarian Bishops might be allowed to write letters in Bulgarian. These concessions which might have been well received some years earlier were now totally inadequate to satisfy the growing demands of the Bulgars for a completely independent Church.

The Council's condemnation had little effect on the Bulgars or their leaders. Undismayed, Ilarion took the service as usual on the following Sunday, and afterwards the Bulgars held a mighty demonstration. It was pointed out that the Patriarch had not excommunicated the Bulgarian Church and that the Bulgarian Church had in any case already disowned the Patriarch and would henceforward be known as the Bulgarian People's Christian Church.[1] The Bulgars asked the Porte to recognize this title, but it refused. In Bulgaria itself, many priests anathematized the Patriarch and burnt the letter informing them of the condemnation of the Church leaders. In some cases the Turks arrested and imprisoned some of the priests but they were freed by the people.

The Uniat Movement

After the Crimean War there was an increase in the activity of Protestant and Roman Catholic missionaries from the West who came into the Turkish Empire side by side with the capitalists who were seeking economic concessions from the Porte. These missionaries enjoyed the support of their respective Governments, who saw their activities as a means of combating Russian influence and for this reason also the Turks allowed them freedom. For a time neither Protestants nor Roman Catholics made much progress among the Bulgars, who preferred their Orthodox faith and who in any case wanted an independent Church of their own, but after the defeat of Russia in the Crimean War, and after it had become clear that the Church movement had reached deadlock in its negotiations with the Patriarch and the Turkish Government, some Bulgars began to consider whether or not the best way out might not be to seek a Uniat with Rome[2] and perhaps win an independent Church with French help. This point of view was encouraged by the negative attitude of the Russian Government towards the creation of an independent Bulgarian Church. The leader of the movement for a Uniat was Dragan Tsankov who was born in Svishtov and who in 1859, with French financial assistance, began to publish a newspaper called *Bŭlgaria*, which advocated a Uniat as the only possible solution. This paper even began to attack and slander the leaders of the Church movement including Ilarion himself. The idea of a Uniat gained considerable support in some quarters and the people of Kukush in Macedonia agreed to accept a Catholic Bishop, although they were later dissuaded by Ilarion on condition they got a Bulgarian Bishop. The Patriarch agreed to this but tried to get Ilarion to go himself, in order to get him out of Constantinople where he was proving dangerous to the Patriarch and to subordinate him to the

---

[1] *Bŭlgarska Narodna Khristiyanska Tsŭrkva.*
[2] A Greek Catholic (Uniat) Church had existed since 1596 in Galicia and Rumania.

hated Neofit Byzantios who was now Bishop of Salonika. The Bulgars were not taken in by this manœuvre and suggested that Parteni Zografsky be given the appointment. The Patriarch was obliged to consent to this and Kukush become the first Bulgarian town to have a Bulgarian Bishop.

Catholicism did not make any significant advances in Bulgaria until after 1860 when the Church movement reached a state of impasse in its relations with the Patriarch. In December 1860, encouraged by Britain and France, Dragan Tsankov signed a Uniat with the Pope by which the Bulgarian Church would keep its own customs and liturgy, but would recognize the Pope as its spiritual head. A house was immediately made into a church and, on the advice of the émigré Pole, Czaikowski, the supporters of the Uniat sought French protection. As a Pole, Czaikowski was, of course, interested in substituting French for Russian influence in Bulgaria. The Uniat was roundly condemned at a special meeting called by the Orthodox Christians, and the whole affair caused such a stir in Constantinople that the Porte asked the Patriarch to take steps to find a solution to the religious problem. The result was the Church Council of 1861 described in the previous section, which resolved nothing.

The Uniat movement, on the other hand, began to advance rapidly. The Uniat Commune in Constantinople was recognized by the Turks who were glad of a solution of the Church problem which did not result in increased Russian influence. The Orthodox Commune of Ilarion and his followers had never been recognized by the Turks, in spite of its authority among the Bulgars. The person chosen to be spiritual head of the new Uniat Church was a somewhat simple, eccentric elderly man named Yosif Sokolsky, who had once been a bandit, but who had become a monk and was now the Abbot of the monastery at Gabrovo. Dragan Tsankov, himself educated by the Jesuits, persuaded Sokolsky that a Uniat would be to the advantage of the Bulgarian people. Then the Jesuits had him sent to Rome and on April 2, 1861, the Pope consecrated him Archbishop and appointed him Papal Representative to Bulgaria, with the promise of making him Patriarch when the Catholics in Bulgaria should number more than 500,000. Napoleon III presented the Uniat Church with twenty chalices, ten of gold and ten of silver, and on April 16th Sokolsky arrived back in Constantinople and began to officiate in the Church.

Having decided to give its support to the New Uniat Church, the Porte prepared to arrest the popular Orthodox leaders, Ilarion, Avksenti and Paisi. The people, however, were ready to defend them.

A crowd of several thousand surrounded the church premises where Ilarion and his companions were, and stood there for three days and three nights to prevent their arrest, while the guilds supplied them with food. In response to the Bulgars' requests, the three Bishops were allowed to remain at liberty until Easter to take the Liturgy, but afterwards on April 23rd, troops commanded by three Pashas came to arrest them. As they left by boat for their prison, Tsankov offered them liberty if they too would sign the Act of Uniat, but they scornfully refused. With the Orthodox leaders safely out of the way, the Porte presented Sokolsky with a *berat* recognizing him as head of the Bulgarian Church.

At this point, the Uniat movement appeared to have gained considerable success, but that success was to prove short-lived. Not long after its apparent victory, the movement was deprived of its leadership by skilful manœuvring on the part of its leading opponents. In the summer of 1861, Sokolsky was smuggled out of the country to Russia where he renounced the Uniat and sent a letter back to Bulgaria advising others to do the same. There are various conflicting accounts of how the affair was managed. One account alleged that Petko Slaveikov and Naiden Gerov, assisted by the Russian envoy, lured Sokolsky with a tale of a bogus meeting at which the three imprisoned Bishops would recognize the Uniat and Sokolsky as Patriarch, and then kidnapped the Uniat Bishop together with his documents from the Pope and the Porte, and conveyed him to Odessa. Another version alleges that Slaveikov and Naiden Gerov persuaded Sokolsky to leave Bulgaria voluntarily, but that he went secretly so that the Turks would know nothing about it until it was too late. Yet another version alleges that after his return from Rome he was kept under very strict surveillance by the Jesuits who would not allow him to come into contact with any of the leading Orthodox Bulgars, and that after about five months of virtual house arrest he fled to the house of the Russian Envoy and besought him to save him from the intrigues of the Jesuits.

With Sokolsky safely disposed of, Slaveikov and his friends then persuaded the other leading figures of the Uniat movement to return to Orthodoxy, and eventually Tsankov himself also renounced the Uniat. Thus the Uniat movement came to an abrupt end, but in accounting for its rapid collapse, it must be remembered that many of those who supported it did so not from religious conviction but purely because they saw in it a way of ending the power of the Patriarch over the Bulgarian Church.

The Church Movement, 1861–1866

The Uniat movement, for all its brief existence, did have one important consequence: the Russians who had hitherto opposed the creation of an independent Bulgarian Church because they believed that a united Orthodox Church in the Balkans was the best way of preserving their influence there, now began to realize that they were in danger of losing their influence as far as the Bulgars were concerned, and eventually decided to give their support to the Bulgarian demands. The Russian leaders, however, hoped that Bulgaria's aspirations could be satisfied by agreement with the Patriarch, thus maintaining Orthodox unity, and from 1864 onwards, Count Ignatiev, the new Russian Envoy in Constantinople, worked skilfully to this end.

The failure of the Uniat also convinced the Turks that the Bulgars would accept no solution short of having their own Church. The Porte began to pursue a policy of acting as mediator between the Greeks and Bulgars, but it also attempted to spin out the negotiations for as long as possible, and to this end it made use of both factions in the Bulgarian Church movement—the 'Old' Party who were in favour of seeking agreement with the Patriarchate, and the 'Young' Party who were opposed to any further talks with the Greeks. The 'Old' Party were more active than the 'Young' at the time, being engaged in endless quarrels and discussions with the Patriarch, seeking a compromise solution and getting nowhere.

In 1862 the political situation in Serbia, Bosnia and Herzegovina became somewhat dangerous for the Turks, and, hoping to avoid further disturbances at home, they set up a joint Greek–Bulgarian Commission to consider the Bulgarian demands. The Commission sat for several months, but no decision was reached. During the whole of the period, the Bulgars were in correspondence with Ilarion who sent them his advice from his place of exile in Asia Minor.

In 1863 a third Church Council deposed the Patriarch Joachim and replaced him by a man named Sophronios who promised to find a solution to the Bulgarian problem. Consequently in 1864 a fourth Council was called, composed of thirty-three clerical and other learned persons, including some Bulgars. Gavril Krŭstevich, one of the leaders of the 'Old' Party, attended as a lay representative. The main demands of the Bulgars were that all Bishops of dioceses within Bulgaria should be Bulgars, and that the Synod should consist of an equal number of Greeks and Bulgars. These demands were rejected by the Greeks and the Council ended without achieving any positive results.

In 1864 the Constantinople Church Commune was reorganized and a Provisional Council was set up with instructions to take new steps for securing the recognition of a national Bulgarian Church and the liberation of the imprisoned Bishops. In the same year, the Russians finally crushed all resistance to their rule in the Caucasus and many Circassians fled to Turkish territory including Bulgaria. The Turks forced the Bulgarians to clothe and feed numbers of these refugees, which was tantamount to levying a new tax. The problem of the Circassian refugees and other grievances relating to taxes caused such discontent in Bulgaria that the Porte became alarmed and decided to release Ilarion and Avksenti, who returned in triumph to Constantinople. The Greek Bishop Paisi was not released until 1868, and, unfortunately, Avksenti died in 1865, the year following his release.

In 1866 a fifth Patriarchal Council was called but it rejected the Bulgarian demands as heretical. Meanwhile in Bulgaria itself the Church struggle was going well. In many towns the Greek Bishops were chased out and Bulgarian Church Communes were set up to deal with Church and educational matters. All the Bishops who were Bulgarian by birth with the exception of Ilarion, Avksenti and Parteni of Kukush, proved to be tools of the Greeks and had to be driven out by force like their Greek colleagues. In these struggles, a reactionary role was played by many of the *chorbadzhii* who took the side of the Greeks against their own people.

The Church Struggle, 1866–1870

By 1867 or 1868, as a result of the successful struggles against the Greek Bishops, the power of the Patriarch in Bulgaria itself had *de facto* ceased to operate in most Bulgarian dioceses, but the Church Communes were not recognized by the Turks and from the legal point of view the whole position remained unchanged. The Bulgars still had to win legal recognition for what had been achieved. Up to 1866 both the Porte and the Patriarch had refused Bulgaria's demands while Russia still hoped to settle the problem by an agreement being reached between the Patriarch and the 'Old' Party. Thus a virtual stalemate existed. In 1866, however, external events brought about a change in the situation. In that year the Greek rising broke out on the island of Crete and lasted until 1869. Relations between the Greeks and the Turks deteriorated and Russia took the side of the Greeks. In order to win the support of the Bulgars for a common fight against the Turks the Greek Government advised the Patriarch to be more sympathetic towards them in future, and the Russians offered the same advice. Apart from the Crete rising the Turks were also alarmed by the appearance in Bulgaria of armed detachments of Bulgarian patriots led by such men as Panaiot Khitov and Filip Totyu (1867) and the celebrated Hadzhi Dimiter and Stefan Karadzha[1] (1868). The Turks were terrified lest general insurrection should break out in Bulgaria and promised that the Church question should be settled to the satisfaction of the Bulgars. The Bulgars also hastened to exploit the situation, although the split between the 'Young' and 'Old' Parties widened and quarrels arose as to how the struggle could best be conducted. The 'Old' Party, led by such men as Gavril Krŭstevich encouraged by the Russian Envoy, were still working for a solution by negotiation with the Patriarch. Dr Chomakov, a member of the celebrated Chalŭkov family and a leader of the Turkophil section of the 'Old' Party, tried to encourage the Turks to look favourably on the Bulgarian demands by sending an address to the Sultan, assuring him of the loyalty of his Bulgarian subjects and making certain attacks on the Greeks and on the rebels in Crete. This letter met with the disapproval of some of the Bulgars. At the beginning of 1867 a body known as the Bulgarian Secret Central Committee was formed among the Bulgarian émigrés in Bucharest. This body issued a memorandum saying that if the Sultan wanted to assure himself of Bulgarian support, he should proclaim the political and religious independence of Bulgaria and should take the title of Emperor of the Ottomans and Tsar of the Bulgars. The Turkophils in Constantinople, who never aimed higher than Church independence with Turkish assistance, did not approve of the memorandum and Ilarion and Chomakov sent a statement to the Press to the effect that the writers of the memorandum had no mandate from the Bulgarian people to make any such declaration. Slaveikov, the leader of the 'Young' Party, while constantly stressing the paramount role of the Bulgarian people themselves in solving the Church problem satisfactorily, nevertheless supported Chomakov since he was trying to obtain a swift settlement and complete independence from the Patriarchate.

In 1867 Patriarch Gregory VI, who had recently succeeded

---

[1] The name exists in two forms: 'Karadzha' and 'Karadzhata'. The suffix '-ta' is merely the Bulgarian definite article.

Sofronios, took the initiative and put forward a scheme approved by the Russians, under which twelve Bulgarian dioceses, excluding all those in Macedonia and Thrace, would be granted autonomy and a Metropolitan nominated by the Patriarch. The 'Old' Party accepted this plan as a basis for discussion and a new mixed Greek and Bulgar Commission was set up but failed to reach any agreement, since the Bulgars wanted the whole of Bulgaria to be included in the proposed autonomous territory and the Greeks refused to improve on their original offer. Then in 1868 the Porte took the initiative and asked the Bulgars for a statement of their demands which was supplied by Ilarion, and produced two projects both of which envisaged the creation of an autonomous Bulgarian Church, embracing all territory with a predominantly Bulgarian population, and sent them to the Patriarch with the request that he choose one or other of them.

The Patriarch rejected both of the projects, saying that the Turks had no right to interfere in Church affairs and that a Universal Church Council was necessary. The Russians, who still adhered to the hope that agreement could be achieved between the Greeks and Bulgars, pressed the Turks to set up another joint Commission. The 'Young' Party had set their face against all further negotiations with the Patriarch and any retreat from the terms of the Turkish projects, but the 'Old' Party took part in the Commission. After months of quarrelling, which revolved mainly round the territorial question, the Commission ended its sitting without any agreement being reached.

At this point the Russians once more changed their ground. The Greek nationalists blamed Russia for the failure of the rising in Crete and began to turn towards the West. The Russian Envoy, Ignatiev, then decided to win the full support of the Bulgars by obtaining a speedy solution to the Church problem in a manner satisfactory to them. It was on the insistence of Ignatiev that on February 28 (old style), 1870, the Porte finally issued a *firman* for the creation of an autonomous Bulgarian Exarchate, covering a wider area than that proposed in the Patriarch's plan of 1867, and with the proviso that any diocese which showed a two-thirds majority vote in favour of joining the Exarchate should do so. The purpose of this last clause was to prolong the possibility of disagreements between the Greeks and Bulgars on the principle of 'divide and rule'. As it gradually became increasingly clear that the Bulgars would win an independent Church, Bulgarian Bishops who had formerly taken the side of the Patriarch, seeing which way the wind was blowing, finally turned against the Greeks, and when the *firman* was issued, the last of these Bulgarian churchmen were won over and declared their support for the Exarchate.

The Creation of the Bulgarian Exarchate

The *firman* did not envisage complete independence since the Exarch was to be approved by the Patriarch, but it was accepted with joy by the Bulgars because it meant the recognition of a principle which they had long sought to establish, i.e. their existence as a separate nation. The trouble, however, was by no means over, for the Greeks could not reconcile themselves to the *firman* while among the Bulgars themselves the differences between the 'Old' and 'Young' Parties continued.

A provisional Council was set up to deal with Church affairs until an Exarch could be chosen, and a provisional Synod was constituted, consisting of Ilarion Makariopolsky, Ilarion Lovchansky, Panaret Plovdivsky, Paisi Plovdivsky and Antim Preslavsky. A Statute for the new Church was prepared by a Commission in which the 'Old' Party, led by Gavril Krŭstevich, played the leading role. On the issue of the Statute, the conflict between 'left' and 'right', so to speak, was also evident, with the 'Young' Party pressing for a greater measure of democracy within the new Church. They suggested, for example, that the Exarch should be elected for a period of four years only, instead of for life, and that the Bishops be directly elected by the people, instead of by the indirect system favoured by the Commission, which would have resulted in the domination of Church affairs by the wealthier *chorbadzhiya* elements. Within the Commission itself, however, only Dr Chomakov stood out for a more liberal Statute.

At the beginning of 1871, a Council was called to adopt the Statute, but most of the delegates, although chosen by the people, proved somewhat timid and fought shy of the more democratic ideas of the 'Young' Party. Of their suggestions, the only one accepted was that which provided for a four-year term of office for the Exarch. The amended Statute was duly passed by the Council and was sent to the Patriarch for approval. The Bulgars wished to proceed at once to the election of an Exarch, but the Turks once more adopted delaying tactics and said that they must wait until the Porte had approved the Statute and the delegates were obliged to disperse.

The Patriarch's reaction was to write to the other Orthodox Churches suggesting that a Universal Council be called to discuss the Bulgarian question. The Patriarch had already broached the subject of a Council before the *firman* was issued, hoping to have the Bulgars condemned for splitting the Orthodox Church. The Bulgars easily refuted these charges, pointing out that the Russians and the Syrians and everybody else had separate Churches from the administrative point of view and no one accused them of splitting the Orthodox Church. Moreover, they pointed out that they themselves originally had their own separate Church which was destroyed, not by decision of any Church Council, but by foreign conquest, and therefore it did not require the consent of any Church Council to restore its independence.

At the time the Patriarch had originally suggested holding a Council, the Serbs had declared their support for the Bulgars, while the Russians had felt that a Council would further complicate matters and that the Patriarch should settle the matter himself. The non-Slav Eastern Churches took up an anti-Bulgarian standpoint. When a Universal Council was suggested for the second time, Russia was still opposed to the idea. The Patriarch then resigned and a Bulgarian delegation went to Constantinople to congratulate his successor on his appointment, hoping that this action might create a more friendly atmosphere, but no such friendly atmosphere materialized. Tension between the Patriarch and the Bulgars rose dangerously as the Bulgars became impatient and discontented over the delay in putting the *firman* into operation. Ilarion and Paisi, who had been forbidden to officiate in church for the last eight years, having vainly asked for permission to conduct the Epiphany Service in Constantinople in January 1872, conducted it, notwithstanding, on the insistence of the 'Young' Party, who wished to provoke the Patriarch and bring matters to a head. Of the Bishops who officiated at the service, Panaret and Ilarion Lovchansky were deprived of their rank, and Ilarion Makarianopolsky was excommunicated by the Sixth Patriarchal Council, and all of them were sent to prison in Asia Minor. A vast Bulgarian protest demonstration and a delegation to the Grand Vizir secured their release after six days, and as the Bulgars refused to accept the validity of the excommunication, a seventh Patriarchal Council was called. This Council informed the Bulgars that they must first condemn the Bishops and only then would the Greeks hold conversations with them. At this juncture the Turks seem to have grown tired of the bickering, for the Porte ratified the Statute and told the Bulgars that they might now choose an Exarch. Of the two most eminent Church leaders, Paisi declined nomination since he was in very poor health and in any case did not speak Bulgarian, while Ilarion Makariopolsky was considered by the Porte to be unsuitable for the post. Ilarion Lovchansky was therefore elected but declined to accept the election, and finally on February 18, 1872, Antim of Vidin was chosen to be the first Bulgarian Exarch. Antim was born in the Lozengrad district and had studied in a seminary at Kharkov and at the Moscow Theological Academy and became Metropolitan of Vidin in 1868. He was in Vidin at the time of his election and journeyed to Constantinople in triumph and with much ceremony, and was presented to the Bulgarian Church Council. On April 12th he was received by the Sultan himself, who sent his royal carriages to fetch the new Exarch and other leading Bulgars. The Greeks refused to admit defeat, and the Patriarch would neither see nor recognize him and forbade him to officiate in church, and all Antim's efforts to secure an interview with him failed. The Patriarch summoned a new Council of all the ex-Patriarchs and all the Bishops in the capital and this Council gave Antim three days in which to consider his sins, after which, if he remained unrepentant, all the Patriarchs in the Turkish Empire would be called upon to condemn his uncanonical actions.

The Bulgars were quite unmoved by this threat and on May 24th, the Feast of St Cyril and St Methodius, Antim held a triumphant service, assisted by the excommunicated Bishops, including Ilarion Makariopolsky, and the *Protosingel* Simeon read out a Declaration to the effect that the Bulgarian Church, under the name of an Exarchate, would henceforward be independent but would still be a true member of the one Catholic and Apostolic Church.

A few days later the Patriarch responded by calling another large Church Council which excommunicated those Bishops not yet excommunicated and anathematized those who had already been excommunicated, and declared the Bulgarian Church to be schismatical. This move did not split the Bulgars as had been hoped. They ignored the Greeks and began appointing Bulgarian Metropolitans. At this point the Grand Vizir, who had been a friend of Russia, was replaced by Midhat Pasha, a friend of Britain. The Patriarch called yet another Council, consisting this time of all the Patriarchs, who also declared the Bulgarian Church to be schismatical. The schism had, in fact, very little validity since it was opposed by three of the largest Orthodox Churches who did not take part in the Council. The Russians, as before, opposed the calling of such a Council right from the start. The Patriarch of Jerusalem opposed the schism, and because of this he was removed from his See, which he had occupied for thirty years, was himself declared schismatical and was sent into exile. The Church of Antioch also opposed the schism. The Greeks now attempted to take advantage of the change of Vizir to persuade the Turks to withdraw the *firman*, to recognize that the Bulgarian Church was schismatical and to confiscate the Bulgarian Churches and monasteries and give them to the Greeks so that they might build new ones for themselves. But Midhat Pasha soon fell from power and violent Bulgarian protests prevented the Turks from giving the Greek demands further consideration, and the Porte promised that the *firman* should be put into practice and that Greek Bishops should be prevented from going to Bulgarian dioceses. It also refused to regard the Bulgarian Church as schismatical.

Thus in 1872 the long struggle for the independence of the Bulgarian Church was brought to a victorious conclusion. Ilarion Makariopolsky, who had contributed so much to make this victory possible, died a few years later on June 4, 1875. As far as the Greeks were concerned, the schism remained in force until 1945 when the Patriarch annulled it and recognized the independence of the Bulgarian Church.

After the Victory

The Church movement had achieved the recognition of Bulgaria as a separate nation and had established religious and cultural self-determination. The whole Bulgarian people—*bourgeoisie*, peasants and artisans, with the exception of a few Graecomane *chorbadzhii*—had taken part in the struggle. For the upper *bourgeoisie* the creation of the Exarchate was the end of the road. They envisaged any further national advance to be achieved through education and legal negotiations with the Turks. For them, the fight against the Phanariots had been primarily a fight with the Greeks for markets. Having won this fight, they were reasonably satisfied with their position within the Turkish Empire, and had no desire to go any further, or to proceed with the next logical step—the political liberation of Bulgaria from Turkish rule. The struggle between left and right, between conservative and revolutionary, had already manifested itself in the controversies between the 'Young' and 'Old' Parties and it grew sharper after the establishment of the Exarchate.

Owing to its official position, the Exarchate kept clear of the revolutionary organization. Some of the Bishops were opposed to the revolutionary leaders, and others who were more sympathetic to them were denounced by the Turks as rebels and were overthrown. The Exarch Antim was himself dethroned and imprisoned in 1877. Church affairs gradually passed into the hands of the Turkophil conservative elements, i.e. the *chorbadzhii* and the upper *bourgeoisie*, while the leaders of the 'Young' Party began to doubt whether the Exarchate now played any positive role in Bulgarian national life. As Lyuben Karavelov put it, 'Freedom does not need an Exarch, it needs a Karadzhata'. Karadzhata was the leader of an armed band of patriots who died in battle with the Turks, and thus Karavelov was saying that national liberation would come not through the creation of an independent Church but by revolution. The Bulgarian people came to share his view. The establishment of the Exarchate made no difference to their economic position and in no way lessened the burden of the Turkish yoke. Indeed the *chorbadzhii* used the Exarchate and their leading position in Church affairs to further their own interests. Now that they were free of the diversion of Church problems, the people began to turn to revolutionary activity culminating in the heroic tragedy of the April Rising of 1876 and the final Liberation of Bulgaria in 1878.

CHAPTER VIII

THE MOVEMENT
FOR NATIONAL LIBERATION

Introduction

The previous chapters have dealt with the struggles of those who saw in education the whole salvation of Bulgaria, whose quarrel was primarily with the Greeks and not the Turks, and who saw a national Church and a national priesthood as the highest possible good. For these people the success of the relatively peaceful battle for a Bulgarian Exarchate represented a confirmation of their belief that further reforms and even political freedom itself might, in the same way, be won gradually through peaceful, legal struggle.

The next two chapters will tell the story of those who considered that while the Church struggle had, in its own way, been progressive and beneficial, the Exarchate no longer had any positive role to play. These men considered that, when all was said and done, an independent Church merely meant that one lot of clergy had been replaced by another, while the people continued to suffer the same oppression and slavery. They opposed the evolutionary theory, believed that educational and cultural progress were themselves impossible without freedom, and sought salvation through the revolutionary overthrow of Turkish rule in Bulgaria.

The years of the great struggle for political freedom form one of the most interesting and inspiring periods of all Bulgarian history. Had Rakovsky, Levsky, Kableshkov or Botev been successful, their names would no doubt be as well known to the world as those of Joan of Arc, Simon Bolivar, Garibaldi and the other great Liberators. Yet those who know their story will agree that their greatness is not impaired by the fact that they themselves failed to drive the Turks from their country. Their appeal and their immortality lie in their selfless devotion to the cause of freedom and in the remarkably advanced democratic theories which characterized their thinking.

F*

Though the revolutionary struggle reached its height in the years immediately following the conclusion of the Church struggle, the two threads had previously run side by side for some time, intersecting only occasionally. The desire of the Bulgarian people for independence was as old as Turkish rule itself. Mention has already been made of the early risings against the Turks, and of the *haidut* movement, which, however, had vengeance as its aim, and was therefore not really political in character. It is generally considered that the modern revolutionary national liberation movement began with the Peasant Risings which took place in the western regions of Bulgaria during the thirties and forties of the last century.

Peasant Risings in Western Bulgaria, 1835-1837

For all their mass character, the Peasant Risings of the thirties were spontaneous, eruptions without proper organization or considered aims. They occurred in the west and south-west regions of Bulgaria and their cause was primarily economic: intolerable taxation and all manner of legalized banditry and terror on the part of the local Turks. Even the official Turkish documents had to admit that the risings were occasioned by the malpractices of their own local authorities. Although the agrarian reform of 1834 officially abolished the *spahi* system, little had changed in the more remote western borderland, and indeed they were additionally burdened by new *spahi* from Serbia who had been settled there after Serbia had gained autonomy in 1830. The Bulgarians thus found themselves being forced to pay taxes both to the State according to the 1834 reform and to the *spahi* who ignored the provisions of the reform and expected their former income. This led to extreme discontent among the peasantry who began to refuse to pay taxes to the *spahi* and perform *angaria*, which was, in fact, abolished under the 1834 Reform. The proximity of the western region to Serbia was another factor in rousing the people there to revolt. The fact that Serbia had won autonomy in 1830 greatly impressed and encouraged the Bulgarian peasants near her border, and Prince Miloš of Serbia, in the interests of his own ambitions, encouraged them to revolt, promising them aid. Unfortunately, when it actually came to the point and the Bulgarian rebels were in desperate need of help, Miloš not only failed to send assistance, but even took part in the suppression of the risings and the persecution of fugitives in order to demonstrate to the Turks that he was a loyal vassal of the Sultan.

In 1835 a deputation of peasants from the regions of Niš, Vidin and Pirot went to Constantinople in an attempt to get the Land Reform implemented. They received certain assurances and returned home to advise those whom they represented against any violent action. These assurances proved worthless and in 1835 there occurred the first armed uprising, about which very little is known, except that sixteen villages in the area of Niš were involved. In the summer of 1836 further risings occurred in the areas of Pirot, Belogradchik and Berkovitsa.

Rather more is known about the 1836 risings. While the main cause for grievance was still economic, a political element was also present, for, according to the official Turkish documents, the rebels wished to create an autonomous Republic. In the Berkovitsa region alone, some three to four thousand people took part in the rising, of whom only about 150 had rifles while the remainder were armed only with axes, scythes and cudgels. The Turkish Government was considerably alarmed by the extent of the rising, and tried to pacify the people by appointing new Governors in Pirot and Berkovitsa. Nothing, in fact, changed and there were further risings later the same summer in Pirot, and again in 1837 in the Pirot and Berkovitsa regions. In spite of the peasants' lack of arms, the Turks were obliged to use troops and artillery to crush the rising.

The Niš Rising, 1841

By 1841 the appalling economic situation and the tyranny of the Turkish administration had been further aggravated by the fact that the *Hat-i-Sherif*, which in 1839 announced far-reaching reforms and equality for all subjects of the Sultan, had remained a dead letter, especially in regions more remote from Constantinople. The Bulgarians were fully conscious of their legal rights and were prepared to insist on them. That the peasants did not intend to oppose the Sultan but merely to protest against the malpractices of the local Governors is evident from a petition signed by 1,000 citizens of Niš, which was sent before the rising started to the Serbian Prince, the Russian Consul in Belgrade and the Commandant there, and read:

'Our most high Sovereign—to whom may the All-High accord years without number—filled with fatherly concern for all subjects in his wide domain . . . has proclaimed the *Gyulkhan Hat-i-Sherif* to rejoice Turks and *raya* alike. We greet this most high *Hat-i-Sherif* as our salvation . . . but how is it possible to assist the most good, the most noble will of our magnanimous lord, if those who rule the country in his name, and who should protect the *raya* as a trust placed in their care, instead trample them under foot?'

Delegations from Niš again went to Constantinople and received all manner of worthless assurances from the Vizir. But the robbing and the violence still went on in the villages, and finally the peasants lost all patience. The last straw was laid on the proverbial camel's back on Easter Day when Turks burst into the village church at Kamenitsa while the people were at prayer and committed various outrages. The authorities did not punish those responsible and the enraged peasants held angry meetings and decided on an armed uprising. They chose as their leader Miloé Jovanović, who had been a member of the delegation to Constantinople. The rising began in Kamenitsa on April 6, 1841, and spread throughout the region of Niš and even as far north as Vidin, where the movement was led by Puyo of the village of Boinitsa.

In spite of the mass character of the rising, the rebels were very badly armed and without proper organization, so that the Turkish authorities had no difficulty in crushing it with their artillery and *bashibazouks* (Turkish irregulars). Miloé himself and fifteen comrades held out in a tower near Kamenitsa to the bitter end and died fighting. The rising was put down with ferocious cruelty. More than 240 villages were burnt, countless people were killed, caravans of girls and children were sent to Constantinople to be sold as slaves, and thousands were obliged to flee to Serbia. In Niš itself, thirty-one severed heads were displayed on the bridge, while in Leskovac sixty stakes were erected for impaling victims.

The atrocities came to the notice of the Powers of Europe, and democratic opinion was incensed, creating considerable embarrassment for those Governments whose policy was to bolster up Turkey under all circumstances. Mikhail, the new Prince of Serbia, like his predecessor Miloš, tried to demonstrate his loyalty to the Sultan by refusing sanctuary to Christian fugitives, but he was forced by the Russian representatives in Serbia to change his policy and nearly 10,000 Christians left their homes and crossed into Serbia. Russia was still the only European Power which supported Bulgaria against the Turks, although it must be said that the Russia of Nicholas I, as a member of the Holy Alliance, stood by the *status quo* in Europe and had little sympathy for independent national liberation movements, except in so far as they served Russia's interests by weakening Turkey.

The First Braila Rising, 1841

The peasants of western Bulgaria were not the only people planning to take up arms against the Turks. Encouraged among other things by Turkey's defeat in the war with Egypt in 1839, by the Bulgarian risings and the formation in Athens in 1841 of the Revolutionary Committee to prepare simultaneous risings in Crete and Thessaly, the Bulgarian émigrés in Rumania and Bessarabia also began to prepare for an armed uprising. Their plan was to organize and equip armed detachments (*cheti*) which would cross the Danube into Bulgaria and rouse the people to revolt. The first *cheta* was organized in the summer of 1841. Its headquarters were in Braila and its organizer was a Serbian captain named Vladislav Tatich from Sabac, who maintained close contact with the Russian Vice-Consul at Galati, and collected money, arms and volunteers. Tatich had as his assistant a Bulgar from Kotel named Vasil Hadzhi Vŭlkov. The volunteers included Serbs, Greeks and Rumanians as well as Bulgars, who formed the majority. As to the type of person who volunteered, little is known except that among the thirty-six who were subsequently tried and who probably provided a cross-section of the *cheta*, there were gardeners, shoemakers, furriers, tailors, and bakers' apprentices and journeymen. Merchants are known to have been privy to the conspiracy and to have helped with the obtaining of arms. Relying on the support of the Russian Vice-Consul, Tatich assembled his men quite openly in Braila at the beginning of July 1841, raised the red flag, and, having been joined by more volunteers, set out for the Danube. The Rumanian authorities, however, were preparing to prevent the passage of the volunteers. When the detachment of about 300 men, accompanied by a further 2,000 men, women and children who had come to see them off, reached the Danube, they found that the large boat in which they had intended to cross the river had been rendered unseaworthy. Rumanian troops then arrived and fired on the rebels and the crowd. In spite of their unfavourable position on the river's edge, the Bulgars fought back all night, losing some eighty men killed or drowned. In the morning, Tatich and twenty-nine of his companions surrendered in return for an assurance that he and his men would go free. The Rumanian authorities did not keep their promise. The rebels were arrested, sent to Bucharest and from thence to hard labour in the salt mines.

The tragic fate of Tatich's *cheta* did not deter the Bulgars from trying again. The situation within Turkey was as bad as ever, the

Greek rising in Crete was still in progress, and Serbian agitators continued their work among the people. Thus, soon after the destruction of the first *cheta*, Bulgarian conspirators in Braila began to make plans for a second attempt. The leader of the conspirators was Georgi Sava Rakovsky, who is regarded as the 'father' of the Bulgarian national liberation movement.

Georgi Sava Rakovsky and the Second Braila Rising, 1842

Rakovsky was born in 1821 in Kotel into a remarkably public-spirited and patriotic family of merchants. His paternal uncles had taken part in the defence of the city against the *Kŭrdzhali*, and his maternal uncle was Georgi Mamarchov. Rakovsky was educated first at the local school in Kotel and then at Raino Popovich's Helleno-Bulgarian school in Karlovo. In 1837 his father, Stoiko Popovich, sent him to a Greek school in Constantinople, where he met Ivan Bogorov and Ilarion Makariopolsky, and also Neofit Bozveli, who, it will be remembered, went to Constantinople in 1839 in connection with the struggle against Panaret, the hated Greek Metropolitan of Tŭrnovo. Rakovsky was greatly influenced by Bozveli and, as a result, played a leading and energetic role in the Church struggle and the campaign to build the Bulgarian Church in Constantinople. In 1841 Rakovsky and Ilarion went to Athens and studied both in the gymnasium and the newly opened Greek University. Here they met the Greek revolutionary youth who were preparing for the risings in Crete and Thessaly, and the Bulgars formed the 'Macedonian Society' to organize a rising in Bulgaria to coincide with those in Greece. For this purpose the two friends toured Bulgaria collecting information on Turkish military positions and other valuable data. Before the Bulgars were ready, however, the risings broke out in Crete and Thessaly, and the two had to find a fresh outlet for their patriotic fervour. At this point, rumours of Tatich's preparations reached Rakovsky and he set off for Braila, while Ilarion remained in Tŭrnovo to provide liaison with Bulgaria itself. By the time Rakovsky reached Braila, disaster had overtaken Tatich's ill-fated *cheta*, but he obtained a Greek passport and remained in Braila, teaching Greek, French and Turkish, and making contact with Bulgarian and Greek revolutionaries in exile. Among his principal colleagues were Georgi Dimitrov Kazak, Petŭr Ganev and Stavri Georgi (Captain Stavri), the envoy of the Thessaly–Epirus Revolutionary Society, who had been sent to organize the Greeks of Braila in support of the Crete rising. A joint Greek–Bulgarian secret society was formed, which was financed from Constantinople through Captain Stavri, and received its instructions from Athens. Although the majority of the members of the Society were Greek, Rakovsky emerged as its leader and chief organizer, and its meetings were held in his lodgings. The aim of the conspiracy was to form *cheti*, with volunteers from Moldavia and Bessarabia who would come through Galati to Braila, gathering forces as they came. The rebels would then disarm the local army unit, kill the Colonel in command of the garrison and set fire to the barracks. When the rebels were fully armed they would then cross the frozen Danube into Bulgaria. For some reason, the rebels decided to go ahead with their plan to overcome the garrison at Braila without waiting for the contingent from Moldavia and Bessarabia. Unfortunately the plot was discovered by the police, who attempted to arrest Rakovsky on the very day when a number of rebels were gathered in his lodgings arming themselves prior to putting the plan into operation. The police were driven off and the rebels then attacked the house of Colonel Engel, the Commandant of the garrison. Here they encountered stiff opposition and both Rakovsky and Captain Stavri were wounded. Although Rakovsky escaped and hid for about ten days, he finally gave himself up to save the others. The 'Capitulations' laid down that no foreign national could be punished in the Turkish Empire, including the vassal States of Walachia and Moldavia, and as the majority of the arrested men had Greek papers, the Rumanian authorities decided to hand them over to the Greek Government in Athens. On the way to Greece, Rakovsky managed to escape and fled to Marseilles. From this time onwards, for reasons of security, he discontinued using his baptismal name of Sava, and called himself Georgi, adding Rakovsky as a surname, after the village of Rakovo where his father was born.

The Third Braila Rising

Although the Second Braila Rising had, like the first, been foiled almost before it had begun, plans were laid in 1843 for yet another. This time the leaders were Andrei Deshev, Petŭr Ivanovich, Nikola Filipovsky (Captain Nikola) and Vasil Hadzhi Vŭlkov, who had fled to Russia after the destruction of Tatich's *cheta*, but had returned to Braila in 1843. The rebels had contact with other towns such as Bucharest, Ploesti and Galati, where there were sizeable Bulgarian colonies. The rebels counted on the outbreak of a war between Turkey and Greece, which would both occupy the Turkish Army and cause unrest in Bulgaria, and once again the essence of their plan was to take control of Braila, raid the garrison for arms and cross into Bulgaria. Once again the plot became known to the Rumanian police on the very eve of the day fixed for the rising. Many arrests were made and finally some twenty-two of them were put on trial. Twelve of them, including Vŭlkov, were sentenced to fifteen years' hard labour in the salt mines.

The Rising in North-West Bulgaria, 1850

Notwithstanding the failure of the earlier risings and the appalling slaughter which ensued, it was not long before western Bulgaria was again seething with revolt. The simple fact was that the peasants found it preferable to risk their lives in insurrection than to endure in silence the conditions under which they were forced to live. The main bone of contention was still the ownership of the land. The Bulgarians insisted that under the reforms the *spahi* estates should be given to them, and that henceforward they should pay taxes merely to the State. The local feudal lords insisted that they should keep the land and not only collected the taxes on it but even added new ones and increased the old ones. In spite of having promulgated the Reforms, it is true to say that the Turkish Government was not particularly anxious to enforce the eviction of the *spahi* on the borderland with Serbia, and so the reform remained unfulfilled. Contemporary documents, including petitions from the peasants of various villages to the Tsar of Russia and the Sultan, give a shocking picture of the sufferings of the peasants. Taxes were enormous; every Turkish official from the local *aga* downwards collected taxes and 'gifts'; the peasants were forced to build bridges without pay, though *angaria* had been officially abolished; internal duties on agricultural produce were still demanded, though these, too, had been officially abolished, and indeed no longer existed in some areas; people who had died were included in the taxation registers, and the dead could not even be buried until a kind of death duty had been paid to the Turks. In some areas the peasants killed their animals, rooted up vines and fruit trees and decreased the area of their cultivated land rather than pay the taxes. Nor were taxes, unbearable as they were, the only form of oppression from which the peasants suffered. The Turks indulged without mercy in terror and plunder, and no one's possessions or daughters were safe from them.

While conditions were worst in western Bulgaria and the clash between peasant and lord in consequence sharper, there was discontent and agitational activity in many other districts as well, including the areas of Pirot, Niš, Sofia, Tŭrnovo, Plovdiv and Adrianople. The actual rising of 1850 was, however, confined to the areas of Vidin, Kula, Belogradchik and Lom in the extreme north-west corner of the country. In 1847 risings had occurred in certain villages in the Kula–Vidin area, under Puyo of Boinitsa, one of the leaders of 1841 Niš Rising. Two years later, in 1849, assisted by his son Vŭlko, and Stanko Atanasov Boyadzhi, another veteran of the Niš Rising, Puyo again persuaded several villages to revolt.

At the beginning of 1850 serious preparation began for a large-scale revolt. Tsolo Todorov of the village of Topolovitsa in the Belogradchik district called representatives from villages in the Vidin, Kula, Belogradchik and Lom regions to a meeting at the Rakovitsa monastery. The meeting decided unanimously to prepare for a rising on June 1st, and chose leaders for the various areas. It is interesting to note that the problem of land had become so acute and the violence of the Turks so insufferable that not only the very poor peasants, but also some of the richer ones, such as Todorov himself, were driven to revolt. The rebels planned to take first the weakly defended town of Lom, then Belogradchik, and finally to attack Vidin with all possible forces. Their aim was to force the Turks to abolish all *spahi* rights in the villages, to end the payment of double tithes, to clear all Turks out of the villages and to implement all the provisions of the *Hat-i-Sherif*. The rebels were thus demanding little more than what was already, on paper at any rate, the law of the land.

On the appointed day the revolt began according to plan. The peasants in the region of Lom assembled and marched on Lom itself. At first the Turks were panic-stricken, for the rebel army numbered at least 1,000, possibly 2,000 men, but when they learnt that the Bulgars were virtually without any firearms, they took heart and sent fifty cavalrymen to attack them. The battle lasted several hours, but, though numerically superior, the unarmed peasants were no match for the Turkish soldiers and 250 of them were killed. Some of the survivors then went home, while one group set out for Belogradchik, according to the original plan. Meanwhile the peasants in the Vidin area had also risen. They too were armed chiefly with axes and scythes, and only about one in forty had a rifle, and they too were defeated by a relatively small but well-armed

Turkish detachment, with heavy loss of Bulgarian life. The rapid defeat of the rebels in the Vidin and Lom regions was due not only to the fact that they were so inadequately armed, but also to the treachery of the *chorbadzhii* in communicating this fact to the Turks, who otherwise would probably not have dared to attack so numerous an army without sending for reinforcements.

The biggest concentration of rebels gathered at Belogradchik, where between 10,000 and 12,000 peasants laid siege to the town for ten days, hoping to starve the Turks out, since they lacked equipment to storm the citadel. After the defeat of the rebels at Lom and Vidin, *bashibazouks* came from all over north-west Bulgaria and attacked the besiegers in the rear. The battle lasted until nightfall when the rebels retreated into the mountains under cover of darkness. The Turks did not dare to follow them and casualties were, therefore, less than they might otherwise have been.

The end of the rising was the signal for the massacres. Men, women and children were mercilessly slaughtered by the *bashibazouks*, and Bulgarian houses were stripped bare. In Belogradchik itself only two Bulgarians escaped the carnage, for the interesting reason that they were sheltered by a Turk. In all some 2,000–3,000 civilians were murdered, and of the 15,000 peasants who took part in the rising, 700 were killed for the loss of only 15 Turks.

The situation continued to be very tense and the rebels who had fled to the mountains at first refused to come down, insisting on their original demands. Ali-Riza Pasha, who had been sent by the Turkish Government to put down the rising and to enquire into its causes, finally persuaded them to do so, promising that they would not be harried and that they might send a delegation to Constantinople to place the people's grievances before the Porte. The Turkish Government was very anxious to settle the matter not only because the unrest had reached such proportions, but also because it feared Russian intervention because of the atrocities, at a time when the Western Powers of Europe were considerably shaken by the revolutions of 1848–1849 and were not in a position to be of much assistance to Turkey. The fact that the peasant leaders were able to send memoranda written in French to the Russian Tsar and the European Envoys in Constantinople further convinced the Porte that outside influences were at work. The State Council decided to end the *spahi* system with compensation to the lords, and it even agreed to pay pensions to the families of those who had died.

The friction did not end there because the delegation was under the impression that the Sultan was making a gift of the *spahi* estates to the peasants and toured the villages telling everybody this, while the Turkish lords maintained that the peasants had to buy the land. This difference of opinion gave rise to fresh friction between the Bulgarian peasants and the Turks, but in the end the Porte upheld the landlords and the peasants were forced to make payment for the land. Because of these payments the economic lot of the peasants did not improve in the way they had hoped once the *spahi* system was ended. Furthermore, the end of the great estates led to greater economic differentiation among the Bulgars themselves since those who were richer were able to buy up more land than their poorer brethren.

While the actual armed risings were confined to north-west Bulgaria, elsewhere in the country, as already stated, there was much discontent and protests of a non-violent character. An example of this was the strike of the grape growers in the Tŭrnovo area in 1851. When the Turks doubled the land tax paid by the grape growers and introduced a duty on grapes, the peasants refused to pick the grapes until the new taxes were withdrawn. The authorities had to give in, but as soon as the grapes were picked, they went back on their word, arrested the peasants' leader, Tsonzarov, with several other people, and sent them to Constantinople charged with inciting the people to refuse to pay taxes. The villainy of the authorities at Tŭrnovo was, however, apparent even to the court at Constantinople, and the men were released.

Bulgaria and the Crimean War

Sufficient material is available in English on the Crimean War to render a detailed account of it unnecessary in the present volume. All that need concern us here is that in 1853 Russia, intent on destroying Turkey, presented the latter with an ultimatum on the guardianship of the 'Holy Places' in Palestine, threatening war should the ultimatum be rejected. Russia had, unfortunately, underestimated the probable extent of Western opposition to her proposals. Since the signing of their highly advantageous 1838 trade agreements with Turkey, Britain and France were even more averse than before to any increase of Russian influence in Turkey. Thus, when Russia declared war on Turkey following the rejection of her ultimatum, she soon found herself fighting Britain and France as well as Turkey. Thirty thousand French and twenty thousand English soldiers were landed at Varna, which became a base for the Western Allies.

Owing to the great distance which separated the Allied Armies from their homelands, they were obliged to obtain all their supplies locally. The sudden large-scale demand had a favourable effect on Bulgarian agriculture and handicrafts, and some Bulgarian traders made considerable fortunes through supplying goods to the Allied Armies. In spite of this positive aspect, conditions in general deteriorated as a result of the war. The Christian population suffered greatly from the heightened religious fanaticism of the Moslems, which expressed itself in murder and violence on a scale which shocked even Turkey's allies. The Bulgarians had to perform *angaria* building fortifications; taxation increased and the money they received from the Allies in payment for their agricultural produce was often taken from them forcibly by the Turks.

The Crimean War, like all other Russo-Turkish wars, filled the Bulgarians with hope that the hour of liberation was at hand. There was much activity among the émigrés in South Russia and also among those in Walachia and Moldavia which were occupied by Russian troops. Petitions and memoranda were sent to the Tsar calling his attention to the heavy lot of the Bulgarians and begging for protection and liberation even before the actual outbreak of war. One such petition from the Bulgarian colony in Constantinople was presented to the special Russian Envoy, Prince Menshikov, who brought the Tsar's ultimatum to the Sultan. Rakovsky was among those who took an active part in the preparation of this petition.

The Russians regarded the activities of the Bulgars with favour and encouraged them. At the beginning of 1854 an organization called the *Epitropia* was formed in Bucharest by a group of rich merchants with Russian blessing. This organization was shortly dissolved and was replaced by a new committee known as the Bulgarian Central Trusteeship,[1] which was in close contact with the Russian High Command and which had as its aim the collection of volunteers and the representation of Bulgaria's interests before the Russians. Similar committees were set up by merchants in Odessa, Braila, Galati, etc.

In Bulgaria itself efforts were being made by Rakovsky and his friends to organize a rising in preparation for what seemed then to be the inevitable coming of the Russian Army. Since the failure of the Braila Rising, Rakovsky had spent eighteen months in Marseilles and then had returned home to Kotel where he and his father

[1] *Bŭlgarsko sredotochno popechitelstvo.*

became involved in conflict between the craftsmen and the local *chorbadzhii*, who were misappropriating public funds. Rakovsky and his father were denounced by the *chorbadzhii* and were sentenced to seven years' imprisonment. They were, however, freed after three and a half years when Rakovsky's mother paid a ransom for them. Rakovsky's father emerged from prison a ruined man, and Rakovsky himself took up law and commerce in Constantinople where he took part in the Church struggle.

After the Crimean War broke out, Rakovsky and his confederates formed a secret society which was in contact with the Russian Command and whose members aimed to enter Turkish service to do what they could to protect the populace, to collect information and to prepare for the entry of the Russians. Rakovsky himself obtained a post as interpreter in Shumen and subsequently visited many towns, although few details are known of this period of his life. The secret society's plan was discovered and betrayed by traitors, including the Metropolitan of Varna. Rakovsky was arrested but escaped and collected a well-armed band of young men who went into the Stara Planina near Preslav, where they roamed about like *haiduts*, hoping to make contact with the Russians and carrying on agitation in villages and monasteries. When the Russians withdrew from the Danube and it became clear that they would not in fact enter Bulgaria, Rakovsky disbanded his men, returned to Kotel and finally crossed into Rumania in 1855.

Preparations for a rising continued in other areas of Bulgaria. In Tŭrnovo there was a conspiracy led by Nikola Filipovsky (Captain Nikola), a tailor specializing in modern European clothes, who had taken part in the Braila Risings and in the revolutionary movement in Bucharest during 1848. Among his co-conspirators was P. R. Slaveikov, who was then teaching in Tryavna. The conspirators, who had links with émigré merchants in Odessa and Bucharest, were drawn from Tŭrnovo and the neighbouring towns and villages, especially Lyaskovets, which sent between one and two hundred armed rebels. They hoped to capture the Turkish barracks in Tŭrnovo, but the Turks were forewarned and strengthened the garrison and the rising failed.

There was also a conspiracy in Vidin. Letters signed by the peasants in the area were sent to the Russian consuls in Belgrade and Vienna, declaring their readiness to take part in the war and their earnest desire that the Russians should liberate them, but the preparations never progressed as far as an actual rising.

The Treaty of Paris, 1856

After the fall of Sevastopol, Russia was obliged to ask for peace, and in March 1856 the Treaty of Paris was signed. Russia lost her control over the left bank of the Danube by the Delta and part of Bessarabia and was obliged to destroy her military installations on the Black Sea. The Treaty also contained provisions to open wide the doors of the Turkish Empire to Western European capital and manufactured goods. Clause nine of the Treaty consisted of the reforms known as the *Hat-i-Humayun* which had been proclaimed by the Porte on British advice even before the signing of the Treaty. The reforms were largely a reiteration and amplification of the *Hat-i-Sherif* and were supposed to safeguard the rights of the Christian population with the understood aim of bolstering up the Turkish Empire and of depriving Russia of cause for intervention. Like the *Hat-i-Sherif*, the *Hat-i-Humayun* remained a more or less dead letter and as before, Western hopes that the proclamation of reforms would quieten the Bulgars were proved vain. While it is true that in the disappointment which followed Russia's defeat the revolutionary movement on the whole temporarily subsided, nevertheless the proclamation of the reforms encouraged the Bulgars to demand the fulfilment of their legal rights. For example, the passages relating to religious freedom were used by the Bulgars as legal support for their demands in the Church struggle.

When the Tax Reforms and the cessation of acts of violence against the Christian population promised by the *Hat-i-Humayun* failed to materialize, there was much discontent among the Bulgars. In Vidin a new conspiracy developed in 1856. The rebellion is known as *Dimitrakieva Buna* after one of its leaders, Dimiter (or Dimitraki) Petrovich from Silistra, and its course reflects the disaffection of the *chorbadzhii* and merchant elements from the national liberation movement which took place after the Crimean War. These elements had counted almost exclusively on Russian help, and the changed political situation resulting from Russia's defeat sapped their enthusiasm for revolt. The Vidin rebellion was betrayed by one of the conspirators, a merchant named Khristo Todorov, and when the rebels gathered at the *rendezvous* near the village of Vlaovich, they were ambushed by Turkish troops and defeated. Dimiter himself with a small band of survivors escaped and roamed about in the mountains, until they realized that the situation was hopeless and crossed into Serbia.

A new conspiracy in Tŭrnovo led by 'Captain' Nikola was similarly betrayed by disaffected merchants, who warned the Turks of the proposed rising. On the appointed day only thirteen persons turned up at the rendezvous in the monastery at Lyaskovets, but 'Captain' Nikola pressed on to Gabrovo where they were engaged by the Turks. Nikola retreated towards Tryavna, but on the way he was betrayed and killed.

Economic Changes after the Crimean War

The Allied victory in the Crimean War greatly increased the influence of the Western Powers over Turkey. The war, which was started allegedly to preserve Turkey's independence, certainly resulted in Turkey becoming for the time being less subject to Russian influence, but at the same time it thrust her into semi-colonial dependence on the West. The process had begun much earlier with the 1838 Trade Agreements, but the influx of foreign capital and goods was enormously accelerated as the result of the war. Alongside the merchants with their manufactured goods came the capitalist speculators seeking to open up the country, to prospect for minerals, establish banks and insurance companies and so on. Efforts were made to improve communications. Even during the war the Western Powers had forced the Porte to install telegraph lines linking Constantinople with Belgrade and thus with Vienna, London and Paris. In 1850 the Turks had begun to build a harbour at Varna, at an estimated cost of 54,000 grosh. After the war in 1861 foreign engineers took charge of the project and enlarged it considerably to include a big quay and a canal to Lake Devna. Turkey was obliged to provide 2,750,000 grosh instead of the original 54,000, together with material from the State Arsenal and 1,000 convict labourers. A foreign company dredged the shallow Maritsa so that in 1859 small boats began to ply between Enos, Adrianople and Plovdiv. After the Crimean War a considerable amount of railway building was undertaken by foreign companies, mainly British. In 1861 the first railway line in European Turkey from Cherna Voda to Constanţa (Kustendzha) was opened and the Varna–Rusé line followed in 1866. The work was undertaken with the dual purpose of opening up the country and of securing a profitable investment. Just how attractive an investment the railways were, can be seen from the fact that the companies insured themselves against all possible risk by forcing the Turks to sign a contract under which the Turks undertook to pay the companies a large sum for every kilometre of track and to indemnify them against possible loss when operating.

It is interesting to note that of the 45,000 shares issued for the Varna–Rusé 36,000 were sold in England and only 9,000 were put up for sale in Turkey. One foreign company which undertook to build a railway from Constantinople to Bosnia made an agreement with the Porte, with the Hungarian Count Zichy acting as intermediary, by which they were given the right to exploit the country's timber, metal and coal reserves for ninety-nine years, conditions which even the Porte eventually recognized as pure banditry and the agreement was torn up in 1872. The two railway companies founded by Baron Hirsch, one for the building of railways and one for running and exploiting them, included the directors of English and Austrian banks, representatives of Dutch and French railway companies, the director of the Paris 'Société Générale' and so on.

The Bulgars themselves derived no immediate benefit from the railways, because not only was the population living beside the line obliged to pay additional taxes, but the tariffs were so high that they virtually prohibited the people from making use of the railway.

Apart from communications, foreign companies entered many other fields of economy. British agencies for life and fire insurance were established in Constantinople and a British company undertook to supply the city with drinking water. Taking advantage of the cheapness of labour and materials, British industrialists had carpets manufactured in the Turkish Empire for export to Britain and America, and the cotton manufacturers did everything they could to encourage the growing of cheap cotton.

Bulgarian agriculture enjoyed a boom during and immediately after the war, because Europe needed grain. Attempts were made to introduce modern machinery, and training courses for technicians were started, but little headway was made owing to the cheapness of labour and the continued existence of *angaria*, and agricultural technique in Bulgaria remained on a much lower level than in the other wheat-growing countries, including Russia and Rumania. Bulgarian wheat was able to compete on the world market only because it was virtually stolen from the producers, who fell more and more into debt. Interest on debts sometimes amounted to as much as 50–60 per cent per annum, and interfered with the peasants' ability to pay taxes to such an extent that the Turks began to open agricultural banks to give cheap credit. Unfortunately, like all Turkish institutions, they rapidly became riddled with corruption, and in any case, those who had most need of loans were unable to obtain them through lack of security.

The Turkish Empire itself fell increasingly into debt after the Crimean War. Even before the war it had no regular budget, and the war left it in a very unsound financial state, fully justifying its nickname of the 'Sick Man of Europe'. Since the beginning of the war, the value of Turkish currency had been steadily falling until after 1856 it was worth only about half of its former value in London. The Turkish Government was obliged to increase taxation and to enter a vicious spiral of obtaining new foreign loans to pay the interest on previous foreign loans. By 1875 Turkey was utterly bankrupt and virtually ceased paying any interest at all. The situation had been aggravated by the fact that during the war, the Turkish Government forbade the export of grain, which was kept at home to supply the Turkish and Allied forces, thus adversely affecting the balance of trade, and also by the fact that the Government printed paper money far in excess of its gold reserves. It must be noted in passing that the devaluation of the Turkish currency was encouraged by foreign capitalists and speculators since it increased the profitability of their investments. The cost of living rose considerably during the war, especially in the towns. The price of meat in Constantinople, for example, was six times higher in 1856 than what it had been before the war. The rising taxes weighed most heavily on those who could least afford them, for the rich *chorbadzhii* who were entrusted with the collection of taxes dealt more lightly with their own friends and relations. The taxation, of course, did not return to the people indirectly in public amenities. The bulk of the money collected in taxation went to Constantinople and the part which remained in the district of collection either went into the pockets of those connected with taxation, or was merely spent on the upkeep of the local administration and army. Feudal rent in the form of *angaria* continued although it had been officially abolished, and the population was conscripted for unpaid labour on railway construction, etc. They were obliged to feed and to build houses, barns and wells for Tartar and Circassian refugees from the Caucasus, more than a million of whom had arrived by 1865. Payment for the work was promised but never materialized, and, to add insult to injury, bands of these Circassian 'guests', who were unaccustomed to peaceful work, took to banditry and later played a savage part in the suppression of the April Rising of 1876.

Economic developments after the Crimean War had two main effects on the Bulgarian population. A certain section of the merchant class became very wealthy through acting as agents for the foreign companies, while the peasants were crippled with debts and the craftsmen engaged in the once flourishing handicraft industries were driven out of business and ruined by foreign factory-made imports. At this time Bulgaria had virtually no factory industry to absorb the ruined peasants and proletarianized craftsmen, and many sought to escape from Turks, Circassians and misery by emigrating. This solution was strongly opposed by Rakovsky, who saw in it a great danger to the future of the nation.

Classes and Parties after the Crimean War

The economic consequences of the Crimean War had the effect of intensifying the process of class differentiation within Bulgarian society. This had a profound effect on the political life of the country in general and on the national liberation movement in particular, for, by and large, adherence to one or other of the various political groupings was not a matter of arbitrary caprice, but was directly related to the social position of the persons concerned and their interest, or otherwise, in the continuance of Turkish rule. Thus at one end of the scale one finds the wealthy *chorbadzhii* who traded throughout the Turkish Empire, piling up fortunes through commerce and corruption, and whose interests coincided with those of the Turks to the extent that they not only desired the continuance of the *status quo*, but were also prepared to betray those of their own countrymen who sought a change, and at the other end of the scale one finds the ruined craftsmen and peasants who had literally 'nothing to lose but their chains' and who therefore preferred to die in insurrection than go on living under conditions which had become totally intolerable. Between these two extremes there were a whole variety of points of view which can, however, all be traced back to the economic interests of the people concerned.

Between the Crimean War and the Liberation, the rural population, apart from the relatively few rich village *chorbadzhii*, who often owned inns as well as land, and engaged in trade and usury, was subdivided into three groups: a continually growing group of small independent peasants, the landless proletarianized peasants who worked on the *chifliks* or on the land of richer peasants, and the dependent peasants who worked someone else's land and paid rent, generally consisting of half the harvest. One of the chief features of the period after the Crimean War was the decay of the *chiflik* system. This was due partly to foreign competition and partly to the contradictions inherent in the *chifliks* which were largely feudal in form, while they produced capitalist-fashion for the market and began to employ more and more hired labour. The owners of the *chifliks* began selling portions of their estates, and these were bought largely by Bulgarians, so that gradually the bulk of the agricultural land passed into the hands of Bulgarian small-holders, a large and ever-increasing section of the population. The position of the peasantry was very difficult. Stripped by taxation and oppressed by usurers, they were often obliged to sell their harvest in advance for a very low price. The peasantry, therefore, had nothing to lose and everything to gain from the ending of Turkish rule, and proved ready to make common cause with the ruined craftsmen in order to cast off their chains.

At this time no separate industrial working class existed in Bulgaria. It is true that there was a small but growing proletarian element in the towns, and, indeed, in the villages, but it was as yet insufficiently developed to constitute a real social force. The Bulgarian *bourgeoisie* was divided into three sections: the big merchant *chorbadzhii*, who were relatively few in number and who had part of their capital in trade, part in usury, and part in the newly developing factory industry, although this was a less important element than trade and usury (misappropriation of public funds, plain robbery, etc., also played an important, though unofficial, part in the enrichment of the *chorbadzhii*); the middle *bourgeoisie*, a fairly numerous but decaying class, consisting of fairly wealthy craftsmen and medium merchants; and the ruined petty *bourgeois* craftsmen, a rapidly growing class, to which for practical purposes may be added the impoverished intelligentsia, who were mainly teachers.

During the thirties and forties of the nineteenth century, the petty *bourgeoisie* had enjoyed a fairly comfortable material position, and the question of national liberation had not seemed a very pressing problem. They concerned themselves mainly with cultural and educational matters, and indeed the cultural struggle was in its time a most necessary and progressive movement. After the Crimean War, when Western competition began to bring ruin to the petty *bourgeois* producers, they turned to revolution as the only way out of their difficulties, and those who stuck to education as the main task now played a very different role from their predecessors in the 'thirties and 'forties. Now, instead of mobilizing the nation, the educationalists diverted people from the task of driving out the Turks by postulating that Bulgaria's salvation lay in evolution through education, not revolution. The educationalists considered that if Bulgaria was to be liberated it must be liberated from outside, presumably by Russia, and while they conceded the usefulness of a rising within the country to support help from outside, they shrank from full-scale revolution as being risky in the event of failure and potentially dangerous in the event of success.

The *bourgeoisie* with its different strata was much divided on the subject of liberation. We have already encountered the groupings known as the 'Old' and 'Young' Parties in the Church struggle. The 'Old' Party, whose adherents were the upper *bourgeoisie*, held views comparable to those of the Conservative *bourgeoisie* throughout Europe, and their view of the future independent Bulgaria never went beyond a vision of a constitutional monarchy. The very richest sections were satisfied with things as they were. The Turkophil section hoped for advance through Church autonomy, to be initiated by the Turks. The Russophils, mainly émigrés in Russia and Rumania, followed Russian foreign policy religiously, and hoped for autonomy through Russian diplomatic intervention. All of these groupings were opposed to the revolutionary movement, not only because they were reasonably comfortable under Turkish rule, but also because they feared what can only be described as the growing Socialist element in the revolutionary movement which threatened their position of wealth and privilege.

The 'Young' Party also had several groupings within it. It took part vigorously in the Church struggle, but in the struggle for national liberation two main tendencies became visible: a moderate, liberal, often opportunist wing, consisting of the middle *bourgeoisie* and those on the way up, and a revolutionary democratic wing, consisting of the ruined petty *bourgeoisie*, the corresponding section of the peasantry and the intelligentsia, who aimed at establishing a Democratic Republic through revolution.

Rakovsky—The 'Patriarch' of the Bulgarian Revolution

After the Crimean War the movement for national liberation developed into an organized revolutionary movement with its own ideology, and the man who did more than anyone else to foster this development was Rakovsky. Rakovsky led the national movement out of the era of spontaneous peasant risings to organized struggle and set before the *haidut* bands the perspective of national liberation in place of private vengeance. Rakovsky greatly admired the *haiduti* —indeed, as we have seen, he was a *haidut* himself for a time—and he idealized them in a poem called *The Forest Traveller* (*Gorski*

Pŭtnik). But eventually he became convinced that the liberation of the country would be accomplished not by the *haiduti* in their present form, but by *cheti* (armed detachments, sing. *cheta*) organized from a centre outside the country and sent in to rouse the people to revolt. The organization of *cheti* became the core of Rakovsky's teaching. Although he realized that internal revolt on the part of the ordinary population was also essential and came to admit the need for Committees in the bigger towns, though purely for agitational work, preparing for the coming of the *cheti*, not for revolutionary organization, he never fully grasped the necessity for revolutionary organization within Bulgaria itself (this was to be the contribution of his disciple and successor, Vasil Levsky), but believed that the people would rise on the arrival of a well-organized, properly trained *cheta*. In the light of this view, he drew up a *Plan for the Liberation of Bulgaria* in 1861, and a Law for the *cheti* in 1867. The *Plan* envisaged the organization in Serbia of a *cheta* of a thousand picked and seasoned men, of which one hundred were to be cavalry, with two cannon and two surgeons. Once in Bulgaria it would be joined by volunteers in sufficient numbers to increase its strength to 150,000 by the time it had reached and taken Tŭrnovo, and to 500,000 by the time it reached the Black Sea. His Law for the *cheti* strongly reflects the romanticism of the *haidut* ideal, as well as his belief in the need for good organization and strict discipline. On joining the *cheta* its members were to swear to eschew drunkenness, lying, stealing from one's comrades and fornication; always to obey the *voivoda* and standard-bearer, to refrain from causing disunity in the group through slanders, quarrels, etc., and to be content with whatever pay the *voivoda* thought fit to give. Death was to be the penalty for any transgression of this law, on the discretion of the *voivoda* and the standard-bearer who was second in command.

Rakovsky's social and economic views were not so well defined as those of his successors, such as Levsky or Botev, who was in fact a Utopian Socialist. But at that time social divisions also were not yet so well defined as they subsequently became. In the towns the population was divided simply into the *chorbadzhii* and the 'people', who embraced the traders and richer craftsmen as well as the poorer artisans, and thus included people who were primarily concerned with education and Church problems as well as those who pinned their faith in revolution. Rakovsky regarded the *chorbadzhii* as the enemies of the people (he had suffered imprisonment for his part in the struggle against them in his native Kotel), and regarded everyone

else as being on the side of the 'people'. He himself reflected the
as yet unseparated strands of education (i.e. evolution), and revolution, in that he took part in the Church struggle and devoted a large
proportion of his time to literary and journalistic activities, as well as
organizing *cheti*. He was himself of the middle *bourgeoisie* by origin,
being born into a trading-industrial family, but he, in fact, espoused
politically the cause of the peasantry and petty *bourgeoisie*. In essence
he was instinctively on the side of all that was progressive. He
wanted to further the economic development of Bulgaria, and
advocated the setting up of joint stock companies for this purpose,
but with Bulgarian shareholders only. Rakovsky loved his country
passionately. His love embraced the people, their native language,
the countryside—everything that concerned Bulgaria. He was the
very embodiment of the Bulgarian Renaissance, interested in everything from schools, newspapers and agricultural machinery to Church
autonomy and revolution that would help his people to throw off the
mediaeval fetters which held them back. He was interested in folklore and philology and, like Paisi, he saw how a knowledge of history
could awake national consciousness and he himself undertook
historical research. Like Paisi, he often idealized Bulgaria's past, but
though his conclusions were sometimes unintentionally a trifle
unscholarly, they were always deeply patriotic. For Rakovsky, to
love one's people and one's land was the highest virtue and to serve
them the supreme happiness.

The First Bulgarian Legion

After the disbanding of his *haidut* unit in 1855, Rakovsky went
first to Rumania and then to Novi Sad in the Austrian Empire and
entered on a period of literary activity. He attempted unsuccessfully
to arrange for the publication of his poem *The Forest Traveller* and
started a newspaper, *Bŭlgarska Dnevnitsa (Bulgarian Journal)*, with
the co-operation of the Serbian publicist Danilo Medakovich. The
paper was directed mainly against the Greek clergy, the Turkish
representatives in Belgrade and the *chorbadzhii*, and not against the
Turkish Government as such. Even this moderate stand annoyed
the Turks, and they persuaded the Austrian authorities to expel
him from the Austrian Empire at the end of 1857. Rakovsky went
first to Rumania, but even there he had trouble with the authorities
and moved to Odessa, where he stayed until 1860, occupying himself
with writing on a whole series of subjects, including ethnography and
philology. He had intended remaining in Odessa but the Holy Synod

of Russia insisted on censoring everything written about the Bulgarian Church question, and he decided to move to Belgrade in 1860.

There he managed to arrange the publication of *The Forest Traveller* and began publishing a new paper *Dunavski Lebed* (*Danube Swan*). This time he confined himself to the Church question and the Turks raised no objection to the paper, and allowed it to circulate throughout the Empire. In spite of great financial difficulties, the paper lasted for more than a year. In 1861, however, Rakovsky abandoned the pen for the sword. At that time, the Serbian Prince Mikhail was preparing to free his princedom from dependency on the Turks who maintained garrisons in the larger towns to enforce their overlordship. Relations between Serbia and Turkey became more and more strained, and war seemed inevitable. Rakovsky fully appreciated the advantages to be gained from organizing a rebellion in Bulgaria to coincide with Turkey's imbroglio with Serbia. He had come to the conclusion that the Great Powers of Europe were motivated entirely by selfish and predatory motives and that the small Balkan countries should get together to defend their own common interests. It was at this time that he produced his *Plan for the Liberation of Bulgaria*. Apart from its military provisions, it envisaged the setting up of a Bulgarian Government to direct operations and to maintain close relations with the Serbian Government. The Provisional Government was, in fact, set up in Belgrade in June 1862 under the chairmanship of Rakovsky. In the meantime Rakovsky had begun the organization of a Bulgarian Legion with the consent of the Serbian Government which intended to make good use of the Bulgarians for its own ends. Rakovsky's paper switched its attack from the Greek clergy to the Turks, and some six hundred volunteers answered his call, including many names which were later to become famous, such as Vasil Levsky and Stefan Karadzha. Large sums of money were sent by émigrés in Braila and Vienna, and Dr Vukovich from Paris offered his services if summoned. The training and maintenance of the Legion was undertaken by Serbia. Thus the Legion was the first Bulgarian detachment to be properly organized and trained on a military basis. At the same time as the volunteers were gathering in Belgrade, Rakovsky sent agitators into Bulgaria itself to prepare the people for the rising, and Committees were formed in the larger towns. Rakovsky not only ensured that his legionnaires were trained militarily and politically, but also that they had uniforms befitting their status. These dashing, if somewhat impractical, huzzar-style uniforms were made of white *shaek*, decorated with rows of green braid, and had green collars and cuffs, and white trousers. A fur cap decorated with the lion emblem of Bulgaria completed the uniform.

Meanwhile, clashes between Turks and Serbians in Belgrade became increasingly frequent, and after a particularly violent one at the beginning of June 1862, the Turks shut themselves up in the citadel and began shelling the city. In retaliation, the Serbs laid siege to the citadel and the Bulgarian legionnaires joined in the fighting with great valour. Expecting war to break out at any moment between Turkey and Serbia, Rakovsky wrote a fiery proclamation to the Bulgarian people, ending:

'Let no one imagine that freedom can be won without blood and costly sacrifice! Let no one wait for some one else to free him. Our freedom depends on us! Let each one inscribe deep in his heart as a holy thing the thrilling words—"freedom or death", and with a flaming sword let him march to the field of battle, under the banner of the invincible Bulgarian lion.'

But the expected war did not materialize. The dispute between Turkey and Serbia was settled diplomatically with the assistance of the Great Powers at a Conference in Constantinople. The presence of the Bulgarian Legion now became an embarrassment to the Serbian Government, and, on British insistence, it asked that the Legion be disbanded and expelled from Belgrade. This incident showed up one of the weaknesses of Rakovsky's theories, i.e. the difficulties inherent in organizing revolution from an outside centre where one was dependent on the whims and diplomacy of a foreign Government.

While the Legion was being organized in Belgrade, preparations for a rising were being made in Tŭrnovo. Early in 1862, the citizens of Tŭrnovo and Gabrovo had heard that the Legion was being formed in Belgrade and sent two representatives to learn more about it. When the representatives came back, they were accompanied by Hadzhi Stavri, a former captain in a Bulgarian volunteer unit during the Crimean War, who had been sent by Rakovsky to lead the rising in the Tŭrnovo area. When the bombardment of Belgrade began, the younger rebels and Hadzhi Stavri decided to rise, in spite of the counsel of those richer traders who had taken part in the conspiracy and who advised waiting until the Serbian Army had actually crossed the frontier. About seventy men joined Hadzhi Stavri in the mountains, hoping to unite with bands from other towns, but prompt

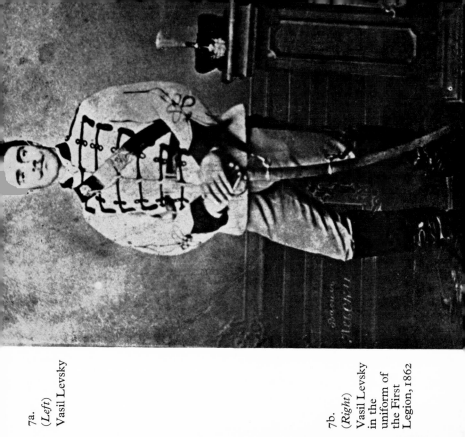

7a.
(*Left*)
Vasil Levsky

7b.
(*Right*)
Vasil Levsky
in the
uniform of
the First
Legion, 1862

8a.
(*Left*)
Georgi
Benkovsky

action by the Turks, together with the rumour of an agreement between Serbia and Turkey, prevented any spread of the rebellion and the detachment was therefore disbanded. Many of those involved were arrested and sent to prison in Diarbekir, a dreaded place of exile in the wilds of Asia Minor. Hadzhi Stavri himself managed to escape to Rumania. At the same time, a *cheta* under Panaiot Khitov, with Hadzhi Dimiter as his standard-bearer, was roaming the mountains between Sliven and Tŭrnovo, with instructions from Rakovsky to prepare the people for the forthcoming rising. Hadzhi Stavri had attempted to make contact with him on his arrival from Belgrade, but had failed. After the Serbs had come to the agreement with the Turks, Khitov eventually came down from the mountains and crossed into Serbia, with part of his *cheta*.

Rakovsky and Balkan Union

Rakovsky remained convinced that the small Balkan nations must form a Union in order to achieve their independence, and after the end of the Bulgarian Legion, he went to Athens in 1863 with the agreement of the Serbian Government, to try to convince the Greeks that Balkan Union was necessary, although he was not very hopeful of success, since he feared that the Phanariot Greeks and the influence of Britain would motivate against any union between the Greeks and the South Slavs. Having seen various important Greeks, he went to Montenegro and then back to Belgrade to report to Prince Mikhail. Rakovsky was becoming more and more perturbed by manifestations of Serbian chauvinism and the desire of the Serbs to annex Bulgaria politically and culturally, but he still hoped that war between Turkey and any one of the small Balkan nations would invoke the intervention of Russia and the subsequent liberation of Bulgaria. Seeing that Turkish–Serbian relations were improving, Rakovsky moved to Rumania, and began to edit a newspaper called *Bŭdeshtnost* (*Future*) which aimed at fostering friendship between Bulgaria and Rumania. The paper also dealt with Church matters, advising the Bulgars to chase out the Greek clergy, and criticized the *chorbadzhii*. This line incurred the wrath of the rich Bulgarian merchants in Rumania who succeeded in making it impossible for him to continue publishing the paper. Rakovsky then began publishing *Branitel* (*The Defender*) in Bulgarian and Rumanian, but only one issue appeared. During 1864 he carried on a correspondence with various leading Serbs and Montenegrins (including the Prince of Montenegro), hoping to bring Serbia and

G

Montenegro closer together. In the same year, he organized small *haidut* bands which crossed the Danube and operated mainly in western Bulgaria. In the following year, 1865, Rakovsky devoted himself almost exclusively to literature.

The Bulgarian Secret Central Committee

It is unfortunate that the Bulgars' high ideals of Balkan brotherhood and co-operation often led them into situations in which neighbouring Governments made use of them and then cast them off when the situation changed. After the abrupt end of the Bulgarian Legion, there was a repetition of the same kind of thing, this time in Rumania. In 1866 the Rumanian Liberal Party formed a Secret Central Committee in Bucharest which overthrew the Rumanian Prince Cuza, who was the Sultan's vassal, and invited the Hohenzollern Prince Carol to take his place. This placed Rumania in a very dangerous position politically for not only did Russia not approve of the *coup*, but it was even rumoured that the Turkish Army would cross the Danube to restore Prince Cuza to his throne. The Rumanian Liberals decided that it would ease their position considerably if the Bulgarians would organize a rising in the rear of the Turkish Army then massing on the Danube, and would thus divert the Turks' attention from Rumania. To this end they approached Rakovsky, who replied that he could easily raise 5,000 volunteers. The negotiations, however, broke down suddenly—in all probability because Rakovsky demanded that the Rumanians should recognize that they would have certain obligations towards the Bulgars. The Rumanian attitude towards Rakovsky changed very rapidly. He was subjected to police supervision, and was finally forced to flee to Odessa. The Rumanians then turned to Ivan Kasabov, who had been a member of the Bulgarian Legion in Belgrade, and who suggested that instead of enrolling volunteers, the Bulgars should form a Committee to organize a rebellion in Bulgaria which was to take place in conjunction with risings in the other Balkan countries. The Rumanians agreed to this suggestion and a Secret Central Committee was formed, and its representatives met members of the Rumanian Committee. It was decided to establish a 'Sacred Coalition' (*Coalitiunea Sacra*) between the Bulgars and Rumanians for joint action against the Turks, and the Bulgars undertook to set up further Committees in Serbia and Bulgaria. Although it was envisaged that the Rumanians should play the leading role in the coalition, even to the extent of giving the word for the commencement of the Bulgarian rebellion, the Rumanian representatives were not over-keen about the whole thing and ultimately refused to sign the agreement. Shortly after this, the Liberal *coup* received European recognition, the danger to Rumania passed and with it the Rumanians' need for Bulgarian support. They discontinued their negotiations with the Bulgarian Committee which continued its work on its own. It did, in fact, set up subsidiary Committees in Shumen, Tŭrnovo and Shvishtov, as well as ten branches in Bucharest. At the end of 1866, Kasabov himself left Bucharest to become a teacher in Ploesti and his place as leader of the BSCC (Bulgarian Secret Central Committee) was taken by P. Kisimov, who represented the richer merchants and whose political ideas were largely those of the 'Old' Party. The idea of a rebellion to liberate Bulgaria completely, in co-operation with other Balkan countries, gave way to various vague compromise solutions, including a future Bulgarian 'Kingdom' dependent on the Turks! One sees in this wavering view-point the influence of the Committee's rich merchant majority who were loth to cut themselves off from the markets of the Turkish Empire. There was, of course, nothing new in this point of view. As early as 1853 the émigré merchants in Rumania had sent a declaration to the Tsar, saying that they did not wish to separate themselves from the Sultan, but merely to obtain some form of representation to safeguard their interests. Another feature of the Committee was its tendency to be anti-Russian, due to the prevailing anti-Russian sentiments of the Rumanians, and therefore to incline towards the Western European Powers.

In 1867 Austria and Hungary set up the Dual Monarchy. The BSCC found this form of government fitted their own aspirations and sent a 'Memorandum' to the Sultan and all European States, suggesting that Bulgaria and Turkey should settle their problems in the same way, by establishing a Turko-Bulgarian Kingdom in which the Bulgarians should have their own National Assembly, administration, courts and army units. The Sultan was to be the head of this dual Kingdom and was to be invited to take the title of Tsar as well as Padishah and to come to Tŭrnovo for the coronation. Although one paragraph of the Memorandum contains words which could be taken to mean that if the proposals were rejected the Bulgarians would resort to a rising, it is quite clear that the BSCC had in fact abandoned any thoughts of a popular uprising and was seeking the goodwill of the Sultan.

While the Memorandum caused some stir, it was not taken

seriously by the Porte or the Governments of Europe. Among the Bulgarians, it evoked the opposition of the Turkophils in Constantinople, but pleased the émigrés in Russia. It also pleased the Russians themselves who fastened on the veiled threat of an uprising, especially in view of the fact that the rising in Crete had sharpened relations between the Turks and Greeks, and therefore between the Turks and Russians, who supported the Greeks. The Russian War Minister offered arms and the émigrés collected funds for the Committee, thus enabling them to start a paper, *Narodnost*, which was edited in turn by Ivan Bogorov, Ivan Grudov and Kasabov himself, and first appeared on September 21, 1867.

No preparations for a rising were in fact made, and the inactivity of the BSCC, plus its compromising 'dualism', lost it the support both of the 'Young' Party and the rich merchants in Russia, who stopped sending it money. When Kasabov undertook the editing of *Narodnost*, the paper became more and more anti-Russian, under the influence of émigré Polish revolutionaries. This lost the Committee further support among the Bulgars. The last number of *Narodnost* appeared on July 24, 1868, and from this date the BSCC ceased to exist.

The Supreme National Bulgarian Secret Citizens' Command

During his stay in Odessa in 1866, Rakovsky attempted to collect money without much success. The rich merchants of that city were then supporting the newly formed BSCC, and in the autumn of 1866 Rakovsky returned to Rumania. He immediately declared his opposition to the BSCC and set to work to win back those members of the 'Young' Party who had been won over by Kasabov in his absence. Soon the majority of the revolutionary émigrés were once more gathered round their old leader and Rakovsky once again began the organization of *cheti*. By now he was disillusioned, as well he might be, with foreign support and directed his whole attention to creating a disciplined properly organized *cheta* movement. At the end of 1866 he set up a new revolutionary body—the Supreme National Bulgarian Secret Citizens' Command,[1] consisting of seven members, whose task was the organization of *cheti*. His 'Law' for *cheti* was issued by the Command on January 1, 1867. In the same year, Rakovsky became ill and died of tuberculosis. His bones were taken to Sofia in 1885 and were kept in the Church of St Nedelya until 1943, when they were moved to his native Kotel.

[1] *Vŭrkhovno narodno bŭlgarsko taino grazhdansko nachalstvo.*

The Dobrodetelna Druzhina

In 1862 the body formed in Bucharest during the Crimean War and known as the *Epitropia* and later as the Bulgarian Central Trusteeship, again changed its name, this time to the *Dobrodetelna Druzhina* (the Benevolent Society), and operated ostensibly as a charitable organization. The *Druzhina* was also known as the Committee of the 'Old'; its leaders were mainly big merchants and farmers and it was completely Russophil in its outlook, dutifully following Russian policy, even when it disagreed with it, as over the Church question. The *Druzhina* did very little before 1866, but in this year Russian foreign policy set itself the task of uniting the Serbs and Bulgars into a South Slav State as a barrier to Austro-Hungarian advance into the Balkans, and the *Dobrodetelna Druzhina* directed its activity towards the achievement of this aim. In January 1867 the *Druzhina* produced a programme providing for the setting up of a Joint State under the Obrenović Dynasty. The programme was approved by the Serbian Government, which, however, considered that the decision had been made by too narrow a circle of people, and therefore in April an extended conference of representatives of the upper *bourgeoisie* from Rumania and Bulgaria met to discuss the programme. The extended conference issued a protocol which followed the lines of the original programme. The Serbian Government did not sign the protocol but merely sent a letter of vague support, urging the Bulgars to prepare for a rising. The *Druzhina* set to work establishing committees in Bulgaria and it was also persuaded to provide money for the *cheti* being organized by Rakovsky and his leading *voivodi* Filip Totyu, Panaiot Khitov, Stefan Karadzhata and Hadzhi Dimiter. An initial grant was made, but eventually it went back on its promise and the original plan had to be revised. Only two *cheti* were sent, under Khitov and Totyu, with orders not to raise a revolt but merely to sound the mood of the people. Rakovsky himself was by now far too ill to join the *cheti* himself.

The Cheti of Khitov and Totyu, 1867

Khitov crossed the Danube on April 28th at Tutrakan with thirty men, including the young Vasil Levsky, who acted as standard-bearer on Rakovsky's personal recommendation. The *cheti* came through the Deliorman to Kotel. They found young men ready to join them, but in accordance with his instructions from the *Druzhina*, Khitov sent them home, advising them to wait. In any case, it was clear to the *cheti* that the people as a whole were not ready either materially or morally to rise. In the meantime, Filip Totyu crossed the Danube on May 17th at Svishtov with thirty-five men. Unlike Khitov, who encountered only a few isolated Turks, Totyu was discovered and attacked by a strong Turkish force in the village of Vŭrbovka near Sevlievo. He escaped with only twelve men and by the time they reached Zlatitsa, the *cheta* had dwindled to four. Here they joined up with Khitov and arrived in Serbia on August 4th.

The *cheti* had a good effect on the morale of the people, not only by their actual presence and the implied existence of a revolutionary leadership, but also because they were reported in the European Press. The Turkophil *bourgeoisie*, however, was utterly opposed to the *cheti*, referred to them as bandits and urged the Government to exterminate them as 'wild beasts'. In fact, not only captured members of the *cheti*, but many other persons in the areas through which the *cheti* passed were hanged or imprisoned by the Turks who were already thoroughly alarmed by the rising in Crete and wished to stamp out any possible trouble in Bulgaria. The Turkophils also sent protests to the BSCC which they erroneously believed to be the organizers of the *cheti*, insisting that the Bulgarians already enjoyed 'beneficent and wise freedom' under Turkish rule.

The Second Bulgarian Legion, 1867–1868

In 1867 the *Druzhina* made arrangements with the Serbs for a military school financed by Russia to be opened in Belgrade to train young Bulgars for the proposed uprising. Some 300 young men enrolled, of whom 200 were Bulgars and the rest were Montenegrins, Serbs and Croats. The Bulgarian group became known as the Second Bulgarian Legion, and included the survivors of the two *cheti*. Apart from the organization of the Legion, the *Druzhina* undertook preparations in Bulgaria itself. Marincho Benli was sent to establish Committees in the major towns, and the Russians sent in arms and gunpowder which were stored in Sofia. The Serbs themselves were preparing for a war against Turkey in the spring of 1868. Unfortunately, once again the weakness of making one's revolutionary centre in someone else's country was made manifest, and the Bulgars' plans again collapsed when there occurred a change of policy on the part of their hosts. The Turks, who were still alarmed by the Cretan Rising, decided to placate the Serbs by removing their garrisons from Serbian fortresses, and relations between Serbia and Turkey once again improved. The Second Bulgarian Legion was now an embarrassment to the Serbs, just as the First had been, and the Serbs began to make things so difficult and unpleasant for the legionnaires that they finally left Belgrade and moved to Rumania. The Second Bulgarian Legion was officially wound up in April 1868.

In 1868 Russian foreign policy also changed. Russia was seeking a revision of the clause in the Treaty of Paris which forbade her to keep a Fleet in the Black Sea. She wished to appear conciliatory toward Turkey and suggested that a conference be called in Paris to consider the question of Crete. This situation demanded an end to *cheti* and other provocations, and the *Druzhina* complied with Russian policy. Encouraged by Russia, the *Druzhina* sent a memorandum to the Paris conference, asking that Bulgaria be granted autonomy under the Sultan with a bicameral Assembly. Thus from federation with Serbia, the *Druzhina* had moved over to a position indistinguishable in essence from the dualism of the BSCC.

The Cheta of Hadzhi Dimiter and Stefan Karadzhata, 1868

In the summer of 1868 on the initiative of a teacher named Zapryanov, a new organization disguised as a cultural and charitable society was founded by the 'young' revolutionary elements among the émigrés in Bucharest. It was known as the *Bŭlgarsko Obshtestvo* (Bulgarian Society), and its leaders included Kasabov, who edited *Narodnost* as the new society's organ. The members of the *Bŭlgarsko Obshtestvo* included Rakovsky's followers, and disillusioned former adherents of the *Druzhina* and the BSCC. Most of its leaders came from the left of the BSCC and represented the middle traders in Rumania. The political aims of the new organization were very vague, and its tactics were no advance on Rakovsky's plan for sending *cheti* into Bulgaria. The *Obshtestvo* is chiefly memorable for being the organizer of the last and most famous of the *cheti*— that led by the veteran *haidut voivodi* Hadzhi Dimiter and Stefan Karadzha. The character of the new *cheta* was somewhat different from all previous *cheti*, since most of its members had been members of the disbanded Second Legion and therefore had received proper military training. The aim of the *cheta* was an ambitious one—to set up a Provisional Government in the Stara Planina and to start a general uprising. The whole idea of the *cheta* was opposed by the *Druzhina* which refused to provide any money and moreover made the preparations for the *cheta* known to the Russian consul, who told the French consul, and rumour of it eventually reached the Turkish authorities who were thus forewarned.

The rebels, who numbered about 120, came in disguise to the assembly point near Petrosani near the Danube, roughly opposite the mouth of the Yantra. There they changed into their blue uniforms, gay with braid and shining buttons, and put on their caps, decorated with the lion emblem and the device 'Freedom or Death'. They crossed the river on the night of July 6th and, on landing in Bulgaria, they had a brush with a Turkish patrol. The firing was seen by a passing Austrian vessel bound for Rusé, and its captain informed the Turkish authorities on his arrival there. The rebels set out as planned for the Stara Planina, heroically fighting off Turkish forces as they went, yet never laying a finger on peaceful Turkish villagers, suffering increasingly from lack of food, water and sleep. After their third battle near the village of Vishovgrad, only sixty-eight of them remained alive, many of them wounded, and in the fourth battle, fought against regular Turkish troops near Kanlŭderé (Sevlievo region), the *cheta* was crushingly defeated. Stefan Karadzha was severely wounded and captured. He was sent to Tŭrnovo and then to Rusé where, in spite of the doctor's orders that he should not drink, because of his stomach wounds, he drank an enormous amount of water in order to deprive the Turks of the pleasure of hanging him, and died in prison. But the Turks hanged his dead body on the gallows to terrify the Bulgarian population.

The shattered remnant of the *cheta*, now only forty strong, struggled on towards the Stara Planina under Hadzhi Dimiter. After several days they reached Mount Buzludzha, and there on the afternoon of July 18th they were surrounded by a large Turkish force, comprising some 700 men including regular troops. In a battle lasting three and a half hours, the *cheta* was wiped out almost to a man. Hadzhi Dimiter himself died there, and his death inspired Khristo Botev to write what is undoubtedly the most celebrated poem in all Bulgarian literature, containing the famous line 'He who falls in the fight for freedom, does not die'.

In spite of its tragic end the *cheta* and the reckless heroism of its members made a great impression both in Bulgaria and abroad. The Turkish Government were sufficiently alarmed to abandon their delaying tactics in relation to the Church problem and to hasten to find a solution acceptable to the Bulgars. It was, however, becoming increasingly clear that it was not possible to rouse the people to revolt and to liberate the country purely or even principally by means of *cheti* organized abroad. Indeed, Vasil Levsky, who had been standard-bearer to Hitov's *cheta*, did not join Hadzhi Dimiter and Stefan Karadzha, partly, it is true, because of ill-health, but also because he had come to doubt the correctness of this form of struggle. The *cheta* involved far too much useless sacrifice, both on the part of the volunteers themselves and on the part of the Bulgarian population which suffered cruelly from Turkish reprisals. New methods were required and a new period began in the history of the Bulgarian Revolutionary Movement, a period dominated by the brilliant personality of Vasil Levsky. Levsky's fundamental theses were that it was useless for Bulgaria to depend on foreign help, that revolution cannot be imported by *cheti*, and that any rising must be organized primarily within the country itself through secret revolutionary committees set up for this purpose.

Vasil Levsky: Early Life

Vasil Levsky was born on July 6/18, 1837, in Karlovo, now called Levskygrad in his honour. Unlike most of the other sub-Balkan towns, Karlovo had a considerable Turkish population, and the town itself and its surrounding territory were *vakīf* land (i.e. land, the income of which was set aside for Moslem religious and charitable purposes). The Bulgarian population were chiefly traders and artisans, and the main industry was the making of *gaitan* (braid), though a wide variety of goods ranging from gunpowder to glass and goldware was also made. Karlovo was also famous for its wine and brandy, and for its attar of roses. The artisans of Karlovo, like their brothers throughout Bulgaria, were gradually being ruined by foreign competition, while the merchants acting as agents for foreign firms retained their wealth and position. Levsky's father, Ivan Kunchev, was a skilled dyer, who also made *gaitan*, and his family of three boys and two girls lived in relative prosperity. In 1844, through the dishonesty of his partner and other difficulties, Ivan Kunchev went bankrupt. Being a sternly upright and honourable man, he was deeply distressed by the failure of his business and had a stroke, as a result of which he gradually became blind. He died in 1851, leaving his wife, Gina, to fend for the family. This she did with admirable fortitude and industry, toiling day and night making *gaitan*.

Vasil was the eldest son (his sister Yana was the eldest child), and his two younger brothers also took part in the national movement. Khristo joined the revolutionary émigrés in Rumania, where he died in 1870 of tuberculosis, while Petŭr was a member both of

G*

the Second Legion in Belgrade and of Botev's *cheta* in the April Rising, and was seriously wounded in the historic battle at Shipka during the War of Liberation.

When Vasil was eight, Gina sent him to a cell school, and the following year he transferred to a 'monitorial' school, where he studied for three years and learnt to read and write. In spite of the family's poverty, Gina hoped to make her first-born son an educated, cultured man, preferably a priest, and for this purpose she placed him in the care of her brother Hadzhi Vasili, a monk from the Hilendar monastery, who had been appointed to perform certain ecclesiastical duties in Karlovo and the surrounding countryside. Young Vasil made himself generally useful to his uncle, assisting him in his work and looking after his horse, in return for which Hadzhi Vasili undertook the boy's education. In 1855 Hadzhi Vasili moved to Stara Zagora where he sent his nephew to a 'class' school, and then to a special course for priests. The boy did very well in his studies, and excelled at church singing, being possessed of a lovely voice which held congregations spellbound. Hadzhi Vasili was very satisfied with his nephew's progress and declared that he would send him to continue his studies in Russia. Buoyed up by this hope, Vasil agreed to his uncle's demand that he should become a monk. In December 1858 he entered the Monastery of St Spas at Sopot under the name of Ignati, and the following year he was ordained deacon by the Greek Metropolitan of Plovdiv.

Once his nephew was safely established in the Church, however, Hadzhi Vasili appears to have forgotten his promise, and the Deacon Ignati waited in vain for its fulfilment. Up till that time Levsky was apparently quite content to submit to his uncle's plans, mainly, no doubt, because it seemed the best way to satisfy his thirst for knowledge. Now, deeply affected by what seemed to him to be faithlessness on the part of his uncle, he reconsidered his mission in life. In the towns and countryside around him, the depressed artisans, petty traders and peasantry were beginning to turn their thoughts from education and Church independence to political revolution, and Rakovsky was already preaching the gospel of national liberation. Levsky stood at the crossroads, and inwardly made new vows, which he was to keep with the steadfast single-minded devotion of a saint. He wrote later on in a letter:

'Already in '61 I dedicated myself to my country, to serve her till death and to do the will of the people.'

One night in March 1862, Levsky departed stealthily on his uncle's stallion, obtained a passport in Plovdiv and rode to Belgrade where Rakovsky was busy propagating his 'Plan for the Liberation of Bulgaria'. He enrolled in the First Legion and received his baptism of fire in the June street fighting, and his nickname 'Levsky'[1] from words spoken by Rakovsky in praise of a mighty 'lion-like' leap performed by the young deacon in the course of his military training.

In the spring of 1863, after the disbanding of the Legion, Levsky went first to Rumania, and then returned home to Karlovo. He evidently made his peace with his uncle, from whom he begged money for a new cassock, and resumed his duties in the Bogoroditsa Church, where his singing once again enthralled the congregation, who, though somewhat astonished, were delighted at his return.

The Turks, however, came to regard him with suspicion, and he was arrested and sent to prison in Plovdiv. After three months, Naiden Gerov secured his release, but since Karlovo now seemed to be too hot for him, he spent the ensuing winter in Plovdiv, returning home again in the spring. His experiences in Belgrade and Plovdiv, his meeting with Rakovsky and the whole new world which had opened up before him now led him to renounce his career in the Church. This time he left Karlovo quite openly. He sang in the Easter Midnight service as usual, but afterwards he cut off his long fair hair, and appeared at the next service in secular clothes.

For the next two years Levsky taught in Voinyagovo, a village not far from Karlovo, where he regaled the youth with tales of the Legion, and encouraged them to drill and to maintain links with the *haiduts* in the mountains. Then he moved and taught for a time in Enikyoi in the Dobrudzha, where he again inflamed the local youth, taking his first steps along the road that was later to take him all over Bulgaria as the mandated 'Apostle of Freedom', preaching a fiery gospel of revolution in every hut, village and town.

Levsky among the Bulgarian Émigrés

In the spring of 1867 Levsky gave up teaching and went to join the revolutionary exiles in Bucharest. He arrived at the time when Rakovsky's supporters were organizing the *cheti* which were to cross into Bulgaria under Filip Totyu and Panaiot Khitov, and he took part in the expedition, as we have already seen, as Khitov's standard-bearer. When the remnants of the *cheti* crossed into Serbia

[1] The name means 'lion-like'.

Levsky went with them and joined the Second Bulgarian Legion
which was then being organized in Belgrade. As the melancholy
history of the Legion moved towards its close, Levsky suffered a
serious illness, the exact nature of which is uncertain, but which
brought him within an inch of death and left him weak and unable
to go out for some time. During this period of enforced inactivity,
Levsky devoted deep thought to problems of the Revolutionary
Movement and its lack of success. The result of his thought was a
new crisis in his outlook, and the beginning of his conviction that
the revolutionary struggle must be organized from *inside* Bulgaria,
and that he must do the organizing. In a letter to Khitov from his
sick-bed, he wrote:

'If I succeed, I shall win for the whole people, if I fail, then I
alone shall perish.'

At the end of April, when the Legion had been finally disbanded,
Levsky went to Rumania, where his old comrades Hadzhi Dimiter
and Stefan Karadzha were preparing for their ill-fated *cheta*.
Levsky's recent illness prevented him from taking part, but he was,
in any case, disillusioned with *cheti* in general, and was thinking
along new lines. Instead of joining them, he went back to Serbia
to search for some of his comrades who had been arrested by the
Serbs, and was promptly arrested himself in Zaichar. His sojourn
in prison completed his disillusionment with the Serbian Government, and he became convinced that Bulgaria must rely on her own
forces. Thus Levsky had already arrived at a point at which he had
begun to formulate in his mind his fundamental theses for revolutionary organization: the revolution must be organized within the
country, embracing the whole people, and, while Bulgaria should
accept any allies she could find ('We shall not refuse help even from
the devil'), she must neither rely on help from outside, nor depend
on the goodwill of others.

After his release, Levsky returned to Rumania, where he was
imprisoned by the Rumanian authorities in the wave of arrests
which followed the departure of Hadzhi Dimiter and Stefan Karadzhata, but he was soon released and spent the next few months
regaining his health and strength and consolidating his new ideas.

By 1868 the rift between the Russophil 'Old' Party and the 'Young'
was complete and even amounted to enmity. Levsky naturally fell
in with the 'Young', who in Bucharest were rallied round the

Bulgarian Reading Room 'Brotherly Love' and the newly formed *Bŭlgarsko Obshtestvo*. The organ of this Society, *Narodnost*, was edited at that time by Kasabov, who was himself, together with his closest associates, an ardent admirer of Mazzini and his 'Young Europe' movement. In fact, in the summer of 1869, Kasabov actually sent a Bulgarian delegation to Zürich to make contact with Mazzini, and after he had heard the report of the delegation, sent Mazzini a letter signed by the 'Brotherly Love' Society, which has been preserved. Apart from the Mazzinist Kasabov and his friends, Levsky made the acquaintanceship of Khristo Botev, with whom he lived for a time in dire poverty, verging on starvation, in a disused windmill on the outskirts of Bucharest.

The *Bŭlgarsko Obshtestvo* provided Levsky with the money necessary to commence conspiratorial work in Bulgaria itself, and on December 6, 1868, he set out by boat for Constantinople. He then toured Bulgaria for about six weeks, visiting Plovdiv, Perushtitsa, Karlovo, Sopot, Kazanlŭk, Sliven, Tŭrnovo, Lovech, Pleven and Nikopol, and returned to Rumania on February 24, 1869. This tour was for purposes of reconnaissance, to test the feeling of the people. Apparently the results were encouraging, for he soon undertook a second tour armed with a mandate and proclamations in Bulgarian and Turkish issued in the name of the 'Provisional Government in the Balkan', a non-existent body, whose name had also appeared on the proclamations distributed by the ill-fated *cheta* of Hadzhi Dimiter and Stefan Karadzhata, and which had therefore acquired a certain sanctity in the eyes of the people. The proclamation is interesting in so far as it was addressed not only to the Bulgarians but also to the Turkish people, calling on them to rise against their rulers and *beys*, who oppressed the ordinary Turks just as they oppressed the *raya*. It promised that in the future 'Free Bulgaria' the Turks and Bulgars should live as brothers enjoying equal rights and religious freedom.

Levsky left Rumania for Bulgaria on May 15, 1869, to begin his task of creating an internal revolutionary organization. He succeeded in setting up the first Committee in Pleven, and the second in Lovech. He also visited Karlovo, Kalofer, Kazanlŭk, Plovdiv, Perushtitsa, Pazardzhik, Sopot, Chirpan, Lyaskovets, Sevlievo, Tŭrnovo and Nikopol and in the majority of these towns he set up Revolutionary Committees. The Turks heard of his activities and attempted to catch him, but in spite of their efforts Levsky always slipped through their fingers, becoming an increasingly legendary figure as the months

went past. He travelled from village to village with unruffled com-
posure, disguised as anything from a monk to a Turkish officer,
setting men's hearts on fire with love for freedom, organizing
committees wherever he went, ever eluding capture by a hair's
breadth, protected by the loyalty and adoration of humble men and
women who risked their lives to shelter the 'Apostle of Freedom',
as they called him.[1]

In July 1869 Levsky returned to Rumania, with his ideas crys-
tallized and with authority, as it were, to speak not only for himself
but also on behalf of the organized people within Bulgaria. For the
next year he remained in Rumania trying to rid the émigrés of their
old ideas on *cheti*, dualism, etc., and to convince them of the correctness of his standpoint. Unfortunately, he did not make much headway. He felt sickened by the disunity and bickering between the
various groups and wanted to return to Bulgaria to get on with the
practical tasks of organizing the revolution. He did, however, make
some progress with the group headed by Lyuben Karavelov, who
had recently come to Bucharest, and Dimiter Tsenovich, who
accepted at any rate the general lines of his thesis, though, as we
shall see, there were important differences between their point of
view and Levsky's.

Lyuben Karavelov: Early Life

As well as being a leading revolutionary democrat, Lyuben Karavelov
was also one of Bulgaria's foremost writers of the pre-Liberation
period, second in importance only to Khristo Botev. He was a publicist, folklorist and a talented writer of narratives and stories on
realistic Bulgarian themes. He was born at the end of 1834 or the
beginning of 1835. His home town, Koprivshtitsa, had like its
neighbour, Panagyurishté, been a military village and therefore had
traditionally enjoyed certain privileges. Sheep dealing, *aba* weaving
and trade were the chief occupations of its citizens, although they
also manufactured arms which were sold as far afield as Abyssinia.
Karavelov's father was a wealthy *dzhelep*, a merchant who sold
sheep in Constantinople, and Lyuben sometimes accompanied him
on trading tours, thus becoming well acquainted with the life of the
people. He attended the school in Koprivshtitsa, where he studied

---

[1] Numerous accounts of Levsky's activities by his contemporaries have
been collected together in *Levsky v Svetlina* by Lyubomir Doichev (Sofia,
1943) and *Levsky v spomenite na Sŭvremennitsite si* by Stefan Karakostov
(Sofia, 1941).

under Naiden Gerov, and in 1854 he was sent to the Greek school in Plovdiv by his father, who wished him to become a merchant. His stay in Plovdiv had a considerable effect on him for he saw the results of Greek influence and the wide gulf separating the poor from the rich whom he learned to hate. In 1857 he went to Moscow hoping to enter the Military Academy, but the scheme fell through and Karavelov attended lectures on philology at Moscow University with the financial help of the largely Slavophil 'Slav Committee' which made a practice of helping Bulgarian students. The intellectual life of Russia in the sixties was very lively and interesting, and Karavelov was influenced not only by his Slavophil benefactors, but also by the great Russian democratic publicists of the period, such as Herzen, Chernyshevsky and Dobrolyubov. In 1861 Karavelov commenced his literary activities by writing for various journals with Slavophil tendencies, and in 1867 he went to Belgrade as the correspondent of several of these papers, including *Golos* and *Moskovski Vedomosti*. His stay in Serbia was a period of intensive cultural and literary activity. He also took a leading part in the new Serbian Radical-Democratic movement which was called *Omladina* (Youth) and which embraced chiefly students and other young people, and which, while not Socialist, was broadly rationalist and humanist. The members of the *Omladina* were under the influence of the ideas of liberation current amongst the progressive *bourgeoisie* of Europe, as expressed in the Italy of Mazzini and Garibaldi, the 'Young Germany' movement, etc. Karavelov worked with the *Omladina* group for the liberation of the Balkan peoples and for political and social justice. Though he championed the poor against the rich throughout his life, he never saw the evils of society being righted through economic and social transformation, as did the Socialists, but saw the hope of the future in science and education, both practical and moral. Karavelov attempted to edit papers, but the Serbian Government would not allow him to do so, and indeed his general activities aroused the suspicion of the authorities to such an extent that he was expelled from Serbia and went to Novi Sad in the Voivodina, which was under Austro-Hungarian rule, but which was a centre of Serbian literary and political thought. In May 1868 Prince Mikhail of Serbia was assassinated, and the Austro-Hungarian authorities arrested a number of Serbs living in the Voivodina. They also took the opportunity of arresting Karavelov, who was held for some seven months in prison in Budapest. Soon after his release in January 1869 the 'Old' Party invited him to come to Bucharest and edit their paper *Otechestvo* (*Fatherland*) and Karavelov agreed. It seems a very odd choice from every point of view, but evidently neither side was clear about the other's standpoint. Karavelov soon realized his error, left *Otechestvo* and in November 1869 he started his own paper, *Svoboda* (*Freedom*). Thus for the first time Karavelov, who had up till then worked in a Russian or Serbian milieu, entered the Bulgarian Revolutionary Movement, and soon became one of its leading figures. Kasabov, incidentally, dropped out of the movement during 1869, and in the following year sought and obtained Rumanian citizenship and began to practise as a lawyer.

Karavelov's Ideology

The prime motive force behind Karavelov's thought and action was an intense love for his country and people. As an example of this one may quote the following short extract from a lyrical description of his native Koprivshtitsa, written while he was in exile in Russia:

'I love you, O my beloved homeland! I love your mountains, forests, sand dunes, cliffs and crystal cool springs. I love you, O my beloved country! I love you with all my heart and soul, even though you may be doomed to bitter suffering and slavery! To this day everything that is good and holy in my poor soul—everything I owe to you! You are the blessed earth that blossoms, that is full of tenderness, radiance and majesty, and therefore it was you that taught me to love and weep over every human misfortune, and that is enough for any man . . .'

This passionate, unqualified love led him to study Bulgarian folklore and also to his participation in the struggle for Bulgaria's independence. His political ideas, however, contained certain illogicalities and shortcomings, especially when compared with the crystal-clear consistency of Levsky's views and actions. Karavelov began as an educationalist and we can see his progress towards a revolutionary standpoint in his newspaper *Svoboda*. In the first number (November 1869) he wrote 'Only blind and uneducated people allow themselves to be led by the nose' (i.e. his original educationalist thesis), but he also added that in order for the Bulgars to be educated they had to be free. By the twenty-third issue he was saying that it was a mistake to think that Bulgaria could overcome her enemies purely by moral pressure, without physical force, and by the thirty-third issue (June 1870) he was writing 'Revolution,

revolution, revolution is our salvation!' For the Church struggle he had little use, and it was he who, following the proclamation of the Exarchate in 1872, penned the famous words: 'Freedom does not need an Exarch, it needs a Karadzha.' Yet in 1873, after disaster had overtaken the revolutionary organization, he was once more to take refuge in educationalism.

Under the influence of the Slavophils and his close connections with Serbia, his political programme was based on Balkan Federation, and he saw the liberation of Bulgaria as being achieved through the help of Serbia. While he agreed with the importance of organizing the people within Bulgaria and therefore joined in Levsky's work, Slav federation and political combination with Serbia were fundamental to his theory of liberation. He had agreed with the *Dobro-detelna Druzhina's* proposals for a Serb–Bulgarian State, and it was probably this which explains the 'Old' Party's otherwise unaccountable invitation to edit their paper. Levsky placed Serbian aid and internal organization in reverse order of importance.

Another issue on which Karavelov and Levsky differed was in their estimation of the Turks. Karavelov did not distinguish between the Turkish people and the Turkish Government. To him every Turk was, in the nature of things, an incorrigible barbarian. In 1869 he wrote in *Svoboda*: 'A Turk is a Turk, and neither God nor the devil can make a human being of him.' This point of view led him to reject all 'dualist' theories and to demand nothing less than full freedom for Bulgaria. He had, however, no definite views on the form of the future 'Free Bulgaria'. On the whole he was a Republican, though occasionally he wavered even on this point. His political ideal did not go much farther than envisaging a Balkan Federation roughly on the lines of Switzerland or the United States, with a parliamentary system. Thus Karavelov did not go much beyond the general liberalism of the epoch, and the educational and philosophical ideas of the French Revolution. The social interests which he reflected were those of the rising trading and industrial class, and although he hated the *chorbadzhii* ('Bulgaria will be delivered only when the Turk, the *chorbadzhiya* and the bishop are hanged on a willow tree—there is no other salvation'), he was never to become even a Utopian Socialist.

Levsky's Revolutionary Ideology

Levsky, as a revolutionary, had several outstanding characteristics. Of all the Bulgarian revolutionaries he was the closest to the people;

his ideology had, as it were, its roots in the soil of Bulgaria, in her people's experience of 500 years of slavery, rather than in the cosmopolitan ideas of freedom current among the enlightened inhabitants of European capital cities; his ideology was flawlessly consistent, and his own life was at one with it, a perfect unity of theory and practice. He was at one and the same time an idealist with a radiant vision of the future, and an intensely practical organizer, with no illusions about the present. By nature he was gentle and compassionate, but he was also capable of whatever ruthlessness the situation demanded.

Levsky was neither an author nor a publicist, and his views are known to us chiefly from the letters he wrote to the Revolutionary Committees he founded throughout Bulgaria, and from the draft 'Statute' which he prepared for the Bulgarian Revolutionary Central Committee which he and Karavelov organized in April 1870.[1] As we have already stated, Levsky took the view that the only way to liberation lay through revolution. For Levsky this revolution was to be not merely a national but also a social revolution. He hoped to sweep away at one blow, not only national slavery but all social injustice and inequality. Levsky was quite definite about the form which the future 'Free Bulgaria' must take—it was to be a 'Democratic Republic (People's Government)'.[2] 'We will have a standard', he wrote, 'with the inscription, a Pure and Sacred Republic.' He even went so far as to propose that anyone who rejected this and organized parties advocating a 'despotic-tyrannical' State, or even a 'constitutional' one (*Konstitutsionna Sistema*, meaning a constitutional monarchy) should be punished by death. Though a great nationalist leader, Levsky was himself untouched by chauvinism and racial hatred, and nothing that he himself or his people suffered at the hands of the Turks, could make him change his view that in the future 'Free Bulgaria' all nationalities, including the Turks, should enjoy complete equality, freedom of religion and an equal voice in voting the laws of the new Republic, and he wrote these provisions into his draft 'Statute'. For Levsky the enemies of the people were the Sultan and his administration and the rich Bulgarian *chorbadzhii*—his brothers were the ordinary people of all

---

[1] Levsky's letters and personal notebook, together with various reminiscences by his contemporaries, have been published by D. T. Strashimirov under the title *Vasil Levsky—Zhivot, Dela, Izvori. Tom I. Izvori.* Sofia, 1929.

[2] The Bulgarian expression is *Demokratska Republika* (*Narodno upravlenie*).

nationalities. Levsky well understood that the success of the revolution depended on good organization, unity and strict discipline within the organization. He therefore paid very great attention to the building up of a closely knit, unified revolutionary organization. He believed that decisions must be taken democratically, but that once taken, they must be binding on all, including any minority, and moreover he practised what he preached even when it was he himself who was in the minority. Side by side with devotion to the principle of democracy, Levsky also insisted on the necessity of constructive criticism and self-criticism. He urged his followers to point out his faults and to be grateful to those who pointed out their own. To leave mistakes uncriticized was in itself a crime, for an evil could grow and in time destroy the people.

Levsky insisted that the Committees accounted for every halfpenny spent and he himself kept a notebook in which he entered every item of his own expenditure, the pathetic modesty of which, incidentally, also gives us an idea of his conscientiousness about public funds. He made most careful, detailed arrangements for the admission of new members, for secret passwords, a secret post between the Committees and even for a secret police to watch over the activities of the Committees and to execute those who transgressed or proved unreliable—a drastic step, but one which was, unfortunately, essential in an organization where secrecy was vital and where one traitor or adventurer could wreck everything and condemn his comrades to torture and death.

Levsky demanded—and gave—complete and selfless devotion to the people's cause, without thought of personal ambition. 'The true man of the people', he wrote to Panaiot Khitov, 'fights as long as he is able to free his people, and if he does not succeed, he must die at his post, working for the people.'

As a person, Levsky was gay, always ready with a joke or a song, infinitely patient, possessed of bewitching charm, superb courage, iron self-control and a serenity which never deserted him, no matter how desperate the situation, or how much others panicked. His faith in the people's ability to carry the struggle to a victorious conclusion was absolute and unassailable. Though he himself was apparently unreligious and totally uninterested in the Church struggle, in spite of—or possibly because of—his monastic upbringing, he brought to the Revolutionary Movement a spirit of dedication and a sense of the sacredness of the cause which was almost akin to a religion. He was deeply conscious of the historic character of the work the Revolutionary Movement had undertaken, and wrote:

'. . . And are we not the fathers and brothers of those to whom we leave behind an eternal memory with every drop of blood we shed for their liberation? Will they not raise monuments to us, record us in the history which we are resurrecting, and to which we are bringing a new age? Will they not remember us in every church in Bulgaria, as long as the name "Bulgarian" shall live, because we shall break Bulgaria's fetters and shall lead our people, with God's blessing, from hell to heaven?'

Yet for himself the Apostle of Freedom asked nothing. To those who asked him what he would be after the Liberation, he replied with all sincerity that he would go to some other enslaved country and help the people there win their freedom also.

Although this picture of Levsky may make him seem impossibly perfect, it is fully borne out by the sources, including the memoirs of those who knew and worked with him. He was undoubtedly one of those very rare beings whose life and character can be subjected to minute examination without revealing a single flaw or shadow.

The Bulgarian Revolutionary Central Committee

It was essential for the network of Committees, which Levsky was busily organizing with considerable success, to have a general centre. Bucharest seemed to be the most convenient place and in April 1870 the Bulgarian Revolutionary Central Committee was founded there. Its first public action was a protest, printed in Karavelov's paper *Svoboda*, against the congratulatory telegram sent by the 'Old' Party adherents in Rumania to the Sultan on the occasion of the publication of the *firman* granting the Bulgarian people an Exarchate. The original leadership of the new Committee included Levsky, Karavelov and Dimiter Tsenovich, and right from the start it contained both revolutionary and educationalist tendencies, represented by Levsky and Karavelov respectively. The educationalist tendency was visible to a certain extent even in the programme of the new Committee, agreed in general terms, and then written by Karavelov and published first in the Russian émigré journal *Narodnoe Delo* (August 1870) and then in *Svoboda* (October 14, 1870). The programme gave as its aim the achievement of 'national freedom, personal freedom, religious freedom, in a word, human freedom'. An important place in the programme was occupied by references to co-operation between the Bulgarian and the other Balkan peoples, and calls for the establishment of a 'Danubian Federation of Free Lands'. Karavelov's influence is also to be seen in the statement that moral persuasion and 'peaceful means', as had been used to win Church independence, were to be used against the Turks, and only in the last resort was violence to be used. The future administration was stated vaguely to be an 'elected Government, which will fulfil the will of the people themselves'. The programme ended by stating that the *chorbadzhii* are to be considered as the enemies of the people.

A fuller version of the programme was issued as a brochure—*Bulgarian Voice*—by Karavelov in the autumn of 1870. The new version was still a compromise between the two groups, but it contained more of Levsky's views than did the original programme. For instance, the idea of 'peaceful means' was entirely dropped, and armed struggle was stated as being the only way to freedom. The future form of 'Free Bulgaria' was also stated to be a Republic.

In the meantime, following the establishment of the BRCC, Levsky had returned to Bulgaria on May 27th via Giurgiu and Rusé, to continue his organization of secret committees. He chose Lovech as the centre for the Bulgarian Committees, owing to its geographical position, which gave easy access to Rumania and to South Bulgaria. The Lovech Committee was first known as the Bulgarian Provisional Government, and later was renamed 'Section 1 of the BRCC—the Provisional Government in Bulgaria' to maintain the principle of centralization, which Levsky considered to be of great importance.

He continued to organize Committees in towns and villages throughout Bulgaria with considerable success, establishing secret communications between them, using code names. He also undertook the task of making military preparations for a rising, and among other measures, he had Serbian military textbooks translated into Bulgarian, and made unsuccessful attempts to get young Bulgarians accepted into the Military Academy in Serbia. One of Levsky's hardest and never-ending tasks was the raising of money with which to buy the necessary arms. Most of the BRCC's supporters were poor, and he resorted to obtaining money from the *chorbadzhii* by sending them letters, some calculated to rouse their patriotic feelings and some purely threatening.

The ever-growing amount of organizational work was beginning to be too much even for a man of Levsky's inexhaustible energy, and in the spring of 1871 the Central Committee chose two assistants for him, Dimiter Nikolich Kosovets, better known as Dimiter Obshti, and Angel Kŭnchev. Obshti was born in Macedonia, and had served in the First Bulgarian Legion, with Garibaldi in Italy, and as a volunteer in the Crete Rising. He was undoubtedly a very courageous man, but Levsky correctly detected in him elements of irresponsibility and adventurism, and did not consider him suitable for important revolutionary work. The Committee at Lovech, however, appointed him as Levsky's assistant by a majority vote, and Levsky, who always honoured the principle of democracy within the organization, accepted the decision. The second assistant, Angel Kŭnchev, was born in Tryavna in 1850. He had served in the Second Legion, and then had studied for a time at an agricultural school in Tabor, Bohemia, before deciding to devote himself to revolutionary work. Kŭnchev was a very different person from Obshti. In spite of his youth and relative inexperience, Levsky received him warmly and hoped that in time he would develop into a reliable assistant. Unfortunately, six months later, he was discovered by the Turks, while trying to cross into Rumania from Rusé, and committed suicide rather than fall into their hands alive.

The First General Assembly of the BRCC, 1872

Levsky felt strongly that in order to maintain discipline and unity within the new revolutionary organization, it was necessary to draw up a proper set of rules, and during 1871 he was working on a draft 'Statute' (*Ustav*) 'for those working for the liberation of Bulgaria'. Apart from a political preamble, expressing his belief in a Revolutionary Republican Government, and in brotherhood and equality between nations, it dealt with constitutional and organizational matters, such as the functions of the Committees and officers of Committees, the enrolment of new members, security measures, the secret post and secret police, the punishment of offenders, etc. Always true to the principles of democracy, Levsky insisted that the Draft Statute must be voted upon by a democratically constituted assembly, and, as a preliminary, he sent copies of the draft to all the Committees in Bulgaria and to the Committee in Bucharest for discussion and comment.

The émigrés wanted the assembly to be in Rumania, with only Levsky attending from Bulgaria, but Levsky indignantly insisted that the movement within Bulgaria should be properly represented, since it was their blood that was going to be shed. He even wanted the Assembly itself to be held in Bulgaria, but gave way in view of the practical difficulties involved. He did, however, get his own way over the representation of the movement in Bulgaria. When the General Assembly of the BRCC began on April 29th, the émigrés had sixteen votes compared to the internal organization's thirty-two (several of the delegates were mandated to represent several Committees and therefore had several votes; the total number of delegates from both sides of the Danube was twenty-one).

The Assembly accepted Levsky's Draft Statute with a few changes, the most important of which was the dropping of political references to the future form of the Bulgarian State as being out of place in such a document.[1] The Assembly also adopted a new programme, which also avoided all reference to the Republic, lest such a declaration should antagonize possible allies. It was simply stated that Bulgaria was to be liberated through revolution, and that the question of the future form of the Bulgarian State should be left open until after the liberation. The programme proclaimed the desire of the Bulgarians to live at peace with their neighbours, including the Greeks, providing the latter abandoned their pan-hellenistic ideas. It also declared that the Bulgarians were opposed only to the Turkish Government and its supporters, and not to the Turkish people—a somewhat weaker formulation than Levsky's categorical statement in his Draft Statute that the Turks should enjoy equal rights with the Bulgars. The *chorbadzhii* were named as the enemies of the people. The Assembly then elected a new Central Committee as follows: Lyuben Karavelov (President), Kiriak Tsankov (Vice-President), Olimpi Panov (Secretary), Dimiter Tsenovich (Treasurer), Panaiot Khitov and Vasil Levsky (members). Other organizational decisions adopted were the abolition of the two Revolutionary Centres at Bucharest and Lovech, and the substitution of a single Bulgarian Central Committee with an unspecified seat, and secondly, the granting to Levsky of a mandate to act for the Committee in Bulgaria with more or less unlimited powers. The Assembly closed on May 5th.

The Arabakonak Incident

Levsky returned to Bulgaria on June 1, 1872. He was well pleased with the results of the Assembly and set to work improving the organization within Bulgaria and collecting money for arms. The

---

[1] The text of the Draft Statute written by Levsky, together with the amended version adopted by the Assembly, can be found in *Vasil Levsky*, by Ivan Undzhiev (Sofia, 1945), pp. 364–73 and 511–20 respectively.

network of Committees had grown to such an extent that the work was becoming more than even he could manage, and there were insufficient responsible *cadres* to help him. He therefore began to decentralize the organization, creating Revolutionary Districts, each headed by a District Committee, responsible for the local committees in its area. Not least of the difficulties with which he had to contend was the undisciplined conduct of his assistant Obshti, who had been forced on him by the Lovech Committee. Obshti, who had always been irresponsible and conceited, now began to intrigue against Levsky and to make serious allegations against him. The whole unity of the organization was threatened and Levsky referred the matter to Bucharest, saying that they must either restrain Obshti or he, Levsky, would hand in his mandate and they must appoint a new representative, under whom he would continue to work. The Committee in Bucharest upheld Levsky, but Obshti did not mend his ways. He now proposed to obtain money for arms by robbing the Turkish mail as it passed through the Arabakonak Pass loaded with bullion. Levsky was not opposed in principle to obtaining money through robbery and terror. He had himself personally obtained 'donations' from *chorbadzhii* at the point of a gun, but he was deeply conscious of the risks involved in such undertakings. If any incautious revolutionary were captured and forced under torture to talk, then the whole organization could be imperilled. Levsky took the view that any such major undertaking required very careful preparation, and therefore he forbade Obshti to rob the mail. Obshti, however, disregarded him, organized a small *cheta*, and successfully robbed the mail on September 22, 1872. At first the Turks thought that it was the work of demobilized soldiers, but later on, owing to the inability of the conspirators to keep their mouths shut, rumours began to fly and the Turks discovered the true nature of the robbery. Mass arrests followed, and Obshti himself was arrested on October 27th. Even now the situation might have been saved had not Obshti and his associates decided to tell everything they knew, partly in order to show the world that the robbery was a political affair and not the work of common bandits, and partly in the hope that the Turks could not hang an enormous number of people and that by mass confession more people would escape. Thus from Obshti and his associates the Turks learned of the existence of the network of Committees and the names of the people involved.

The news of the disaster reached Levsky while he was busy

organizing Revolutionary Districts in southern Bulgaria. Panic and paralysis were spreading like wildfire through the organization. Levsky himself remained as calm as ever, and, although Obshti's disclosures had made his position extremely perilous, he went on doing what he could to prevent the situation from deteriorating still further.

Panic had also spread to Bucharest and the Central Committee wrote to Levsky, ordering him to attack the prison on Sofia where the conspirators were awaiting trial, in an attempt to liberate them. Levsky himself felt that such an action might prejudice the general rising which was the aim of the revolutionary organization, and he took no immediate action. The following day, the Central Committee changed its mind and ordered Levsky to start a rising, in the hope that Serbia and Montenegro would give their support. The Committee, like Obshti, did not want Europe to imagine that the robbery was the work of bandits, and it felt that unless an immediate rising was proclaimed, the Bulgarian people would lose confidence in the Central Committee, and could never be persuaded to revolt in the future. Levsky did not agree with any of this, having always been opposed to a premature rising since 'we are playing with the lives of 7,000,000 Bulgars'. He did not, therefore, proclaim a rising, but in the meantime, in order not to be accused of indecision and of ignoring the collective decision of the Committee, he asked the Committees in Bulgaria to state whether or not a rising should be started immediately. The Stara Zagora Committee, in a reply to the Central Committee, wrote that it was impossible to organize a rising at such short notice, and expressed doubts as to whether any help from Serbia and Montenegro would, in practice, materialize. But in view of the fact that there existed two schools of thought within the organization, Levsky decided to go himself to Bucharest to thrash the matter out, and in the meantime, he told the Committees to make all possible preparations for a rising.

The Death of Levsky

On his way to Rumania, Levsky decided to go to the old revolutionary capital at Lovech in order to do what he could to put the shattered Committee on its feet and to retrieve the revolutionary archives which were kept there. To go to Lovech where the police were extremely vigilant and where treachery was already stalking the streets, was a very dangerous undertaking. Nevertheless, Levsky felt he had to go, and arrived there on Christmas Day 1872. He found the position of the Committee even worse than he had feared. He managed to obtain the archives, but failed to see the President of the Lovech Committee, the local priest, Pop Krŭstyu, whom he already suspected of treachery. Krŭstyu had been arrested by the Turks on November 18th, as a result of Obshti's disclosures, but had unaccountably been released the following day. He was also in financial difficulties with payments on a house he had bought on credit, and had 'borrowed' Committee money. He was therefore understandably eager to avoid an interview with Levsky.

Levsky left Lovech for Tŭrnovo on December 26th, accompanied by a loyal member of the Lovech Committee, Nikola Tsvetkov, and spent the night in the village of Kŭkrina, at an inn kept by another Committee member, Khristo Latinets. Early in the morning, the inn was surrounded by Turkish police, acting evidently on information received from Krŭstyu. Levsky attempted to escape, but was wounded and captured. He was bound hand and foot and was taken in a cart back to Lovech together with Tsvetkov and Latinets. From Lovech, he was sent in chains to Tŭrnovo, and then to Sofia, to face the Special Court which was already trying the Arabakonak prisoners. Before the court, Levsky behaved with characteristic calm and courage. He did not give away a single name, and he answered the judges' questions with long involved statements, carefully compounded of truths, which told the Turks nothing which they did not already know, and lies designed to conceal the true nature of the revolutionary organizations, in the hope that even at this critical hour the organization could be saved from utter destruction.

Although Levsky's skill in answering, or rather not answering, their questions confounded his judges, there was little he could do in the face of the wholesale confessions of Obshti and the weaker revolutionaries who gave way under torture. The Court found the accused guilty. Obshti was hanged on January 15, 1873, and the less important prisoners were exiled for life to Diarbekir, the infamous prison in the mountain wilderness of Asia Minor. Levsky himself was also sentenced to death and was hanged on February 6th on the spot in Sofia where his monument now stands.

But this was not the end of the story. In spite of the apparent destruction of Levsky's organization, the foundations remained and formed the basis for future organization. The April Rising of 1876, which resulted in Russian intervention and the final liberation of Bulgaria, would have been unthinkable without Levsky's revolutionary theories and practical work, and his final heroism in protecting what was left of the organization by betraying nothing to the Turks, although he knew everything.

The Revolutionary Movement after Levsky's Death

The history of the revolutionary movement immediately after Levsky's death clearly demonstrated just how much the Central Committee and the movement itself had owed to Levsky's clear-sighted and undeviating leadership. The wholesale panic which had pervaded the movement since the Arabakonak incident was followed, on Levsky's death, by a period of organizational and tactical confusion. Although Levsky had consistently taught that the date of the rising must be dependent on the preparedness of the organization, the Central Committee clung to the idea of organizing a rising in the immediate future, in spite of the fact that some of the best Committees in Bulgaria were shattered, and that the primary task must be the restoration of the internal revolutionary network. The Türnovo Committee, which Levsky had charged with the responsibility of liaison with Bucharest after the collapse of the Lovech Committee, also favoured a speedy rising, and, acting semi-independently of the Central Committee, though they first wrote letters to Karavelov and Khitov, sent a representative to Belgrade to find out from the Serbian Foreign Minister what the prospects were of Serbian help in the event of a rising. The Minister advised them against any precipitous action, and doubtless gave the same answer to Karavelov, who also approached him. Karavelov was extremely incensed by the unilateral action of the Türnovo Committee, which he regarded as contrary to the Statute, and had indeed forbidden their representative to approach the Serbian Foreign Minister—an interdiction which was ignored. Panaiot Khitov, on the other hand, approved their action, saying that they should listen to the people, not the Central Committee, and the representative from Türnovo advised his Committee to listen to Khitov, not to Karavelov, thus adding to the confusion and lack of unity. In this situation, there was a simultaneous revival of the idea of basing revolution on outside help on the part of the Committees, and of the anarchical tactics of the *cheti*, on the part of the old *voivodi*, who had never quite reconciled themselves to Levsky's insistence that they were outdated. Thus there was every danger of the clock being put back to pre-Levsky revolutionary theory.

In March 1873 the Türnovo Committee called an Assembly of delegates from Committees in Bulgaria. Only six delegates, representing three or four towns, attended. They decided that another Assembly with delegates from both sides of the Danube should be called in Bucharest. About the same time the Central Committee also took a decision to call an extended meeting with representatives from Bulgaria. In an effort to restore the internal organization, Atanas Uzunov, a teacher from Sliven, was chosen to replace Levsky. He visited Bucharest during March 1873 and met members of the Central Committee. In April he returned to Bulgaria and began his first and last tour of the Committees. A month later, while attempting to kill the *chorbadzhiya* Hadzhi Stavri, who had been sentenced to death by the Khaskovo Committee, he was captured by the Turks, who also arrested many other people in Khaskovo. At his trial, Uzunov copied Levsky's technique of attempting to disguise the true nature of his activity. He was fairly successful, for no general catastrophe followed, and of the forty-four people arrested, no one was hanged, and only twenty-four, including Uzunov himself, were sent to prison in Asia Minor.

The proposed meeting of representatives from Rumania and Bulgaria took place from May 11 to May 12, 1873. Only two representatives from Bulgaria were present. The meeting approved the accounts, and took certain other decisions, which were kept secret. From a note written in Karavelov's hand on a copy of the Statute, it appears that this was revoked. The meeting decided to send a *cheta* into Bulgaria under one of Khitov's old comrades-in-arms, S. Sofiisky, to test the feeling of the people—an action which showed just how out of touch with reality in Bulgaria the Central Committee had become. After the meeting the Central Committee more or less lapsed into inactivity. Henceforward, the initiative was taken by the Committees in Tŭrnovo and Rusé who maintained relations with the émigrés via Khitov, not the Central Committee. These two Committees called a new meeting in Bucharest from August 20 to August 21, 1874 which was attended by three delegates from Bulgaria and ten émigrés. A new temporary Central Committee was elected, consisting of Karavelov, Kiriak Tsankov, Olimpi Panov, Todor Peev and Khristo Botev, who now became a member of the Central Committee for the first time. The new Committee was charged with the organization of another Assembly with greater representation from the Bulgarian Committees. The meeting gave the Rusé Committee the responsibility for resuscitating the Committees in Bulgaria and for preparing them to send delegates to the proposed Assembly. The Rusé Committee chose Stefan Stambolov to replace Uzunov, and he began a tour of the Committees in November. Unfortunately, the work was too much for this young and inexperienced man, and he crossed into Rumania the following month. In January, he returned to Bulgaria, but was soon forced to flee to Constantinople, from whence, with the aid of the Russian Envoy, Count Ignatiev, he went to Odessa.

Karavelov Leaves the Central Committee

Levsky's death and the catastrophic collapse of the Committees had affected Karavelov deeply. His whole faith in the possibility of organizing the people for revolution was undermined and began to crumble. His paper *Svoboda* had ceased publication in February 1873, and he had begun to publish *Nezavisimost (Independence)*. On October 12, 1874, he announced in what was to be the last number of *Nezavisimost* that he intended to give up his publicist activities. In order that the Revolutionary Movement should not be left without a paper, Botev began to publish *Zname (Banner)* from December 7, 1874. Karavelov did not, however, resign from the Central Committee and attended the Assembly, which was held in Bucharest on December 26, 1874. At this meeting the two tendencies —the Liberal and the Revolutionary—which had long existed, and which Levsky had succeeded in holding in temporary abeyance, reappeared in full force, and internal rivalries and controversies began to consume the whole energy of the Committee. Now the Liberals were headed by Karavelov and the Revolutionaries by Botev. The Liberal wing of Karavelov and his supporters wanted authority to be given to one person, who would direct the work of the Committee and conclude agreements with foreign Powers. Karavelov, who pinned his main hope of liberation on help from Serbia and Montenegro, apparently hoped to be elected to such a post himself. The idea was not accepted for in the meeting, the revolutionary wing under Botev was in the majority. No agreement was reached, and it was decided to call a new Assembly in March 1875. A Commission, consisting of Karavelov, Tsankov, Ivan Adzhenov, Toma Panteleev and one representative from Bulgaria, was elected to prepare for the March meeting and to lead the organization during the intervening months. The Commission had a Liberal majority and did nothing in spite of the efforts of Khristo Botev, who subsequently replaced Panteleev but who was constantly hindered by the chairman, Karavelov. The latter's unwillingness to act stemmed from his dependence on the foreign policy of the Serbs who did not want any 'premature' action on the part of the Bulgars. Botev himself was extremely unwilling to let the Bulgarian Revolution become a mere adjunct to a Serbian war against the Turks, for he feared lest the Serbs should annex part of Bulgaria as the price of their 'help'. Karavelov, on the other hand, was becoming increasingly pan-Slav, and continued to look to Serbia and not to the Bulgarian people themselves to accomplish the liberation of the country. Soon after the December meeting, he reverted completely to his old theories of educationalism which he had never wholly abandoned, and began to publish a new journal, *Znanie* (*Knowledge*), which was purely a scientific and literary publication. Karavelov also forbade Botev, as secretary of the Committee, to send out invitations for the March Assembly.

Relations between Botev and Karavelov and their respective groups became increasingly strained, especially after Botev had criticized Karavelov in his paper *Zname*. Although Botev insisted that the quarrel was not personal, but one of principle, relations between the two leaders were eventually broken off completely. The young revolutionary regarded Karavelov's inactivity and delaying tactics as utterly unpardonable, especially at a time when, in the face of Turkey's economic crisis and ever-increasing taxation, the Bulgarian people were once again turning to revolution as the only way out of their misery.

The outcome of the struggle among the émigrés was that Karavelov was eventually forced to leave the Committee, and the leadership passed to Khristo Botev.

Khristo Botev: Early Life

Khristo Botev was born on December 25, 1848/January 7, 1849 at Kalofer. His father, Botyu Petkov, who had studied in Odessa, was one of the most celebrated teachers in Bulgaria. Botev began his schooling in Kalofer, and in 1863 his father sent him to Odessa to continue his education, with a grant from the Russian Government. Unfortunately, after two years, he lost his grant, apparently owing to discrimination on the part of the conservatively inclined influential Bulgarian émigrés. He remained in Odessa, and thirteen months later, in the autumn of 1866, became teacher in the Bessarabian village of Zadunaevka, where there were many Bulgarian émigrés from the Sliven district. In the spring of 1867 he returned to Kalofer to teach in place of his father, who was ill.

Botev's stay in Russia was very important for his ideological development. He became profoundly influenced by the Russian Revolutionary Democrats and Utopian Socialists such as Alexander Herzen, Chernyshevsky, Dobrolyubov, etc. In contrast to the Western Utopian Socialists who set great store by the example of philanthropists (e.g. Robert Owen), the Russian Utopian Socialists believed in revolutionary struggle. Owing to the backwardness of their own country, and the absence of an industrial proletariat, they hoped that Russia might avoid passing through the stage of capitalism and jump straight to Socialism. They therefore saw the peasantry as the chief force behind the revolution and the village commune as the basis of the future Socialist order of society. Apart from the influence of the Russian democrats, Botev was also considerably affected by the Polish Rising of 1863, and he maintained connections with Poles and during 1866 he lived with a Polish family.

As a teacher in Kalofer, Botev continually criticized the established order and propagated the ideas of Socialism. He even drilled his pupils. His agitational activity reached a climax when, at the 1867 celebrations to mark the festival of St Cyril and St Methodius, he made an extremely fiery and daring public speech, which infuriated the *chorbadzhii* and delighted the youth. Much alarmed by the possible repercussions that might follow the speech, and worried by the fact that his son had not completed the course at Odessa, Botyu Petkov sent him back there. Botev, however, did not go to Odessa, but to Bucharest, drawn by the news of the existence of the Secret Committee there, and the organization of the *cheti*. He was very short of money and left Bucharest after three or four months for Braila where he worked for a printer. He also did Russian translations and wrote his own poems but failed to find a publisher who would print them.

In the autumn of 1868 he returned to Bucharest, hoping to get work as a teacher, but did not succeed. There then began for him a period of dire poverty, when, as he put it, his clothes became so tattered that he was ashamed to go into the streets by day. He decided to return to Bulgaria, but could not raise a loan to pay for the journey, so he spent the winter in the derelict mill on the outskirts of Bucharest where he was joined by Levsky. Sometimes they went hungry for two and three days at a stretch, and Botev records how Levsky kept up their spirits by singing from the moment they woke to the moment they went to sleep. In spite of the hardships and difficulties, Botev continued his literary and publicist work. He gave talks at the 'Brotherly Love' Reading Room, and wrote for the humorous journal *Tŭpan* (*Drum*) which was founded by the younger émigrés at the beginning of 1869. During 1869 Botev managed to obtain a post as a teacher, first in Alexandria (in Rumania) and from August 1869 onwards in Ismail, where he met the famous Russian revolutionary Sergei Nechaev and assisted him in his work. After Nechaev was arrested and sent back to Russia, Botev went first to Galati, then to Belgrade and then to Braila, where in June 1871 he began to publish his own paper *Duma na Bŭlgarskite Emigranti* (*The Word of the Bulgarian Émigrés*). After five issues, the paper failed through lack of funds, and Botev moved to Bucharest. Here he worked closely with Karavelov on *Svoboda* and *Nezavisimost*, and from May 1873 he began to publish his own satirical paper *Budilnik* (*Tocsin*). As we have already seen, after *Nezavisimost* ceased publication, Botev brought out *Znamé* to ensure that the Revolutionary Movement had its own paper.

Khristo Botev's Ideology

Botev's views are most accurately reflected in *Duma* and *Znamé*, the two papers which he edited himself, and in which he was absolutely free to express himself, uncurbed by anyone else's editorial prerogative. In these papers Botev reveals himself as the most advanced thinker of pre-Liberation Bulgaria. A devoted patriot, filled with grief for his people's sufferings and with hatred for their oppressors, Botev believed, like Levsky, that freedom could be achieved only through revolution organized within Bulgaria. He did, however, consider that once the revolution had been proclaimed, a useful, supporting role could be performed by *cheti* organized among the émigrés. Because he believed revolution to be the only way to liberation, he was bitterly hostile to all contrary trends: to the Dualists, who would perpetuate Turkish rule; to the educationalists, whose efforts were powerless to better the lot of the people, so long as they lacked political and economic freedom; to those who hoped that the Turkish Empire would die of itself or who sought liberation through outside intervention either diplomatic or military, for this, he insisted, would merely lead to the substitution of one alien rule for another. In a blistering attack on the educationalists in *Znamé* (January 5, 1875) Botev wrote:

'It is true that we do have schools, reading rooms and newspapers, bookshops and literature, but all this has brought this people to such a degree of happiness that it is able to write down fairly correctly

. The Cross and Bible used by the rebels who took the oath at Oborishté in April 1876

9b. One of the cherry-tree cannons used in the April Rising

10a. The Dryanovo Monastery where Bacho Kiro held the Turks for nine days during the April Rising

10b. The arrival of Botev's *Cheta* on Bulgarian soil

(From a painting by Professor Dimiter Gudzhenov)

when there was a famine in Turkey, when there was an epidemic, when the Sultan's men[1] passed, when the Circassians[2] came, when a tax[3] was levied on babes in arms, when . . .'

Among the worst enemies of the Bulgarian people Botev numbered the *chorbadzhii* and the upper clergy, whom he hated almost as much as he hated the Turks:

'The same hatred which the Bulgar cherishes against the Turk (possibly even deeper since it is of longer standing) he also cherishes against the *chorbadzhii* and the clergy, that still unremoved Byzantine stench, which had sold and ruined the people, and which today wears around its neck the keys of their fetters' (*Duma*, June 10, 1871, Year 1, No. 1).

Botev himself was a convinced, militant atheist, who not merely objected to the upper clergy on social grounds, but believed that religion was a barrier to true human freedom, and compared it to 'Plague, cholera and war', the causes of so much human suffering. Accordingly, Botev looked forward to an Age of Reason in which religion 'will decay and give place to . . . a scientific world outlook, the clergy will make their exit and give place to freedom and equality'.

Botev's burning, self-sacrificing patriotism led him not to chauvinism, but to internationalism, to love for all suffering and oppressed humanity:

'First of all we must be human beings, and only then Bulgarians and patriots.'

'He who dies for freedom, dies not for his own country alone, but for the whole world.'

'Everyone knows that want and suffering bring people closer to each other and unite them, make them sincere with each other, and make them help each other to save themselves from the common evil. All poor workers of whatever nationality, wherever they live, are brothers . . .' (*Zname*, Vol. I, No. 24, August 3, 1875).

In arriving at this lofty concept of international solidarity, Botev abandoned his original view that all Turks were by definition incorrigible, and came to believe, like Levsky, that freedom must be

[1] Bulgars had to provide free food, fodder, etc., for the Sultan's men.
[2] A reference to Circassian bandits.
[3] A reference to the extension of the poll tax levied on persons over fifteen.

H

indivisible, and that even the Turks were divided into oppressor and oppressed:

'Let anyone say what he pleases, but we think that if the oppressed and tormented Turkish nation gives up its fanaticism and, without paying attention to the religious and national differences which exist between it and our nation, if it desires to unite itself with us, in order to rid itself of the common enemy—the Government, we would be bound to receive it with open arms, without considering the historical enmity which tends to disunite us. The present social order, which permits the existence of Sultans and capitalists, is the source of the sufferings of both Turks and Bulgars, therefore everyone, who is unjustly treated by this order, who is condemned by it to struggle with want and hunger, who detests his bestial situation and wishes to save himself from it, is our friend, our brother.' (*Zname*, Vol. I, No. 24, August 3, 1875).

Botev's internationalism led him to hope for the creation of a brotherly union of the Balkan peoples, to whom he wished the same freedoms as he sought for Bulgaria. He was, of course, as we have seen, under no illusions as to the predatory character of the existing Balkan Governments, but he considered that these governments were 'not a true and reliable expression of the will, needs and aspirations of the people', and looked forward to a future transformation there also. He regarded a Balkan Union, based on true democracy and popular government, as a guarantee of the future freedom of the Balkan peoples from outside interference and new slavery. He recalled how disunity in the Balkans had facilitated the Turkish conquest and warned that future disunity could very easily lead to the coming of 'other uninvited guests . . . some other civilized horde.'

Like Levsky, Botev saw the revolution as being both national and social, but with his superior education and wider knowledge of European affairs, Botev evolved a more defined and developed social theory. He was a convinced Socialist who hated the capitalists as he hated the *chorbadzhii* and the Turkish ruling class. He began his publicist work in earnest in 1871, the year of the Paris Commune, which he welcomed with whole-hearted enthusiasm, and to which he sent a telegram of congratulations. In April of the same year he wrote his beautiful *Creed of the Bulgarian Commune:*

'I believe in the united common strength of the human race on earth to create good.

'And in the united Communist order of Society, saviour of all peoples from age-long oppression and misery through brotherly labour, freedom and equality.

'And in the bright, life-giving spirit of reason, strengthening the hearts and souls of all people for the success and triumph of Communism through revolution.

'And in the united and indivisible Fatherland of all peoples and the common ownership of all property.

'I profess united, glorious Communism, the corrector of the faults of society.

'I await the awakening of the peoples and the future Communist order in the whole world.'

Yet Botev was not, in fact, a Communist in the strict sense of the word, i.e. one who accepts Marx's theory of Scientific Socialism. Though Botev was acquainted with some of the writings of Marx, including *Capital*, and was almost certainly influenced by the Communist Manifesto when he wrote his *Creed*, he remained a Utopian Socialist, whose views were a mixture of those of Chernyshevsky and Proudhon. Indeed, it would not have been possible for Botev, living as he did at a time when Bulgaria was an agrarian, semi-feudal country without capitalist industry and without an industrial proletariat, to have accepted Marxism in its entirety. Botev saw the miseries that capitalism in the West had brought to the working people, and he hoped that in the Slavonic countries the stage of capitalism might be avoided altogether. Limited by the stage of development then reached by Bulgaria, he could not grasp the Marxist thesis that capitalism, for all its evils, was in its own era a step forward, a necessary, inevitable stage in economic development, and that only capitalism could produce the class which would build Socialism, i.e. the industrial proletariat. While Botev did develop beyond his earlier theory that the basis for Socialism in Bulgaria was the 'special character', the 'special physiognomy' of the Bulgarian people, with its communes, guilds, etc., given freedom from Turkish slavery, and came to believe under the influence of Scientific Socialism that Socialism would be created by the working people acting in unison against 'Tsars and capitalists', he never came to see Socialism as historically necessary for resolving the contradictions of capitalism, but rather as something morally desirable, and the 'proletariat' which he counterposed to the hated capitalists and *chorbadzhii* was not the industrial proletariat of Marx—there being no such class at that time in Bulgaria—but the 'people' in general, and the peasantry in particular. Moreover, for his ideal society Botev did not look forward to the Socialist transformation of an industrial society, but back to the 'Golden Age' of the decentralized village communes. He even opposed the introduction of modern inventions, because he saw the evils that industrialization had brought to the West, and he was afraid lest modern inventions would bring similar ills to Bulgaria. Furthermore, he observed that such inventions in the main benefited the rich and not the poor, and therefore he rejected them, not perceiving that it was not the things themselves but the nature of their ownership that was at fault.

'Each discovery and improvement in science and industry, if it cannot be applied in practice by everyone and be of equal use to the poor as well as to the rich, is injurious to the progress of freedom and therefore to the happiness of humanity. During the last century the natural, physical and mathematical sciences have indeed achieved great successes in their development, but from all their results we see that part of humanity, which has always lived well and has never done any work and has always sucked the blood of millions of unfortunate human creatures, makes the most use of them. Look at all the civilized countries of Europe, lend an ear to those groans and sufferings which are heard behind the official screens of human progress, pay serious attention to the desperate struggle between labour and capital in Europe as well as in America, and you will be convinced of the truth of our words, and you will say together with common sense that in the present social and political order of humanity the poor man is everywhere a slave and the slave is everywhere a poor man.' (*Zname*, Vol. I, No. 17, May 23, 1875.)

In particular Botev was opposed to the building of railways—a thing understandable enough in Bulgaria's case, since the railways facilitated foreign economic penetration and the subsequent ruin of the Bulgarian artisans who could not compete with cheap Western competition:

'For us the railways are harmful in every way. Economically they are harmful because they will increase the export and import of goods— the former, since it consists entirely of raw materials, will exhaust and impoverish our land which will soon resemble Palestine, and the second will kill our handicrafts and industry.'

The shortcomings in Botev's Socialism were quite natural and inevitable in view of the economic and social conditions then prevailing in Bulgaria, and they in no way alter the fact that Botev's ideology marks the highest point reached by any pre-Liberation Bulgarian thinker.

Although apart from being a great revolutionary, Botev is considered to be Bulgaria's greatest poet, there is no room in a history of this kind to discuss Botev's poetical works. They are relatively few in number, about twenty in all, but are exceptional in quality and beauty. Almost all reflect the revolutionary struggle, the agony of slavery, Botev's passionate desire to work and fight to the death for his country's liberation, his hatred of the oppressors, his contempt for the indifferent. His heroes are the legendary fighters for freedom: the *haidut voivoda*, Hadzhi Dimiter and Vasil Levsky. The poems are deeply popular in form and content—an attribute which possibly may be due in no small measure to the influence of Botev's mother who knew four hundred folk songs, which she sang to her children. Botev's most famous poem *Hadzhi Dimiter*, which tells of the heroic death of the *cheta voivoda*, has been set to music and remains to this day one of Bulgaria's most popular songs, sanctified not only by Botev's own death in similar circumstances, but also by the blood of countless latter-day martyrs for freedom who have gone to their deaths singing the celebrated fifth verse: 'He who falls in the fight for freedom does not die . . .'

For Botev literature was one of the weapons in the struggle for freedom. It must both mirror present reality and point the way to the future.

'Learning and literature and poetry and journalism, in a word, all the spiritual activity of their [the people's] leaders should assume the character of political propaganda, i.e. should conform to the life, the aspirations and needs of the people, and should no longer be learning for learning's sake, art for art's sake, or journalism for chewing over the cud of the old, rotten, long since discarded European dunghill.'

Botev's own poetry and other writings certainly lived up to this definition, and as a revolutionary poet and publicist he was unsurpassed. But although he agreed with Levsky that a Revolutionary Party was necessary, he was himself a prophet rather than an organizer. He lacked Levsky's patience, his ability to build brick by brick, year by year. Botev's fiery temperament craved immediate revolution and he was ready, even eager, to lay down his own life for the cause. It was not only his impatient nature that made him over-hasty. Under the influence of the Russian *Narodniks*, Botev believed that the mass of the people was always instinctively ready for revolution and merely awaited leaders to direct and set a personal example. It was, of course, true that a potentially revolutionary situation existed within Bulgaria, but, as subsequent events were to prove, far more organizational work and patient preparation than Botev and his companions realized was necessary to make proper use of this situation.

The Economic situation in Turkey, 1874–1875

During 1874–1875 the economic situation in Turkey, which had steadily deteriorated as a result of Western exploitation since the Crimean War, took a sharp turn for the worse. Turkey's foreign debts rose from 0·75 milliard francs in 1854 to 5·3 milliard francs in 1875, in which year 60 per cent of Turkey's State Budget went on paying the interest on foreign loans. Year by year the budget deficit had increased and in 1875 Turkey was obliged to declare herself officially bankrupt.

In an effort to extricate the country from the bottomless pit into which it was inexorably sliding, the Porte adopted a series of desperate measures which included confiscating part of the income from *vakīf* lands, cutting expenditure and raising tithes and taxes. The first two antagonized many Turks, and increased sympathy for the Young Turk Movement, founded by Midhat Pasha, which hoped through reforms to make Turkey a modern State with a constitutional Government. The third measure, which did yield money, nevertheless acted as a serious brake on economic development. Apart from that, it brought increased misery to the Christian people already overburdened with taxes of all kinds. Even without extra taxes, 1874 and 1875 were disastrous years for the peasantry. A drought in the summer of 1874 was followed by a severe winter, which led to serious difficulties in finding fodder for cattle. Even the straw off the roofs had to be used for this purpose, and still the cattle died in large numbers from cold, disease and starvation. According to the Bulgarian Press in Constantinople, people also died of starvation, and when the spring finally came, they were without seed for sowing or food to last until the harvest. Unfortunately, drought struck again in the summer of 1875, and the people reached the lowest depths of destitution. The moneylenders, however, 'had never had it so good'. They bought the grain from the peasants at an artificially low price while it was still standing in the fields, and sold it back to them at a much higher price. The journal *Napredŭk* of Stara Zagora described how a peasant might sell his grain in advance for 25 *grosh* a kilo, and would later have to buy it back at 81–91 *grosh* a kilo, when the normal cash price was 50 *grosh* a kilo, so that in fact the peasant might pay up to 66 *grosh* interest on a 25 *grosh* loan.[1]

The peasants were not the only ones who suffered. High taxation and inflation also affected the merchant and manufacturing *bourgeoisie* and led to a slump in trade. In 1875 the famous Unzundzhovo Fair closed down. In addition the population suffered from the banditry of the 100,000 Circassians who had been resettled in the Turkish Empire, and, it goes without saying, the usual corruption and outrages continued unabated.

The New Central Revolutionary Committee, 1875

By 1875 the desperate plight of the Bulgarian people had given rise to a situation which was extremely favourable for the organization of a general revolution. The explosive situation was further enhanced by the outbreak of a revolt in Bosnia and Herzegovina (during June of 1875) provinces which like Bulgaria had suffered from the great drought and the increased taxation. The rising roused tremendous interest on the part of the Bulgarians, and the Bulgarian Press in Constantinople printed detailed reports of the progress of the rising and the diplomatic reactions of the Great Powers, especially Russia's support for the rebels. Botev greeted the rising with unbounded enthusiasm:

'In this deep night', he wrote in *Zname*, 'in which we count the days of our endless Passion Week, south-west of us in the homeland of Vukalovich, our oppressed Herzegovinian brothers have raised the banner of freedom, and, without any kind of outside help, have gone forth to do battle with our common tyrant. What South-Slavonic heart will not begin to beat at this signal of revolution? What young hero will not twirl his moustaches and seize his rusted sabre?' The time had come for Bulgaria to act: 'We cannot but turn to our Revolutionary Party and remind it that it has an obligation to follow the example of our Serbian and Montenegrin brothers. Now

[1] Kosev, *Lektsii po Nova Bŭlgarska Istoriya*, p. 214.

is the time for us also to add our strength and to proceed to the cutting of the Gordian knot . . . Now is the time to call the people to revolt and, by splitting the forces of our common enemy, to help both ourselves and our brothers. Now! But are we ready? Have we anything worked out, assembled, and organized?—Shame and reproach on us, brother émigrés! Shame and reproach on our idleness! . . . But the people have worked, and nothing can bring about a general revolution other than common suffering and misfortunes. The idea of freedom is all powerful and love of it can achieve all things. Think on this, unhappy sons of Bulgaria and do not let slip the opportune moment. . . . Now is the time to show that we are men and not cattle.'

And one of the Bulgarian revolutionaries imprisoned in Diarbekir expressed the same hope in the folllowing message, which was also printed in *Znamé*:

'Have we not here, in the rising in Herzegovina, the beginning of the sacred struggle of the people and the Slavs for freedom and equality? O tremble, you reptiles, as my heart now trembles, as I recall that in this ferment of Slavonic power, the Bulgarian people are no longer sleeping.'

Fully believing that the rising in Herzegovina was the beginning of the end for Turkey, Botev and his comrades began to organize for a rising in Bulgaria to take full advantage of the situation. Botev and Stambolov, who had returned to Rumania in April 1875, formed a Commission for the purpose of reuniting the Revolutionary Movement inside and outside Bulgaria, and called for an Assembly with representation from all the Committees. The internal Committees approved their initiative and agreed to send Nikola Obretenov, the youngest son of Baba Tonka, the dauntless old lady of Rusé, who was herself a leading member of the revolutionary movement, who had boldly sheltered and assisted Levsky, and whose two elder sons had taken part in the *cheta* of Stefan Karadzhata and Hadzhi Dimiter. Botev and Stambolov also won the support of the veteran *voivoda*, Panaiot Khitov, who helped them to send letters to the Committees in Rumania.

The delegates met on August 12, 1875. A new Central Committee was elected, consisting of Dragoi Shopov (Treasurer), Ivan Drasov, former Secretary of the Lovech Committee and a comrade-in-arms of

Levsky, Dr Khristo Chobanov, Dimiter Tsenovich and Botev himself. It was apparently not considered necessary to elect a secretary or chairman, but it was decided to send 'apostles' into Bulgaria to raise a revolt and the following were sent to the various districts: Nikola Obretenov to Rusé, Shumen, Varna and Razgrad; Stambolov to Stara Zagora; Tanyu Stoyanov and Sava Tanasov to the Sliven district; Mikhail Sarafov and Petŭr Volov to Tŭrnovo and Stoyan Dragiev to Lovech. In addition, Stoyan Zaimov and five others, including Georgi Benkovsky, were sent to Constantinople to set fire to the city in order to create panic and confusion among the Turks. Dimiter Tsenovich was sent to Belgrade, presumably to make contact with the rebels in Herzegovina, while Botev was sent to Odessa to collect money for arms and to try to persuade Filip Totyu to join in the struggle. It was also hoped that Botev would be able to persuade Bulgarian officers in the Russian Army to resign their commissions and return to Rumania to help, and that influential Bulgars in Odessa would prevail upon the Russian Government to supply 12,000 rifles. The general plan of the revolt envisaged that apart from the burning of Constantinople and the risings within Bulgaria itself, several *cheti* should be organized from outside, including one of 2,000 men under Khitov, who was to cross from Serbia, or from Rumania, if the Serbs objected.

The Stara Zagora Rising, 1875

Unfortunately, although the plan looked impressive on paper, the hard facts of the matter were that the preparations for their realization were totally inadequate. Levsky alone seemed to have been sufficiently unromantic to appreciate the fact that the people were not perpetually on the brink of revolt, awaiting only the word to rise. He realized only too well that they had to be convinced, inspired, welded into a disciplined organization and properly armed. His life had been devoted to this task and he had achieved a remarkable degree of success. After his death, however, the Committees collapsed and the iron discipline had rusted. Both the period of inactivity for which Karavelov was responsible, and the inexperience of Levsky's successors had also contributed to the unsatisfactory conditions of Levsky's network of Committees. The foundations remained, but the damage would take time to repair, and the new Central Committee, eager to take advantage of the political situation, did not allow sufficient time for the rebuilding of all that had been destroyed. The centralized discipline was not fully restored and the

H*

'apostles' worked in their own separate areas without adequate liaison and co-ordination. The problem of obtaining arms, which had been one of Levsky's greatest difficulties, still remained unsolved, for Botev's efforts to obtain money and arms were largely unsuccessful. Here again the Central Committee took a rather romantic, unrealistic view. 'Even a small rising will do good. . . . If there are no cannon and rifles, let the people rise with scythes and cudgels.'

The two *voivodi* did absolutely nothing about organizing the *cheti*, and in Khitov's case, this was probably due to the influence of the Serbian Government whose policy at that time was opposed to any rising in Bulgaria. Finally, the party sent to set fire to Constantinople were unable to do so because they lacked sufficient money and helpers. Thus the rising was a complete failure from the outset.

On September 14th the Committee in Tŭrnovo announced that they would rise on September 16th, and urged Stara Zagora to do the same. In Stara Zagora, Stambolov, who had proposed on his arrival there that they prepare for a rising in the very near future, encountered a certain amount of opposition from people who considered that insufficient preparations had as yet been made. Nevertheless, when they received the message from Tŭrnovo Stambolov, supported by the peasants in the surrounding villages, declared that they would rise on September 16th. The *chorbadzhii* had learnt of the arrival of Stambolov, and informed the Turks of the rising, so that fears of reprisals engulfed the population, including some of the committee members, and only twenty people turned up at the rendezvous. Undismayed, the little band marched off with songs, hoping to join up as arranged with other detachments of rebels from Sliven, Chirpan, Plovdiv and Tŭrnovo. Unfortunately, the haste and lack of proper preparation produced the same results everywhere. At the last moment Tŭrnovo decided to postpone the rising, but the news reached Stara Zagora too late. In Rusé some twenty-five to thirty men formed a *cheta*, but betrayal and the news that Tŭrnovo had not risen forced them to disband. From Shumen about twenty men set out but soon dispersed when they heard that no rising had materialized in Sliven. Everywhere it proved impossible to rouse the people to revolt and the rising ended abortively almost before it had begun. The only fighting took place between a small *cheta* of villagers under Rusi Bakŭrdzhi and some armed *bashibazouks* near the village of Elkhovo. Bakŭrdzhi was killed at the beginning of the engagement and his *cheta* dispersed. Stambolov escaped to

Tŭrnovo and from thence managed to return to Rumania. An interesting sidelight on the rising is provided by the proclamation issued by the Central Committee urging the rebels in no way to harm peaceful Turks whom it calls 'our neighbours and fellow sufferers. . . . The honour, property and life of peaceful Turks should be as precious and sacred to you as it is to them'. This did not prevent the Turks from taking cruel vengeance on the Bulgarians. In Adrianople (Edirne), for example, two hundred were arrested, and ten were hanged. In Stara Zagora itself, seventy-eight were arrested, of whom seven were hanged.

CHAPTER IX

THE APRIL RISING
AND THE LIBERATION

Bulgarian Society on the Eve of the April Rising

A correct picture of Bulgarian society in the 1870's is essential if one is to understand why the revolutionary fervour of some sections of the Bulgarian people rose again like the phoenix from the blood and ashes of each successive failure, while other sections went to great lengths to undermine the Revolutionary Movement and to sabotage its efforts. Let us start with the peasantry as the most numerous class at that time. Mention has already been made of the natural disasters of 1874–1875 and the extent to which the peasants were falling into debt, but the real problem was more fundamental, and was aggravated, not caused, by the dry weather. In essence, the problem arose from the fact that the Turkish regime with its feudal system of tithes, taxes and usury carried to the limit by law and corruption, had reached the point where it was not possible for the peasant to make a living from the land. The problem for the Bulgarian peasant was not lack of land. Each peasant, however poor, had his own house, garden, vineyard, plot of land and livestock. Not all the available land was even being cultivated. The problem was that no matter how hard the peasant worked, most of his harvest was taken from him in tithes and taxation, which embraced every possible branch of village economy. In theory the Bulgarian peasant was an independent smallholder—in practice, with his whole harvest mortgaged in advance at an artifically low price, sometimes with even the title-deeds to his land itself in the hands of the usurers, he was no longer the owner of his land and the fruits of his labour, but merely the hired labourer of his creditors, a kind of rural proletarian. Theoretically the Bulgarian peasant had the means of supporting himself and his family through his own labour on his own land. In practice, Turkish rule rendered this impossible. Some gave up trying to gain a living from their own land and sought work as hired labourers on the Turkish *chifliks*, but these were by now relatively few in number and the demand for labour was small. Others drifted in search of work to the towns, to the wharves of the Danube ports, to the new railway construction sites. The economy could not absorb all the surplus labour and wages were consequently very low. Some of the proletarianized peasants sought work abroad as gardeners, labourers, drovers, etc., leaving home in spring and returning in the autumn. Some even went as far as France.

The position in the towns was not much better. Some craftsmen carried on agriculture as well as a trade, but this was not possible in the mountain towns where the soil was poor, such as Troyan, Gabrovo, Karlovo, Sopot, Koprivshtitsa, Panagyurishté, Batak, etc. As the competition of the cheap imported European goods ruined the local craftsmen, unemployment in these towns grew, since the backward economy could not absorb all the idle hands. The men would leave home for months or even years on end, to work in the towns in the plains or even abroad, sending home what money they could. The women and children worked at home, spinning and weaving with material supplied by merchant capitalists who put work out at very low wages. The struggle which these families had in order to live is perhaps best illustrated by the fact that in these mountain towns where people could not grow much and had to buy more or less all their food, dishes unknown in the plains were prepared from such things as snails, nettles and docks, which could be gathered free.[1] Even those who for the time being survived foreign competition were ruined by Turks who took goods 'on account' without the slightest intention of ever paying, or obtained 'loans' from Bulgarian craftsmen and petty traders without ever returning the money, knowing full well that the wretched Bulgars would not dare to complain for fear their shops would be burnt or they themselves imprisoned. It is no accident that the centres of the April Rising were precisely these mountain towns where the sheer physical impossibility of living any longer under Turkish rule was most keenly felt.

Another section of the community stricken with unemployment was the intelligentsia. Owing to the opening of schools and the increased opportunities for Bulgars to study abroad, the ranks of the intelligentsia had swollen considerably, but the low level of culture which prevailed throughout the Turkish Empire, the concentration

[1] Professor Doctor Kh. Gandev, Aprilskoto Vŭstanie, *Narodna Mladezh*, 1956, p. 23.

of the administration in the hands of the Turks, the lack of cultural institutions, etc., meant that the intellectuals could not find suitable posts. One of the few openings available to the Bulgarian intellectuals was the teaching profession, which was over-crowded and very poorly paid. Some intellectuals were driven to seek material security in the priesthood or the monasteries.

For these sections of the population, Turkish rule not only made life impossible in the present, but also represented a barrier to all possible improvement in the future. For them the only solution to their problems was the immediate ending of Turkish rule. But there were other sections, fewer in number but socially and economically powerful, which were able to make use of the special conditions of Turkish rule to enrich themselves, i.e. the *bourgeoisie* and, in particular, the upper *bourgeoisie*, including industrialists, large-scale traders, tax farmers, bankers, moneylenders, etc.

The most important section of the *bourgeoisie* were the owners of industrial capitalist enterprises, who were relatively few in number, only some 1,500–2,000 throughout the country. Since the beginning of the century, capitalist relations had been creeping in, even while the guilds were still an active force, in the form of the giving out of work by traders to people who worked at home for a wage. The next stage was the building of workshops where hired labour was employed. Capitalism was most advanced in the textile industry. Much of the production of *aba* and *gaitan* was already organized on capitalist lines. *Gaitan* workshops, for example, accounted for most of the production in the main handicraft towns, such as Karlovo, Kalofer, Kazanlŭk, Sopot, Panagyurishté. The average number of people employed varied from 15 to 30, although Dobri Zhelyazkov's former textile mill in Sliven, now under State control, employed between 500 and 1,000 people. In Karlovo, Ivan Grosev's factory used iron looms and steam power, although others still used wooden looms and water power, or even looms worked by hand. During the seventies, the Rasheevs, *gaitan* manufacturers of Gabrovo, decided to build a textile mill and even went to France in order to examine machinery, and other *gaitan* manufacturers were thinking along the same lines. Capitalist manufacture was also developing in other industries such as tanning, flour milling, spirit distilling, etc.

The big traders who dealt in European imports and raw materials for export with a network of middlemen all over the country, were also capitalists in essence. Bulgarian industry depended to a very great extent on foreign imports, especially steel, cast iron, non-ferrous metals, glass, paper, kerosene, sulphuric acid, vitriol, etc., and import and export firms existed in all the main ports. In Svishtov, for example, there were a hundred such firms. These traders, unlike the ruined craftsmen, had no objection to Western industrial penetration, for their fortunes were made through acting as agents for Western goods. In addition to their usual business, the capitalists were often, at the same time, usurers.

To the upper *bourgeoisie* belonged also the *dzhelepi*, who engaged in large-scale sheep trading, and those who bought the right to collect taxes. These people had no reason to be dissatisfied with Turkish rule, and the tax collectors, in particular, benefited from the innumerable taxes and the general corruption.

Apart from the large-scale capitalists, there was also a middle *bourgeoisie*, which was in part the ally of the upper *bourgeoisie*. The middle *bourgeoisie* was a much more numerous class, consisting of the owners of large inns, taverns, wine cellars, the petty capitalists, usurers, tax collectors responsible for only two or three villages, small cattle dealers, shopkeepers, etc. While it is true that petty commodity production was still predominant in Bulgarian economy and that the petty *bourgeoisie*[1] was the predominant class numerically, and while capitalism had hardly penetrated at all into most of the handicraft industries, nevertheless the upper *bourgeoisie*—the capitalists—had gained control over the most important and profitable branches of the economy. Apart from their economic power, they gained political power when the Turks, in the course of reforms on the basis of the *Hat-i-Humayun*, allowed the setting up of official Bulgarian municipalities, or Communes, with competence over all manner of local matters. The members of these Communes were, in theory, to be elected, but, in practice, only a minority were able to vote, and the Councils usually consisted of rich traders, bankers and other members of the upper *bourgeoisie*. Thus the Councils were the obedient tools, nay, bosom friends, of the Turks. The rich escaped the worst oppressions of Turkish rule, and, in any case, they had sufficient wealth to bribe their way out of any unpleasantness. Their position was threatened, not by the Turks, on whose rotting administration they lived like parasites, but by revolution, and consequently their attitude to the Revolution was one of bitter hostility, which increased as the tide of revolt rose.

[1] The term 'petty *bourgeois*' is applied to minor property owners, producing on a small scale for the market. It includes poor and middle peasants, craftsmen and petty traders.

The Crisis in the BRCC

After the failure of the Stara Zagora Rising, a crisis developed in the affairs of the BRCC which resulted in Botev's resignation on September 30, 1875, and the subsequent collapse of the Committee. The basic reasons for the crisis were the failure of the Stara Zagora Rising, but the seeds of the trouble had been sown even before the actual rising took place and arose in part from the Committee's perennial lack of funds. It had always been the case that while money was by no means lacking among the Bulgarian émigrés, it was concentrated in the hands of those opposed to revolution. The Liberal middle *bourgeoisie* had adopted a negative and non-co-operative attitude towards the new BRCC, and since many of the Committees in the towns throughout Rumania were largely under Liberal control, these Committees refused to pay the contributions required of them. In this situation, the BRCC was forced to make a compromise with the Liberals, and on August 20, 1875, two Liberal representatives—Ivan Kavaldzhiev, and Kiriak Tsankov, one of Karavelov's foremost supporters—joined the BRCC. Tsankov also had certain connections with the 'Old' Party and the Committee hoped that through him they might be able to obtain financial support from the rich upper *bourgeoisie*.

No sooner had Tsankov joined the BRCC than he set up another organization called *Bŭlgarsko Chelovekolyubivo Nastoyatelstvo* (Bulgarian Humanitarian Committee), and subsequently won over to it two other members of the BRCC, Kavaldzhiev and Shopov, who had been one of the original members of the new BRCC. Tsankov insisted that the aims of the Bulgarian Humanitarian Committee were purely charitable, but it was perfectly clear to Botev, at least, that it was intended to be a rival Liberal political organization, and he said as much in a letter to Drasov, written while he was on his way to Russia to do his part in the preparations for the Stara Zagora Rising. In Botev's absence, the growth of the Liberal influence in the BRCC became apparent in the Committee's paper *Zname*, which lost the vigorous militancy imparted to it by Botev.

The Committee was further undermined by the fact that while Panaiot Khitov was outwardly a loyal member of the Committee—indeed, he had acted as Chairman at the foundation meeting on August 12th—he was, in actual fact, as we have seen, wedded to the policy of the Serbian Government, having been a Serbian pensioner since 1868.

In offering his resignation to the Committee, Botev was guided by many considerations. He felt that the Committee had capitulated to the Liberal *bourgeoisie* and the pro-Serb element, and he had a serious disagreement with Drasov who, together with him, had been the life and soul of the Committee, doing the bulk of the work. The disagreement was over the question of whether or not they should try to continue the rising in spite of its lack of success. Botev was opposed to any attempt to continue it. Apart from differences of policy, another factor influenced Botev's decision to resign: the deliberate slander campaign whipped up by the upper *bourgeoisie* and aimed at discrediting the BRCC and disrupting the revolutionary camp. As we have seen, the Bulgarian upper *bourgeoisie* in Rumania was opposed to revolution in any form, not without reason, in view of the repeated statements by revolutionary leaders that the liberated Bulgaria was to be a 'People's' Bulgaria without *chorbadzhii*. The rich *émigrés*, headed by Evlogi Georgiev, directed their attack primarily against Botev, whom they rightly regarded as the key man in the BRCC. They put out various slanderous rumours about him, hoping to blacken his character in the eyes of his comrades.

In such a situation in view of Liberal undermining, disagreement with his closest colleague, Drasov, who had won Tsenovich for his point of view, Khitov's two-faced conduct and the slander campaign, Botev felt his position to be impossible and offered his resignation on September 30th. About the same time Chobanov, Shopov, Tsankov and Kavaldzhiev also resigned, though no doubt for very different reasons, leaving only Drasov and Tsenovich of the original Committee. On October 1st there was a meeting of the BRCC at which, in addition to Drasov, Tsenovich and nine other people, there were present the two 'Apostles', Stambolov and Nikola Obretenov, who had returned from Bulgaria. The meeting discussed the possibility of continuing the rising. It was pointed out that Khitov's failure to cross with a *cheta* as planned had contributed to the failure of the Stara Zagora Rising, and the two 'Apostles' insisted that it was impossible to organize a rising without *voivodi*. Finally it was decided that Stambolov and Filip Totyu, who was present at the meeting, should cross into Bulgaria with a few men, and if the people reacted favourably, a rising should be proclaimed. Plans were made for the collecting of funds, but nothing came of them. The Committee's lack of success gave rise to bitter recriminations, which split and weakened it still further, and by the beginning of November 1875 it had more or less ceased to function.

The Gyurgevo Committee

When the remainder of the 'Apostles' returned undaunted to Rumania, ready both to analyse the reasons for the failure of the Stara Zagora Rising and to make plans for the next attempt, they found that the BRCC was already a corpse, paralysed by internal dissensions and the skilful manœuvres of the 'Old' Party. They therefore left Bucharest and went to Giurgiu (in Bulgarian Gyurgevo), a town on the Danube opposite Rusé. Here, with the financial help of two merchants, they rented a house on the outskirts of the town and began to consider what the next step should be. By the middle of November, the following people were assembled in the 'barracks', as they called their house: Nikola Obretenov, Stefan Stambolov, Stoyan Zaimov, Panaiot Volov, Ilarion Dragostinov, Khristo Karaminkov, Georgi Apostolov, Nikola Slavkov, Georgi Benkovsky, Georgi Ikonomov, Georgi Obretenov (Nikola's brother) and Georgi Izmirliev. The twelve leading revolutionaries were also supported by Ivan Hadzhi Dimitrov, one of the active members of the Türnovo Committee since the days of Levsky, Ivanitsa Danchov, Sava Penev and Yanko Angelov, who taught at the Bulgarian school in Giurgiu.

The so-called Gyurgevo Committee sat from November 15th to December 25th (old style). Unlike all previous Committees, its members were unanimous on major questions of policy: all were agreed that another rising must be organized and that all their efforts must be directed toward this end. The unity of the Committee was further strengthened by the fact that almost all its members were seasoned revolutionaries, experienced in practical work, and on the friendliest terms with each other personally.

The difficulties involved in organizing a successful rising were enormous. Apart from the purely organizational problems such as finance and the collection of arms, the revolutionaries faced a situation in which they had to contend with the active treachery, or, at best, the passive non-co-operation of the richest and the most influential of their fellow countrymen; they would be faced with well-equipped professional soldiers, whom, in view of national differences, they could not hope to win over to their side—in many other revolutions the demoralization of the Army was an important factor for success—and in addition, they would have to contend with armed Turkish civilians who would not hesitate to massacre any Bulgar on whom they could lay their hands, without reference to age or sex. The greatest difficulty of all was the totally inadequate time during which all the preparations had to be made. The date of the rising was dictated by the international situation. Serbia and Montenegro were expected to declare war on Turkey in the spring; the rising in Bosnia and Herzegovina would flare up again as soon as the snow melted, and since a Tripartite Conference between Russia, Austro-Hungry and Germany to discuss the whole question of autonomy for the Slav provinces of the Turkish Empire was scheduled to take place in May, it was felt that a rising before that date would bring the Bulgarian question to the notice of the Great Powers and reinforce Bulgaria's claim for freedom.

The Gyurgevo Committee decided to divide the country into four independent Revolutionary Regions, and to send Apostles to each to prepare for the rising. The four Regions by no means covered the entire country, nor were they contiguous. Lack of time and cadres made it necessary to concentrate only on certain key areas. In selecting the four regions, the Committee chose mountain areas, which provided a suitable base for military operations, and avoided the plain where the population was predominantly Turkish. They also avoided areas where the old Committee organization had been badly disrupted as a result of the Arabakonak incident and Levsky's capture.

The four Regions chosen were Tŭrnovo, Sliven, Vratsa and Plovdiv. The first Region, that of Tŭrnovo, also included the districts of Gabrovo, Tryavna, Dryanovo, Sevlievo and Gorna Oryakhovitsa, and the Apostle appointed to this district was Stefan Stambolov, with Khristo Karaminkov and Georgi Izmirliev to help him. Izmirliev had been a cadet at the Military School in Odessa, and had been persuaded by Botev to return to help in the struggle. The second Region included the districts of Sliven, Yambol and part of the districts of Nova Zagora and Kotel, and the chief Apostle chosen was Ilarion Dragostinov, with Georgi Obretenov and Stoil Voivoda as his assistants. The third Region embraced north-west Bulgaria from Vratsa to the district of Lom, and was entrusted to Stoyan Zaimov, with Georgi Apostolov, Nikola Obretenov and Nikola Slavkov as his assistants. The fourth Region, that of Plovdiv, is better know as the Panagyurishté Region, since early on the organizational centre shifted from Plovdiv to Panagyurishté. It included an area bounded on the east by a line from Karlovo to Plovdiv, on the north by the Stara Planina, on the south by the northern slopes of the Rhodope taking in the villages of Batak, Perushtitsa, Peshtera, etc., and on the west by a line through Samokov. The chief Apostle for the fourth Region was Panaiot Volov, assisted by Georgi Benkovsky and later by Georgi Ikonomov, who was transferred from the Sliven region to which he had originally been assigned.

This arrangement of Regions, as we have already noted, left large areas of the country outside the organization. Such important areas as the Dobrudzha, the districts of Varna, Burgas, Khaskovo, Chirpan, Stara Zagora, Svishtov, Vidin, Lovech and even Sofia, had to be left unorganized. It was, however, hoped that since in many of these districts the old Committees founded by Levsky still survived, they would join in the rising once it had been proclaimed. In any case, apart from risings within the Regions, it was planned to cut all telegraph lines and the Adrianople–Belovo railway, and to set fire to Constantinople, Adrianople, Plovdiv and Pazardzhik. Botev was informed of the decisions of the Gyurgevo Committee by Nikola Obretenov and Georgi Apostolov, and promised to help when the rising started. Early in January the Apostles left Giurgiu for their districts, crossing the frozen Danube on the ice. A few of the Committee members remained in Rumania, but from this point onwards the Committee virtually ceased to exist as a centralizing body.

Preparations in the Tŭrnovo Region

The organizational centre of the first Region was Gorna Oryakhovitsa, not Tŭrnovo itself, since the former was not only well situated geographically, but was far more free of Turkish police than the ancient capital. Stambolov himself soon moved to the village of Samovodené, north-west of Tŭrnovo, and apart from visiting two or three villages to found Committees, he left that side of the work to his helpers, devoting his time to general leadership and liaison with Rumania, from whence he not only obtained guns, etc., but also recruited a number of new and valuable assistants. Because of this, the work in the villages went ahead well. Everywhere the Apostles were well received by the villagers, and, although they were seldom able to re-visit any village, they managed to inspire local leaders to carry on with all the necessary organizational work, maintaining contact by courier or by calling local representatives to discussions in Gorna Oryakhovitsa. In Tŭrnovo itself the work was less successful, owing to the opposition of the wealthy upper *bourgeoisie*. On the whole the work went well throughout the Region; there emerged plenty of excellent local leaders, possessed of inspiration and ability, but even so the agitational work and therefore the scale of the preparations was inadequate for the task.

The greatest organizational problem was how to obtain guns. Lead bullets were being cast in all the villages where there were local Committees, but while the Region had plenty of money collected in donations, it was proving wellnigh impossible to buy rifles in large enough quantities. Gunpowder was another problem. It could be bought on the 'black market' in Turkish villages, but soon the Turks began to suspect what was afoot, and they started to adulterate the powder.

Preparations in the Sliven Region

The first two representatives of the Gyurgevo Committee, Georgi Ikonomov and Stoil Voivoda, arrived in Sliven in the middle of February 1876. Ikonomov only stayed in Sliven for a short time, because as a native of the town, who had already fallen foul of the Turkish police and their spy, Saruivanov, the owner of a textile mill, he was obliged to remain in hiding. By the middle of March, he had made contact with the local revolutionary-minded youth and had formed a Regional Committee. He then moved first to Gorna Oryakhovitsa and then to Plovdiv, where they needed more Apostles and where he was not known to the police. Shortly afterwards, Ilarion Dragostinov and Georgi Obretenov arrived from Giurgiu to lead the organization. Unfortunately, differences of opinion arose between some of the local revolutionaries and the newly arrived Apostles. The local Committee wanted to form *cheti* which would operate in the mountains, and leave all the actual villages outside the organization, hoping in this way to avoid unnecessary slaughter and destruction. The Apostles, on the other hand, adhered to the Gyurgevo plan, which was to involve the whole population in the rising. The local revolutionaries evidently felt that they could not rouse the whole population, and Stoil Voivoda, who shared their point of view, began to prepare an armed camp in the mountains, with the intention of adopting *cheta* tactics in the forthcoming rising. Obretenov and Dragostinov were unable to persuade the Sliven Committee to alter its tactics, and therefore, under the circumstances, they made the best of a bad job and visited the villages and towns in the area, organizing committees to recruit young men for the *cheti*. Unfortunately, Kukumyatkov and Sŭbev, who were given the task of organizing the villages round Kotel, aroused the suspicions of the *chorbadzhii* of Gradets through their inexperience and were arrested. Although the two were released again, the Turks began to search the district with the aid of Bulgarian spies and found out about the camp in the mountains and the presence in Sliven of Stoil Voivoda himself. In order to avoid capture, Stoil and some of his comrades moved to the camp itself, where on April 23rd they had a clash with a Turkish Army unit, which fled after Stoil had shot the commander. Only now did the Sliven Committee begin hurriedly to collect arms and powder, but they had not got very far before the rising broke out, as we shall see later, in the Sredna Gora towns of the Plovdiv Region.

Preparations in the Vratsa Region

Of the four, the Vratsa Region proved to be the weakest organizationally. Here the work began in January when Stoyan Zaimov arrived with Georgi Apostolov, Nikola Obretenov, Ivanitsa Danchov, Spas Sokolov and Nikola Slavkov. Unfortunately, Nikola Slavkov was soon apprehended in the Teteven district, because of his immense stature, a danger which Stambolov had foreseen in Giurgiu, but which the others had decided to risk in view of Slavkov's pleading. Since the Turks were now keeping a watchful eye on all strangers, Nikola Obretenov was unable to do any organizational work round Teteven, and, after hiding in Vratsa for a month, he returned to Rumania. Most of the other Apostles were also forced to return to Rumania for one reason or another, leaving Stoyan Zaimov virtually single-handed. He toured Lom, Berkovitsa, Byala Slatina and various other towns and villages, reviving the old Committees and setting up new ones. While in some places good activity was developed, especially in Byala Slatina where F. Simidov, a teacher, did excellent work, the preparations never attained the level of drawing in the mass of the peasantry. The military preparations were particularly weak. Although considerable sums of money were available, and a number of guns were purchased, it proved impossible to bring them across the Danube, and there were no military instructors. In Vratsa itself, the difficulties were made greater by quarrels within the Committee, the members of which included quite a number of merchants and craftsmen, accustomed to having everything their own way. It was after a quarrel with the Vratsa Treasurer that Georgi Apostolov returned to Rumania, and even Zaimov himself was on the point of departing because of the constant bickering, but was persuaded to stay.

Preparations in the Panagyurishté Region

The picture in the Panagyurishté Region was very different. Panaiot Volov and Georgi Benkovsky, the Apostles assigned to the Region, were the first to reach Bulgaria, arriving in the first days of January. Plovdiv proved to be too full of Turkish police and spies and too much subject to the paralysing influence of the upper *bourgeoisie* to make a suitable revolutionary capital, and the centre of gravity soon shifted to Panagyurishté and Klisura. In the Panagyurishté Region there existed a combination of favourable circumstances: discontent among the peasants and the ruined artisans of the former handicraft centres, such as Karlovo, Sopot, Panagyurishté, Koprivshtitsa, Perushtitsa, and Batak, was approaching boiling point, while several brilliant leaders came to the surface to canalize and direct this discontent towards a definite goal. Benkovsky and Volov were soon joined by Georgi Ikonomov from Sliven, and Zakhari Stoyanov, and they found many more excellent revolutionary leaders in the localities, in particular Todor Kableshkov of Koprivshtitsa, a young man whose vision, enthusiasm and genius for organization invite comparison with Levsky.

The four Apostles toured the area, reviving Levsky's Committees and creating new ones where none had previously existed. Everywhere they ceremoniously swore in new revolutionaries and set in motion preparations for the great uprising. Their approach in the villages was a new and interesting one. They boldly approached the rich, influential citizens, together with the mayor, the teacher and the priest, and once having won such men for the cause, as they often did succeed in doing, the problem of drawing in the mass of the population was made much easier. Benkovsky himself personally visited Plovdiv, Karlovo, Klisura, Koprivshtitsa, Pazardzhik, the north Rhodope villages, and many other places. A native of Koprivshtitsa, whose real name was Gavril Khlŭtov, Benkovsky had received a scanty education and, starting life as a tailor's apprentice, he had been driven by poverty and unemployment to emigrate to Anatolia in search of work. Politically he belonged to the extreme left wing of the National Liberation Movement. Like Levsky he was a Republican, and he shared both Levsky's faith in revolution and his ability to inspire faith in others. Now in the heat of the preparations, he showed such qualities as an organizer that Panaiot Volov voluntarily relinquished his post of chief Apostle to him, as the more able leader.

Benkovsky's fiery eloquence and brilliant organizing ability, coupled with correct tactics, won trader, priest, teacher and peasant alike, and welded them into healthy, active Committees closely linked to the central leadership under the Apostles. Whereas in the other regions the Apostles had, on the whole, remained in their 'capitals', and had failed to involve the peasantry, the Panagyurishté leadership left the towns to the local Committees and concentrated on the villages. Usually they were eagerly received by the inhabitants, who in some cases had already been preparing for a rising on their own initiative, inspired by the rumour flying round the country that, in the spring, 'Russia will audit the accounts of the Sultan', presumably based on the news of the proposed Tripartite Conference. In one village, Sotir, Zakhari Stoyanov found a large number of people gathered in a house for a traditional 'working party', but instead of doing the usual domestic or agricultural tasks, the guests were filling cartridges with gunpowder and casting lead bullets in the hearth!

Apart from involving the mass of the people, the Panagyurishté Apostles also gave great attention to the question of military preparations, which tended to be the weak link in the other Districts. In the Panagyurishté Region, statistics were collected of the numbers of Bulgars able to bear arms, and the probable numbers of Turks with whom they would have to contend. Benkovsky demanded that each rebel should have a rifle, a knife, a sword, a pistol or revolver, 300 cartridges for the rifle and a 150 for the pistol, 50 grammes of gunpowder, and suitable clothing, including a uniform. He laid great stress on the provision of uniforms because of the impression that they would make on all who saw them, and the uniform that he chose was of white *shaek*, similar to the Russian uniforms, with white foot-wrappers tied with black thongs, and a black fur hat, adorned with a peacock feather and the lion emblem. Uniforms for Benkovsky himself and his comrades were made by Deyan Belishky, a tailor of Panagyurishté, who also made a banner for the rising to Benkovsky's specifications. It was of silk, green on one side and red on the other, and it was subsequently embroidered, also to Benkovsky's specifications, by Raina Georgieva (Futekova), a Panagyurishté teacher, with the device 'Freedom or Death' and a lion trampling on the Crescent.

Arrangements were made for the formation of units of from ten to a hundred men, according to the size of the villages, Commanders were appointed and training was carried out in the mountains and forests. It must be stressed that the Panagyurishté rebels had no *voivodi* and no professional officers with military training, and that all their Commanders, including Benkovsky himself, were ordinary civilians with some knowledge of firearms and tactics.

Great care was given to the collection of firearms and gunpowder, but although funds were collected in voluntary donations, even here, in this otherwise well-organized Region, the whole question of obtaining arms remained a difficult and relatively unsolved problem. Modern artillery was out of the question, but the Bulgarians manufactured home-made cannon from cherry trees, bound with metal hoops and lined with copper from the pipes of the vats used for distilling rose-oil. Gunpowder was obtained on the black market from the Turks and Albanians, but here, too, the traders began to adulterate their goods so that it hardly burned. Most of the rifles were, in any case, very old ones.

Apart from the all-important problem of arms, the business of assembling stores and equipment went ahead splendidly. In Panagyurishté, merchants provided flour, wool, lead, iron, leather, etc., against ious. Two hundred people were working under three master tailors sewing uniforms, and a further thirty-five were making leather sandals, satchels, cartridge belts, etc. By March and April, practically the entire population in such towns as Panagyurishté, Koprivshtitsa, and Bratsigovo had abandoned their usual work in the fields and workshops to devote their particular skills to the cause of revolution. Even the women and children were baking biscuits, rolling bandages and preparing ointments.

Benkovsky revived the disciplined revolutionary organization created by Levsky: within the Panagyurishté Region, security was protected by a secret mail and a Secret Police, and in both Panagyurishté and Koprivshtitsa and even in some of the villages, night patrols were organized to apprehend suspicious-looking persons and to give warning of danger. A Secret Police also operated, though to a lesser extent, in the Tŭrnovo Region.

Oborishté

When the preparations were well under way, Benkovsky and the Panagyurishté Apostles decided that since the Gyurgevo Committee had agreed that the rising should take place as soon as possible, preferably on May 1st, it was time to call a Delegate Meeting to make the final arrangements. The urgency of the matter was further accentuated by the fact that with so many people taking part in the preparations, it would not be possible to keep the secret from the Turks indefinitely. Once they discovered what was being prepared under their noses, there would follow a series of arrests which would hamstring the whole organization. It was therefore necessary to proclaim the rising before the secret leaked out.

The meeting was called for April 12/24, 1876, but since some delegates were late in arriving, it did not actually start until April 14/26th. It was held near Panagyurishté in a narrow, wooded valley called Oborishté, where, guarded by a double line of patrols, some fifty-six delegates met in conference for two days and two nights. The total number of people at Oborishté, including patrols, cooks, etc., was between 300 and 350.

The first matter to be discussed was the question of leadership. Benkovsky asked that full powers be given to Volov and himself, as the Apostles of the Gyurgevo Committee, and that the Panagyurishté Regional Committee be recognized as something approximating to the Provisional Government. Although this proposal amounted to little more than a recognition of what was already the case, there was some disagreement among the delegates. Certain of those present felt that it would be more democratic to delegate responsibility to the various Committees. The majority, however, realized the necessity of a centralized leadership, and Benkovsky was given a written mandate with unlimited powers. Reports were made from the various areas on the position of forces, supplies, etc., and the discussion passed to questions of tactics. Here again there was disagreement. Some favoured *cheta* tactics, while Benkovsky and, as it turned out, the majority stuck to the original idea of a general uprising involving the whole people. The meeting decided to concentrate all their forces in a few armed camps in the mountains to which the entire population would withdraw, having set fire to their villages. The population of the Rhodope villages would go to a camp near Batak and to another farther east, while the population on the plains to the east would go to Panagyurishté and Koprivshtitsa, and the villages of the Pazardzhik district to a camp in the Sredna Gora. The camps would then be defended for as long as possible. By involving the whole population in this way, the Bulgars hoped to demonstrate to the rest of the world their single-minded desire for freedom, and to make it harder for the Turks to pretend that they were merely taking legitimate action against bandits. The tactics chosen, while correct in as far as they were aimed at uniting the whole people in a simultaneous rising, were mistaken in as far as they were based on defence and not on attack, and this proved to be one of the fundamental errors of the leadership.

The meeting confirmed the date of the rising as May 1st, but in view of the fact that the Turks, either through treachery or through putting two and two together, might learn of the rising before the appointed time, it was decided that should this happen and should mass arrests start in any town or village, the local Committee should at once proclaim the rising and inform all other Committees.

Finally, when all the decisions had been made, those present, led by the Priest Gruyu Bansky, bared their heads and took a solemn oath. The delegates then departed and Benkovsky informed the other three Revolutionary Regions of the decisions of the meeting at Oborishté.

The Betrayal

Unfortunately, in spite of the great care taken in verifying the credentials of the delegates—some were even sent home again because of irregularities in their papers—a traitor, Nenko Stoyanov, of Baldyovo near Pazardzhik, managed to attend the meeting. How this happened is not known, although it is probable that he came as one of the very large band of helpers, who patrolled the area, cut wood, cooked for the delegates, etc. There was no Committee in his village, so he could not have come as a delegate. Nenko Stoyanov was a rich farmer, who ingratiated himself with the Turks, and behaved like a Turk towards the peasants in his village. As soon as the meeting was over, this man immediately informed the Turks of the preparations for the rising. The authorities in Pazardzhik at once reported the news to Plovdiv. The news that a rising was being prepared did not come as a complete surprise to the Turks, who had for some time been aware of suspicious activity on the part of the Christian population. The *chorbadzhii* of Koprivshtitsa had attempted to inform the authorities in Plovdiv of the preparation for the rising, but their courier had been intercepted by the Revolutionary Committee's 'Secret Police'. Two other *chorbadzhii* had subsequently managed to reach the authorities. In view of the international situation and the forthcoming Tripartite Conference, the Turkish Government was anxious to avoid having to make mass arrests or indulge in violent suppression when, to all outward appearances, the population was behaving in a law-abiding manner, and there was little definite information to go on. The news brought by Nenko Stoyanov was of a very different character, for not only did it give the date of the rising, but it also revealed how the rising could be touched off prematurely, so that the situation could be transformed from the twilight world of suspicion, in which little could safely be done, into the clear daylight of open armed rebellion against which Turkey might take stern measures without fear of unfavourable international repercussions. It is possible that even now the Turkish Government did not take Nenko's revelations very seriously, for it merely ordered the local authorities in Plovdiv to nip the revolt in the bud. The Turkish population was armed, while two detachments of *zaptiehs* (police), under Ahmed Aga and Nedzhip Aga, set out for Panagyurishté and Koprivshtitsa respectively to arrest the rebels. Ahmed Aga delayed on the way, either through lack of enthusiasm or through fear, but Nedzhip Aga went resolutely to Koprivshtitsa with the intention of arresting the revolutionary leaders there, and, in particular, Todor Kableshkov.

Todor Kableshkov, 1851–1876

Kableshkov was one of the exceptions to the rule that members of wealthy families were opposed to the revolution. He was the son of a rich *chorbadzhi* family, whose exquisite house is one of the glories of Bulgarian national architecture and remains one of the showpieces of Koprivshtitsa, now preserved in its entirety as a Museum of Architecture and Revolution. His mother died when he was very young and her place in the household was taken by his father's sister Pena, who was the wife of Doncho Vatakh, a legendary *haidut voivoda* who not only helped Bulgarians but even distributed money from *beys'* estates to needy Turks after the manner of Robin Hood. Pena was a wonderful story-teller and it was probably from her tales of Doncho's exploits that Todor learnt his first lessons in patriotism.

He went to school initially in Koprivshtitsa, and then in Plovdiv where he first encountered and learnt to hate the chauvinism of the Greeks, and felt the full weight of the Turkish yoke, which had seemed comparatively tolerable in Koprivshtitsa with its purely Bulgarian population. In 1868 he was sent to the French Lycée in Constantinople, where teaching was conducted in French and Turkish. Certain of the French teachers were sympathetic to Bulgarian national aspirations, and one, at least, was an ardent supporter of the Paris Commune, and expounded revolutionary ideas to his pupils. In the spring of 1871 Kableshkov became seriously ill and returned home to Koprivshtitsa. All his short life he was to wage his own private struggle against tuberculosis, as well as the great public struggle in which he never spared his frail and fever-ridden body. Kableshkov became acquainted with the organized Revolutionary Movement in Koprivshtitsa, and when, towards the end of 1871, Levsky and Angel Kŭnchev arrived in Koprivshtitsa, Kableshkov rose from his sick-bed and went out through the snow to meet the Apostle of Freedom—a meeting which made an abiding impression upon him.

On January 1, 1872, not long after Levsky had left, Kableshkov founded a Co-operative Society with cultural and economic aims. Economically the Society aimed at mechanization of handicrafts in order to meet Western competition, and some machinery was actually bought. The Society also obtained consumer goods for its members. Soon Kableshkov had drawn the flower of the young people of Koprivshtitsa into the Society, and thence into the Revolutionary Committee. Here he began to encounter the opposition of the *chorbadzhii*, and those of them who had originally joined the Co-operative Society now backed out and demanded their money back.

During the summer of 1872, with the approval of the Committee, Kableshkov toured the villages in the area, talking with the peasants, speaking to them about the evils of drunkenness, the benefits of education and so on. At the beginning of 1873, he went to Adrianople to work as a trainee-telegraphist on Baron Hirsch's railway. Here, too, he continued his agitational work, gathering the schoolboys and young people around him, firing their patriotism with talk of freedom and stories of Levsky's exploits. The highlight of his stay in Adrianople was the organization of a demonstration of young people who appeared in church wearing red ties and sang a revolutionary song, in which a military band, staffed by Bulgarians,[1] joined, to the consternation of the priests and *chorbadzhii*.

Soon after this Kableshkov went to Plovdiv as a telegraphist and then to Belovo, where he became station-master. Unlike Botev, Kableshkov was greatly in favour of railways, because communications brought the people of Bulgaria closer together, and also made it easier for Europe to learn of their plight.

In Belovo Kableshkov continued his agitational work. Reading-rooms were set up both in Belovo itself and in the neighbouring village of Golyamo Belovo. Kableshkov also contacted people who had been members of Committees set up by Levsky, and political work went on side by side with education and culture. His work bore fruit, for in April 1875 the Reading Room Committee in Golyamo Belovo transformed itself into a Revolutionary Committee. Kableshkov similarly combined culture and revolution in his frequent visits to Tatar Pazardzhik.

[1] Sadŭk Pasha (the emigré Pole Czaikowsky) made efforts to bring Bulgarians in the Turkish Army, without any real success.

In the spring of 1875 Kableshkov resigned from his post as station master and began to work ostensibly as a merchant, based on Tatar Pazardzhik, and toured the towns and villages in the Samokov, Sofia and Pirot areas. In Pirot he set up a Revolutionary Committee. But in the autumn of 1875 his health deteriorated to such an extent that he had to return home to Koprivshtitsa. As soon as he was a little better, he set to work again, visiting villages to establish reading-rooms and to revive the Committees founded by Levsky. In the spring of 1876, he toured the area east of Koprivshtitsa with Volov, visiting Klisura, Sopot, Karlovo, Kalofer, Shipka, etc.

The Beginning of the Rising

Nedzhip Aga arrived in Koprivshtitsa on April 19th and established himself in the *konak* (the seat of local government). On the following day he endeavoured to arrest Kableshkov by cunning, calling at his house and pretending that he had brought him a letter from his father in Plovdiv. Although Kableshkov was, in fact, at home ill, he suspected Nedzhip Aga's real intentions, and the Turks were informed that he was out. As soon as they had gone, Kableshkov slipped out to the house of Rashko Stoichev, where the Committee met in urgent conclave. The meeting had to decide whether to bide their time, and thus risk the arrest of some of their number, or to declare an immediate rising. They decided that Braiko Enev, one of the elders, should test the situation by going voluntarily to the *konak*. If he were arrested, the others would attack the *konak* to free him and the rising should be proclaimed. The conspirators then dispersed to clothe themselves in their uniforms and to prepare their arms. Braiko Enev duly presented himself at the *konak* and was detained, whereupon Kableshkov sent two men to ring the church bells to summon the people to arms, and two groups of rebels, one under Kableshkov and the other under Georgi Tikhanek, set out to attack the *konak*, while a third went to guard the road to Plovdiv. As the group under Tikhanek approached the Kalŭchov bridge over the River Byala, they encountered a hated Turkish *zaptieh*, named Kara Hussein, and Tikhanek shot him dead. In so doing, he had fired the first shot of the April Rising.[1]

Then as the church bells pealed forth their call to arms and freedom, and the rebels dressed in their white uniforms came surging into the streets, Kableshkov mounted his father's horse, and took command.

[1] Visitors to Koprivshtitsa may see a monument outside the Lulchov House, marking the spot where this incident took place.

The banner of revolt was triumphantly unfurled and the rebels surrounded the *konak*, trapping the *myudyur* (the Turkish Governor) Nedzhip Aga and the police. They demanded, and obtained, the release of Braiko Enev and Georgi Tusunov, who had been arrested earlier. Kableshkov then called on the Turks to surrender, but they refused. When the Bulgars then prepared to set fire to the *konak*, the Turks succeeded in escaping by a ruse: they opened the gates to draw the fire of the Bulgars, who imagined that the Turks were attempting to break out, then rode out themselves a few seconds later when the Bulgars were re-loading their ancient guns. In this way, the majority of the Turks, including Nedzhip Aga himself, escaped, while the *myudyur* and one *zaptieh* were killed and four Turks were captured.

Free Koprivshtitsa

Koprivshtitsa was free. Kableshkov's first action was to write his celebrated letter (with a postscript by Karadzhov) to Benkovsky at Panagyurishté, telling him of the great events in Koprivshtitsa:

'Brothers!
'Yesterday Nedzhip Aga arrived in our village from Plovdiv, intending to imprison several people including myself. Since I had been informed of your decision taken at the Oborishté meeting, I called together several young men, and after we had armed ourselves, we set out towards the *konak* where we killed the *myudyur* and several *zaptiehs*. . . . Now, as you receive this letter, our banner is flying in front of the konak, the guns are thundering to the echo of the church bells and the young men are kissing each other on the streets. . . . If you, brothers, are true patriots and Apostles of freedom, then follow our example in Panagyurishté also. . . .
Koprivshtitsa, April 20th 1876.
T. Kableshkov.

'I was an eye-witness when everything described above in Todor's letter took place. I am leaving for Klisura to do the same.
'N. Karadzhov.'

Kableshkov then drew a cross on the letter with the blood of the *myudyur*, and the couriers departed. Karadzhov carried a similar 'bloody letter' to Klisura, and letters were also sent to other Committees.

The Bulgarian Military Council, with Kableshkov as its elected

Chairman, now took over the government of the town. Preparations for battle were resumed: swords were forged, rifles repaired and bread baked. Units were posted on the roads into the town, trenches were dug, and the rebels' four cannon were placed in position, including one made from the cherry tree which had formerly grown in the garden of Kableshkov's house. On Kableshkov's orders the taverns were closed and sealed, and all consumption of spirits forbidden, presumably to avoid a situation in which the victory celebrations might result in the people being unfit for further battle.

April 21, 1876, was a day such as Bulgaria had not seen for more than 500 years. All the people gathered, the rebels with their weapons, the children with bunches of flowers, the priests in all the splendour of their finest vestments and carrying crosses, candlesticks and church banners, for the blessing of the green silken flag embroidered by Evlamia Bekilova with the golden lion and the inscription 'Freedom or Death', which together with the little red flags of the various units now fluttered proudly over free Koprivshtitsa. After prayers led by the priests Nikola Belchev and Ilya Katsarov, the flag was presented to the standard bearer, and Kableshkov, who arrived on horseback with a naked sword in his hand, kissed the flag and addressed the people. Then Pop (priest) Doncho Plachkov sprinkled holy water and congratulated the people, wishing them success, and finally Pop Nikola walked through the crowd, swearing in new rebels and distributing little lion cap badges made of lead which he had cast himself.

After the rejoicing a general meeting was held at which all essential stores and material in the town were declared to be public property to be administrated by the Military Council, who distributed them to everybody, according to need, and gave receipts for all goods to the owners. The meeting also approved the composition of the Military Council, which now set up its headquarters in Dr Spas Abrashev's pharmacy.

The Rising in the Panagyurishté Region

Ahmed Aga finally arrived in Panagyurishté despite his dilatory progress, and put up at an inn owned by Naiden Drinov. The arrival of the Turks caused great consternation among the members of the Committee since Drinov was one of their number, and the gunpowder was stored at his inn. Benkovsky ordered that the inn should be surrounded by rebels who would take up their positions in neighbouring houses, and that should Ahmed Aga make any

11.
The
suppression
of the April
Rising in
Batak

NEUTRALITY UNDER DIFFICULTIES.

BULL. "BULGARIAN ATROCITIES! I CAN'T FIND THEM IN THE 'OFFICIAL REPORTS'!!!"

12b. Neutrality Under Difficulties

Drawing by John Tenniel from Punch, August 5, 1876. Reproduced by kind

12a. Execution of Bulgarians in the streets of Philippopolis

move against the Committee, the whole inn should be blown up together with its Turkish guests.

It was at this juncture that Kableshkov's 'bloody letter' arrived from Koprivshtitsa. It aroused such emotion in Panagyurishté that it was at first passed from hand to hand before anyone managed to control himself sufficiently to read it out aloud. Once its contents were made known, Benkovsky ordered that the rising be immediately proclaimed. Amid the clanging of the church bells, the revolutionary units assembled and the following proclamation was published throughout the area:

'The brutal tyranny which we have suffered for 500 years under oppressive Ottoman rule has come to an end. Each of us has awaited this moment with impatience. . . . Forward, brothers! Seize your arms and with them let us together fight bravely against the might of Turkey. O Bulgarian! Prove that you are alive, show that you know how to value your freedom. Arise, win today your freedom in struggle and with your blood. Henceforward, in the name of our people we declare before the whole civilized world that we will have complete freedom or death. . . .'

A Bulgarian unit under Georgi Ikonomov cleared the *konak* of Turks, and power passed into the hands of the Bulgars. The subsequent events paralleled those which took place in Koprivshtitsa. The rebels made their way to the central square, to the sound of bells ringing and shots being fired into the air, accompanied by women and girls weeping for joy and garlanding the men with flowers. The Regional Committee was augmented by the inclusion of several leading citizens and was transformed into a Supreme Military Council and Provisional Government combined. The largest house in the town was commandeered for its headquarters and the houses round it for stores and workshops for making armaments. Benkovsky, as Supreme Commander, sent couriers to the villages in the Panagyurishté Region to inform them that the rising had started.

On the same day, April 20th, Klisura rose. Sharp fighting broke out in Strelcha, a large village to the east of Panagyurishté, where the Turkish population were well-armed professional bandits who had long terrorized the neighbourhood. The Turkish quarter passed into Bulgarian hands, but a group of Turks shut themselves up in the mosque and could not be dislodged. A *cheta* under Vorcho Voivoda

I

was sent from Panagyurishté to Strelcha, but still the Turks held out, and, indeed, they continued to do so until the end of the rising.

Benkovsky himself with a mounted *cheta* set out to the westward to rouse the villages there, and passed through Mechka, Poibrené, Petrich, Mukhovo, Tserovo, Slavovitsa, Lesichevo and other villages. Here the rising was magnificently supported by the peasantry on a truly mass scale. The women and children were evacuated, some to Panagyurishté itself, some to Mount Eledzhik in the Ikhtiman Sredna Gora. The resolution of the peasantry can be gauged from the fact that, in some places, they burnt their own houses before setting out for the rallying points. On reaching Eledzhik, the rebels fortified their camp and elected a Military Committee headed by Gené Teliisky. Benkovsky took groups of well-armed young men from each village and returned with about two hundred men to Panagyurishté where he received a tumultuous welcome from the exultant people. On April 22nd, Pop Gruyu ceremoniously blessed the rebels' banner and gave it into the keeping of Raina Georgieva, who had embroidered it. Benkovsky then set out again with a mounted *cheta* to tour the villages and to encourage the people.

In the meantime, Kableshkov was also trying to collect the civilian population together. Villagers from Sindzhirlii, Eleshnitsa, Tsaratsovo and many other places, with their cattle and with their carts loaded with possessions, converged on Koprivshtitsa, where they were received by Kableshkov himself. As many as possible were billeted in the houses and temporary shelters were erected for the others.

A *cheta* under Naiden Stoyanov was sent from Koprivshtitsa to Strelcha to reinforce the Panagyurishté *cheta* in their siege of the mosque, and Volov and Ikonomov, who had accompanied Vorcho Voivoda, left Strelcha to go via Koprivshtitsa to rouse the Karlovo district. Soon, however, Turks from other villages came to the aid of those besieged in the mosque and there was some very sharp fighting. The women and children of Strelcha, together with the cattle and what few possessions they could carry, were evacuated towards Koprivshtitsa, convoyed by Naiden Stoyanov's *cheta*, while Vorcho returned to Panagyurishté leaving Strelcha in flames behind him.

When the rising began, Vasil Petleshkov, the leader of the Bratsigovo Committee, happened to be in Panagyurishté, and thus he was able to take the proclamation to Bratsigovo, Peshtera, Batak and the other villages in the northern Rhodope. Perushtitsa received news of the rising from Khristo Todorov, a teacher from Plovdiv. The villages all rose, with the exception of Peshtera, where there was a large Turkish population, and where the merchant members of the Committee were too much afraid to take action. Some of the more resolute members left the village and went to Batak or Bratsigovo in order to join in the rising.

In the two main towns of the region, Plovdiv and Pazardzhik, no rising took place. These were towns with a large Turkish population—a fact which had an intimidating effect on the conspirators. The premature declaration of the rising took the Committee by surprise, and they panicked and went into hiding. In Plovdiv the plan to set fire to the town was not carried out owing to opposition from the majority of the members of the Committee, and further activity was paralysed by the presence of *bashibazouks*. Only a few rebels left the town to take part in the rising, among them Kocho Chistemensky, who went to Perushtitsa with his whole family.

The Beginning of the End

At the very start of the rising, serious errors had been made which affected the whole course of the rising. The failure to gain control of, or burn, the chief towns, such as Pazardzhik, Plovdiv and Adrianople, left the Turks with convenient bases from which to operate. The failure to cut the railway lines facilitated the movement of Turkish troops, one of the factors on which Botev based his objection to the building of railways. But the fundamental error lay in the strategy of the rising which was based on defensive, not offensive, warfare. The population was withdrawn from the villages and concentrated in camps for defence. Even when the *bashibazouk* units forced the Bulgars to withdraw from Strelcha, no immediate attempt was made to re-take it, although it was of great strategic importance for both Koprivshtitsa and Panagyurishté.

Another factor which contributed towards the difficulties of the Bulgars—though it was one which was entirely beyond their control —was the deterioration in the weather. On April 22nd and 23rd heavy rain began to fall, soaking the rebels' gunpowder and rendering it useless, while having little effect on the more modern weapons of the Turks.

At the time when the rising began, the Turkish regular troops were concentrated in the west, towards the frontiers with Serbia and Montenegro. The garrisons within the country were relatively small and the Turkish authorities began arming the local Turkish and Circassian population and forming them into *bashibazouk* (irregular) units.

When news of the rising reached Karlovo, Tosun Bey unfurled the sacred banner of Islam outside his *konak*, and, with the aid of drums and trumpets, roused the fanaticism of the Turkish population to fever point. On April 26th, he led a mob of several thousand well-armed *bashibazouks* to Klisura, promising them *giaour* blood and booty. The Bulgarian defenders, with their ancient firearms and cherry tree cannon fought heroically, but in vain. With the village in flames, a few of them carried on a desperate rearguard action, while the population fled towards Koprivshtitsa. Over 200 women, children and old men, who could not run away, were slaughtered by the Turks.

As soon as the news of the Turkish attack on Klisura reached Koprivshtitsa, Volov, who was back in the town, set out at once with a *cheta* of sixty men. Kableshkov followed him with 200 men, but when they saw the smoke rising from the ruins and met the weary, despondent, rain-soaked refugees, they realized that there was nothing that they could do. Four thousand more homeless and hungry people had to be accommodated in Koprivshtitsa, which was now itself in grave danger.

Kableshkov sent a letter to Benkovsky, informing him of the destruction of Klisura. A large *cheta* under Volov was sent to rouse Sopot and Karlovo in Tosun Bey's rear, but they failed to reach their objective. Everywhere the villagers were afraid that they might share the fate of Klisura. With the pouring rain soaking into its gunpowder, the *cheta* was obliged to return to Koprivshtitsa. A second *cheta* under Ikonomov, which hoped to rouse the population of Pirdop, likewise had to turn back with their weapons rendered useless. Between 2,000 and 3,000 regular troops with artillery, commanded by Khafŭz Pasha, and accompanied by large numbers of *bashibazouks* now marched from Pazardzhik to Strelcha, thus cutting off communications between Panagyurishté and Koprivshtitsa. On April 28th, they began their offensive on Panagyurishté itself.

Benkovsky was at the camp on Mount Eledzhik, and the defenders of Panagyurishté were commanded by Ivan Sokolov. He had earthworks dug on the south of the town, expecting the attack to come from the direction of Pazardzhik. But Khafŭz Pasha, having gained control of Strelcha, attacked from the east. For four days the Bulgars heroically resisted the superior might of the relatively modern Turkish Army, but on April 30th the Turks finally took the revolutionary capital and set it on fire. Many of the Bulgars, including innocent women and children, were killed, and the remainder withdrew under Pavel Bobekov into the mountains towards Koprivshtitsa.

The End in Koprivshtitsa

In the meantime, things were going badly in Koprivshtitsa. At the beginning of the rising the local gypsies had been disarmed and they had apparently agreed to work in support of the rebels. When, however, it was learnt that in Klisura the gypsies had been among the first to set fire to the village, it was decided to investigate the position in Koprivshtitsa. Gypsy houses were searched and among the objects found were arms, cans of paraffin and a *zaptieh*. Some of the gypsies actually admitted that it had been their intention to set fire to the town and to seek arms and help from nearby Turkish villages. The guilty gypsies and about eight armed Turks, who had been caught in various places, were executed, but the old people, the women and the children, as well as innocent Turks and gypsies were not harmed.

But the gypsies were not the only people plotting against the revolution in Koprivshtitsa. The upsurge of patriotic feeling had not touched the hearts of the *chorbadzhii*, whom the rebels had magnanimously, but unwisely, left unmolested and at liberty. These *chorbadzhii*, led by Ivan Madzharov, Kosta Karavelov and others, hoped to salvage something from the ruins by proving themselves loyal subjects of the Sultan. They played on the alarm and depression which the fate of Klisura had brought among the people, and attempted to turn public opinion against Kableshkov and the other revolutionary leaders. Kableshkov realized that the town could not be held against an attack by the Turks, and on April 28th he put forward a proposal, which was unanimously accepted by the Committee, that the rebels should withdraw into the Stara Planina with supplies for several months and should carry on the fight from there. When the proposal was put to a meeting of all the rebels, the majority refused to leave their families. Only about 600 agreed to go, but heavy rain delayed their departure.

The *chorbadzhii*, whose agitation had won over some of the simpler peasants, especially those whose villages had been burnt, now staged a counter-revolution. With the aid of a crowd of peasants, they began to arrest and disarm the rebels, binding their hands and

locking them up with the intention of handing them over to the
Turks. Kableshkov refused to allow his men to fire on the crowd
and shed Bulgarian blood, and thus he himself, together with Volov
and Ikonomov and other leading members of the committee were
locked up in the pharmacy.

On April 30th, Pavel Bobekov arrived from stricken Panagyurishté
with a handful of rebels, including Vorcho Voivoda. By pretending
that a great victory had been won, that troops had arrived from
Serbia and that hundreds of rebels were marching towards Koprivshtitsa, they struck such fear into the hearts of the *chorbadzhii*
that they were able to liberate the imprisoned rebels unhindered. To
the latter they told the awful truth that in fact Panagyurishté had
been reduced to ashes, and it was decided that there was nothing left
to do except withdraw into the mountains. About ninety rebels,
including Kableshkov, Volov, Ikonomov, Naiden Stoyanov, Bobekov
and Vorcho, left with their banner for the Stara Planina to carry on a
guerrilla warfare against the Turks. Many of them, however, turned
back, and only twenty-seven of them remained when, on May 1st,
they reached the Stara Planina. They made their way along the
mountains aiming to reach Svishtov and thus to cross into Rumania.
But Vorcho was captured by the Turks and Volov and Ikonomov
were drowned while trying to swim agross the Yantra. Only some
three members of the *cheta* including Bobekov succeeded in reaching
Rumania, where they arrived at the end of August.

Kableshkov himself had fallen ill soon after they had reached the
mountains. He found shelter in a peasant's hut near Troyan, and
begged the others to go on without him. Three of them, however,
including Naiden Stoyanov, stayed with him. On May 8th they
were surprised by the Turks who killed two of them and captured
Kableshkov and Stoyanov alive. They were taken first to Troyan,
then to Lovech, and finally to Tŭrnovo. Here Stoyanov, who had
been mercilessly beaten and kicked by the Turkish *zaptiehs* during
the journey from Lovech, died in Kableshkov's arms. Kableshkov
himself behaved with the utmost courage and dignity. Neither the
cruelty of his captors nor the sickness of his own weak body could
break his proud spirit. Together with Vorcho, who had also been
brought to Tŭrnovo jail, Kableshkov was dispatched to Gabrovo,
en route for Plovdiv where he was to stand trial. Knowing that
nothing awaited him in Plovdiv but torture and the gallows, he
contrived to seize a revolver in the police station at Gabrovo and shot
himself (June 16th).

So died the Apostle of Koprivshtitsa. But freedom had already long been dead in Koprivshtitsa itself. The Turks had first appeared outside Koprivshtitsa on May 1st, and with the revolutionary leaders gone, the *chorbadzhii* surrendered the town. They could not prevent the Turks from looting, but they were able to prevent the town from being burnt to the ground by paying the Turks a substantial sum of money. For this one act posterity may be grateful to these people whose treachery was otherwise unmitigated.

The Death of Benkovsky

As we have already seen, Benkovsky was not in Panagyurishté at the time of its fall. With his so-called 'Flying *Cheta*', he toured villages in the west of the region, including Belovo, where Kableshkov had once been station-master. Here a number of Serbian and Dalmatian workers joined the rebels. Benkovsky then rode back to the camp at Eledzhik, which was being threatened by an army of *bashibazouks* and, under his leadership, the peasants were able to fight off the enemy. On April 30th, the rebels at Eledzhik saw the flames of burning Panagyurishté. On May 1st Benkovsky set out to the aid of the stricken town, but there was nothing that he could do. He hoped to form a larger *cheta* with which he could retake the town, but when news came of the fall of Koprivshtitsa, he realized that this, too, was impossible. In his absence the 700 defenders of Eledzhik were attacked by 7,000 well-armed Turkish regulars, brought by Hasan Pasha from Niš. The Bulgars—men, women and children—were mercilessly slaughtered. Gené Teliisky, the commander of the camp, died with them after fighting to the end with exceptional bravery. The same fate overtook another camp near the village of Petrich. Fire and slaughter swept over the Fourth Revolutionary Region. On Mount Lisets, looking down helplessly on his former capital, now in flames, Benkovsky said: 'We have achieved our aim', meaning that the appalling destruction and murder must surely bring the plight of Bulgaria to the notice of the world and that Russia at least would be obliged to come to her aid.

Benkovsky had no other course open to him than to withdraw into the mountains and attempt to get through into northern Bulgaria. Everywhere there were Turkish units. Food was impossible to obtain. Heavy rain brought despondency and illness. To increase their chances of escape, the *cheta* broke up into smaller groups. Benkovsky's group consisted of one of the Dalmatians from Belovo, Zakhari Stoyanov, who later wrote an epic account of the whole rising, and Father Kiril, abbot of the Kalugerovo monastery. This small group fought its last fight with the Turks near Teteven; Benkovsky was killed and the others were captured.

The Rhodope Villages

In the Rhodope preparations for the rising had been really effective only in Perushtitsa, Bratsigovo and Batak. The plan agreed at Oborishté had been for all the rebels to leave their villages and to concentrate in the mountains near Batak to wage a defensive war. This plan was never fully carried out and the rebels remained in isolated groups. Peshtera failed to rise and only a few people left for Batak and Bratsigovo. An attempt to evacuate the inhabitants of Bratsigovo failed when the column of baggage horses sent from Batak was attacked and dispersed by *bashibazouks*.

The tragic events in Perushtitsa constitute one of the most celebrated and heart-rending episodes of the whole rising. Here the chief organizers were Petŭr Bonev, the teacher, Spas Ginev, a peasant, and Kocho Chistemensky, a shoemaker, who had come from Plovdiv after the rising had failed to materialize in that town. News of the rising in Koprivshtitsa and Panagyurishté had reached Perushtitsa on April 22nd, and the local Turkish and *Pomak* population began to arm themselves. On April 26th Ahmed Aga Tümrüshliyata surrounded Perushtitsa with a mob of *bashibazouks*, to whom he promised booty and Bulgarian girls. The local *chor-badzhii* persuaded some of the people to surrender, and, deaf to the warnings of the rebel leaders, some 200 men, women and children set out, accompanied by priests, for the camp of Ahmed Aga Tüm-rŭshliyata. Here seventy of them were immediately mown down by the *yatagans* of the *bashibazouks*, and the remainder fled back to the village.

There could now be no question of further negotiations or of surrender. From well-placed positions the rebels repulsed the encircling Turks so bravely and so successfully that Tümrŭshliyata was obliged to send to Plovdiv for regular reinforcements. But even the arrival of artillery did not put an end to the Bulgarian resistance. Most of the village was now in flames, but the people congregated in and around the stone church of the Holy Archangel, firing back at the Turks from the windows and from the belfry. Bonev had already been killed, and Chistemensky and Ginev, hoping to save some of the people from certain death, sent 300 people out under cover of darkness during the night of April 29th–30th, and a further

100 the following night. Most of them succeeded in arriving safely in Plovdiv.

Before the remainder could attempt to follow them, the Turks brought their cannon closer and began to bombard the church precincts at a range of only 100 yards. The belfry was destroyed and it became clear that it would be only a matter of time before the whole building collapsed on the heads of its defenders. The peak of the tragedy was reached on May 2nd when, rather than fall alive into the hands of the Turks, the leaders Ginev and Chistemensky shot their own wives and children, and a number of other women and young girls who asked them to do so, and finally killed themselves. When the Turks entered the church it already resembled a tomb. They robbed the bodies of dead and living alike. Those who were left alive were sent to Plovdiv, and the village was burnt. The present-day visitor to Perushtitsa may see the church still preserved in its semi-destroyed state. The roof is half gone, and the interior of the building is protected by a wooden covering. In the crypt lie the skulls of some of those who died in the holocaust.

On April 30th, the *bashibazouks* of Ahmed Aga Barutanliyata began to attack Batak, the defence of which was organized by Petŭr Goranov and Stoyan Trendafilov. Here, as in Koprivshtitsa, the *chorbadzhii* played a treacherous role. Already, by persuading the Committee to negotiate (April 25th–27th) with the Turks, who were at that time relatively weak in numbers and would easily have been defeated by the rebels, they had wasted valuable time, time during which the Turks were able to bring up huge *bashibazouk* reinforcements. Now the *chorbadzhii* sought to disrupt the defence of the village by going out to the well-placed rebel positions outside the village and persuading them that it was better to defend themselves in the houses. They argued that in this way they would appear as peaceful defenders of their homes and would escape political responsibility and consequent punishment for the rising. Unfortunately, many of the villages succumbed to this argument and withdrew. While Goranov and Trendafilov were convincing one group of the strategic folly of this step and persuading them to return to their former positions, the *chorbadzhii* were pouring their poison into the ears of another group and so on. In this way, the original, sound defence system collapsed, and the rebels were obliged to take cover behind the walls of the buildings. Once they were inside the village, the *chorbadzhii* attempted to arrest the leaders, with the intention of handing them over to the Turks, in the hope of gaining

I*

thereby a pardon for themselves. They did not succeed in this plan, since they could find little support among the people.

Within the village the rebels reformed into two groups under Goranov and Trendafilov, Kolyo Tsŭrpov and Todor Kolchov, and fought back heroically. Goranov even managed to mount a cherry tree cannon and bombarded the Turks until he and almost all his companions were killed by enemy crossfire. But the withdrawal into the village had already sealed their fate from the military point of view. House by house, the Turks advanced into the village. During the night of May 1st–2nd, many of the defenders fled under cover of darkness, and next morning Barutanliyata offered to spare the remaining defenders' lives if they would lay down their arms. This they did, though not without considerable misgivings, on the insistence of *chorbadzhiya* Angel Karlakov. Their misgivings proved to be well founded, for Ahmed Aga then ordered the *bashibazouks* to slaughter the whole population. For three days the massacre continued. The victims were first undressed so that their clothes, which formed part of the victors' spoil, should not be soiled with blood. Apart from those murdered in the streets and houses, a large number of men, women and children were burnt to death in the church.

Finally, Barutanliyata, having watched the slaughter, left Batak for Bratsigovo. Here the populations of several other villages had gathered under the leadership of Petleshkov. The defence of the village was entrusted to Gocho Angeliev of Radilovo, and so well did he carry out his duties that from April 28th–May 6th, the Turkish *bashibazouks* were repeatedly repulsed with heavy loss of life. But when regular troops equipped with artillery arrived from Plovdiv, the rebels surrendered to Hasan Pasha on May 7th, having received a promise that the civilian population would not be massacred nor would the village be burnt. In general this promise was kept, but Petleshkov was roasted between two fires to force him to tell the names of the other leaders. This he refused to do, saying: 'I am alone . . . there are no others.' He died shortly after of self-administered poison.

Chronologically this was the final episode of the rising in the Fourth Revolutionary Region.

The Rising in the Tŭrnovo Region

Benkovsky's letter arrived in Gorna Oryakhovitsa, centre of the Tŭrnovo Revolutionary Region, on April 25th. A conference was to have been called to decide on a date for the rising, but the Turks managed to capture a courier from the Sliven Region, who gave them information, and arrests began. Between April 25th and April 27th, many of the members of the Gorna Oryakhovitsa and Lyaskovets Committees were arrested, together with their military instructor, Georgi Izmirliev, who was hanged.

Stambolov, chief Apostle for the region, abandoned the idea of a conference, and, after some hesitation, proclaimed the rising, without any proper plan having been made. He himself took no further part in the rising, and remained in Samovodené, whither he had withdrawn during the period of preparation, until August, when he returned to Rumania.

The rising began on April 28th in the village of Musina, where a large *cheta* of some 200 rebels from the surrounding villages gathered under Pop Khariton, with Petŭr Parmakov, a native of Gradets, Kotel district, and an ex-officer in the Russian Army, as military instructor. Over half the rebels came from Byala Cherkva under Bacho Kiro Petrov.

The *cheta* set out through the mountains for Gabrovo, but on the way they were attacked by *bashibazouks*, and took refuge in the monastery at Dryanovo on April 29th. The stout walls of the monastery presented an insuperable obstacle to the Turkish irregulars, and fierce fighting continued for three days. Then two regular units under Fazlŭ Pasha were sent to their aid, making a total of 10,000 besiegers. On the fourth day of the siege Pop Khariton and several others were fatally burnt in an explosion in the gunpowder store, which occurred through carelessness on the part of one of the rebels. Parmakov and Bacho Kiro took over the command and carried on the struggle.

Eventually the Turks became convinced that it was impossible to capture the monastery and enlisted the help of the local *chorbadzhii*, hoping to persuade the rebels to surrender. The Dryanovo *chorbadzhii* wrote the following letter to the defenders of the monastery:

'You do ill to take up arms against our sovereign. You have done wrong, but our sovereign is merciful and will pardon you. We beg you for the first time, do not cause the destruction of the monastery. It would be better if you surrendered. Let the monks go before you, and behind them, go you yourselves, each to your own house, without let or hindrance. All will go free and will be pardoned by the Pasha.
'The *chorbadzhii* of Dryanovo.'

The rebels received this letter with the contempt it deserved. The Turks replied by bringing up two new steel cannon to replace the old-fashioned one which they had previously been using, and the Pasha sent a note to the rebels saying that if they did not surrender, the monastery would be reduced to dust and ashes. To this the rebels replied:

'Pasha, we have risen against you in order to defend our people, who are tormented by the Turkish authorities. . . . The people want their rights and are determined to win them, with their lives, even, if need be. We have not risen against the peaceful population, no—we require the Government to recognize our rights as a people, and until this is done, we will not surrender ourselves alive into the hands of our tormentors—we have resolved to die and we will keep our vow. And you will answer to Europe for your tyrannies.

'The rebels in the Dryanovo Monastery.'

The new cannon breached the walls of the monastery and set the buildings on fire, and the rebels decided to break out. Unfortunately, they did not know exactly where the enemy was placed, and they emerged at a point where the Turks were concentrated in large numbers. In a violent engagement, Parmakov and many others were slain, and only some forty men escaped, including Bacho Kiro. The rest of the rebels, who remained in the monastery, were killed when the Turks entered it. Bacho Kiro's freedom was short-lived. He and the remainder of his men were hunted down and captured. Bacho Kiro was hanged in Türnovo, after he had behaved with exemplary courage at his trial, expressing his contempt for his judges in extempore Turkish verse.

The news of the formation of Pop Khariton's *cheta* reached the Committee in Gabrovo via Tsanko Dyustabanov, a member of the Committee who was a Government clerk and who, as such, had seen a telegram referring to the rising and to the fact that an army unit was to be sent to hunt the rebels down. The Gabrovo Committee decided to form a *cheta* and leave the town secretly for the mountains where they would rouse the villagers and support Pop Khariton. It was suggested that instead of forming a *cheta*, they should seize control of Gabrovo and draw all the townsfolk and the peasants from the surrounding villages into the rising. At the time it would have been relatively easy to seize the town but the suggestion was rejected by Dyustabanov and the majority of the Committee, who feared the influence of the *chorbadzhii* and, even more, the possibility of the town being destroyed and their families slain.

One hundred and twenty-two rebels left Gabrovo and passed through several mountain hamlets, gaining in strength until they numbered over two hundred. They halted at the Gabrovo monastery, and it was decided to divide the *cheta* into two groups in order to carry out more widespread agitation. One of these groups was to be commanded by Dyustabanov, who had been elected *voivoda*, and the other by G. Bocharov. Both the detachments, however, proved to be sadly lacking in organization and discipline. Recruits alternately joined and left, and Dyustabanov himself had no understanding of military matters.

In Sevlievo to the north-west of Gabrovo, Stefan Peshev, the Chairman of the Committee, had been arrested and no rising took place in the town itself. Nevertheless, some villages in the district, including Novo Selo and Krŭvenik, had risen on May 1st and 2nd, so Dyustabanov and Bocharov set out towards them. When they came to Batoshevo, the peasants rose here also, and Bocharov remained there with a group of rebels, who together with the Batoshevo peasants numbered 480, of which only 40 to 50 men had firearms. The rest of the rebels continued on their way to Novo Selo and Krŭvenik where two large *cheti* of 200 and 300 men respectively, led by Doncho Feschiev and Yonko Karagyozov, had already been formed. The Turks marched against them with a vast horde of *bashibazouks* and Circassian horsemen, and the rebels fought back heroically, using a wooden cannon, and rolling rocks down the mountainside against the enemy. Even women took part in the fighting, and the name of one of these heroines has come down to us, that of Stoyana Draganovska, who, armed with a rifle, repulsed the attacking *bashibazouks*. But heroism, however great, could not compensate indefinitely for poor equipment and inexperienced leadership. Dyustabanov failed to concentrate the rebels, and this enabled the Turks to tackle and destroy the various groups one by one.

Batoshevo was the first village to fall, on May 6th. *Bashibazouks* looted and burnt the village, murdering not only captured rebels, but also the civilian population, including women and children. Then they swept on to Novo Selo and Krŭvenik where, up till their arrival on May 9th, the rebels had managed to hold their own. At Krŭvenik the Gabrovo *cheta* failed to give the rebels adequate support and the village was taken. Then came the turn of Novo Selo.

Here, until May 9th, the defenders, under Yonko Karagyozov, assisted by the Gabrovo *cheta* under Dyustabanov, had successfully held off the enemy, but now the whole strength of the Turks was concentrated on the village, and Dyustabanov ordered the rebels to withdraw into the mountains. The *bashibazouks* poured into the village and here, as in Batoshevo and Krŭvenik, they looted, burned and murdered. No one was spared. Even pregnant women were ripped open and left to die in agony.

The rebels continued to fight in the mountains with exceptional bravery. On May 10th and 11th Dyustabanov's *cheta* was engaged in very heavy fighting with Circassian bands near Mount Mara-Gidik, and the rebels were utterly defeated and scattered. Dyustabanov and Karagyozov were both captured and hanged, the former in Tŭrnovo and the latter in Sevlievo. Now that all resistance had ended, the *bashibazouks* roamed through the forests, killing all who had taken refuge there.

In the Tryavna district attempts were made to rouse the villages, but the organization was very weak, and some of those who originally took up arms dispersed to their homes again. Finally a *cheta* of 120 assembled near the village of Nova Makhala, with Khristo Patrev, an old comrade of Hadzhi Dimiter, as *voivoda*, and Todor Kirkov and Stefan Gŭdev as his assistants. On May 9th the *cheta* was defeated and dispersed by *bashibazouks* and regular troops. Small groups of the rebels continued to resist, moving east through the mountains. Kirkov was betrayed and captured near Elena, and was subsequently hanged. Patrev died fighting heroically near the village of Chengé, Provadiya district, while Gŭdev managed to elude capture and hid in his native village of Shipka until he was able to escape to Rumania.

No other risings took place in the Tŭrnovo Revolutionary Region. In Tŭrnovo itself and the other towns, the moderate *bourgeois* elements gained the upper hand in the Committees, advising caution, which resulted in nothing being done.

The Rising in the Sliven Region

As we have seen, the Sliven Committee decided on *cheta* tactics right from the start, and prepared an armed camp in the mountains. The Turks came to know about the preparations for the rising and arrested the Chairman of the Committee, Neno Gospodinov. The two Apostles, Georgi Obretenov and Ilarion Dragostinov, went to Stoil Voivoda's camp in the mountains, and it was decided to collect all their supporters from the surrounding villages to form a *cheta*. About sixty people rallied, mainly from the villages of Neikovo and Zheravna, but also from Yambol, led by Georgi Drazhev. During the first days of May the *cheta* set out in the direction of Neikovo and Zheravna. Near Neikovo they were attacked by a strong Turkish unit and Circassian cavalry, and in the bloody battle that ensued Georgi Obretenov was killed. The *cheta* withdrew, but encountered another Turkish unit and this time Dragostinov was killed. Stoil Voivoda continued to retreat with the remainder of the *cheta*, some of whom began to desert, but on May 10th he was slain, and the remainder of his companions, including Drazhev, were captured and executed.

Shortly after, a small *cheta* of fifteen men under Tanyu Stoyanov, one of Levsky's former comrades, which had crossed from Rumania to take part in the Sliven Rising, was completely annihilated by Turkish troops on its way from Tutrakan to Razgrad.

In the Vratsa Region, owing to the difficulties already described, no rising took place.

Khristo Botev's Cheta

Although after leaving the Central Committee Botev played no further part in the leadership of the Revolutionary Movement, he was by no means inactive, and kept in touch with all that was going on through his friends Nikola Obretenov and Georgi Apostolov, who were members of the Gyurgevo Committee. Botev considered that a well-armed *cheta* organized abroad could play a very useful role in supporting the internal revolutionary movement once the rising began, and that it was the duty of all émigré patriots to join such a *cheta*. He, too, was certain that a large-scale uprising would have beneficial international repercussions and force the Powers to consider the plight of Bulgaria. The news of the beginning of the rising spurred him on to increased activity. He began to publish a new paper, *New Bulgaria*, and with the help of his friends he began to organize his *cheta* in earnest. For once, arms were no great problem, for they were able to make use of the arms which the Vratsa Committee had obtained but had been unable to transport across the Danube. The *cheta* numbered about 200 men, the majority of whom were ordinary workers, gardeners, drovers, clerks, teachers, etc., with a sprinkling of professional revolutionaries, including Nikola Obretenov, Georgi Apostolov and Levsky's youngest brother, Petür. There were also two officers from the Russian Army,

N. Voinovsky of Gabrovo and Captain Radionov, a Russian émigré from St Petersburg, who had served as a volunteer in the rising in Herzegovina.

According to the plan worked out by Botev, the rebels would cross the Danube by seizing control of the *Radetzky*, an Austrian passenger ship, sailing up-stream from Braila—a method of acquiring transport which had, to Botev's knowledge, been used successfully by Polish and Italian revolutionaries. On May 16th the 200 rebels boarded the *Radetzky* in small groups at various Danube ports, disguised as itinerant gardeners bound for Kladovo in Serbia, with their uniforms and arms packed in trunks which were stowed as luggage aboard the ship. The whole plan was brilliantly conceived and put into operation. Some way out from the Rumanian port of Beket, Botev gave the eagerly awaited signal. The rebels changed into their uniforms and went to their posts. They arrested Captain Englender and his second-in-command, treating them with firm courtesy, took control of the engine-room and placed all the sailors under guard.

Resplendent in a gold-braided uniform, with a golden lion on his black fur cap, Botev received Captain Englender politely, handed him a letter in French, and proudly introduced himself as the leader of the Bulgarian rebels. He demanded that the captain place his ship at the rebels' disposal to convey them to the Bulgarian shore, and, said that, should he refuse, they would be obliged to use force. At first the captain did refuse, but then, realizing that the rebels would carry out their plan in spite of him, and fearing for the safety of his crew and the other passengers, he finally agreed, and was allowed to resume his duties. No one on board the ship was harmed, including two Turks—the *kaimakan* (local governor) and Port Director of Oryakhovo. The ship was brought to the shore near Kozloduy and the rebels disembarked, unfurled their banner and kissed the soil of their beloved country.

This was, perhaps, the happiest moment of Botev's life, in spite of the fact that he had left behind in Rumania his wife, Veneta, whom he had married less than a year before, and his new-born daughter, Ivanka. Gone were the frustrations of exile and of being constantly hampered in his journalistic activity by lack of money. At last the hour had come when he could give himself utterly to the cause of liberating his country. Even the prospect of dying for this cause filled him with unbounded joy, as we can see from the letter which he wrote on the ship to his friends in Bucharest. He also sent a farewell letter to his wife, and telegrams to the newspapers *Journal de Genève* and *La Republique Française*, since he considered that drawing the attention of Europe to the struggle of the Bulgarian people was almost as important as the struggle itself. The telegrams informed the newspapers of the events on the *Radetzky* and the aims of the *cheta*, and ended: 'They [the Bulgars] are confident that the civilized European peoples and Governments will stretch out a brotherly hand to them.'

Once on Bulgarian soil, however, the romance of the seizure of the ship faded away into stern reality. The spectacular method by which the rebels had crossed the Danube meant that they had forfeited the advantages of surprise and secrecy. The two Turks on board naturally informed the authorities at the next port of call, and thus, from the beginning, the approximate whereabouts and strength of the *cheta* were known. Botev had imagined that when the *cheta* arrived in Bulgaria, it would be the signal for a general rising in the area and that it would receive considerable support and reinforcements. But it was now May 17th, and everywhere the rising had already been crushed. *Bashibazouks* and Turkish Army units were everywhere. No support was forthcoming from Vratsa where no rising had taken place.

The *cheta* set out for the mountains. In the first few villages through which they passed, only two people joined it. On May 18th from a rising called Milin Kamŭk, they fought all day against companies of Turkish troops and a large number of Circassians and *bashibazouks*, sustaining some thirty casualties, including the standard-bearer, and during the night of May 18th–19th they slipped away under cover of darkness and hid in the vineyards on Mount Veslets near Vratsa. The wounded, who had to be left behind in peasant huts, were subsequently burnt alive by the Turks. A letter was sent to the Committee in Vratsa, requesting food and support from a Vratsa *cheta*, but although they waited all day, no reply came, for the army of Hasan Pasha had just arrived in Vratsa from southern Bulgaria. On May 20th they took up their positions in a long line below Mounts Vola, Kamarata, Okolchitsa and Kupena. Tortured by thirst, they fought heroically all day against regular troops, *bashibazouks* and Circassians. The firing ceased with nightfall, but when a Turkish trumpet sounded, Botev stood up to find out what was happening, and fell dead with a bullet in his heart.

When his companions had recovered somewhat from the initial shock of their loss, they removed all the insignia of his rank, so that the Turks should not mock his body, kissed his forehead and departed.

Bereft of their leader, they broke up into smaller groups. Voinovsky commanded the biggest of these groups, and some weeks later he was killed fighting heroically near Shipkovo in the Troyan district. Most of the others were soon betrayed and captured, including Nikola Obretenov, who, however, survived captivity and lived to see the Liberation.

The Reasons for the Failure of the April Rising

Various factors contributed to the failure of the rising. Not all the heroism of the rebels and their leaders could compensate for the fact that the preparatory work was totally inadequate and the overall leadership weak. The rising was prepared in a very short space of time, because of the international situation, and as a result, very few localities were ready, either morally or materially, to rise. Moreover, once the Gyurgevo Committee had made its general propositions, it ceased to exist and there was no General Staff, as it were, for the leaders were all scattered over the country working independently in their own districts, without very efficient liaison. Thus the risings, when they started, were piecemeal, instead of simultaneous and co-ordinated. Then one must take into account the treacherous role of the *chorbadzhii*, and the almost equally paralysing effect of the timid, vacillating conduct of the *bourgeois* elements on the Committees, i.e. the medium-scale traders and minor industrialists. The actual geographical position of Bulgaria, close to Turkey, easily accessible to Turkish troops and already inhabited by large numbers of Turks and Circassians, created difficulties for the Bulgarian rebels which the rebels in more distant Herzegovina never had to face.

All this produced very unfavourable conditions for the rebels from the start, but the difficulties were made worse by the tactics adopted. Instead of exploiting their initial success by taking the offensive against the Turks, who were ill-prepared to fight back, the rebels based their whole strategy on defence, more or less waiting for the Turks to assemble forces and attack them. In some areas, such as Sliven, the old outmoded *cheta* tactics were substituted for a general uprising. Even the few offensive elements contained in the original plan were not carried out: the railways were not cut and the towns were not burnt. No attempt was made to obtain arms from the enemy. Finally, among the factors contributing to the apparent failure of the rising, mention must be made of the heavy continuous rain which wrought havoc with the rebels' arms, and affected both health and morale.

The Significance of the April Rising

For all its shortcomings, the April Rising represented the highest point of the Bulgarian struggle for national liberation. It was a *bourgeois* democratic revolution in that it was an attempt to throw off the fetters of feudalism in the name of a more progressive form of society, but in the particular situation prevailing inside Bulgaria, the upper *bourgeoisie* and part of the middle *bourgeoisie* had found it to their advantage to ally themselves with Turkish feudalism, and had done all they could to sabotage the rising, while other sections of the middle *bourgeoisie* had taken part in the preliminary organization, but had backed out at the eleventh hour. The basic driving force of the April Rising was the peasantry, who accounted for more than two-thirds of those involved, plus the ruined craftsmen and the intellectuals who threw in their lot with the people. They were led by the left wing of the Revolutionary Party founded by Levsky and organized according to the pattern which he had evolved. The aims of the leaders at least went far beyond the timid limits set by the *bourgeoisie*—hence their last minute vacillation and retreat.

While one may criticize their tactics, no praise can be too high for the heroism of the leaders and the rank and file rebels. Time and again they demonstrated that the words of their banners—'Freedom or Death'—were no empty slogan but their innermost conviction, the very fabric of their being. And we now know that their sacrifice was not altogether in vain, for although the rising was outwardly a failure, costly beyond comprehension in blood and suffering, yet it achieved its aim: it forced all Europe to consider Bulgaria; it demonstrated to all who were not too bigoted to see that Turkey was completely incapable of governing the country other than by the sword and it set in motion the train of events which resulted in Russian intervention and the eventual liberation of Bulgaria. Benkovsky had spoken the truth when, gazing down at burning Panagyurishté he had declared that they had inflicted upon Turkey a wound from which she could never recover.

'Government by Yatagan'[1]

The crushing of the rising was followed by weeks of terror as the *bashibazouks* and Circassians roamed the country, fearful lest fresh

[1] This phrase was coined by Zakhari Stoyanov.

risings should break out, drunk with blood and fanaticism. By September some 30,000 people had been massacred, mostly cut to pieces with *yatagans*, and 10,000 more had been imprisoned. Eighty villages had been burnt to the ground and 200 others sacked. More than 300,000 head of cattle and sheep were stolen.[1]

Lest anyone should conclude that the appalling carnage was the result of local fanatics running wild rather than of the deliberate policy of the Turkish Government, it must be pointed out that the Government promoted and decorated precisely those Commanders who were responsible for the worst atrocities, and demoted those who had shown some signs of humanity. Tosun Bey (Klisura), Khafŭz Pasha (Panagyurishté), Barutanliyata (Batak) and Tŭmrŭshliyata (Perushtitsa) were all either decorated or promoted, while Hasan Pasha, who had kept his promise not to burn Bratsigovo or harm its inhabitants, was made to suffer for his mercy.

Some measure of responsibility for what happened must be borne by the British Government of the day, whose Envoy in Constantinople, Sir Henry Elliot, in pursuance of his Government's policy to maintain the Turkish Empire, encouraged the Porte to crush the rising at all costs. On May 7th, for example, Elliot sent the following dispatch: 'About 5,000 troops have been dispatched from here (Constantinople) and I believe no exertion should be spared for assuring the immediate suppression of a movement which, if allowed to spread, will become extremely serious.' On May 19th the Foreign Secretary, Lord Derby, sent a dispatch to Constantinople complaining of 'the weakness and apathy of the Porte in dealing with the insurrection in its earlier stages'.

Foreign Reaction to the Atrocities

When news of the massacres reached other countries abroad, progressive opinion throughout Europe expressed its horror and its sympathy for the Bulgarian people. From Italy, Garibaldi sent a telegram to the Bulgarian Central Charitable Society[2] in Bucharest, and several public protest meetings were held. In France, Victor Hugo spoke in defence of Bulgaria, and the celebrated publicist Girardin wrote several articles devoted to the April Rising and the sufferings of the Bulgarian people. In Bohemia and Slovenia, then still under Austrian rule, poets wrote verses against the Turks and

[1] Gandev, *Aprilskoto Vŭstanié*, p. 156.
[2] This was Tsankov's former Humanitarian Committee which had been renamed in July 1876.

the British Government which supported them. In Rumania, a number of artists and poets, as well as the early Socialists, joined their voices to the general protest.

In Russia, even the conservative papers which were, in principle, opposed to revolution, spoke in defence of Bulgaria. In some places the workers and peasants collected money to help their Bulgarian brothers. Many of the most eminent Russian scholars and writers, such as Dmitri Mendeleev, Dostoevsky, Tolstoy, Turgenev, Ivan Aksakov and Garshin expressed their support for Bulgaria. In *Anna Karenina*, Tolstoy sent his hero Vronsky to fight as a volunteer against Turkey, and Turgenev built his famous novel *On the Eve* round a Bulgarian hero. Turgenev also wrote a bitter denunciation of Queen Victoria and her Government in his poem *Croquet at Windsor*. Among the artists who were moved by the sufferings of Bulgaria were K. E. Makovsky, who painted a famous picture called *Bulgarian Martyrs*, which depicts Bulgarian women being seized by Turks by the altar of a church, and V. V. Vereshchagin, who later accompanied the Russian Army in the war against Turkey.

British Reaction to the Atrocities

While the British Government adhered to its traditional policy of upholding the 'integrity' of Turkey in order to avoid any increase of Russian influence in the Balkans, even to the extent of minimizing the scale and significance of the atrocities, the British people were not slow to react, and a strong campaign developed against the Government's policy on the Eastern Question, as it was called.

The British people first learnt of the atrocities when the *Daily News* published a dispatch from its correspondent in Constantinople, J. A. MacGahan. MacGahan's appalling revelations were dismissed by the Prime Minister, Disraeli, who described them as 'to a large extent inventions', and cynically rejected the stories of torture as unlikely since Turkey usually adopted 'more expeditious methods'. But the ghastly truth could not be kept dark, and by August and September the protests began to swell into a flood.

Following Russian approaches to the West, demanding that energetic steps be taken to force Turkey to grant Bulgarian autonomy, and declaring that in the event of nothing being done she would have to take other steps, the British Government decided to make an official inquiry into the atrocities. Sir Walter Baring, Second Secretary to the British Embassy in Constantinople, was sent to tour the affected areas. With him went Schuyler, the American

Consul in Constantinople, the Russian Consul in Plovdiv and Mac-Gahan, the *Daily News* correspondent. The reports made by the investigators make heart-rending reading.

'At a short distance from Ireni, upon one of the thousand stream-lets which empty themselves into the Maritsa, there is a water mill; for five days the mill could not work because the stream was blocked up by dead bodies which stopped the wheels.' (*Daily News*, August 2, 1876.)

'I have just seen the town of Batak with Mr Schuyler. Mr Baring was there yesterday. Here is what I saw. On approaching the town on a hill there were some dogs. They ran away and we found on this spot a number of skulls scattered about, and one ghastly heap of skeletons with clothing. I counted from the saddle a hundred skulls, picked and licked clean; all women and children. We entered the town. On every side were skulls and skeletons charred among the ruins, or lying entire where they fell in their clothing. There were skeletons of girls and women with long brown hair hanging to the skulls. We approached the church. Here the remains were more frequent, until the ground was literally covered with skeletons, skulls and putrifying bodies in clothing. Between the church and the school there were heaps. The stench was fearful. We entered the churchyard. The sight was more dreadful. The whole church-yard for three feet deep was festering with dead bodies partly covered —hands, legs, arms, and heads projected in ghastly confusion. I saw many little hands, heads and feet of children of three years of age, and girls, with heads covered with beautiful hair. The church was still worse. The floor was covered with rotting bodies quite uncovered. I never imagined anything so fearful. There were 3,000 bodies in the churchyard and church. We were obliged to hold tobacco to our noses. In the school, a fine building, 200 women and children had been burnt alive. All over the town there were the same scenes . . . The town had 9,000 inhabitants. There now remain 1,200 . . . Many who had escaped had returned recently, weeping and moaning over their ruined homes. Their sorrowful wailing could be heard half a mile off. Some were digging out the skeletons of loved ones. A woman was sitting moaning over three small skulls with hairs clinging to them, which she had in her lap.' (*Daily News*, August 7, 1876.)

In contrast to this terrible indictment of Turkish barbarity, MacGahan also mentions in his report that he had found no proof that a single Turkish woman or child had been killed by the Bulgars.

Public horror at the revelations expressed itself in a protest meeting convened in Manchester by the Mayor of that city on August 9th. On August 12th, the *Beehive*, a trade-union weekly, also printed an account of Batak, with bitter comment:

'Among the scenes of fire and slaughter visited by Mr Baring was the town of Batak . . . It had 9,000 living inhabitants, of whom but 1,200 remain alive . . . Everywhere the eye meets with skulls and mutilated corpses, half eaten by dogs . . . In the school 200 women and children had been roasted alive; 7,000 bodies had been lying in the sun since May 12th . . . The fiend who perpetrated all this, Akhmed Aga, has received promotion . . . These are what the First Minister of the tenderhearted Queen Victoria has the hardihood to style "imaginary atrocities".'

On August 22nd the *Daily News* printed a very strong article by MacGahan, in which he refuted the suggestion that the Bulgars were a savage people:

'I think people in England and Europe generally have a very imperfect idea of what these Bulgarians are. I have always heard them spoken of as mere savages, who were in reality not much more than the American Indians; and I confess that I myself was not far from entertaining the same opinion not very long ago. I was astonished, as I believe most of my readers will be, to learn that there is scarcely a Bulgarian village without its school; that these schools are, where they have not been burnt by the Turks, in a very flourishing condition; that they are supported by a voluntary tax levied by the Bulgarians on themselves, not only without being forced to do it by the Government, but in spite of all sorts of obstacles thrown in their way by the perversity of the Turkish authorities; that the education given in these schools is gratuitous; and that all profit alike by it, poor as well as rich; that there is scarcely a Bulgarian child who cannot read and write; and finally that the percentage of people who can read and write is as great in Bulgaria as in England and France. Do the people who speak of the Bulgarians as savages happen to be aware of these facts? Again, I had thought that the burning of a Bulgarian village meant the burning of a few mud huts that were in reality of little value and that could be easily rebuilt. I was very much astonished to find that the majority of these villages are in reality well-built towns, with solid stone houses, and that there are in all of them a comparatively large number of people who have attained to something like comfort, and that some of the villages might stand a not very unfavourable comparison with an English or French village. The truth is that these Bulgarians, instead of the savages we have taken them for, are in reality a hardworking, industrious, honest, civilized and peaceful people.'

On August 29th the *Daily News* printed a report on Panagyurishté by Schuyler, the American Consul:

'Old men had their eyes torn out and their limbs cut off, and were then left to die, unless some more charitably disposed gave them the final thrust. Pregnant women were ripped open and the unborn babies carried triumphantly on the point of bayonet and sabre, while little children were made to bear the dripping heads of their victims.'

Schuyler also stressed, as MacGahan had done, that no Turkish women or children had been killed in cold blood, none had been violated, none tortured, neither had any mosques been desecrated or destroyed, nor had any Turkish house been pillaged.

Although he was a Turkophil and played down the atrocities as far as he could, even Baring was obliged by sheer weight of evidence to admit that certainly 12,000 people, mostly women and children, had been killed. The British Government was obliged to abandon its unreserved support for Turkey, but in actual fact, it shifted its ground very little. Disraeli himself intimated in Parliament that while the killing of 12,000 people (Baring's figure; the actual figure was 30,000) was indeed a terrible occurrence, it was not sufficient reason to force the British Empire to change its traditional policy. British interests in India, the acquisition of the Suez Canal shares, and the purchase by Britain of a large number of Turkish Bonds, all outweighed the sufferings of the Bulgarian people in the estimation of the British Government and its supporters.

The British people, through their local Liberal Associations, Radical and Nonconformist groups and working-class organizations thought otherwise. Protest meetings were held throughout the country. On September 4th there were meetings in nine towns, on

September 5th in seventeen, and on September 6th in twenty. On September 9th the *Beehive* stated:

'The public demonstrations against the Turkish atrocities in Bulgaria and elsewhere are, day by day, maintaining a unanimous character and gradually assuming full national proportions. No meeting, perhaps, has been held at which the conduct of our Government has not been condemned as emphatically as the cruelty and abominable acts of the commissioned instrument of that of Turkey . . . The recall of Sir Henry Elliot from the Embassy is universally demanded, also compensation for the injured, to come, says Canon Lidden with general approval, out of the Treasury of the Porte, if it be not literally bankrupt . . . Most frequently calls are made by unanimous resolution for the punishment of the perpetrators . . .'

The rising tide of opposition to the Government brought William Gladstone into action. He had retired from the leadership of the Liberal Party after the Tory victory in 1874, and the Bulgarian issue offered an excellent platform for a political comeback. He wrote a pamphlet, denouncing Turkey in extremely violent rhetoric, which contained the following celebrated words:

'An old servant of the Crown and State, I entreat my countrymen, upon whom far more than perhaps any other people it depends to require and to insist that our Government, which has been working in one direction, shall work in the other, and shall apply all its vigour to concur with the other States of Europe in obtaining the extinction of the Turkish executive power in Bulgaria. Let the Turks now carry away their abuses in the only possible manner, namely by carrying off themselves. Their *Zaptiehs*, and their *Mudirs*, their *Bimbashis* and their *Yuzbashis*, their *Kaimakams* and their *Pashas*, one and all, bag and baggage, shall, I hope, clear out from the province they have desolated and profaned. This thorough riddance, this most blessed deliverance, is the only reparation we can make to the memory of those heaps on heaps of dead; to the violated purity alike of matron, of maiden and of child; to the civilization which has been affronted and shamed, to the laws of God, or, if you like, of Allah; to the moral sense of mankind at large. There is not a criminal in a European gaol, there is not a cannibal in the South Sea Islands, whose indignation would not arise and overboil at the recital of that which has been done, which has too late been examined, but which remains unavenged, which has left behind all the foul and fierce passion that produced it, and which may again spring up, in another murderous harvest, from the soil soaked and reeking with blood and in the air tainted with every imaginable deed of crime and shame. That such things should be done once, is a damning disgrace to the portion of our race which did them, that a door should be left open for their ever-so-barely-possible repetition would spread that shame over the whole. Better, we may justly tell the Sultan, almost any inconvenience, difficulty, or loss associated with Bulgaria "Than thou reseated in thy place of light, the mockery of thy people and their bane".[1] We may ransack the annals of the world, but I know not what research can furnish us with so portentous an example of the fiendish misuse of the powers established by God "for the punishment of evil doers, and for the encouragement of them that do well". No Government ever has so sinned, none has so proved itself incorrigible in sin, or which is the same, so impotent for reformation. If it be allowable that the executive power of Turkey should renew at this great crisis, by permission of authority of Europe, the charter of its existence in Bulgaria, then there is not on record, since the beginnings of political society, a protest that man has lodged against intolerable misgovernment, or a stroke he has dealt at loathsome tyranny, that ought not henceforward to be branded as a crime.'

Gladstone followed up the pamphlet by addressing an enormous meeting on Blackheath, where, however, his language was slightly more moderated:

'You (the Turks) shall receive your regular tribute, you shall retain your titular sovereignty, your Empire shall not be invaded, but never again . . . shall the hand of violence be raised by you, never again shall the flood gates of lust be open to you, never again shall the dire refinements of cruelty be devised by you . . .'

Thus in September popular feeling against Turkey became so strong that Lord Derby was obliged to inform Turkey that outrages had 'aroused a universal feeling of indignation in all classes of English society, and to such a pitch has this risen, that in the extreme case of Russia declaring war on Turkey, Her Majesty's Government would find it practically impossible to interfere in the defence of the Ottoman Empire'.

[1] Tennyson's *Guinevere*.

The Bulgarian National Liberation Movement after the April Rising
One of the salient features of the national movement was the absence
of the left wing of the 'Young' Party, for the simple reason that
nearly all its leading members had been killed in the fighting.
The politically active émigrés in Bucharest now consisted, in the
main, of the moderate revolutionaries, such as Kiriak Tsankov and
Olimpi Panov, who were in close touch both with Karavelov and
with the 'Old' Party under Evlogi Georgiev, who had been, and
still was, opposed to revolution in any form.

While the rising was in progress, various other events of importance to the Balkans had been taking place. During May 1876 the
Tripartite Conference to discuss the situation in the Balkans
had met in Berlin. The Austro-Hungarian representative, Count
Andrassy, supported by Bismarck, insisted on so many amendments
to the Russian plan for autonomy for the Slavonic provinces that
the final proposals laid out in the so-called Berlin Memorandum
amounted to little more than Andrassy's original programme of
maintaining the *status quo* with certain administrative reforms,
which had already proved unacceptable to the rebels in Bosnia and
Herzegovina. But even these new proposals were too radical for
Britain, who rejected them and thus nothing came of the Berlin
conference. Serbia and Montenegro, weary of the fruitless deliberations of the Great Powers, formed an alliance, and began to prepare
for a war against Turkey in support of Bosnia and Herzegovina,
confidently expecting Russian assistance. Thus, shortly after the
crushing of the April Rising, the long expected war between Serbia
and Turkey broke out on June 19, 1876. Between four and five
thousand Russian volunteers joined the Serbs and their commander,
General Chernaev, was appointed Commander-in-Chief of the
Serbian Army.

The suppression of the April Rising and the events in Serbia
naturally evoked great interest and activity amongst the Bulgarian
émigrés. Even the 'Old' Party in Rumania and the *bourgeoisie* in
Constantinople, including Dragan Tsankov, and the Exarch Antim,
who had been totally opposed to the April Rising, began to talk
eloquently about the sacrifices of the people and to indulge in
political activity, spurred on by the hope that in the event of Russian
intervention and the liberation of Bulgaria, they might take office
in the new administration.

Kiriak Tsankov's Bulgarian Humanitarian Committee, which had
done very little prior to the April Rising, had been resuscitated early

in May, and formed branches in many Rumanian towns to collect money for the victims, and it became clear that the Committee proposed to play a political role.

When the war with Serbia began, some of the veteran *voivodi*, such as Panaiot Khitov, Filip Totyu and Khristo Makedonsky, at the invitation of the Serbian Government, collected Bulgarian volunteers and formed *cheti*, which included survivors of the April Rising.

Another feature of the movement following the destruction of the internal revolutionary organization was the unanimous turning of the Bulgarian people and the émigrés to Russia as their only salvation. For their part, the Slavonic Committees in Moscow and St Petersburg were very active in trying to reconcile the various groupings among the Bulgarian émigrés in order to organize them to the best possible advantage in the struggle against Turkey. As early as May, the St Petersburg Committee sent Nikolai Kiraev to try to resuscitate the old Revolutionary Central Committee, with the participation of both 'Young' and 'Old'. In this he failed, because the 'Old' were still opposed to any form of revolutionary activity. In June, after the Serbo-Turkish War had begun, the Moscow Committee sent Vladimir Ionin to Bucharest with the same task. On July 10, 1876, Ionin called together the members of Tsankov's 'Humanitarian Committee' and the latter was transformed into a new Revolutionary Central Committee, but it was decided to give it the innocent name of 'The Bulgarian Central Charitable Society' (BCCS) to avoid any political embarrassment to the Rumanian Government. Officially the organization existed to aid the victims of the April Rising, but, in actual fact, its main task was the recruitment of volunteers to serve in Serbia. The Officers of the new Committee were Ionin (Honorary President), Kiriak Tsankov (Chairman), and P. Enchev (Secretary). Two representatives of the 'Old' Party joined the Committee, but were forced by the leaders of the 'Old' Party to resign. Subsequently various other people joined the Committee, including Ivan Vazov, the writer, Olimpi Panov and Stambolov.

Ionin and Enchev went to Serbia and arranged with General Chernaev for the Bulgarian volunteers to serve as a separate unit. The Serbian Government, who wanted the Bulgars to serve in Serbian units under the Serbian flag, did everything they could to prevent the formation of the separate Bulgarian unit, but Chernaev was able to insist.

By the middle of September some 2,500 volunteers had arrived in Serbia, and were formed into three battalions under Russian officers. As part of Chernaev's detachment of Russian volunteers, the Bulgars took a leading part in the fighting and conducted themselves with great bravery.

While continuing to collect volunteers, the Committee in Bucharest made further plans which included organizing a revolt in Bulgaria itself, should the war take a favourable course, and asking the Slavonic Committee to obtain permission from the Russian Government for the organization of a *cheta* in southern Russia, which would go to Bulgaria by sea, when the time seemed opportune.

Unfortunately, the war did not take a favourable course. The Serbian Army was defeated at Aleksinac and Deligrad, and by October 20th the road to Belgrade lay open to the Turks. Serbia was saved from complete catastrophe by the intervention of Russia, who sent Turkey an ultimatum, demanding the cessation of military operations. Turkey accepted the ultimatum and an armistice was signed with Serbia, but Montenegro and the rebels in Bosnia and Herzegovina refused to make peace. General Chernaev was obliged to hand over his command to Colonel Hervatovic and left Serbia with his Russian volunteers. The Bulgarian volunteers also had no further cause to remain in Serbia and returned to Rumania. The departing Bulgars were very badly treated by the Serbs who even took away their clothes, so that many of them died of cold and hunger.

As it became increasingly clear that there would eventually be war between Russia and Turkey, the Central Charitable Society continued to recruit volunteers, concentrating them in Rumania, where they were trained by Russian instructors. The Central Charitable Society also attempted to revive the Committees within Bulgaria, through the Rusé Committee, which was to act as liaison. The Rusé Committee was asked to do all it could to get the population to send petitions to Russia asking for help, and to prepare the people for the arrival of the Russians. Not a great deal of progress was made, because the Revolutionary Movement within the country had not recovered from the consequences of the April Rising.

On November 18, 1876, the Central Charitable Society held a National Assembly in Bucharest under the chairmanship of Ionin. The Assembly adopted a programme which declared that their main aim was the liberation of Bulgaria from Turkish rule. Of the form which the future Government of Bulgaria should take, little was said, apart from mentioning that the country was to be governed constitutionally and that complete freedom of conscience should prevail. In fact, most of the leaders of the Central Charitable Society were in favour of a constitutional monarchy, although this was not stated in the programme. Against the *chorbadzhii* nothing was said, probably in order to avoid conflict with the 'Old'. The Assembly, consisting of émigrés in Rumania, was very unlike the 1872 Assembly with a majority of revolutionaries from Bulgaria itself, which had voted the programme of the old Central Committee, and the new programme was a very far cry from the Democratic Republic of Levsky and Botev, and from their ideal of social as well as national revolution. But one has to bear in mind the close dependence of both the Committee and its plan on Tsarist Russia and its consequent desire to offend neither Russia nor the 'Old'. In any case, few of the adherents of the Central Charitable Society had ever been very 'left', with the possible exception of Stambolov, so the 'Programme' did not represent for them personally an ideological retreat. The convinced Republicans were almost all dead. In spite of its obvious limitations the Central Charitable Society performed quite a useful function, especially in relation to the recruitment of volunteers.

After the Assembly, the Central Charitable Society did very little, apart from sending the 'Programme' and a *mémoire* to the Governments of the Great Powers, asking for support, and, in addition, letters and telegrams to various individuals and organizations abroad. During the Constantinople Conference (December 1876–January 1877), the Central Charitable Society sent petitions to the foreign consuls in Rusé, asking that Bulgaria should become an Autonomous State, headed by a Prince, who would recognize the overlordship of the Sultan.

After the Russo-Turkish War broke out, the Central Charitable Society ceased to function.

The Events Leading up to the Russo-Turkish War

The intricacies of European diplomacy are too complex to be unravelled in a book of this kind, and therefore the events leading up to the Russo-Turkish War will be described only in outline form. The position of the major Powers of Europe may be summarized as follows: Russia, in her perennial striving to gain control of the Dardanelles, desired to restore her influence in the Balkans which had been in eclipse since her defeat in the Crimean War; moreover, successful intervention against Turkey would do much to increase the prestige of the Government at home, and thus weaken the revolutionary forces there; thus a large autonomous Slavonic State in the Balkans under Russia's protection would contribute greatly to Russia's influence in the vital area of the Dardanelles; Austria-Hungary who ruled the Slovenes and Croats, found all moves for freedom or autonomy in the Balkans a menace to herself, and it goes without saying that she was opposed to any increase in Russian influence there, and therefore desired to maintain the *status quo* in the Balkans; Germany was quite happy to see Russia and Austria in conflict in the Balkans, because they would weaken themselves and thus strengthen Germany. The position of Britain has already been made sufficiently clear so as to need no further comment.

When the Serbian-Turkish War first began, Russia hoped to avoid further war, and even when General Chernaev was first appointed Commander-in-Chief of the Serbian Army, it was against the will of the Russian Government. Later, the Russian Government, not wishing to lose her influence in the Balkans, decided to support Serbia and Herzegovina, even at risk of antagonizing the other Great Powers, and began to prepare for war with Turkey.

On June 26, 1876, Tsar Alexander II, accompanied by his chancellor, Gorchakov, had met the Austrian Emperor, Franz Josef, and Count Andrassy at Reichstadt in Bohemia. They discussed the war and came to a general agreement about a common policy in the event of a Turkish defeat or a Turkish victory. The agreement was, however, purely verbal and open to various interpretations. During October, as we have seen, the position in Serbia deteriorated, and to maintain her prestige, Russia was obliged to intervene. Partial mobilization was ordered and the ultimatum was sent to Turkey at the end of October.

In the meantime, the *bourgeoisie* in Constantinople had roused themselves to political action. While the minority Turkophil section (Dr Stoyan Chomakov, etc.) still advocated dualism, the Russophil section (Exarch Antim, Naiden Gerov, etc.) hoped that with Russian help Bulgaria would gain liberation or at least some form of autonomous government in which they would play the leading role. With the approval of Count Ignatiev, the Russian Envoy in Constantinople, the Russophil merchants presented to the representatives of the European States a *mémoire* setting out their version of Bulgaria's aspirations. They also sent a delegation consisting of Dragan Tsankov and Marko Balabanov to tour the capitals of Europe. In August the delegates reached Vienna, and after a short stay in Paris they went to London where they had discussions with the British Foreign Secretary, Lord Derby, and with Gladstone. After that they visited Rome and Berlin. Everywhere they were received sympathetically, but no promises were given. The climax of their pilgrimage came when they visited St Petersburg, where they were warmly welcomed. The Tsar himself received the delegates and repeated the declaration that he had made in Moscow on October 29th/November 11th, that if the Great Powers could reach no agreement on the granting of autonomy to Bulgaria, Russia would take unilateral action, i.e. war.

Alarmed by the prospect that Russia might do precisely this, the Great Powers agreed to hold a Conference in Constantinople. The Conference opened on December 11/23, 1876, and was attended by Great Britain, Germany, Austro-Hungary, France, Italy, Turkey, and Russia. Russia was represented by Count Ignatiev, and Britain by the Marquis of Salisbury and Sir Henry Elliot. Great Britain proposed that Bulgaria be divided into two Autonomous Regions, an Eastern Part centred on Tŭrnovo and a Western Part centred on Sofia, each with a Christian governor, not necessarily a Bulgarian, appointed by Turkey with the agreement of the Great Powers. Bosnia and Herzegovina were to receive autonomy. The main purpose of dividing Bulgaria was to weaken future Russian influence in the Balkans, but in spite of the fact that the plan by no means satisfied Russia, she was prepared to accept it because she was confident that the two parts would eventually unite. But behind the scenes, Britain was secretly urging Turkey to reject the plan, and the Sultan Abdul Hamid[1] threw a thunderbolt among the delegates by announcing with much pomp and circumstance that the deliberations of the Conference were superfluous since a new constitution would be introduced, assuring all Turkish subjects equal rights and freedom. Thus the Conference closed early in January having achieved nothing.

In the course of the Conference, the Porte attempted to organize Bulgarian support for itself, through the Turkophil *bourgeoisie* who collected signatures for an address to the Sultan, declaring that the Bulgars were satisfied with Turkish rule and the new Constitution, and would not recognize the decisions of the Conference. It goes without saying that little support was forthcoming for this address,

---

[1] In May 1876, Abdul Azis had been dethroned by the Young Turk Party under Midhat Pasha, who became Grand Vizir to the new Sultan Murad V. The latter was declared mad and forced to abdicate after only three months, and Abdul Hamid II took the throne.

13. The Eastern Question: Conference at St James Hall—Mr Gladstone speaking
(From the Illustrated London News, December 16, 1876)

14. Russian soldiers making themselves at home in a Bulgarian cottage

(From the Illustrated London News, March 9, 1876)

but the Turks did succeed in engineering the dethronement and imprisonment in Asia Minor of the Russophil Exarch Antim I and his replacement by Yosif I.

While she continued to seek agreement with the Great Powers, Russia had no illusions about the inevitability of a war between herself and Turkey. Since the autumn of 1876, she had been secretly negotiating with Austria to secure the latter's neutrality in the event of such a war, and shortly after the end of the Constantinople Conference, agreement was reached in Budapest on the basis of the recognition of Austria's right to occupy Bosnia and Herzegovina in exchange for neutrality. Russia had also been conducting long negotiations with Rumania to allow the passage of Russian troops through that country, negotiations which were successfully concluded on April 12, 1877.

Russia continued to try to neutralize the Great Powers as far as possible, and in March after much diplomatic activity on the part of Count Ignatiev, the six powers signed the London Protocol, a rather vague document which called on Turkey to introduce certain reforms. Counting on secret Western support, whatever might be said in public declarations, Turkey rejected the Protocol as an unwarranted interference in her internal affairs.

It was obvious that nothing further could be achieved by diplomatic means, and on April 12th (Old Style), 1877, in Kishinev, the Tsar signed a manifesto declaring war on Turkey. Russian troops entered Rumania on their way to the Danube and also crossed into Turkish Armenia in the Caucasus.

British Reaction to the Russo-Turkish War

As we have already seen, there was fairly unanimous public support for Bulgaria against Turkey during the summer and autumn of 1876. When it became obvious that there would be a war between Russia and Turkey, the position became very much more complicated. The main factor here was the traditional dislike of the British progressive movement for Russian Tsarism, which it regarded as little better than Ottoman despotism. In this connection we may quote the words of the radical Joseph Cowen, spoken somewhat later, on February 11, 1878, in the House of Commons:

'. . . there is a ring of Christian Pashas at St Petersburg as corrupt and cruel as the ring of Mohammedan Pashas at Constantinople . . . They have the ferocity of barbarism with the duplicity of civilization. Their

K

first word is gold, the second the sword, the third Siberia. Bribery, bayonets, banishment are the triple pillars upon which their politico-military-ecclesiastical system stands. . . .'

Indeed, a section of the progressive movement believed that a military defeat for Russia was desirable because it would weaken Tsarism. The true character of Russian Tsarism had not escaped the notice of the Bulgarian revolutionaries either, but nevertheless they accepted the possibility of obtaining Russian help in liberating Bulgaria. Botev had worked closely with the Russian Revolutionaries who aimed at the overthrow of Tsarism, and Levsky had commented on the persecution suffered by Republicans in Russia.

In a paradoxical situation where the objectively reactionary Tsarist Government was playing a progressive role as far as Bulgaria was concerned, both trends of British progressive opinion can be said to be in part correct, but in practice, the existence of a division served to strengthen the hand of Disraeli. The dilemma of British progressive opinion was reflected in the *Beehive* on October 7, 1876:

'There are two barbarisms to deal with, and the English Government as well as the English people would do wrong if they encouraged or confided in the one rather than the other.'

On the whole, opinion was crystallizing into a demand for non-intervention in any war between Russia and Turkey. John Bright addressed the Manchester Reform Club in this vein, and on October 20th the Labour Representation League[1] resolved that:

'should Russia make war on Turkey, it will be the duty of the English people to oppose any action of the Government which has for its object any defence of the Ottoman Empire, or which shall prevent the establishment of such an independent Government for the Turkish provinces of Eastern Europe as shall be in accordance with the wishes of the people of these provinces.'

On November 9th at a Guildhall banquet Disraeli made an extremely bellicose speech, inspiring the famous music hall song which gave the word 'jingoism' to the English language. On December 8th

[1] A body formed to promote the candidature of working men to Parliament and which was falling increasingly under Liberal influence.

the opponents of British intervention held a conference in St James Hall. The speakers included Anthony Trollope, the Duke of Westminster, Henry Richard (a pacifist), Samuel Morely (a Radical M P), George Howell, Henry Broadhurst and William Gladstone. The calling of the meeting infuriated Queen Victoria, who wanted the Attorney General to take action against the speakers. ('It can't be constitutional'; 'This mawkish sentimentality for people who hardly deserve the name of real Christians . . . forgetting the interests of this great country, is really incomprehensible.')[1] As a result of this conference, the Eastern Question Association was officially established, with A. J. Mundella, Radical M P for Sheffield, as Chairman and William Morris as Treasurer. The Duke of Westminster and Lord Shaftesbury also supported the Association, which made contact with the Labour Representation League. On the eve of the Russian declaration of war, the latter resolved:

'That should an attempt be made to involve this country in the conflict in support of Turkish interests, either direct or indirect, it will be the duty of the people of this country to take such steps as will prevent English Blood and the People's Taxes being employed in such an unworthy and hopeless cause.'

Once the war had begun, the two organizations began to act jointly, with William Morris in the forefront of the activity. Many meetings against the involving of Britain in the war on the side of Turkey were held. On May 2, 1877, Henry Broadhurst called a meeting of 'Workmen's Political Associations and Trade Societies of the Metropolis' at Cannon Street Hotel in support of the anti-Turkish motions which Gladstone had tabled in the House. On May 7th another conference under the auspices of the Eastern Question Association was held at St. James Hall. Later, when the victorious Russians were threatening Constantinople, and the danger of British intervention became even more acute, a large meeting was held on January 16, 1878, in Exeter Hall. For this occasion, William Morris wrote a special song which was sung by a choir. Clashes occurred between 'jingoists' and those opposed to war. In the spring of 1878, following the Treaty of San Stefano, which established an independent Bulgarian State, when Britain was pressing for its revision, agitation continued against any military intervention. In a leaflet signed by F. W. Campin, Daniel Guile and Henry Broadhurst,

[1] G. E. Buckle, *Life of Disraeli*, 1920, Vol. VI, pp. 107, 130.

addressed to the Working Men of the United Kingdom and issued on April 4, 1878, there occur the following words:

'What has England to go to war for? Is it to fasten anew the fetters of a hateful despotism around the necks of a now free people in Eastern Europe, and to set upon its legs that revolting power called the Ottoman Empire? When England draws the sword let it be on the side of liberty to the oppressed and down-trodden. Fellow workers, the noisy minority who are now shrieking for war are not moved by feelings of sympathy for the enslaved or the free. The motive power is their millions invested in Turkish bonds. As they have wrung their wealth from our bones and muscles, so they would not hesitate to deluge foreign lands with our blood to thwart political and social progress at home for the next twenty years, in order to get back their gold. Let the money-mongers suffer the just penalty of their inordinant love of gain and want of patriotism. England's greatest men believe that all just aspirations which the country should have in settlement of the Eastern Question can be obtained without war. We also believe it.'[1]

The Beginning of the Russo-Turkish War, 1877–1878

The news of the declaration of war was received very differently in various quarters. Great Britain and Austria received it with natural hostility, and the Pope ordered prayers to be said for Turkey—an action which provoked demonstrations against the Pope in Prague. Rumania allied herself to Russia and also declared war. In Russia itself the news was received with joy, and in Bulgaria with wild rapture. The Bulgarian Central Charitable Society renamed itself the Bulgarian Central Committee and issued an appeal calling on the people to be ready to welcome the Russians and to take part in the struggle side by side with them. Bulgarian volunteers, in all about 7,500, flocked to join the army in Russia and Rumania, and they were formed into separate Bulgarian units with mainly Russian officers under General Nikolai Stoletov. A few of the officers were Bulgars who had served in the Russian Army. The Bulgarian volunteers were presented with a special banner by the town of Samara (now Kuibishev). As always, those ready to lay down their lives for liberty were largely farm labourers (*ratai*), workers and intellectuals. The rich *bourgeoisie* in the 'Old' Party were so afraid of revolution

[1] From the Howell Collection. Quoted in *Labour's Formative Years 1849–1879*, Lawrence and Wishart, p. 193.

that their leader, Evlogi Georgiev, even tried to prevent the formation of separate Bulgarian units, and they refused to let their own sons and servants take part.

The Russian Army was smaller and less well armed than the Turkish Army which had the latest German artillery, and English and American rifles. The Russian Army had the additional difficulty of having to maintain long lines of communication and supply. Moreover, although the Russians had many talented Generals, some with a democratic outlook into the bargain, their task was made very difficult by the fact that the High Command was in the hands of the Tsar, his relations and the Generals of his retinue. The Turks themselves lacked skilled artillery and other specialist officers, but they had many foreign instructors from France, Germany and England. The Turkish Fleet, which was commanded by the English Admiral Hobart, also had an immense advantage over the Russian Fleet in size and weight, but this did not prevent the Russians from winning a victory over it on the Danube and Black Sea. In spite of all the handicaps on their side, the Russians possessed one priceless advantage: regardless of whatever motives the Tsarist Government may have had, the ordinary Russian soldiers saw the war as a just war of liberation, and therefore their enthusiasm and heroism overcame all difficulties and hardships. They had yet a further advantage: they were fighting on friendly soil where the people had waited 500 years for their coming.

On June 15, 1877, the main body of the Russian Army crossed the Danube near Svishtov and took the city. The liberation of Bulgaria had begun.

The Course of the War

From Svishtov the Russians fanned out in several directions. One section of the Army went east to Rusé, where the main Turkish Army was enclosed in the rectangle Shumen–Rusé–Silistra–Varna, one went west to Nikopol while a third, commanded by General Gurko, and including the Bulgarian volunteers, marched south to Tŭrnovo and the Stara Planina. On June 25th Tŭrnovo, the ancient capital of Bulgaria, was liberated amid scenes of unimaginable rejoicing. This is how the correspondent of the Russian *Illustrated Chronicle of the War* (No. 28) describes it:

'On the 30th of June at about noon the Grand Duke arrived here. He was welcomed so enthusiastically by the population that it is difficult if not impossible to relate it in words. This enthusiasm can only be comprehensible to you if I tell you that the dawn of Liberation has been awaited by the Bulgarians for five whole centuries. At last that day has come! Men, women and children with tears of happiness in their eyes, embrace every Russian they meet on their way. The Russian and Bulgarian flags, adorned with myrtle and olive branches, fly over every Christian house. The Bulgarians invite every Russian to their homes, offering him the richest entertainment they can afford. The entertainments, lunches and dinners are still in progress and are not likely to stop soon! The entire population is jubilant, *Te Deums* are sung and the people walk around our camps which echo to the songs of choirs, military bands and Russian songs; they rejoice at the Russian soldiers and bring hay and fodder for the horses of our troops, free of charge.'

Exactly the same picture, though described with understandably less enthusiasm, came from an English journalist:

'Not for one minute must we forget that the Russians are here as welcome guests. The poor people are literally crying, praying and throwing themselves on the necks of their liberators. . . . From the English point of view, of particular importance is the fact that the doors of all the houses are opened with joy to the victors, and that all who can provide them with food and drink refuse all payment.'

Everywhere the Russians were greeted with wild enthusiasm, flowers and the traditional offering of bread and salt. T. G. Vlaikov in *What I have Lived Through* describes how his village went out *en masse* to welcome the Russians:

'The next morning we heard the gongs being beaten, both the wooden and the iron ones. They were being beaten solemnly, as on important holidays. Was there to be a service because of the arrival of the Russians? No, they were sounding to gather the people together to go and meet the Russian Army. . . . In front of Hadzhi Petrov's inn and all around it, the place was black with people, the whole village was out. The priests were at the head of the population, dressed in their gold vestments, and before them marched the choristers with the censers and church banners. After them and all round them came a crowd of men, women, young people and children—there was no end to them! Nothing was to be seen on the road to town. But at one time a peculiar sound was heard in the distance, a rhythmical thudding. And after a while the head of a moving mass appeared around the bend in the road. "The Army! The Army! The Russian Army!" a shout went up. . . . There it was, approaching. The serried ranks of the soldiers were already to be seen, all with their rifles on their shoulders. The measured tramp of their footsteps along the frozen road was already clearly to be heard. And further on, as far as the eye could see, there was nothing but rifles. . . . They swayed up and down. A tall, elderly man, without a rifle, but with a long sword at his side and shiny shoulder straps, was marching at their head—their commander. He looked grave and important. Behind him there were several more, also with the same shiny straps on their shoulders. When he reached the priests who were standing in the middle of the road, the commander stopped. The column stopped too. Father Kiril, who was at the head of the priests, raised the cross he held in his hand on high and, trembling with emotion: "Blessed be ye in the name of the Lord!" he said, then in a quavering voice he added: "We bid you welcome, our saviours!" The great man took off his cap, crossed himself and kissed the cross, then bending, kissed father priest's hand. He too said several words. Then turning to the soldiers, he shouted something. A full-throated "Hurrah-ah-ah!" broke from the whole column. The people, startled at first by the thunderous shout that they were hearing for the first time in their lives, were imperceptibly carried away and joined in. And the whole countryside rang again to inspired and incessant "Hurrah-ah-ahs! . . ." After this wave of enthusiasm, a lass came forward and handed her nosegay to the commander. He thanked her, smiling, rising his hand to his cap in salute. Then he turned again, signed to his soldiers and set off. The crowd parted and made way for them, and the lasses began to shower their nose-gays on them. A ceremony never seen before in its imposing enthusiasm.'

But the road to Constantinople was strewn with thorns as well as roses, and the Russian Army experienced not only the welcome of the Bulgarian people, but also bitter fighting and heavy losses. In the north-west, the Russian troops who had taken Nikopol failed to press on to Pleven before the Turks there were reinforced by the army of Osman Pasha from Vidin. Twice the Russian forces attacked Pleven, but both times they were repulsed with heavy losses and failed to capture the town. In the meantime General Gurko, who had crossed the Stara Planina by the Hainboaz Pass, took Kazanlŭk, overcame the Turkish troops guarding the Shipka Pass and captured Stara Zagora (July 10/22, 1877). Among the crowds who left Stara Zagora to welcome the Russians was Dimiter Blagoev, who later became the founder of the Bulgarian Communist Party. At this point, however, the Russians were obliged to go over to defensive fighting on all fronts owing to their difficulties at Pleven and also in north-east Bulgaria. The Turks had received reinforcements in the shape of the army of Suleiman Pasha, which had been transferred from the Montenegrin front with the help of English ships, and now arrived in the area of Nova Zagora, greatly outnumbering the Russians under General Gurko. After very heavy fighting in which the Bulgarian volunteers, with the Samara banner, played a heroic role, Gurko was obliged to withdraw from Stara Zagora (July 19th/31st), which was then sacked and burnt by the Turks.

General Gurko was now given a new command, while General Stoletov with a Russian-Bulgarian force of some 6,000 to 7,000 men was ordered to hold the Shipka Pass at all costs to prevent Suleiman Pasha from crossing into northern Bulgaria, and it was at Shipka that one of the most famous and most heroic battles of the war was fought. On August 9th/21st, the 40,000 strong Turkish Army began its attack, but was repeatedly hurled back by the defenders. Violent fighting continued all the next day, and General Stoletov sent a plea for reinforcements to General Radetsky. On August 11th/23rd the position of the defenders was becoming increasingly critical. Ammunition ran out, but the Russians and Bulgars fought with the butts of their rifles, hurling stones, trees and even the bodies of their dead comrades at the Turks below. At the eleventh hour, when all seemed lost, General Radetsky arrived with reinforcements and the Turks were once more repulsed. Fighting continued for the next three days, but then Suleiman Pasha realized that it was impossible to take the pass, and called off his attack. The Shipka Pass had been held at the cost of 3,773 Bulgarian and Russian dead and wounded, but the Turks had lost over 10,000 dead and wounded. All through the months to come, including the bitter Balkan winter, the Shipka Pass remained closed to the Turks, a factor which was of great importance to the final success of the campaign in northern Bulgaria. This historic battle at Shipka is commemorated by a massive tower standing on what is now called Mount Stoletov. On the front of the monument is a bronze lion, 12 metres high, and the inscription 'Here Dawned Bulgaria's Freedom!' At the foot of the pass, there is an exquisite church with golden cupolas, designed by the Russian architect A. N. Pomerantsev, and built as a memorial to the Russians who gave their lives for Bulgaria's liberation, and for whom requiem is still held daily.

The battle at Shipka, in which Bulgarian and Russian fought side by side, served to strengthen still further the Bulgarians' century-old trust in *Dyado Ivan*, and their conviction that the Russians were their blood brothers. The Bulgarian contribution was not confined to the enlistment of volunteers. Everywhere the civilian population did what they could to help, transporting food and supplies, clearing roads, acting as guides and taking care of the wounded. They gave especially valuable assistance in providing the Russians with information about Turkish troop movements, and, indeed, Suleiman Pasha complained bitterly about this, remarking that he could never get any information about Russian troop movements from Bulgarians. Another aspect of Bulgarian participation in the war was the formation of numerous *cheti*, some of which were formed on Russian initiative, and others of which sprang up spontaneously and operated partisan-fashion in the rear of the enemy. Among the leaders of these *cheti* there were many famous names such as Panaiot Khitov and Zhelyu Voivoda. The *cheti* did much to protect the civilian population from the wrath of the Turks, but they were not able to prevent many frightful massacres, comparable to those which followed the April Rising. In all some 16,000 civilians were killed and many towns were looted and burnt.

While the Russians and Bulgarians were holding the Shipka Pass, the Russians north of the Stara Planina were fighting bitter battles with the forces of Mehmet Ali Pasha in the Rusé–Silistra–Varna–Shumen rectangle, and with those of Osman Pasha in Pleven. At the end of August a third assault on Pleven failed, in spite of outstanding heroism on the part of the troops commanded by General Skobolev. In September reinforcements arrived from Russia and the celebrated General Totleben was summoned from St Petersburg to direct a systematic blockade. Troops under General Gurko cut the Turks' communication to the west with Sofia, Orkhanié (Botevgrad) and Vidin, and thus the huge Turkish forces in Pleven were placed in a critical position. On the night of November 27th–28th (old style), the Turks took the only course open to them and attempted to break out. The attempt was unsuccessful and they were obliged to surrender. The prisoners taken included no less than 11 pashas, 2,000 officers and 37,000 men.

K*

Then the Russians began a grand offensive. In spite of the appalling winter conditions, they crossed the Stara Planina with their artillery. On December 23, 1877/January 4, 1878, General Gurko liberated Sofia, while on December 28th (old style) Radetsky inflicted a resounding defeat on the forces of Veisel Pasha at Sheinovo below the Shipka Pass. Gurko continued his advance towards Plovdiv and defeated the army of Suleiman Pasha, who left his artillery and fled. Adrianople fell to the Russians on January 8, 1878 (old style). In north-west Bulgaria, also, the Turks suffered a series of defeats and fell back to Varna and Burgas, whence they were evacuated by sea to Constantinople. In the Caucasus, too, the Russians were victorious, and to complete the catastrophe which had engulfed the Turks they inflicted a crushing blow on the Turkish Fleet.

Now General Gurko and General Radetsky began the final march on Constantinople itself and arrived at San Stefano, a small town some seven miles from the Turkish capital.

The Treaty of San Stefano

Russia's spectacular successes against Turkey and the imminent collapse of Turkey in Europe naturally aroused dismay and consternation on the part of the Western European Governments, who prepared to take action in defence of Turkey. The British Mediterranean fleet was ordered to the Dardanelles, while Austria considered military action. In this situation, Russia did not risk war with the West by pressing on to take Constantinople, but granted Turkey the armistice for which she asked, and on February 19/March 3, 1878, a Peace Treaty was signed at San Stefano.

The main provision of the Treaty of San Stefano was the setting up of a large Autonomous Bulgarian Princedom, including more or less all the territory recognized as Bulgarian at the Constantinople Conference, but this time united into one State, instead of being divided into two. The new Bulgarian State included almost all Macedonia as far west as Okhrid and Tetovo, and as far south as Kostŭr (Kastoria). It had an outlet to the Aegean Sea from the Struma to a point south-east of Xanthi. In the Dobrudzha, the frontier ran from Cherna Voda to Mangalia. The northern Dobrudzha passed to Rumania in exchange for part of Bessarabia, which now became part of Russia. In the south-east, although Adrianople was left in Turkish hands, Lyuleburgas was included in the new Bulgarian State. In all the new Bulgaria comprised about 160,000 sq. km. and was to be provisionally administered by Russia for two years. In addition to the liberation of Bulgaria, the Treaty of San Stefano provided for Serbia, Montenegro and Rumania to be completely independent States, and for Bosnia and Herzegovina to have self-government, though remaining Turkish Provinces.

The signing of the Treaty of San Stefano is regarded by the Bulgarians as the official end of 500 years of Turkish rule. Although this Treaty was subsequently set aside, the date on which it was signed is still celebrated annually as the Day of Liberation.

THE TREATY OF SAN STEFANO AND THE TREATY OF BERLIN, 1878

CHAPTER X

BULGARIAN CULTURE
DURING THE RENAISSANCE

Education

The early period of the development of Bulgarian education has already been described in sufficient detail to require no further elucidation. After the Crimean War, there was a considerable expansion in education until there were few sizeable villages without a school. By 1876 there were approximately 1,479 primary schools of which 72 were in towns and 1,407 were in villages. Class schools existed not only in towns but also in some villages such as Strelcha and Klisura. From evidence collected prior to the Liberation, there existed a total of about 50 class schools, including two-class schools in 11 towns (1872–1873); three-class schools in 15 towns (1873–1874); four-class schools in 11 towns (1874–1875); five-class schools in 9 towns (1875–1876) and full gymnasia in Plovdiv, Gabrovo, Stara Zagora and Bolgrad (Bessarabia). Great efforts were being made to transform the class schools in Svishtov, Shumen, Tŭrnovo and several other towns into full gymnasia. Class schools for girls were also set up in Shumen, Gabrovo, Stara Zagora, Rusé, Plovdiv and Kazanlŭk. A training college for primary school teachers was opened in Štip (Macedonia) by Iosif Kovachev in 1868. Interest in economic education also began to grow. Lessons in agriculture and commerce were introduced into certain of the class schools, a commercial school was opened in Svishtov by D. Shishmanov in 1875, and in the same year there were discussions on a plan to open a commercial college in Constantinople. Russian influence was very strong in Bulgarian education, especially after the Crimean War. Most of the teachers were educated in Russia, and the teaching methods as well as most of the textbooks were those used in Russian schools.

One of the great shortcomings of Bulgarian education in the early days was a lack of any real co-ordination or standardization of syllabuses and teaching methods. The Bulgarian educationalists were aware of this shortcoming, and they began to hold teachers' conferences. The idea was first mooted by P. R. Slaveikov in the paper *Makedonia*, and the first Conference took place in Stara Zagora in 1869. A second Conference in Stara Zagora and other conferences in Plovdiv, Kazanlŭk and other towns followed. After the setting up of the independent Bulgarian Church, the Exarchate played a part in the calling of such conferences. The question of a professional organization for teachers was also raised.

In many cases the teachers in the Bulgarian schools were supporters of the Revolutionary Movement and the schools were therefore cradles of national consciousness. This was realized by the Turks, and in 1869 Midhat Pasha, Governor of the Danube region, put forward a plan to merge Turkish and Bulgarian schools into united State schools. The implications of this proposal were fully understood by the Bulgarians who rejected it with vehemence, and the plan was dropped.

The 'Reading Rooms'

The development of reading-room clubs was one of the most important and most typically Bulgarian phenomena of the period following the Crimean War. Their avowed aim was to work against illiteracy, to encourage reading and cultural activity, but they also stimulated national consciousness and love for liberty. It is not surprising, therefore, that in many cases they became undercover centres of revolution. The following description by Zakhari Stoyanov of an incident which he witnessed in the reading room at Rusé illustrates their dual purpose:

'One day, an unknown monk came into the reading room, in such a ragged state, that seeing him, a few dandies, who had come, not to read but to see each other, began to giggle and to say: "What is the fox doing at market?" But the humble father payed no attention to this. He greeted those present and sat down at the table with newspapers. Two or three days later the same monk came again to the reading room with my friend when I was there alone. They went into the library, locking the door behind them. I could not restrain myself and peeped into the library through a small hole, and what did I see! The humble, ragged monk had taken off his cassock and was binding a dozen revolvers, which my friend was handing him one by one, round his waist. I was deeply impressed by this sight. That monk, whose name I learned afterwards, was

Father Matei Preobrazhensky, author of the book *Stories* and one of the active members of the Revolutionary Committee. There was no longer any doubt that my two friends led the Ruschuk (Rusé) Bulgarian Committee, and the Reading-Room *Aurora* served as a meeting place for this Committee.'

The hundred or so rebels from Byala Cherkva who came with Bacho Kirov to join Pop Khariton's *cheta* were all members of the Byala Cherkva Reading-Room Club, in the affairs of which Bacho Kiro himself played a very active part.

The first reading room was opened by Emanuil Vaskidovich in Lom in 1856, and in the same year two more appeared in Shumen and Svishtov. By the Liberation their number had increased to over 130. Reading rooms were also started by Bulgars abroad. In Bucharest there was one called 'Brotherly Love', and in Constantinople the reading room published its own journal.

Considerable struggles for the control of the reading-room clubs developed between the 'Young' and 'Old' Parties. The latter wanted the reading rooms to confine their activities to strictly legal cultural and educational matters, while the 'Young' wished to develop their role in the movement for political liberation.

Literature

Bulgarian literature was relatively late in developing and it was not until the middle of the nineteenth century that there appeared any literature in the modern sense of the word. When it did develop it was much influenced, as one might expect, by the giants of Russian literature such as Karamzin, Pushkin, Lermontov, Gogol, the Ukrainian poet Shevchenko and such writers and critics as Belinsky, Pisarev, Herzen and Chernishevsky. Various Western European writers, such as Schiller, Hugo, Defoe and Molière, were also known in Bulgaria in translation.

The first Bulgarian poem of any real artistic merit was Naiden Gerov's *Stoyan and Rada*, published in Odessa in 1845. The next important poet was Dobri Chintulov (1822–1866) of Sliven, whose revolutionary poems set to music were extremely popular as songs among the younger generation of patriots. Rakovsky himself wrote poetry, though his most important work *The Forest Traveller* is, like Father Paisi's *History*, more memorable for the revolutionary inspiration it imparted than for its intrinsic worth.

The real father of modern Bulgarian verse was P. R. Slaveikov of Tŭrnovo (1827–1895). He was much influenced by the Russian poets, by Pushkin in particular, but he also drew his inspiration from Bulgarian folk songs. His works included humorous poems, fables and love poems, as well as patriotic poems.

Two other writers, who, though best known for their prose, were also poets, were Lyuben Karavelov and Ivan Vazov (1850–1921). The latter was a native of Sopot (Vazovgrad) who began writing verse under the influence of Pushkin and Lermontov. After the April Rising he went to live in Rumania. His most famous work is his novel *Under the Yoke*, which tells the story of the April Rising, and has been translated into many languages and has also been filmed.

By far the greatest poet of the period was Khristo Botev, whose work has already been discussed in as far as the limitations of the present book permit.

The first real Bulgarian *belle-lettriste* was Vasil Drumev of Shumen (1841–1901), whose realistic story of the *Kŭrdzhali* period, *An Unhappy Family*, appeared in 1860. Drumev was also Bulgaria's first real playwright.[1] His historical drama *Ivanko, Assassin of Asen I*, appeared in 1872, and is still performed. Undoubtedly the finest pre-Liberation prose writer was Lyuben Karavelov, whose stories confirmed the realist, humanist trend of Bulgarian literature.

Theatre

The development of the theatre was originally linked closely to the class schools. Teachers wrote dialogues and scenes to be performed by their pupils at the end-of-term 'speech days'. P. R. Slaveikov was one of those who wrote such dialogues. The first real Bulgarian theatrical performance took place in a tavern in Shumen on August 15, 1856. The play performed was *Mikhail the Mouse-eater* by a teacher named Sava Dobroplodni, who also produced it. The actors were his pupils. In the same year a translated play, *Long Suffering Genevieve*, was presented in Lom under the direction of Khristo Pishurka, who himself took the title role, as women did not as yet appear on the stage. In 1865 Dobri Voinikov, who had been obliged to emigrate to Rumania, formed an amateur theatre group in Braila, which performed a number of plays including several written by himself. In Bulgaria itself, the practice developed

[1] Dobri Voinikov, a teacher in Shumen, was actually the first Bulgarian to write plays, but, since they were without artistic merit, Drumev is regarded as the father of Bulgarian drama.

of giving plays at the reading rooms, usually in support of the local schools. In some cases, on Levsky's recommendation, plays were performed to raise money for the revolutionary organization. In spite of the extremely primitive conditions under which the plays were performed, the frequently poor quality of the actual dramas and the amateur status of the actors, who were generally teachers and schoolboys, the theatre was very popular, and, owing to the fact that the plays often had historical and patriotic themes, they did much to rouse the national pride of the audiences.

Music

Music, like the drama, developed in Bulgaria through the schools. Here again we find the name of Dobri Voinikov, the enterprising teacher from Shumen. He had learnt music from a Hungarian émigré named Mikhail Shafran, who had come to Shumen in 1850 and had founded an orchestra composed of Polish and Hungarian émigrés, who played marches, Polish *mazurkas* and folk songs. In 1859, Voinikov himself began to write school songs, and to organize music lessons. He also formed a school orchestra. When he moved to Braila, he always had an orchestra to play during the intervals in his theatre.

Architecture

The rise of a Bulgarian *bourgeoisie* naturally gave a considerable impetus to the development of architecture. The rich merchants built themselves dignified, comfortable houses worthy of their status. In spite of the destruction caused during the April Rising and the Russo-Turkish war, enough of these old houses have survived to provide eloquent testimony to the craftsmanship and good taste of the Bulgarians of that day. Fine old houses can be seen in Plovdiv, Samokov, Tŭrnovo and other towns, above all in Koprivshtitsa (the Oslekov House, 1854, the Kableshkov House, 1845, etc.). The typical Bulgarian houses of that day had two or three stories and the upper stories frequently overhung the ground floor, which was used for storage purposes. There are few windows in the outer walls which face the street, and high walls, roofed with tiles, surround the gardens like a rampart, so that the houses seem to turn their backs on the outside world, and have a forbidding appearance when seen from the street. But once inside the heavy gates, one finds oneself in a veritable paradise. The gardens with their vine pergolas, cool fountains and brilliant flowers are havens of peace and beauty, and the façades of the houses, with stairways leading up to the living rooms on the first floor, are full of windows and exquisitely ornamented with frescoes and wood-carving.

Now that there were no longer such strict prohibitions against church building, many fine churches were built, including the church at Pazardzhik, the churches at the Bachkovo and Preobrazhensky monasteries and Sveta Nedelya in Sofia. The brightest jewel of the architecture of the Bulgarian Renaissance is the Rila Monastery, rebuilt in 1834–1837 after it had been almost totally destroyed by fire in 1833. The men who built it were a group of local master builders, who combined in the mediaeval manner the professions of architect and builder. They included Milenko from the village of Blateshnitsa, Aleksei Rilets from Rila itself and Pavel from Krimin, who was responsible for the Church of the Virgin which stands in the courtyard.

During the period of the Renaissance many fine public buildings, clocktowers, etc., were erected. Particular mention should be made of the school at Gabrovo, built by Usta Gencho Kŭnev, and inspired by the Rishelevsky Lycée in Odessa. One of the most famous master builders of the period was Nikola Fichev (Kolyu Ficheto), 1800–1880, who was a native of Dryanovo. Among his finest works are the covered bridge at Lovech, the bridge over the Yantra at Byala and various buildings in Tŭrnovo, including the Inn of Hadzhi Nikoli.

Painting

During the nineteenth century Bulgarian painting began to free itself from the traditions of Byzantium and to be influenced by Western European and Russian painting. An increase in church building led to a flowering of ecclesiastical painting. Three schools of ikon painting were founded: in Samokov (by Khristo Dimitrov, d. 1835, of the village of Dospei), in Bansko (by Toma Vishanov Molera) and in Tryavna (by Pop Vitan). Of these, the most celebrated was the Samokov School, and one of its most famous representatives was Khristo Dimitrov's youngest son, Zahkari Zograf (1811–1853), some of whose most interesting ikons and frescoes can be seen at the Preobrazhensky monastery near Tŭrnovo, and at the Bachkovo and Rila monasteries. Even in his religious paintings, there are many social and realistic elements. For example, in his fresco of the Last Judgment at the Bachkovo monastery, he has drawn portraits of the *chorbadzhii* of Plovdiv among the sinners, and has dressed some of the adultresses in the fashions of the day. His hatred for the rich can also be seen in other frescoes, such as Dives and Lazarus and the Devil taking the soul of the rich man. Zakhari Zograf also painted many fine portraits, as frescoes, and also with water-colours on paper and with oils on canvas. His elder brother Dimiter Zograf was also a painter and some of his finest painting is at the Rila monastery.

Dimiter Zograf's son, Stanislav Dospevsky (1827–1877), was one of Bulgaria's finest portrait painters of the period. He studied in Kiev and Odessa, and finally at the St Petersburg Academy of Art, and was therefore much influenced by Russian art. Although his work includes ikons as well as portraits and landscapes, he represents a further step in the decline of ecclesiastical and the growth of secular art. There is reason to believe that he had connections with the Revolutionary Movement. Be that as it may, he incurred the suspicions of the Turks and died in a Constantinople prison.

Another very important painter of the period following the Crimean War was Nikolai Pavlovich of Svishtov (1835–1894). He studied in Vienna and Munich, and his works include ikons, portraits and lithographs. Some of his most famous pictures are scenes from Bulgarian history, including *Asparukh crossing the Danube*, *Krum sacrificing before the walls of Constantinople*, *The Baptism of the Court at Preslav*, and various scenes from the life of Princess Raina. He also painted the décor for Voinikov's production of *Long Suffering Genevieve* in Braila. He was the first Bulgarian artist to see the important role that art could play in the education of the young, and wrote several articles for the Press, urging that art be included in the curricula of the schools.

Another leading portrait painter was Khristo Tsokev of Gabrovo, who studied art in Moscow and died of tuberculosis in 1883.

Very great popularity was enjoyed by the émigré Polish artist, Henryk Dembicki, who came to Bucharest after the Polish rising of 1863, and who was a friend of Botev. Dembicki's lithographs included Bulgarian patriotic and revolutionary subjects: Tsar Simeon before the walls of Constantinople, the suicide of Angel Kŭnchev, Hadzhi Dimiter and Karadzhata, Filip Totyu, Rakovsky and other contemporary heroes.

Woodcarving

Side by side with the flowering of domestic and ecclesiastical architecture, there was a national flowering of woodcarving, for many houses were built largely of wood, and wood was used extensively for interior decoration and for the ikonostases of churches. There were three main schools of woodcarving. The oldest was the school of Tryavna, where an organization of builders and woodcarvers existed as early as 1804. Here the arts of ikon painting and woodcarving were frequently practised by one and the same master, and groups of workers under one master would undertake all the work connected with the building and interior decoration of a church. The main motifs were plants and flowers in symmetric compositions; animals and birds appeared occasionally; people were rarely shown. The second school was that of Samokov, which was connected with the school of Mount Athos. Master Andoni of Mount Athos made the central part of an ikonostasis for the church at Samokov. Wings for the ikonostasis, in keeping with the design of the central part, were later made by local carvers under the direction of Master Atanas of Salonika, and this ikonostasis thus became the model for the particular style of the Samokov school. The finest works of the Samokov masters are in the Rila Monastery, including the ikonostasis made under the direction of Master Atanas. Clusters of grapes, birds, monsters and human figures, as well as roses and other flowers and plants, appear in the rich work of the Samokov masters. The third school was the Miyashka school in Macedonia, better known as the Debŭr school, from the town in which it flourished. One of the finest works of the Debŭr school is the ikonostasis of the Church of the Virgin in Pazardzhik, which was completed in 1854. Hidden in a tropical profusion of foliage, roses, acanthus, daffodils and narcissi, are human figures and scenes from the Bible, as well as birds, wolves, lions and griffins.

Apart from the ornamentation of churches, the woodcarver found ample scope for his art in the homes of the day. Behind their high walls, in their inner sanctuaries, hidden from the Turks, the Bulgars filled their houses with beauty and ornament. The doors, cupboards and, above all, the ceilings, were richly carved. Often the centre piece of a ceiling would have an elaborate carving representing the sun and its rays. The pillars supporting the verandah, which is so typical of Bulgarian houses, were usually decorated with carvings, and so were numerous household articles, such as cradles, candlesticks, distaffs, chests and so on.

CHAPTER XI

THE FORMATION OF
THE NEW BULGARIAN STATE

The Congress of Berlin

Although, with an eye to Western reactions, the Russians had left much territory still under Turkish rule under the terms of the Treaty of San Stefano, the Western Powers could not accept the creation of a large united Bulgarian State, which would undoubtedly be friendly toward Russia, and they set to work to annul the Treaty. On March 6, 1878, Austro-Hungary, supported by Great Britain and Germany, proposed that a Conference be called to review the Treaty. After a tough and exhausting war, Russia was in no position to refuse, and the Conference opened in Berlin on June 13, 1878, under the chairmanship of Bismarck, the self-styled 'honest broker'. The Balkan peoples were not represented.

At the Conference, the Western Powers were able to insist on a return to a divided Bulgaria. Without regard for the aspirations and sacrifices of the Bulgarian people, the country was brutally dismembered. Only the territory north of the Stara Planina, and, on Russian insistence, the Sanjak of Sofia (Kyustendil, Dupnitsa, Samokov, Slivnitsa, Breznik, Trŭn, Tsaribrod, Bosilevgrad), gained autonomy as a vassal principality. The remainder of the country, comprising the territory south of the Stara Planina, was made an Autonomous Province of Turkey, with a Christian Governor to be nominated by the Sultan every five years, and its capital at Plovdiv. Southern Thrace and Macedonia were returned to Turkey. Austria gained the right to occupy Bosnia and Herzegovina for thirty years and Britain won from Turkey, as her commission in the affair, the dubious prize of Cyprus. Russia gained some Turkish territory in eastern Anatolia.

It is interesting to note that in the interval between the Treaty of San Stefano and the Congress of Berlin, when there was once again danger of British military action against Russia, there was a revival of the anti-war movement in England. On March 27th the Government decided to call out the reserves, and on April 17th it was revealed that an expeditionary force of 700 to 800 men was being sent to the Mediterranean from India. On April 29th there was a 'Working Men's Peace Conference' at Liverpool, to which Gladstone sent a message of encouragement, strongly criticizing the Government. On April 30th an anti-war delegate assembly took place in Manchester, followed by a public meeting in the evening at which John Bright spoke. There was a similar gathering in Birmingham at which the speaker was Joseph Chamberlain.

In actual fact, the Berlin Treaty was not such a blow to Russian policy as might seem at first sight. While the Bulgars thought of Russia as 'Grandfather Ivan', their protector and liberator, and while the ordinary Bulgars and Russians regarded each other as blood brothers, the brutal truth of the matter was that the Tsarist Government was no more concerned with the welfare of the Bulgarian people than it was with the welfare of the Russian people. Since it was clearly not going to be possible for Russia to occupy Bulgaria, it was in the interests of the expansionist policy of the Tsarist Government to encourage and perpetuate the Bulgars' belief in the liberating mission of Russia. The setting aside of the Treaty of San Stefano did nothing to undermine this belief. On the contrary, it confirmed the Bulgarian conviction that Russia and Russia alone had Bulgaria's interests at heart, and therefore it could be utilized in the furtherance of the Tsarist Government's long-term ambitions. On the Bulgarian side, this heightened Russophilism, which gave rise to the view that nothing could or should be done without the approval of the Tsar, played a very important role in Bulgarian politics during the years immediately following the Liberation.

Provisional Russian Administration in Bulgaria

One of the effects of the Congress of Berlin was to shorten the length of Russian post-war administration in Bulgaria from two years to nine months. Even before the beginning of the war, a special commission had been set up to deal with the administration of liberated Bulgaria. It was headed by Prince Vladimir Aleksandrovich Cherkassky, who then proceeded to organize a civil administration in every district liberated. He appointed Russian Governors in each district, but at the same time he prepared for the eventual withdrawal of the Russians by appointing Bulgarian Deputy-Governors, and by trying to train Bulgarian administrative cadres. The first district to be formed was that of Svishtov, where Naiden Gerov, for many years Russian consul in Plovdiv, was appointed Governor with Dragan Tsankov as his deputy. With very few exceptions, the Bulgars whom he brought into the administration were people of conservative views connected with the 'Old' Party. Local Councils were formed of officials and elected representatives. In the elections and on the Councils, sharp struggles continued between the *chorbadzhii*, and the peasants and poorer townsfolk. In a few districts, the peasants won an overwhelming majority in the elections, but the Russian authorities discouraged such revolutionary manifestations, and annulled the elections in such cases.

Prince Cherkassky did not complete his work of organizing the administration of Bulgaria, for, on the very day that the Treaty of San Stefano was signed, he died. He was succeeded by Prince Aleksandr Mikhailovich Dondukov-Korsakov.

Dondukov-Korsakov had instructions to complete the temporary organization begun by Cherkassky, to set up a central administration, to form a Bulgarian Army and to prepare for the calling of a Constituent Assembly which would adopt a Constitution for the Bulgarian Principality. Dondukov-Korsakov did not possess the wide experience of Cherkassky, but he followed his instructions closely and took considerable notice of the advice of his Bulgarian helpers, in particular of Marin Drinov, the Bulgarian scholar and historian, who had been a professor at Kharkov University. Dondukov-Korsakov set up a Government Council of seven members, each heading a department. The seven departments were: internal affairs, finance, justice, education, military affairs, diplomatic relations, and posts, telegraphs and communications. Drinov was put in charge of education.

Under the Treaty of San Stefano, Plovdiv was to have been the capital of Bulgaria, but after the Congress of Berlin, Dondukov-Korsakov was obliged to transfer his administration to Sofia, and his task of creating an administration was made harder by the fact that now everything had to be completed in nine months instead of two years.

The creation of the Bulgarian Army went ahead very successfully. The Bulgarian youth was eager to join up in order to bear arms in the defence of their newly liberated country, and by the end of the period of Russian administration, over 30,000 young men in the Principality alone had undergone military training. Some were sent for special training in Russia, and a school to train Bulgarian officers was opened in Sofia.

The system of taxation was to a large extent overhauled. The military tax paid by Christians was abolished, taxes in kind were replaced by taxes in money, and other taxes which were retained were collected in more reasonable proportions. Tax-farming was also abolished. To assist the economy, a Bulgarian National Bank was established in Sofia with 2,000,000 francs capital, and attempts were made to resurrect the agricultural banks.

In addition to organizing the administration, the Russians replaced the feudal Turkish courts with a new system similar to that introduced into Russia in 1864. A postal service was organized; a public library was set up in Sofia; hospitals and dispensaries were opened; schools were opened, new syllabuses were prepared and a system of school inspection was instituted.

The Russians also gave considerable aid to refugees and to those who had suffered during the war. Many were settled on land that had belonged to Turks who had fled. Large sums of money were given to assist in the rebuilding of towns which had been burnt, such as Stara Zagora, Karlovo, Klisura and Kalofer.

Opposition to the Treaty of Berlin

The Treaty of Berlin was naturally a bitter disappointment to the Bulgars, especially to those in eastern Rumelia and Macedonia who were to remain under Turkish rule. Demonstrations and even rebellions broke out in various parts of the country. As always, two tendencies were visible in the opposition movement: a moderate wing representing the *bourgeoisie*, who were content with diplomatic methods, the compilation of memoranda, petitions, etc., and an extreme wing, representing the peasants and poorer townsfolk, who were prepared to resort once more to an armed uprising in order to win their freedom. In Sofia and various other towns, Unity Committees were set up under the guise of charitable organizations. The aim of these Committees was to organize *cheti* to take part in a Macedonian Rising. In Macedonia, where Russian troops had never penetrated and where the Turks were able to wreak vengeance on the Christian population, conditions were particularly bad and many people had been forced to emigrate. In the proposed Principality, *cheti* were formed under Adam Kalmykov, a former Russian officer, and Ludvik Voitkevich, a Polish émigré who posed as a French staff officer. In Macedonia itself, peasant *cheti* were formed under Stoyan Voivoda, and Dimiter Pop Georgiev was declared 'Chief of Staff of the Macedonian Rising'. In September 1878, the rising began in the village of Kresna. Supported by the local population, the rebels overcame the Turks and liberated several villages. The rebellion spread to the whole area round Melnik, and at the beginning of November there was a rising in the Razlog region. Unfortunately, disagreements developed between the rebels and the Committee in Sofia, which was not wholeheartedly behind the rising as such, but saw it merely as a lever for the diplomatic struggle. The leadership from Sofia became hesitant and finally acted as a brake on the rebellion. Stoyan Voivoda was murdered and Pop Georgiev was relieved of his command. In such a situation, the Turks were able to crush the rebellion, helped as they were by the British Government, which arranged for British ships to transport Turkish troops from Constantinople to Salonika.

In eastern Rumelia, there were numerous demonstrations and protests, especially after the European Commission, which had been set up to work out a Statute for the province, moved from Constantinople to Plovdiv. Eastern Rumelia included the towns of the Fourth Revolutionary Region, which had fought so courageously during the April Rising and had suffered so much. To the people of these towns it was inconceivable that they should be handed back to their oppressors. Protests poured in to the Commission, including one from 864 widows of Karlovo, which ran:

'Gentlemen of the Commission, ask the Turkish judges for the court protocols, so that you may see the fault of our hanged husbands and sons. You ought to do this so that you can see the moral character of the Government which you now want to bring back to our wretched country . . . But this shall never be! We will never allow these butchers to come among us, and we swear to you that Turkish troops shall never enter Bulgaria, except over the dead bodies of the widows of Karlovo.'

During November, thousands of peasants from the Plovdiv and Pazardzhik districts gathered in Plovdiv to demonstrate against the Treaty of Berlin. Some of the angriest demonstrations were directed against the man whom the Commission appointed to be Director of Finance in Rumelia. He was a German named Schmidt, who had formerly served for many years in the administration of the Ottoman Bank, and the news that a Turkish official was to tour the Province inspecting finance aroused great fury among the people. In Plovdiv, Nova Zagora, Khaskovo, Yambol and Sliven, Schmidt was greeted by hostile demonstrations. In Sliven the demonstrators included a large number of women and girls, and the mood of the crowd was such that Schmidt was obliged to flee from the town. He later returned with a military escort, but subsequently gave up the idea of further tours.

The Constituent Assembly

According to Article 4 of the Treaty of Berlin, an Assembly of leading Bulgars was to meet in Tŭrnovo to draw up an Organic Statute for the new Principality, prior to the election of a Prince. Dondukov asked S. I. Lukianov, head of the new Department of Justice, to prepare a draft for the forthcoming Assembly, and the Draft was then sent to St Petersburg for approval. The Draft Statute vested great power in the Prince and made the Assembly an advisory body rather than a Parliament in the Western European sense of the word. To a large extent it was based on the Serbian and Rumanian Constitutions. In St Petersburg, however, it was decided that the Draft Statute must be made more liberal and that greater power must be given to the National Assembly. For example, where the original Draft proposed that a law could be promulgated with the 'approval' of the Assembly, the St Petersburg Draft laid down that no law could be promulgated, amended or rescinded without its being discussed and accepted by the National Assembly. Where the original Draft proposed a complicated indirect system of election of deputies, the St Petersburg Draft proposed that the election be direct, on the basis of one deputy for every 20,000 persons.

At first sight it may seem extraordinary that a Government as reactionary as that of Tsarist Russia should insist that Bulgaria should have a Constitution, which for its day, was extremely progressive. The reason for this lay in the rivalry of the Great Powers for influence in Bulgaria, and Russia's desire to keep Bulgarian hopes orientated towards St Petersburg. The Russian Government was aware of the revolutionary mood of the Bulgarian people and realized that to offer them anything other than a relatively liberal Constitution would be to lose their confidence. And, indeed, many efforts were being made by the Western Powers to drive a wedge between the Bulgars and their liberators. Hints were dropped that the reunification of the two parts of Bulgaria might be achieved with Western help, providing that the Assembly did not elect a Russian candidate as Prince. These manœuvres had little success, for the Russians had played their cards well, and Bulgaria's traditional Russophilism was not to be undermined.

On February 10, 1879, the Assembly opened in Tŭrnovo under the chairmanship of the former Exarch Antim. It was composed of 231 members, who may be divided into three categories. The first comprised those there 'by right', i.e. notables, 118 in all, who included the Bulgarian Exarch and his Bishops, the Greek Metropolitan of Varna, the Turkish *Mufti*, the Jewish Rabbi, representatives of the courts and of the Regional and City Councils. The second category comprised 89 representatives of the people, elected on the basis of one deputy for each 10,000 of the population. The third category consisted of people nominated by Dondukov, as the Tsar's Commissioner, and included 11 representatives of the Turkish minority, one representative each from the Rila monastery and the Bulgarian organizations in Odessa and Vienna, and 10 other eminent Bulgars, among them the poet Petko Slaveikov, who otherwise would not have been present.

Right from the beginning the division of Bulgarian opinion between the 'Old' and 'Young' Parties showed itself. The 'Old' Party now became the Conservative Party. It had little support among the people, but disproportionate strength in the Assembly, since many of the notables as well as some of the deputies appointed by Dondukov were 'Old' by persuasion. The Conservatives represented the big *bourgeoisie*—the *chorbadzhii*, usurers and merchants—and they also had the support of the upper clergy. The 'Young' Party which now became the Liberal Party, was a much less homogeneous group. Even before the Liberation it had contained various tendencies, though the left wing democrats had kept the upper hand. After the April Rising, in which most of the Revolutionary Democrats had died, the leadership of the Party passed to those middle and petty *bourgeois* elements who believed that the Liberation would come about through Russian intervention and not through revolution. After the Liberation, the population of Bulgaria was largely middle or petty *bourgeois*, so that almost all the elected deputies and even many of those there 'by right', including the representatives of the Local Councils and the courts, were middle or petty *bourgeois*. The Liberals, led by Dragan Tsankov, Petko Karavelov and Petko Slaveikov, had an overwhelming majority in the Assembly.

The popular anger roused by the Treaty of Berlin found its reflection in the Assembly, where the problem of the division of Bulgaria was immediately raised. Some even wanted to dissolve

the Assembly until the Great Powers permitted the unification of
Bulgaria. This could have led to a very difficult situation for Russia,
but Dondukov, who was present throughout the deliberations of the
Assembly, managed to persuade them to abandon any such action.

The Tŭrnovo Constitution

By a small majority and against the wishes of the Liberal leaders,
who wished the Draft to be discussed by the whole Assembly, it
was decided to appoint a Commission of fifteen to report on the
general principles of the Draft Statute. The Commission consisted
largely of Conservatives and the proposals which it made were a
definite step backwards in comparison with the St Petersburg Draft.
It proposed a two-chamber system in which the Senate, to be
appointed in the main by the Prince, would stand above the National
Assembly, with the franchise limited by a property qualification.
These proposals, which reflected the upper *bourgeoisie's* fear of the
people, and their desire to limit their political influence as far as
possible, were violently attacked by the Liberal spokesmen. A
particularly fine speech was made by Petko Slaveikov, who declared:

'What is this that the Commission has produced? What rubbish
have we here? All our enemies contend that we are not sufficiently
mature for freedom. But here we have a Commission of the National
Assembly confirming their words, since it has declared by the
spoken word and in print, that we are not yet ready for full freedom,
when for this freedom so much precious blood has been spilt by our
brothers, the Russian people, and when so many costly sacrifices
have been made by our own people. The Commission wants to
give us freedom like the Sacrament—in small quantities, as though
we had weak stomachs . . . You want a free people, but you take
freedom from them; you want a strong and stable Government,
but you take away its strength; you are afraid of contact between
the Government and the people, and you erect a barrier between
them. I propose that we return immediately to the Draft Statute
since this Constitution which the Commission offers us is even
worse than that of the Turks . . . As a People's Representative and
in the name of the people, I cannot accept the report . . . I move that
the report be rejected.'

The Assembly did reject the report, but this did not prevent the
Conservatives from again proposing the creation of a Senate during
the discussion on the Draft Statute. Again the proposal was rejected.

The Constitution finally adopted defined the new Bulgarian Principality as a 'hereditary and constitutional monarchy with a people's government'. The Prince was to have wide powers including the right to dissolve the National Assembly, to order new elections and to confirm laws. He was also to be Commander-in-Chief of the Armed Forces. The Ordinary National Assembly was to consist of deputies elected by all male citizens over the age of twenty-one on the basis of one deputy to every 10,000 voters, and was to concern itself with the routine activities of a Parliament—drawing up legislation, approving the Budget, etc. In addition, provision was made for a Grand National Assembly composed of two deputies for every 10,000 voters. This Grand National Assembly was to be called when it was necessary to elect a Prince, amend the Constitution, or alter the frontiers of the Principality.

The Constitution, as adopted by the Tŭrnovo Assembly, followed the general lines of the St Petersburg Draft, but embodied certain changes which made it more democratic than the original. For example, the Draft had proposed that the National Assembly should consist, like the Tŭrnovo Assembly, of notables, who sat 'by right', as well as elected members, whereas the Constitution provided for an Assembly of elected members only. The Assembly added entirely new Articles, which declared that there should be no division into social categories and no titles or other orders, apart from a decoration for bravery in time of war. They also wrote into the Constitution the following Article: 'Any slave of whatever faith, sex, race or origin who enters the territory of the Bulgarian Principality shall become free.' In accordance with traditional Bulgarian practice, they added the words 'and free of charge' to the Article of the Draft which laid down that primary education should be compulsory. Certain important changes and additions were made to the Articles dealing with civil liberties, such as freedom of assembly and freedom of the Press, which had certain limitations in the Draft. In the new Constitution, all censorship of the Press was forbidden, and to the Article guaranteeing freedom of peaceful assembly, there was added the right to form societies and associations.

The amendments made to the Draft caused considerable alarm in St Petersburg, where they were regarded as far too radical, especially in view of the rising tide of revolution in Russia itself. Particular exception was taken to the articles on freedom of the Press and of association. Dondukov reassured his Government that they were exaggerating the dangers, and that there was not a hint of

Socialism in the Article on freedom of association. His Government appear to have remained unconvinced, because a subsequent letter from St Petersburg expresses the fear that 'Bulgaria may in time become a hot-bed of international and revolutionary propaganda, if suitable measures are not taken to avert this'.

The Constitution was approved by the Assembly on April 16, 1879, and was signed by all the deputies. Notwithstanding the complete abandoning of the Republican form of government, which had been the political ideal of the old Revolutionary Democrats, and the great power given to the Prince, the Tŭrnovo Constitution with its rejection of titles and of any form of Upper Chamber or unelected deputies, was one of the most democratic Constitutions of its time, and its adoption represented the victory of the 'Young' or Liberal Party over the 'Old' or Conservative Party.

The First Grand National Assembly

After it had adopted the Constitution, the work of the Tŭrnovo Assembly was over, and it was closed by Dondukov. On the following day, April 17, 1879, the First Grand National Assembly met to elect a Prince. According to the Treaty of Berlin, the Prince could not be a member of the ruling dynasties of the Great Powers, and had to be elected by the Bulgarian people and approved by the Great Powers and the Porte. The final choice fell on Alexander of Battenberg, a German princeling who was a nephew of the Tsaritsa. He had been educated in the German Cadet Corps, had served in the Hessian Regiment of Dragoons and in the Prussian Life Guards. His candidature was approved by all the Great Powers and he was elected Prince of Bulgaria unanimously and without discussion by the Grand National Assembly. Alexander of Battenberg was an extreme reactionary by upbringing and inclination, who desired to rule as an autocrat. His first action on being elected Prince was to travel to Russia to ask the Tsar, Alexander II, for his support for the abrogation of what he called this 'perfectly ridiculous Liberal Constitution'. The Tsar, who was aware of the mood of the Bulgars and their trust in Russia, wisely refused. Alexander then visited Vienna, Berlin, Paris, London and Constantinople, and finally appeared before the Grand National Assembly on June 26, 1879, where he swore allegiance to the Constitution. Shortly after this he travelled to Sofia and took over the Government from Dondukov. In July 1879 the Russians withdrew from Bulgaria.

Eastern Rumelia

The European Commission charged with preparing an Organic Statute for Eastern Rumelia began sitting in Constantinople in September 1878. A month later it moved to Plovdiv, the future capital of the Province, where it became the centre of demonstrations against the partition of Bulgaria. The working out of the Statute took place in an atmosphere of struggle between Russia on the one hand, and Turkey and the Western Powers on the other, and, as we have already seen, angry demonstrations against the whole principle of partition. The Commission's work was completed on April 14, 1879, and the final result was a Statute far less democratic than the Tŭrnovo Constitution. The new Province was to be ruled by a Governor-General as the Sultan's representative, who would govern with the aid of a Privy Council. The Legislative body was the Provincial Assembly of 56 deputies, of which 36 were elected, 10 were appointed by the Governor-General, and 10 sat 'by right'. It was only on Russian insistence that the majority of the deputies were elected, and even so the franchise was limited by property qualification. On Russian insistence, too, Bulgarian was made the only official language of the Province, although Britain wanted Greek and Turkish to enjoy equal status with it. The Governor-General, chosen by the Sultan with the approval of the Great Powers, was Aleko Bogoridi, a Bulgarian by origin, who had, however, served so long in the Turkish Diplomatic Service that he had forgotten how to speak Bulgarian. He set out from Constantinople, wearing a fez, but *en route* he became so conscious of the strong national feelings of the Bulgars that he hastily donned a Bulgarian fur hat.

Agrarian Development, 1878–1885

The Russo-Turkish War of 1877–1878 resulted in the final liquidation of the remnants of feudalism in Bulgaria. The Turkish landlords fled and their land passed into the hands of the peasants, who also annexed the former State lands. In the south-west where the system still prevailed, the peasants stopped paying *ispolitsa*, and *kesim*, thus becoming *de facto* the owners of the land which they tilled. In this way the land passed into the hands of Bulgarian smallholders, and petty commodity production became the chief form of production.

The Liberation also resulted in a changed distribution of the population. People who had lived in the mountains came down to the plains which had been largely inhabited by the Turks in the past. The movement of the population, as well as the peasants' new freedom to buy land privately where they would, led to a change in the character of the village communes. No longer were they closed units, primarily economic, imposing obligations on the individual peasant. Instead, they became purely administrative, similar to the town communes, dependent on the State Organs and controlled by them. The movement to the plains spelt the end of the village communes based on the *zadruga*, which had survived since ancient times in the mountain regions.

At first the Russians did not intend that the peasants should seize the land. At the very most they saw it as a temporary measure to ensure cultivation. When, after the Congress of Berlin, the Western Powers encouraged the return of the Turkish landowners, the Russians began to look at the problem differently, seeing it as part of the struggle for influence in the Balkans, and they did everything possible to prevent the return of the Turkish landowners. One of the most effective measures taken by the Russians to prevent their return was a decree declaring that all returning Turks, who were guilty of murder, rape, arson, etc., would be brought before a court-martial. This decree was a sufficient deterrent for the majority of Turks, few of whom were guiltless, but those who did return were obliged to produce documentary evidence of their right to the land, something which few of them could do. The clash of Russian and British policies over Turkish fugitives can be seen in the cases of Hadzhi Arif Aga and Hadzhi Shaban Aga. These men were both big landowners from Plovdiv, who returned to Bulgaria immediately after the Congress of Berlin. The Russians arrested them, tried them in public and condemned them to death in spite of British opposition. Eventually, the British managed to put sufficient pressure on the Tsar to get the sentence commuted to banishment, but even so, the case proved very effective in discouraging other Turkish landowners from returning. Many Turks, of course, did not want to live under a Bulgarian Government and were willing to sell their land cheaply and return to Turkey. H. Berkeley, writing in *The Times*, advised readers who wanted to buy land overseas to go to Bulgaria, where, he explained, the soil was fertile and labour and land was cheap.

Most of the land changed hands through private transactions, but in some cases it was done with the aid of State loans. Great difficulties arose over the repayment of the loans by the peasants, for the peasants felt that since it was Bulgarian land, it belonged to them by right. The opposition parties encouraged the peasants not to pay, and, in any case, the dire poverty of the peasants increased the difficulties of repayment. Land belonging to Bulgars, which had been given to Tartars and Circassians after the Crimean War, was returned to its former owners without any payment.

The agrarian changes after 1877 did not result in a more equitable distribution of the land. The richer peasants were in a position to buy more land, and the poorer ones who borrowed money to do so fell into the clutches of the moneylenders, and subsequently had to sell some of their newly acquired land. The extent to which the peasants were being fleeced by the moneylenders can be seen from the fact that in 1880 a law was passed which forbade the buying of produce 'in the green', i.e. before it was even harvested. Apart from debts, the peasantry was still much burdened with tithes. Even the replacing of tithes in kind by tithes in money (1880) did not help because agricultural prices had fallen very low, and indeed many peasants now preferred tithes in kind.

At the other end of the scale there began to develop a class of rich farmers, farming on capitalist lines, and showing considerable interest in the introduction of machinery. Imports of agricultural machinery increased from 21 tons in 1882 to 133 tons in 1887, but its introduction was still very limited, partly because of the lack of people who could repair such machines, and partly because labourers refused to work on farms where there was machinery for fear that the machines would take their jobs from them. The basic implement remained the wooden plough.

Handicrafts and Industry, 1878–1885

Handicrafts continued to decline after the Liberation. The Treaty of Berlin left in force the 'Capitulations', and Western factory-made goods continued to flood onto the Bulgarian market. During the 1880's more than half Bulgaria's imports came from Britain and Austro-Hungary. The Bulgarian craftsmen had now lost the Turkish market which had offered considerable scope before the Liberation, and more and more people were developing a taste for factory made goods. Some branches of industry, such as *gaitan*-making died out almost entirely after the Liberation. Many craftsmen were obliged to close their shops and enter the administration or go to work in the new factories which were being built in Bulgaria and which caused the ruin of still more craftsmen. In the Stara Zagora region, for example, there had been 660 workshops in 1877. In 1885 there were only 263.[1] The number of master coppersmiths in Stara Zagora declined from the pre-Liberation figure of 42 to 14 in 1885. Master shoemakers declined from 35 to 6, tailors from 20 to 5, furriers from 18 to 4, woollen weavers from 50 to 7 and saddlers from 35 to 8.[2] The same picture was typical of many other towns. Jireček records that in Samokov the 456 workshops that existed in Turkish times were reduced to 58 during the post-war years. With the decline of the handicraft industry, the old guild system disintegrated.

Factory industry did not develop very rapidly in the first years after the Liberation. Although the hindrances of feudalism had been removed, and there was plenty of labour available, the Turks had taken a great deal of money out of the country, and there was as yet insufficient capital accumulation for any widespread growth of industry. There was a limited amount of factory building. In 1879, 20 industrial enterprises existed in Bulgaria, of which one was concerned with metal working, 10 with alcoholic drinks, 4 with textiles and 5 with tanning. Only 3 of them were real factories, and these 3 all produced textiles. The first post-war factory was a textile mill built in Gabrovo by Ivan Kalpazanov in 1882, and a second mill was built there in 1883. In Sliven the factory founded by Dobri Zhelyazkov and now leased by a joint stock company from the East Rumelian Government, was producing 230,000 metres of cloth annually. Jireček wrote the following account of the factory:

'The machinery is driven by water from a mountain stream with the aid of two wooden wheels; there are about 240 workers, Bulgars, Turks and Gypsies of both sexes. It is now the foremost industrial enterprise in Bulgaria. The samples which I was shown were as good as any Western work. Not far from the factory a small industrial school had also been opened and in order to perfect the factory the management had brought two dyers from Reichenberg.'

Factories were also opened in Sofia, Tryavna, Samokov and other towns, and by 1887 there were about 37 major enterprises in the country. The Government made some effort to attract foreign capital, and leased certain enterprises to foreign companies, but in general, it had no clear economic policy and this also served to hold up the economic development of Bulgaria in the years immediately following the Liberation.

[1] *Bulg. Hist.*, Vol. II, p. 32.   [2] *Sov. Hist.*, Vol. I, p. 388.

L

Classes and Parties, 1879–1885

The main political battles of the period raged around the Constitution. The Conservative Party of the big *bourgeoisie* had been against the Constitution from the first. They objected to its wide franchise, its freedom of assembly and of the Press, because they regarded the mass of the people as immature politically, unfit to govern and susceptible to demagogy. They believed that in order to maintain the dominant position of their relatively small class, it was necessary to do away with such democratic practices—to amend the Constitution. Thus they were in close alliance with the Prince who had also fought against the Constitution almost from the very moment of his election. Both believed in a strong monarchy, with even greater powers than the Tŭrnovo Constitution permitted. The Conservatives objected even to the very existence of the Liberals. Their ideologists denied the existence of classes and therefore the need for parties. To them the division into rich and poor resolved itself into a differentiation between the hardworking and thrifty, i.e. the big *bourgeoisie*, and the lazy, i.e. everybody else. Under this reasoning, it was obvious that the hardworking and thrifty were the only people fit to rule the country and that no other parties were necessary.

The corner stone of the Liberals' policy was the defence of the petty *bourgeois* social and economic system created after the Liberation and hence of the Tŭrnovo Constitution. But the Liberals, as we have seen, were a very mixed collection of people. Their policy therefore lacked consistency, and their newspapers advanced very varied and often contradictory points of view, ranging from the defence of private property to radical Socialist and *Narodnik* ideas, which called down upon their heads charges of 'Communism' from the Conservative Press.

The First Conservative Government

Althought it was quite clear from the Tŭrnovo Assembly that the Liberals enjoyed the support of the majority of the people, the Prince chose a Conservative Government. It consisted of Todor Burmov (Prime Minister and Foreign Minister), Dimiter Grekov (Minister for Justice), M. Balabanov (Minister for Internal Affairs), G. Nachovich (Minister for Finance), General Parensov (Minister for War) and Dr Atanasovich (Minister for Education). Parensov was a Russian, and indeed up till 1885 the Bulgarian Minister for War was always a Russian General, and the Bulgarian Army had many Russian officers. In the struggles which developed round the

Constitution, Parensov sided with the Liberals, which is not difficult to understand if one remembers that not only had the Tŭrnovo Constitution been approved and upheld by the Tsar, but also that Battenberg was anti-Russian as well as anti-Constitution. Apart from his Conservative cabinet, Battenberg furnished himself with several German councillors. He also appointed several German officers to posts in the army, without consulting Parensov, who promptly relieved them of their command without consulting the Prince.

The first inroad on the Constitution came immediately after the appointment of the Government. The Constitution laid down that the Prince should be addressed as 'Your Serenity' (*Svetlost*), but the new Government addressed Battenberg as 'Your Highness' (*Visochestvo*), arguing that he had had this title since birth. It was apparently a minor point, but it was not without its significance in view of what was to come. Next the Government allowed the Prince to appoint half the members of the Sofia City Council.

All these things aroused strong criticism from the Liberals and great discontent throughout the country. When in the autumn of 1879 elections were held for the First Ordinary National Assembly, the Liberals won an overwhelming majority. Contrary to normal parliamentary practice, the Conservative Government did not resign, and endeavoured to delay the calling of the new National Assembly. The Prince sought Russian permission to suspend the Constitution, but this was refused, and he was obliged to call the National Assembly. The Liberal leader, Petko Karavelov, brother of Lyuben Karavelov, was elected Chairman, and in its reply to the 'speech from the throne', the Assembly declared that it had no confidence in the Government. When the latter realized that it was impossible to win over the Assembly, it was finally obliged to resign. Still the Prince manœuvred. At first he refused to accept the resignation of the Government, but was finally obliged to do so. Then he refused to accept the reply to the speech from the throne because it referred to him as 'Serenity', instead of 'Highness', and dissolved the National Assembly on November 24, 1879.

The Conservative Government of Metropolitan Kliment

On the day following the dissolution of the National Assembly, the Prince formed a new Government, headed by Kliment, Metropolitan of Tŭrnovo, and once again composed of Conservatives. Evidently satisfied that a crisis had been averted, Battenberg went to Russia early in 1880, once more bent on obtaining the Tsar's

L*

consent to the suspension of the Constitution. The Liberal Press, which up until the dissolution of the National Assembly had spared the Prince and concentrated their attack on the Conservatives, now began to criticize Battenberg himself. The Conservatives continued to call the Liberals 'nihilists', 'Communists' and 'office seeking egotists,' and made use of the criticisms of the Tŭrnovo Constitution which were appearing in the particularly reactionary Russian journals, thus exploiting Russia's paradoxical role, which made her at one and the same time the guardian of democracy and freedom in Bulgaria, and the most authoritarian State in Europe.

The new Conservative Government was quite unable to cope with the tasks that faced it. In spite of a shortage of food in Bulgaria owing to the drought of 1879, the Government continued to allow the export of wheat. Its incompetence was realized by the people, and the elections held in January 1880 resulted in an increased majority for the Liberals.

Battenberg's mission to St Petersburg proved a failure. The Tsar still refused to allow him to suspend the Constitution, although he agreed to recall Parensov, and sent General Ernrot in his place. Metropolitan Kliment's Government was obliged to resign on March 22, 1880, and the Prince asked Dragan Tsankov, one of the more right wing Liberal leaders, to form a Government.

Dragan Tsankov's Liberal Government, 1880

The Government consisted of Tsankov (Prime Minister and Minister for Foreign Affairs), Petko Karavelov (Minister for Finance), Khristo Stoyanov (Minister for Justice), G. Tishev (Minister for Internal Affairs), Ivan Gyuzelev (Minister for Education) and General Ernrot (Minister for War). Now that Karavelov was Minister for Finance, the Assembly elected Petko Slaveikov as its Chairman in his place.

The new National Assembly passed a series of laws dealing with various spheres of national life, all of a moderate character, including the replacement of tithes in kind by tithes in money. The Finance Minister insisted that the tax be collected regularly, a move which caused considerable disappointment among the peasantry, since, when in opposition, the Liberals had agitated for lower taxes and had even incited the peasants not to pay taxes. It is true that the new Government did lower the taxes a little, but not to any very great extent. One of the laws passed by the Second National Assembly was of some historic interest: the law of May 27, 1880, which provided for the minting of Bulgarian money in the form of *leva* and *stotinki*. One *lev* consisted of one hundred *stotinki*, and at the time was equivalent to one franc. Prior to this Bulgaria had used Turkish and Russian money.

As far as the Prince was concerned, Tsankov's Government pursued a policy of appeasement in the hope of winning his confidence and co-operation, but unfortunately it did not have the desired result. Moreover, he was receiving encouragement in his Russophobia and his drive towards autocracy from the envoys of France, Germany and Austria.

The Liberals feared the possibility of a *coup*, and wishing to have reliable troops at the disposal of the Government, decided to form a National Militia of all electors under the age of forty, and commanded by two officers chosen by the National Assembly. Legislation for this purpose was initiated by Stambolov, while Battenberg was in Russia during May 1880 for the funeral of his aunt, the Tsaritsa. The law evoked violent opposition from the Conservatives, who renewed their accusations of 'nihilism' and 'Communism,' while General Ernrot equated the Militia with the Paris Commune. On his return from Russia, Battenberg refused to ratify the law, and the Liberals caved in. He subsequently did ratify the law, but only after it had been amended to his liking.

Foreign Policy and Railways

The foreign policy of the Tsankov Government was aimed at safeguarding Bulgaria's independence as far as possible. The task was made very difficult by the rivalry between the Western Powers and Russia for influence in the Balkans, and by the fact that while Tsankov looked to Russia for support, Battenberg pursued a pro-Western line.

The main clash arose over the question of railways. The Western States had long regarded Bulgaria as a potential colony. Austro-Hungary, in particular, having lost Italy, wanted to expand eastwards since her economy was booming, and she was very anxious to complete the railway line from Vienna to Constantinople. She won Serbian support for the scheme and began putting pressure on Bulgaria. At the same time Russia sought to gain control of the Bulgarian railways, and proposed to build a line linking Sofia and Tŭrnovo with Svishtov, i.e. northwards towards Russia. Great Britain's position in the railway controversy was also one of opposition to exclusive Austro-Hungarian control of the railways, which would undoubtedly have an adverse effect on Britain's commercial interests in that part of the world. The Tsankov Government supported the Russian plan and agreed that the Sofia–Tŭrnovo–Svishtov railway should be built first. The Prince supported Austria, and relations between him and the Government worsened.

In the autumn of 1880 Austria raised the question of navigation on the lower reaches of the Danube—a matter as important to Austrian commercial interests as the railways—and put certain proposals to a Danube Commission which met in Galatis to discuss the problem. Acceptance of the Austrian plan would have meant giving Austria the decisive voice in all matters of Danube navigation. Battenberg demanded that the Bulgarian delegate, Kiriak Tsankov, be mandated to accept the Austrian plan. Dragan Tsankov was opposed to this, but, wishing to avoid a clash with the Prince, he gave the Bulgarian delegate official instructions to vote for the plan, and private orders to vote against. The ruse was discovered, and Dragan Tsankov was forced to resign. On November 29th, a new Government was formed with Petko Karavelov as Prime Minister. Tsankov was given the post of Minister for Internal Affairs, but Austrian pressure forced his resignation from that post also and it was then given to Petko Slaveikov.

The new Government concerned itself mainly with home affairs, such as improvements in administration. As far as railways were concerned, it still opposed the Austrian plan, and produced one of its own which proposed to link Tŭrnovo with Stara Zagora, and Sofia with Skoplje via Kyustendil.

Tsankov's resignation was the signal for renewed Conservative attacks on the Liberals, and for new accusations of 'anarchism', 'nihilism' and 'Communism', aimed at discrediting them in the eyes of Russia and other foreign powers.

The Coup d'État of 1881

In the middle of this violent battle between the Liberals and Conservatives, which was being fought principally through the Press, a *Narodnik* secret society, the '*Narodnaya Volya*' (People's Will), assassinated the Russian Tsar Alexander II. This was followed by a period of reaction and repression in Russia, which was reflected in that country's foreign policy and therefore in her attitude towards Bulgaria. Battenberg went to Russia for the funeral of the late Tsar, and raised the question of the Constitution with the new Tsar, Alexander III. In an atmosphere charged with fear of nihilism and popular movements in general, Battenberg at last found a sympathetic ear for his complaints about the dangers of such a Liberal Constitution. While the Tsar did not actually agree to the suspension of the Constitution in so many words, yet Battenberg came away convinced that there would be no objection from St Petersburg if the Constitution were, in fact, to be suspended. On his way home, he visited Berlin and Vienna, where he found support for his schemes of autocracy. Armed with the approval, either tacit or spoken, of three of the Great Powers, Battenberg lost no time. On April 27, 1881, he began his *coup d'état*, assisted by Ernrot, the Minister for War, whose participation Battenberg hoped would convince the people that the *coup* was sanctioned by Russia, although Ernrot was, in fact, acting without orders from St Petersburg. The Government was dismissed, the Constitution was suspended and the National Assembly dissolved. The country was placed under virtual martial law, with Ernrot as provisional head of the administration, holding the portfolios of War, Foreign and Internal Affairs. The other members of the new Government were all foreign subjects: Georgi Zhelyazkovich (Finance), Porfiri Stamatov (Justice), Konstantin Jireček (Education). The latter, a Czech by birth and an Austrian subject, was a Slavonic scholar of considerable stature, who made a special study of Bulgarian history.

Battenberg then demanded that a Grand National Assembly be summoned to vote him special powers, including the right to govern by decree, with the aid of a State Council, for seven years, at the end of which time a Grand National Assembly would be called to review the Constitution in the light of experience. He threatened to abdicate should his demands be refused.

The *coup* found the Liberals completely unprepared. They failed to rally the people and merely sent telegrams to various statesmen abroad, and sought help from the British and Italian Consuls. The Conservatives were jubilant. They held a banquet in Sofia, and then, headed by the Metropolitan of Sofia, they went in a body to the palace to render thanks to their Prince. The Metropolitan made a speech in which, drawing support from Holy Writ, he praised the Prince's deed and blessed him. Then the Metropolitan led those present in a *horo*, or chain dance, such as are performed in Bulgaria on all joyous occasions.

Dictatorship

In order to make certain that an obedient Grand National Assembly was elected, the Conservatives resorted to open terror. The Press was muzzled; military courts were set up to try 'inciters to rebellion', i.e. Liberal propagandists; people were appointed to 'observe', i.e. 'cook' the elections; a system of collective voting was instituted under which all the inhabitants of a ward could declare that, with the exception of so-and-so, they all supported the Prince's proposals; the Liberal leaders Karavelov, Slaveikov, Tsankov and Suknarov were arrested and released only on the eve of poll. On polling day itself, there were widespread disorders and clashes between police and Liberals. In some areas, such as Pleven, Nikopol, Gabrovo, etc., no election took place at all because of opposition from the mass of the people. In a few areas, such as Tŭrnovo, Liberals were returned, but over the country as a whole, terror had done its work, and together with the wholesale rigging of the ballot, ensured the election of an obedient Assembly, ready to do the Prince's bidding. It must be admitted that the Prince did enjoy some popular support, based entirely on the fact that he claimed to be acting with Russian approval. Bulgarian confidence in Russia was such that many of the people were prepared to accept anything as being in their interests, providing they thought it had the blessing of Russia. In some villages the people had become so befuddled by everything that was going on that they voted to have the Tsar as their representative! During the crisis, Battenberg made full use of the effect that the assassination of the 'Tsar-Liberator' had had on the Bulgarian population, and endeavoured to equate the Liberals with the 'nihilists' who had killed him. Liberal attempts to prove that the suspension of the Constitution was not the will of Russia were undermined when the Russian Government indicated its support for Battenberg once the *coup* had been successful.

Fearing popular demonstrations if the Assembly met in Tŭrnovo or Sofia, Battenberg convened it in Svishtov. He arranged to have a boat waiting at the quay, and threatened to board it and depart should the Assembly refuse to vote him the special powers for which he asked. Even now, after the elections, such terror was used against the Liberal deputies that some of them were obliged to leave Svishtov before the Assembly opened. Dragan Tsankov, who held his ground and remained, was not permitted to enter the Assembly. Under these conditions, it is not surprising that on July 1, 1881, Battenberg was voted dictatorial powers for seven years.

A new Government was formed under the chairmanship of the Prince, who also created a State Council with five nominated and ten elected members as an advisory organ. The Government was allegedly 'non-party', a designation which was really a euphemism for loyal supporters of the *coup*. The posts of Minister for Internal Affairs and Minister for War were given to two Russian officers, Lt. Colonel Remlingen and General Krylov. The former State Procurator, Georgi Teokharov, became Minister for Justice, and Dr Vŭlkovich, a former officer in Eastern Rumelia, became Foreign Minister.

The new Government continued its policy of terror against the Liberals. On leaving Svishtov, Karavelov went to Rumania and then to Eastern Rumelia. The other two Liberal leaders, Tsankov and Slaveikov, were met everywhere they went by popular demonstrations, and they were therefore arrested and interned. The Liberal papers *Nezavisimost* and *Rabotnik* were closed down. Slaveikov was elected to the State Council, but refused to serve on what he regarded as an unlawful body. In September, Slaveikov joined Karavelov in Plovdiv and began publishing a new *Nezavisimost* there.

The Government of the Russian Generals

In spite of its unlimited use of terror, Battenberg's Government was far from secure, and it was only too clear to him and the Conservatives that it had no popular support. Moreover, there were clashes between the Prince and the Conservatives on the one hand, and the Russian Envoy, Khitrovo, on the other, over the old question of who was to build railways where, and over Khitrovo's efforts to form volunteer *cheti* to help Herzegovina in her rising against Austria.

In the summer of 1882, Battenberg once more went to Russia, where he persuaded the Tsar to recall Khitrovo and Krylov (Remlingen had already been ousted from the Government and replaced by Nachovich). He obtained the services of two reactionary Russian Generals, L. N. Sobolev and A. V. Kaulbars, whom he intended to use as he had used Ernrot. His move in requesting the Russian Generals killed several birds with one stone. He hoped to demonstrate both to the Tsar and to the Bulgarian people his loyalty to Russia, and to rid himself of any direct responsibility in the worsening situation. On July 27, 1882, a new Government was formed with Sobolev as Prime Minister and Minister for Internal Affairs, and Kaulbars as Minister for War. In addition there were some Conservative ministers, including Nachovich, Grekov, Stoilov and Vŭlkovich. The Government produced a new electoral law which limited the franchise with property and educational qualifications, and reduced the number of deputies. The Prince's view of the ideal National Assembly was expressed in his remark that he wanted deputies elected who would 'vote like a company of soldiers'.

It was not long before the Prince and the Conservatives came into conflict with the Russian Generals over the long-standing affair of the railways, which at bottom was a question of whether Russia or Austria was to be the dominant influence politically and economically in Bulgaria. The new National Assembly, which met at the end of 1882, was composed mainly of Conservatives, many of whom were closely connected with Western European capital, and several deputies attacked the Russian Generals. It now became clear to Sobolev that it was the Prince and the Conservatives who formed the opposition to Russian influence in Bulgaria, a fact of which they had been informed by the Liberals on their arrival and which they had then chosen to ignore. As a result of clashes between the Russians and the Conservatives, Stoilov, Nachovich and Grekov were forced to resign and were replaced by Teokharov, Kiriak Tsankov and T. Burmov, who in the past had been known as Russophils.

Battenberg now realized that the Russian Generals were his enemies, and made use of his visit to Russia in the spring of 1883 to attempt to persuade the Tsar to remove them. In this he was supported by a Conservative delegation which went to Moscow to offer their congratulations on the occasion of the Tsar's coronation. The Tsar, however, was now fully aware of the real situation in Bulgaria, and not only refused to remove the Generals, but even began to consider the removal of Battenberg himself.

The Restoration of the Constitution, 1883

The Prince and the Conservatives realized that they were in a very difficult position, opposed by both Russia and the mass of their own people. They therefore tried to strengthen their position by a *rapprochement* with the moderate wing of the Liberal Party, whose leader, Dragan Tsankov, was released from his detention in Vratsa and returned to Sofia amid popular rejoicing, with his reputation enhanced by his 'martyrdom'.

In August 1883 an agreement was reached between the Conservatives and Tsankov by which the Conservatives agreed that the Constitution be restored, while Tsankov agreed to make certain amendments which would make it more acceptable to the Conservatives. For their part, the Generals began to woo the left wing of the

Liberal Party, who opposed Tsankov's agreement with the Conservatives, and who demanded that the Constitution be restored without any amendments. This demand Sobolev supported, although it was not long since his Government had passed legislation of a character totally incompatible with the Constitution. It was absolutely clear to everyone that the Prince's period of dictatorship was coming to an end, and it was now only a question of who would emerge on top.

It was the Prince who moved first, to undermine the Generals and rid himself of them. Making use of the 'tame' majority in the National Assembly, which met in September and which, in its reply to the speech from the throne, dutifully begged the Prince to restore the Constitution, he immediately declared his readiness to fulfil the 'will' of the people and issued a Manifesto to this effect on September 4th. The Constitution was to be the amended version agreed between Tsankov and the Conservatives.

Battenberg had stolen a march on the Generals. There was now nothing for them to do except offer their resignations and return to Russia.

Tsankov's Coalition Government, 1883

A coalition Government of Conservatives and moderate Liberals was formed by Tsankov on September 7, 1883. It included one other Liberal, D. Mollov, and four Conservatives: Nachovich, K. Stoilov, M. Balabanov and T. Ikonomov. A Russian General, M. A. Kantakuzin, was Minister for War.

One of the first things this Government did was to reverse the policy on railways in favour of Austria, in spite of fierce opposition from the Left Liberals. Then it proceeded to the amendment of the Constitution. According to the agreement between the moderate Liberals and the Conservatives, the Third National Assembly, which had been elected in an unconstitutional manner during the period of the dictatorship, was not to be dissolved and was even to discuss the amendments to the Constitution. Tsankov expected fierce opposition from the Left Liberals, and attempted to win some of them over, but failed. The amendments put forward included two of the Conservatives' traditional aims: a limited franchise and an Upper Chamber, consisting of senior civil servants nominated by the Prince, three bishops and two elected representatives from each region. Naturally this evoked a storm of protest from the Left Liberals, and, because of this, the Government introduced the

L**

legislation on December 5th without prior warning to an Assembly sitting behind closed doors. Two deputies who protested against such procedure were thrown out. The amendments were accepted by the obedient Conservative majority and the Assembly was then dissolved. It was indeed a sorry end for Tsankov, who had suffered 'martyrdom' to defend democracy and the Constitution.

The Split in the Liberal Party

The years following the Liberation were years during which trading and finance capital, the heralds of capitalism, began to accumulate in the hands of a special trading section of the middle *bourgeoisie*, whose interests were opposed to those of the depressed petty *bourgeoisie* and the peasantry. Politically this new rising class of trading industrialists and entrepreneurs formed the moderate wing of the Liberal Party, the Tsankovists. The middle *bourgeoisie*, which had originally been in alliance with the petty *bourgeoisie*, now shifted its ground closer to the Conservatives, a change which was reflected in Tsankov's agreement with them. The Liberal Party, even in its pre-history as the 'Young' Party, had always contained both moderates and extremists. Now in 1883, Tsankov's compromise with the Conservatives threatened to split the Party. The Left leaders did their best to preserve the unity of the Party. A Liberal Congress was held on November 18th, i.e. after Tsankov had reached agreement with the Conservatives, but before the extent of his sell-out had become apparent. At this Congress an understanding was reached between the two factions: the Left Liberals recognized Tsankov as the Party Leader, while Tsankov assured them that the changes to be made in the Constitution would be insignificant. The events of December 5th, when reactionary legislation was rushed through an unconstitutional National Assembly, opened the eyes of the Left Liberals to the true position of Tsankov. Karavelov and Slaveikov, who had arrived from Plovdiv, led the attack on Tsankov, and Slaveikov founded a new paper called *Tŭrnovo Constitution*.

Finding that Tsankov was doing their job for them as well as they could do it themselves, the Conservative members of the Government resigned, thinking that in this way they could help Tsankov to win greater support from his own Party, and a new Government consisting of moderate Liberals was formed by Tsankov on December 31, 1883. This move was strongly opposed by the Left Liberals, who insisted that Tsankov must, according to the Constitution, hold elections four months after the dissolution of the

National Assembly. Tsankov refused to order elections, and, in order to force him to do so and to demonstrate that he was out of step with the majority of the Liberals, the Left Liberals called a Party Congress in February 1884, which almost unanimously demanded the holding of elections. Shortly after the Congress, the Liberal Party split into two separate Parties, the Moderates under Tsankov, and the Left Liberals under Karavelov and Slaveikov. The rising tide of opposition forced Tsankov to hold elections in May 1884, and in these elections the Left Liberals won an overwhelming majority.

The Government of Petko Karavelov, 1884–1886

At first the Prince refused to accept Tsankov's resignation, but when it became quite plain that Tsankov could not win over the deputies of the new National Assembly, which elected Karavelov as its chairman, he was obliged to ask Karavelov to form a Government. The new Government also included Petko Slaveikov (Minister for Internal Affairs), Iliya Tsanov (Minister for Foreign Affairs), V. Radoslavov (Minister for Justice) and R. Karolev (Minister for Education). General Kantakuzin remained Minister for War, the post he had held in the Tsankov Government. The first action of Karavelov's Government was to restore the Constitution in its original form, without any amendments. The Government followed a policy of developing the productive forces of the country without admitting foreign capital. For this purpose they brought in legislation to make the Bulgarian National Bank a State enterprise without foreign capital, and to give the State the sole right to build, own and exploit railways in Bulgaria. Their foreign policy was orientated towards Russia, which they considered to be the sole country with the right to have influence in Bulgaria. Even so, they were opposed to Russian interference, and national independence was the key-note of their policy.

As far as the Prince was concerned, the Government was at first inclined to think that he would have to go, but later they came to the conclusion that they were sufficiently strong to hold him in check. The Russians, however, had now definitely decided that Battenberg must go, and their new Envoy in Bulgaria, A. Koyander, had instructions to prepare the ground for his dethronement. Battenberg was aware of the danger which threatened him, and took all possible steps to win popular support. At this point, all other considerations became overshadowed by events in Eastern Rumelia.

The Economy of Eastern Rumelia

The Liberation brought similar economic changes in Eastern Rumelia to those it had brought in the Principality. Land passed into the hands of Bulgars, partly by seizure, but in the main by the Turks selling their land in order to return to Turkey. As in the Principality, the richer peasants bought most of the land, while the majority of the peasants were able to buy only small amounts, and found freedom from feudal exploitation only to become the slaves of the moneylenders. The ruin of the peasantry was hastened by taxation and low agricultural prices, and many lost their land, which resulted in the growth of a rural proletariat and the concentration of the land in the hands of the village *bourgeoisie*. Agriculture began to assume a capitalist character. Not only grain, but also grape and tobacco products were produced for the market. Rose-oil was produced in vastly increased quantities. In the Kazanlŭk district, the area of the rose fields doubled between 1879 and 1885.

The richer farmers, anxious to increase production, introduced a certain amount of machinery, but the poorer peasants continued to farm on the three-field system, using wooden ploughs.

Of the two halves of the country, southern Bulgaria was the more fertile and more advanced economically, containing such important towns as Plovdiv, Sliven, Burgas, Koprivshtitsa, Karlovo, etc. The *bourgeoisie* strove to develop industry, organizing courses for technical cadres and giving scholarships to young people to study abroad. Various factories, mainly distilleries, breweries, textile mills and tobacco works, were opened. The population of the towns increased, especially that of Plovdiv, which rose from 24,000 in 1880 to 33,400 in 1885. But the economic development of the country was much hampered by the artificial division of the country, and the existence of customs barriers and tariffs between the two halves. For example, before 1879 most of the wool for southern Bulgaria came from the north and thus became dutiable as a result of the division, considerably adding to the cost of the finished article. This together with the competition of foreign imports and developing factory industry contributed to the downfall of the old handicraft industries and manufactories.

The economic effect of the customs barrier was so crippling that the Governments of the two countries were obliged, in defiance of the Berlin Agreement, to lift the tariffs on most goods of local origin, until by September 1885, when north and south reunited, tariffs remained only on salt and tobacco. This measure lessened but did not eliminate the economic difficulties attendant on the division of the country.

Classes and Parties in Eastern Rumelia

In Eastern Rumelia, as in the Principality, the vast majority of the people were middle or petty *bourgeoisie*, but there was also a small but powerful big *bourgeoisie*. At first party politics were unimportant. The struggle against the Berlin Treaty, the danger of Rumelia becoming an ordinary Turkish Province, the struggle to prevent Greeks, Turks and other foreigners from gaining the upper hand in the administration put all political differences in the background.

On his arrival in Plovdiv, Aleko Bogoridi formed a Privy Council or Directorate, consisting of Gavril Krŭstevich, one of the leading figures of the 'Old' Party in the Church Struggle in Constantinople, (Chief Secretary and Director of Internal Affairs), Y. Gruev (Director of Public Education), and T. Kesyakov (Director of Justice). The hated Schmidt was retained as Director of Finance, and General Vitalis, a French adventurer in Turkish service, was appointed by the Sultan to be Head of the Militia and Gendarmerie, where he proceeded to give all the posts to French, English and other adventurers. Popular opposition to the brutal and anti-Bulgarian behaviour of these two men soon led to their dismissal. Schrecker, a German in Turkish service, replaced Vitalis, and a Bulgarian, Dr Stransky, replaced Schmidt.

The first elections were held on October 17, 1879, and for the reasons given above, the campaigns were fought on national rather than political lines, by Parties representing the Bulgarian, Greek and Turkish communities. The Bulgarian Party was also supported by the Jewish and Armenian minorities. Efforts were made by the Turks, Greeks and other Western supporters to represent the Bulgars as forming a much smaller proportion of the population than they actually did, but the results of the election demonstrated to the world that Eastern Rumelia was undoubtedly Bulgarian. Even in Plovdiv, which had always been a stronghold of Hellenism and Islam, the Bulgarian candidate won 2,345 votes to the Greek's 511 and the Turk's 1,651. In all, the Bulgars won 31 seats, the Greeks 3, and the Turks 2. Even when, according to the Organic Statute, the National Assembly was augmented by 10 persons who sat 'by right', and 10 appointed by the Governor-General, the Bulgars held 40 of the 56 seats.

It was only now, when it became generally recognized, as a result of the elections, that Rumelia was clearly Bulgarian, that Conservative and Liberal Parties appeared, representing the big *bourgeoisie* and the middle and petty *bourgeoisie*, respectively. In the intervening period, however, the chief posts had been taken by representatives of the big *bourgeoisie*, who, because of the national struggle, had encountered no opposition. The Chairman of the Provincial Assembly was Ivan E. Geshov, a member of a big landowning merchant family, who, in the words of contemporaries, soon turned Rumelia into its 'family estate'. Geshov was also chairman of the Permanent Committee, the third organ of Government in the Province, consisting of ten appointed persons and three persons chosen by the Provincial Assembly.

According to the Organic Statute, half the Provincial Assembly was to be renewed every two years, and in 1881 the Liberals refused an alliance with the Conservatives and produced their own list of candidates. The Conservatives relied mainly on the credit that their leaders had gained by establishing the Bulgarian character of the Province. These included I. E. Geshov and Gavril Krŭstevich, and their policy was one of unqualified support for Tsarist policy in the Near East. The Liberals, led by Dr Stransky, Dr Chomakov and others, were relatively weak and had no newspaper, until the arrival of Karavelov, Slaveikov, Zakhari Stoyanov and other Liberal émigrés from the Principality, when *Nezavisimost* began publication in Plovdiv. Bogoridi, the Governor-General, supported the Liberals because he was on bad terms with the Russian representatives in Rumelia. Chomakov had always been anti-Russian, and while the Liberal émigrés were not anti-Russian in general, they objected to the Tsarist Government's support for Battenberg's special powers. The 1881 elections resulted in considerable Liberal gains, which gave them about the same number of seats as the Conservatives. Two years later, in 1883, they won a majority. When the émigré Liberals left, however, the Liberals began to lose ground again. In 1884, Bogoridi's five-year term as Governor-General came to an end, and it became necessary to appoint a new Governor-General. The Liberals supported Bogoridi for a second term of office, while the Conservatives put forward Gavril Krŭstevich. As far as the people were concerned, the election centred round the attitude of the candidates towards Russia. It is an interesting indication of the feelings of love which the Bulgarian people had for their liberator, that this point could be the overriding consideration in their choice of candidate. In Bogoridi's case, his quarrel with the Russian representatives lost him much popular support, while Krŭstevich, who enjoyed Russian approval, was able to exploit this so as to win great popular support. The Conservatives, who had for some time past called themselves 'Unionists', also made great play with the slogan of uniting the two halves of Bulgaria.

The Porte, on Russian insistence, appointed Krŭstevich as Governor-General. He dissolved the National Assembly, and in the new elections held on September 23, 1884, the Unionists won. A new Unionist Directorate and Permanent Committee replaced the previous, mainly Liberal organs.

During this and all previous election campaigns, both Parties made great use of the popular slogan of the reunification of Bulgaria, but once the elections were over, it was usually forgotten. So it was with the Unionists after the 1884 elections, and they laid themselves wide open to Liberal attacks and accusations of being 'False Unionists' who used the slogan of union merely to gain power. The Liberals began a noisy campaign for reunification, and this coincided with the rise of a new movement in both halves of Bulgaria for reunification through an armed uprising.

The Bulgarian Secret Central Revolutionary Committee

After the initial wave of protests against the arrangements made at Berlin, the movement died down and everybody became more occupied with inter-Party struggles. The desire for reunification remained but little action was taken. In 1880 and 1882 attempts were made to form secret unity organizations, but nothing concrete came of either attempt. At the end of 1884 and the beginning of 1885, spurred on by reports of Turkish violence against the Christian population in Macedonia, former members of the National Liberation Movement began intense activity to achieve the liberation of Macedonia and the reunification of Bulgaria through an armed uprising. Committees were set up in Rusé, Sofia, Varna and Plovdiv with the task of sending *cheti* into Macedonia and the Plovdiv Committee was elevated to the status of being the Bulgarian Secret Central Revolutionary Committee. Apart from demonstrations, the BSCRC also undertook the organization of *cheti* to go into Macedonia, a task which proved very difficult in view of Government opposition in both halves of Bulgaria. The first *cheta* which entered Macedonia was immediately destroyed by the Turks, and the members of the second were arrested by the East Rumelian police in Stara Zagora. The leading figure of the movement was Zakhari Stoyanov, who edited *Borba* (*Struggle*), the Committee's organ. Outwardly the organization of the movement, as well as its programme, was modelled on the old Bucharest Committee, and its adherents considered themselves to be the disciples and heirs of Levsky, Botev and Benkovsky. Thus the organization won great support among the people, who attributed to it the profoundly democratic, almost Socialist character of the pre-Liberation Committees, and saw in it an instrument not only for the reunification of the country, but also for the solution of all the problems of social and economic inequality which afflicted them. In reality, Zakhari Stoyanov had already moved away from his former revolutionary, democratic standpoint, of which little remained but high-sounding, demagogic phrases, and in June 1885 there was a change of policy in the organization due to the fact that the leadership of the BSCRC passed to the trading *bourgeoisie*. Prior to 1885, the *bourgeoisie*, though desiring reunification, regarded any action on their part as too risky, and preferred to wait until reunification could be brought about either by Russian or Western intervention. By 1885, however, there had developed a new, wealthy, trading *bourgeoisie*, whose ambitions were being severely cramped by the division, especially by the tariff barriers between north and south. For them reunification was an immediate economic necessity. They began to take a lively interest in the BSCRC, and directed its activity primarily towards the reunification of north and south, and away from the liberation of Macedonia, which they regarded as a dangerous proposition, which might prejudice the chances of achieving reunification.

The initiative of the trading *bourgeoisie* had the support of Battenberg, who, after his quarrel with Russia, was seeking support elsewhere. Through commerce, the trading *bourgeoisie* had links with the Western Powers, especially Britain and Austro-Hungary, and Battenberg also hoped that by espousing an obviously popular cause, he might gain much needed popularity within Bulgaria. Zakhari Stoyanov had by now departed far enough from the ideals of Levsky and Botev publically to invite the Prince to lead the movement for reunification. He also managed to persuade his comrades that priority should be given to reunification and that the liberation of Macedonia should come later. On Stoyanov's insistence, Dr Stransky and various high-ranking officers in the East Rumelian Army were brought into the organization.

In July the traditional meeting held on Mount Buzludzha in memory of Hadzhi Dimiter and his comrades became the occasion for an impressive demonstration for reunification. Shortly after the demonstration, there was a meeting of the BSCRC at which the change in the character of the organization was legalized. A new Committee was elected with Stoyanov as its chairman, and a new policy statement declared that the aim of the organization was to unite North and South Bulgaria under the sceptre of Prince Alexander. The original plan to achieve the Committee's aims through a revolutionary armed uprising was now quietly dropped and the emphasis was now primarily on the use of the Army.

The Declaration of Union, September 6, 1885

During August 1885 the BSCRC and its Local Committees organized a series of demonstrations against the East Rumelian Government. Particularly heated demonstrations occurred in the village of Golyamo Konaré, where the people under Chardafon Veliki actually took control of the village for a time, and in Panagyurishté, where on September 2nd public pressure forced the authorities to release two young men, who had been arrested in a previous disturbance, and to return their banner which had been confiscated. Demonstrations on a smaller scale took place in Chirpan, Sliven, Pazardzhik and Karlovo.

While Rumelia was being swept by a wave of demonstrations, the BSCRC supporters among the army officers, led by Major Nikolaev, were preparing to overthrow the Government. Battenberg was fully aware of what was going on, although to avoid international complications, he pretended to know nothing. He received a delegation from the BSCRC, accepted their plans and agreed to recognize the Union once it had been proclaimed.

The Committee met on September 3rd and fixed the Rising for the night of September 5–6th. The early date was dictated not only by the wave of demonstrations, but also by the need to utilize the concentration of the military forces of both North and South for manœuvres. The manœuvres in Rumelia were due to begin on September 6th, and Major Nikolaev was in command not only of the troops in the Western Area (Plovdiv) but also of the reception camp for the militia near Plovdiv. In the Principality, the manœuvres had ended on August 30th, and while the Prince had agreed to delay issuing the order for demobilization, he could not do so indefinitely without arousing suspicion abroad.

Immediately after the meeting of the BSCRC, orders went out to all the Local Committees to mobilize their members to seize power locally and march to Plovdiv, to arrive there on the evening of September 5th–6th. Chardafon Veliki was ordered to organize a rising in Golyamo Konaré and to advance on Plovdiv with an army of armed peasants. This he did with great efficiency. En route for Plovdiv, he encountered a cavalry squadron and the shots that were exchanged served as the signal for general action, and Major Niko-laev also marched on Plovdiv. At dawn the rebels surrounded the town hall where Gavril Krŭstevich, the Governor-General, was living. He was arrested and sent to Golyamo Konaré. The BSCRC set up a Provisional Government with Stransky as chairman, and Dr Chomakov as deputy-chairman, and called all reservists to the colours.

All over Bulgaria the events in Plovdiv were greeted with en-thusiasm and exultant public meetings. On September 8th, Prince Alexander officially declared his recognition of the Union, and de-clared that in future he would be known as Prince of North and South Bulgaria. On September 9th he arrived in Plovdiv and appointed Stransky as his mandated representative until the question of the reunification be settled internationally.

The Serbo-Bulgarian War and the Recognition of Union

Immediately following the reunification the international position of Bulgaria became very difficult. Turkey began to concentrate troops on the frontier. The Tsar viewed the events with disapproval because he had not been kept informed and because the reunification had undoubtedly strengthened the position of Battenberg. A special Bulgarian delegation sent to Russia was told by the Tsar that Bulgaria could expect no help from Russia while Battenberg remained on the throne. To emphasize his disapproval, the Russian officers serving with the Bulgarian Army were withdrawn.

An international conference met in Constantinople on October 24th to consider the Union, which had to be regarded as a breach of the Treaty of Berlin. At this conference it was Britain who took the line most favourable to Bulgaria. Disraeli had died in 1881, and his views were not altogether shared by the new Prime Minister, Lord Salisbury, who realized that the Bulgarians would never voluntarily renounce the newly achieved reunification. Britain now proposed that the Sultan name Battenberg as Governor-General of Eastern Rumelia, hoping in this way to drive a wedge between Bulgaria and Russia. The conference had reached no decision when, on November 2nd, King Milan of Serbia unexpectedly declared war on Bulgaria. Although Serbia had long cherished expansionist ambitions towards Bulgaria's western frontiers, and doubtless considered the moment opportune to realize these ambitions, nevertheless it is clear that she was encouraged to act by Austro-Hungary, on whom she was more or less economically and politically dependent, and who considered that the weakening of Bulgaria through war would facilitate Austrian expansion into the Balkans.

The Serbian Army, though less numerous, was better armed than the Bulgarian Army, which had lost its Russian officers, and was concentrated on the Turkish frontier, several days' journey from the western frontier. Everybody expected a swift and easy Serbian victory, but they had reckoned without the tremendous patriotic fervour which now swept Bulgaria. Having sacrificed so much for the Liberation of their country, the Bulgarian people were ready to sacrifice anything in order to defend their freedom and unity, and the young men flocked to the colours.

The Serbs, who had been led to believe that they were preparing for war against Turkey in order to liberate those Serbian lands still under Turkish rule had no enthusiasm for a war against Bulgaria, and the Serbian Army, well armed though it was, was no match for the Bulgarians fighting with the deepest conviction in defence of their newly liberated country.

Milan's dream of a 'stroll to Sofia' was shattered as the Bulgarians inflicted defeat after defeat upon his armies at Slivnitsa, Pirot and Belogradchik, drove them out of Bulgaria and entered Serbia. Only the intervention of the Austrian Government on November 16th saved Serbia from total defeat. Austria threatened military intervention, and pointed out to Battenberg that this would give Russia an excuse to intervene, and that she would probably occupy Bulgaria and remove him from the throne. The threat was effective. Military operations were suspended and an armistice was signed on December 7th. This was followed by a Peace Treaty signed in Bucharest on February 19, 1886.

Bulgaria's unexpected victory had a very favourable effect on her international standing, and therefore on the ultimate course of the Constantinople Conference. The Conference took advantage of Austria's intervention in the war to attempt to reimpose Turkish rule, an attempt which Britain did not support. On November 19th two Turkish delegates arrived in Plovdiv with a proclamation calling on the Bulgarian people to accept the restoration of the *status quo*. They were greeted with such demonstrations of hostility that they were obliged to leave without even publishing the Sultan's proclamation.

Discussions continued at Constantinople and on January 20, 1886, agreement was reached between Bulgaria and Turkey that the Sultan appoint Prince Alexander as Governor-General for five years, that the administration of Rumelia be fused with that of the Principality, and that Turkey should receive the Kŭrdzhali district south-east of Plovdiv. This formed the basis for the final agreement, with the important difference that, on Russian insistence, the 'Bulgarian Prince', and not Battenberg personally, was named as the Governor-General. The final agreement was signed on April 5, 1886, and the Union of North and South Bulgaria was thus formally recognized by the Great Powers.

CHAPTER XII

POSTSCRIPT

The year 1885 is a convenient date at which to pause. The long struggle which had begun in 1393, reaching its heroic climax in April 1876, had been crowned with final victory, and the worst injustices of the Treaty of Berlin had been set aside. The whole political atmosphere of Bulgaria had changed. Almost all the old revolutionary leaders were dead, and the few who had survived had become respectable politicians. It was true that most of Bulgaria had been liberated from the Turks, but there was little else in Battenberg's Princedom which Levsky and the men of the April Rising would have recognized as the things for which they had fought and died. Only in Macedonia, which remained under direct Turkish rule, did politics retain, for a time, the honest democracy and simple idealism that had characterized the old Bulgarian revolutionary movement. Levsky would have felt at home in the IMRO[1] of Gotsé Delchev and Yané Sandansky, before the organization was corrupted, through the chauvinist poison of the Supremists, into the evil force which later bedevilled Bulgarian public life. Kableshkov and Benkovsky would have found much to remind them of Koprivshtitsa and Panagyurishté in the little town of Krushevo where a Republic was proclaimed, when Macedonia, in her turn, rose against the Turks in the Ilinden Rising of 1903. Elsewhere everything was already different.

When the revolutionary movement reappeared, though it was no less honest than before, it already belonged to a new age in which politics were no longer so simple and clear-cut as they had been before the Liberation. In this new age a struggle was to be fought to the death between Labour and Capital, though in 1885 few in Bulgaria even realized the existence or understood the nature of either.

In 1885 Dimiter Blagoev returned to Bulgaria from Russia, where,

[1] Internal Macedonian Revolutionary Organization.

as a student, he had helped to form one of the first Marxist circles in St Petersburg. In 1891 he founded the Bulgarian Social-Democratic Party[1] at a secret congress on Mount Buzludzha, not far from the place where Hadzhi Dimiter had met his death. In 1904, on the initiative of the Social-Democratic Party, the individual Trade Unions joined together in the General Workers' Trade Union—the Bulgarian equivalent of the T.U.C.

For a long time after the Liberation the bulk of the population were peasants, and the formation of the Agrarian Union in 1899 was therefore a very important event, although, for much of its history, it is debatable how far the Union could be considered a revolutionary organization. In 1923, however, when a fascist *coup* overthrew the legitimate Agrarian Government, the Communist Party and the Agrarian Union joined forces in the world's first anti-fascist uprising. The two organizations continued their co-operation in the Resistance during the Second World War, and, in September 1944, they were the two main parties in the Fatherland Front Government formed when the fascists were overthrown. In September 1946 one of the most cherished aims of the old National Liberation Movement was achieved when, after a Referendum, Bulgaria was proclaimed a Republic. Yet another dream of the nineteenth century became reality in May 1953 when the Bulgarian Patriarchate was restored. The schism imposed on the Bulgarian Church by the Greek Patriarchate in 1872 had already been lifted in 1945.

Recent years have also seen the full implementation of the Bulgarian Revolutionary Central Committee's principle of equality for those Turks who wished to remain in Bulgaria. Before 1944, the Turkish minority were treated as second class citizens and their standard of living was below that of the rest of the population. Only 15 per cent of Turkish children attended school and no books were published in the Turkish language. Today virtually every Turkish child attends school, the number of Turkish schools has risen from 404 in 1944 to 1,152 in 1959, and over 1,000 separate titles have been published in Turkish since 1944. The Constitution of 1947 makes all forms of racial discrimination punishable by law, and guarantees the right of national minorities to be taught in their own language.

Although so much has changed, the years of the Turkish Yoke remain the key period for an understanding of Bulgaria. It was

---

[1] The Party was renamed the Bulgarian Communist Party at its Congress in 1919.

then that Bulgaria's national consciousness and character were formed. It was in those dark centuries of slavery that her traditional architecture, her national costumes and dances, most of her folk songs and much of her folk art were created. That typically Bulgarian institution, the Reading Room, was invented as a means of re-establishing Bulgaria's cultural independence, and today the Reading Rooms, multiplied in number, equipped with film projectors and expanded to include symphony orchestras, choirs and dance ensembles among their many activities, are still the centres of cultural life in town and village.

There are few countries in the world where the past is so much a part of the present as in Bulgaria. Every year on May 24th all people in any way connected with culture—from the members of the Academy of Sciences to the cinematograph workers and school-children—march in procession through the streets of Sofia to celebrate the Day of Culture and Slavonic Writing on the traditional feast of Cyril and Methodius. Every year those who fought and died in the struggle against the Turks and against fascism are remembered collectively with torchlight processions and fireworks, on June 2nd, the anniversary of Botev's death, and individually on their own anniversaries. The uniforms of the April Rising are still worn at memorial meetings and episodes of the heroic past are re-enacted in pageant form. This catalogue of living links with the past could be continued indefinitely, for every Bulgarian is steeped in the traditions of that legendary era; every Bulgarian sings Botev's songs, and regards Levsky, Benkovsky and Karadzhata not as fossils from the schoolroom, but as his elder brothers. There is nothing extraordinary in this, for there is much in Bulgaria's past of which she can be proud, and the story of how she recovered her national identity and fought to regain her freedom is undoubtedly one of the most stirring epics in human history.

NOTE ON THE TRANSLITERATION AND PRONUNCIATION OF
BULGARIAN WORDS

А	a	rather shorter than the 'a' in 'graph' or 'car'; roughly similar to the 'u' in 'bunker' or to the italian 'a'
Б	b	as in 'big'
В	v	as in 'van', except final 'v' which is as 'f' in 'cliff'
Г	g	invariably hard as in 'gate'
Д	d	as in 'dog'
Е	e	as in 'met'
Ж	zh	as 's' in 'measure'
З	z	as in 'zoo'
И	i	as 'ee' in 'meet'
Й	i medially and finally y initially	as 'y' in 'boy' and 'yet', occurring only in diphthongs
К	k	as in 'king'
Л	l	as in 'lad'
М	m	as in 'man'
Н	n	as in 'no'
О	o	as in 'or'
П	p	as in 'pin'
Р	r	as in 'ran'; always pronounced as separate letter
С	s	as in 'song'
Т	t	as in 'tin'
У	u	invariably long as 'oo' in 'roof'
Ф	f	as in 'fox'
Х	kh	as 'h' in hunt, or 'ch' in Scottish 'loch'
Ц	ts	as in 'cats'
Ч	ch	as in 'cheese'
Ш	sh	as in 'ship'
Щ	sht	as 'shed' in 'wished' or 'finished'
Ъ	ŭ	an indeterminate vowel, similar to that in the final syllable of 'soda' or 'little', or as the 'u' in 'turn'
Ь	y	as in 'yet'
Ю	yu	as 'u' in 'use'
Я	ya	as in 'yard'

In certain words where there already exists a generally accepted English form of spelling, this has been used in preference to above system of transliteration. In particular, the more familiar '-sky' ending for personal names has been used instead of the more correct '-ski', and the spelling 'haidut' in place of 'khaidut'.

Serbian spelling has been used for towns which are now in Yugoslavia. Final 'e' is always pronounced in Bulgarian, and is accented in the text.

Aba	A type of heavy woollen cloth.
Angaria	Compulsory unpaid labour; corvee.
Bashibazouks	Turkish irregular troops.
Beglichiya (plural: Beglichii)	A person responsible for collecting the tax on sheep and goats.
Boyar	A nobleman in mediaeval Bulgaria.
Caravanserai	An inn for merchants.
Cheta (plural: Cheti)	An armed detachment.
Chiflik	A large, privately owned farm.
Chorbadzhiya (plural: Chorbadzhii)	A rich peasant, or 'kulak', frequently residing in a town.
Dzhelep	A wholesale cattle dealer.
Dyado	Grandfather
Firman	A decree signed by the Sultan.
Gaitan	A kind of braid for ornamenting clothes.
Gaz-i-Mülk	Land granted in perpetuity to a person thought by the Sultan to be deserving.
Giaour	A derogatory Turkish term for non-Moslems.
Haidut	A patriotic outlaw, conducting guerrilla warfare against the Turks.
Hodja	A Turkish priest.
Kadi	A Moslem judge.
Konak	The seat of Turkish local government.
Kŭrdzhali	Bandits who ravaged Bulgaria at the end of the eighteenth century and the beginning of the nineteenth century.
Londzha	The general council of a guild.
Miri	A Turkish term for land held by the State Treasury, and allocated by the Sultan as he thought fit.
Mülk	A Turkish term for land held in full private ownership.
Myudyur	A local Turkish Governor.
Pomak	A Bulgarian who has adopted the Islamic faith.
Raya	A Turkish term for the non-Moslem subject population.
Shaek	A type of light woollen cloth.
Sheriat	Moslem religious law based on the Koran.

Spahi	Horsemen of Turkish Army, who received incomes from allotted estates in return for military service.
Tapia	A title deed to land.
Usta-Bashiya	The chief master or president of a guild.
Vakïf	A Turkish term for land, the income from which is bequeathed in perpetuity for charitable purposes.
Voivoda	The captain of an armed band; also occasionally used to denote a local governor.
Yatagan	A large Turkish sabre.
Zadruga	A large patriarchal family, owning and cultivating the land in common.
Zaptieh	A Turkish policeman.

SELECTED BIBLIOGRAPHY

This list contains only the more important works consulted. It does not include newspapers, for which references are given in footnotes, or works for the periods summarized in Chapters I and XII. The general works are given first, followed by the more specialized ones.

Istoriya Na Bŭlgariya   *Bŭlgarska Akademiya na Naukite.* Sofia. Vol. I, 1954; Vol. II, 1955. (A History of Bulgaria. Bulgarian Academy of Sciences.)

Istoriya Bolgarii   *Akademiya Nauk, SSSR.* Moscow. Vol. I, 1954; Vol. II, 1955.

DERZHAVIN, N. S.   *Istoriya Bolgarii.* Moscow. Vols. I–IV 1945–1948. (A History of Bulgaria.)

SAXENA, H. L.   *Bulgaria Under the Red Star.* Delhi, 1957.

NATAN, ZHAK   *Bŭlgarskoto Vŭzrazhdane.* Sofia, 1949. (The Bulgarian Renaissance.)

KOSEV, D.   *Lektsii po Nova Bŭlgarska Istoriya.* Sofia, 1951. (Lectures on Modern Bulgarian History.)

STANEV, N.   *Bŭlgariya pod Igo.* Sofia, 1935. (Bulgaria under the Yoke.)

KONDAREV, NIKOLA   *The Reading Rooms in Bulgaria.* English language pamphlet issued by the Ministry of Information and Art. Sofia.

TSVETKOVA, BISTRA   *Kharakterni cherti na osmanskiya feodalizŭm v bŭlgarskite zemi. Istoricheski Pregled.* No. 4–5, 1951, p. 380. (Characteristic Features of Ottoman Feudalism in the Bulgarian Lands.) *Pozemlenite otnosheniya v bŭlgarskite zemi pod osmansko vladichestvo. Istoricheski Pregled.* Year 7, Vol. 2, p. 158. (Agrarian relations in the Bulgarian lands under Ottoman rule.)

GANDEV, KH.   *Prichini za upadŭka na turskata imperiya v period ot XVI do XIX vek. Istoricheski Pregled.* Year 3, Vol. I, p. 76. (Reasons for the decline of the Turkish Empire during the 16th–19th centuries.)

Tsvetkov, Andrei — *G. S. Rakovsky.* Sofia, 1949.

Pancharov, Khristo — *Stefan Karadzhata.* Sofia, 1956.

Vasev, Vasilen — *Hadzhi Dimiter.* Sofia, 1956.

Undzhiev, I. — *Vasil Levsky.* Sofia, 1945.

Strashimirov, D. T. — *Vasil Levsky—Zhivot, Dela, Izvori.* Tom I, Izvori. Sofia, 1929. (Vasil Levsky—Life, Deeds, sources. Vol. I, Sources.)

Dimitrov, M. — *Khristo Botev. Idei—Lichnost—Tvorchestvo.* Sofia, 1946. (Khristo Botev. Ideas—Personality—Works.)

Undzhiev, I. — *Khristo Botev.* Sofia, 1956.

Botev, Khristo — *Sŭchineniya.* Sofia, 1949–1950. (Collected Works. 3 Vols.)

Gandev, Kh. — *Aprilskoto Vŭstanie.* Sofia, 1956. (The April Rising.)

Stoyanov, Z. — *Zapiski o Bolgarskikh Vosstaniyakh.* Moscow, 1953. (Notes on the Bulgarian Risings.)

Maccoby, S. — *English Radicalism.* 1853–1886. Allen and Unwin, 1938.

Thompson, E. P. — *William Morris.* Lawrence and Wishart, 1955.

Marriot — *The Eastern Question.* London, 1940.

Konstantinov, G. — *Nova Bŭlgarska Literatura.* Sofia, 1947. (Modern Bulgarian Literature.)

Gladstone, William — *The Bulgarian Horrors and the Question of the East.* 1876.

INDEX

GEORGE ALLEN & UNWIN LTD
London: 40 Museum Street, W.C.1

Auckland: 24 Wyndham Street
Bombay: 15 Graham Road, Ballard Estate, Bombay 1
Buenos Aires: Escritorio 454–459, Florida 165
Calcutta: 17 Chittaranjan Avenue, Calcutta 13
Cape Town: 109 Long Street
Hong Kong: F1/12 Mirador Mansions, Kowloon
Karachi: Karachi Chambers, McLeod Road
Madras: Mohan Mansion, 38c Mount Road, Madras 6
Mexico: Villalongin 32–10, Piso, Mexico 5, D.F.
New Delhi: 13–14 Ajmeri Gate Extension, New Delhi 1
São Paulo: Avenida 9 de Julho 1138–Ap. 51
Singapore: 36c Prinsep Street, Singapore 7
Sydney: N.S.W.: Bradbury House, 55 York Street
Toronto: 91 Wellington Street West